ATLAS

a WORLD of MAPS
from
THE BRITISH LIBRARY

NITISSIMA.VICTA.EXPUGNATA
DITA. BAVARORUM.ELECT.FOR
ISSIMO.PLAMM:HOSTIL.ULTORI.
GUILELMI.III.M.B.R.AUSPIC.KAUG.
VIRTUTE.HEROICA.LABORE.HERCUL
REPR:CXX MILL.HOST.IRRITO.PRO
OBSESSIS.TENTAMINE.A°. MDCXCV.
NOB.MO SPECT.MO PRUD.MO DOM: DOM.O ANTONIO HEINSIO
AT. REIP. COM. ET MIN: PRI: MAG. SIC. CANC. FEUD. CUR.
IND. SOC. DIRECT. D.D.D. ROMANUS DE HOOGE.
Gemblours
Peruwes
Ascheen
Meux
de Mehaigne fl
St. Denis
Ime le Dame
le Falise
Grote Cassey
St. Antonis Heremitage
de beek Verderin
St. Carels berg
Meel berg

ATLAS
a WORLD of MAPS
from
THE BRITISH LIBRARY

TOM HARPER

BRITISH LIBRARY

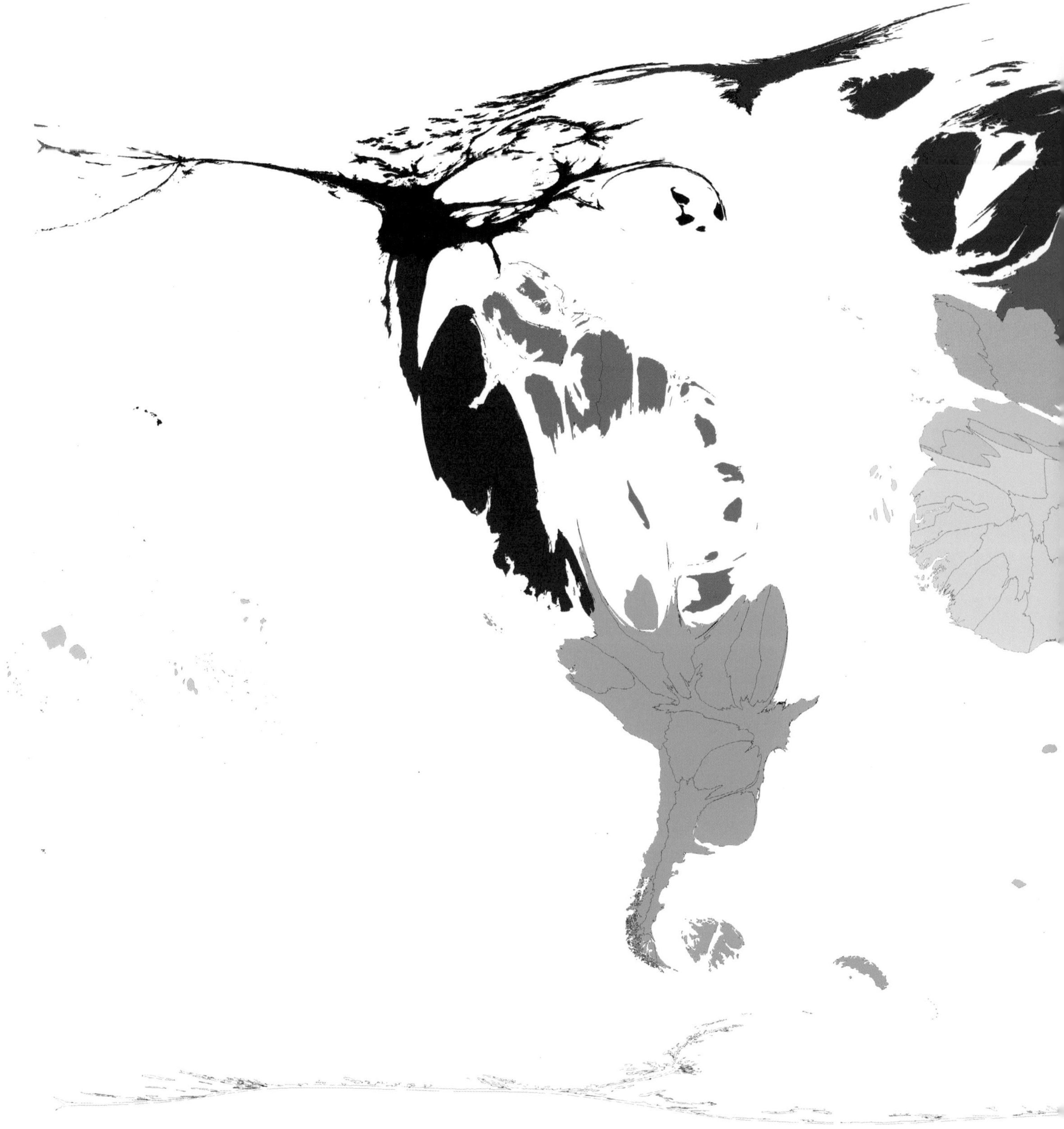

WORLD MAP

AREAS COVERED BY THIS ATLAS

This is a world cartogram by the geographer Benjamin Hennig of worldmapper.org. It has been created by taking the number of times territories are featured in this atlas and converting it into a world map in which more frequently covered territories are visualised as bigger in size.

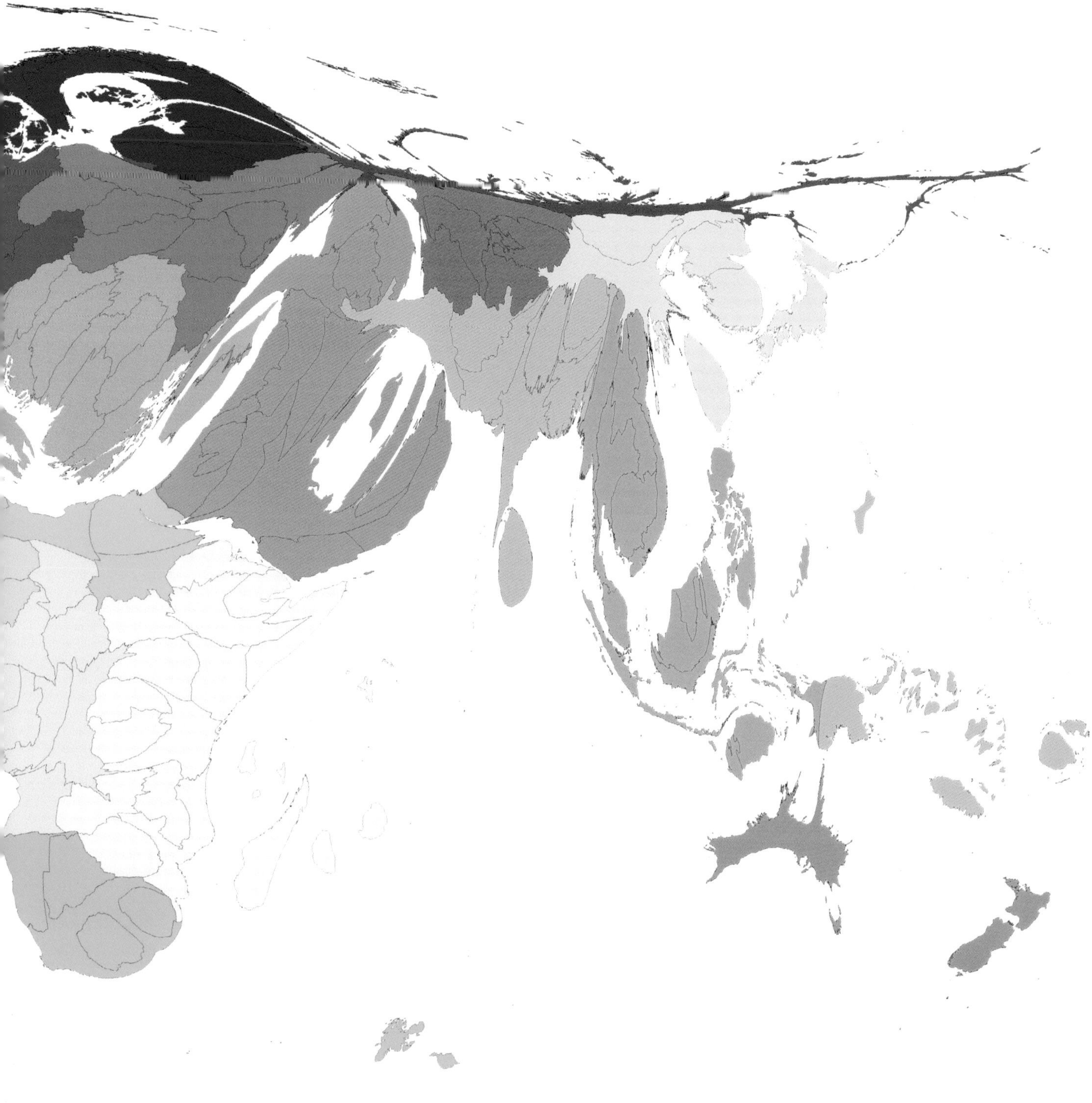

First published in 2018

This edition published in 2020 by
The British Library
96 Euston Road
London NW1 2DB

ISBN 978 0 7123 5332 8

Cataloguing in Publication Data
A catalogue record for this publication
is available from the British Library

Designed by Jason Anscomb
Printed and bound in Malta
by Gutenberg Press

Cover design: Georgie Hewitt
Cover illustration: Thomas Jefferys, *The Virgin Islands from English and Danish surveys*, 1797. [Maps 188.o.2.(1.)]

Frontispiece: Romeyn de Hooghe's etching depicting the
Siege of Namur, from the Beudeker Atlas, 1695. [Maps C.9.d.1]

Contents

ATLAS
SIVE
COSMOGRAPHICÆ
MEDITATIONES
DE
FABRICA MVNDI ET
FABRICATI FIGVRA.
Gerardo Mercatore Rupelmundano,
Jllustrißimi Ducis Julię Clivię & Mõ-
tis &c. Cosmographo Autore,
Cum Privilegio.

OPPOSITE: The title page of Mercator's *Atlas* of 1595 [Maps C.3.c.3]

Introduction

The first 'atlas' was produced by the Flemish cartographer Gerhard Mercator (1512–94) and published posthumously in 1595.[1] By that time books containing maps had been in existence for centuries, but the title of Mercator's book of maps – named after Atlas, the mythical geographer king of Mauritania – stuck. From then on it became the universally adopted title of a book containing accurate, uniform, up-to-date and evenly spread maps of all or some of the world.

This is an atlas with a difference. It is different because the maps in it were made by different people at different times for different reasons. As a result there is very little uniformity among them, and few could reasonably be called 'accurate' in the modern sense. Unlike the atlases we are accustomed to using, this one could almost certainly not be used to plan a journey, research a current geopolitical situation or even peruse future holiday destinations. However, this atlas can help us to travel in a way that regular atlases do not, because by looking at the old maps and getting to know their stories we can be transported back to the times in which they were made. You could almost call it an atlas of time travel.

The value of older maps

Old maps, early maps or even 'antiquarian' maps are defined as maps which are not contemporary. That is, they were produced at a time other than the present. 'Historical' maps such as those in *The Times Atlas of European History*[2] are not old because, although they show the geography of an earlier age, they are contemporary productions. Map collections, such as the one in the British Library where the maps in this book come from, have collected and preserved maps over the centuries and saved them from what tends to happen to old and out-of-date things, like being thrown in a rubbish bin.[3]

Saved for posterity, they appeal to new generations of people. In a book published in 1953, the head of the British Museum's (since 1973, the British Library's) map collection, Edward Lynam, wrote that 'early maps, which have lately become very popular, are full of varied interest. Their geographical information is often as delightful as it is incorrect; their Utopias such as Brazil and the Southern Continent recall the aspirations and labours of bygone generations, not yet disillusioned by knowledge.'[4] Allowing for the tendency, typical of the time, to see the present generation as the most enlightened, Lynam's delight at the rich possibilities of maps is plain to witness. There is both light-hearted enjoyment and serious historical insight to be had from maps.

Exactly how old maps manage to conjure such delights has a lot to do with their complex abilities as things. Maps are not merely images. They are also objects. And, like other things which have played a role in human history, they are carriers or vehicles of meaning. If we look at each of these attributes in more detail we can see how maps work.

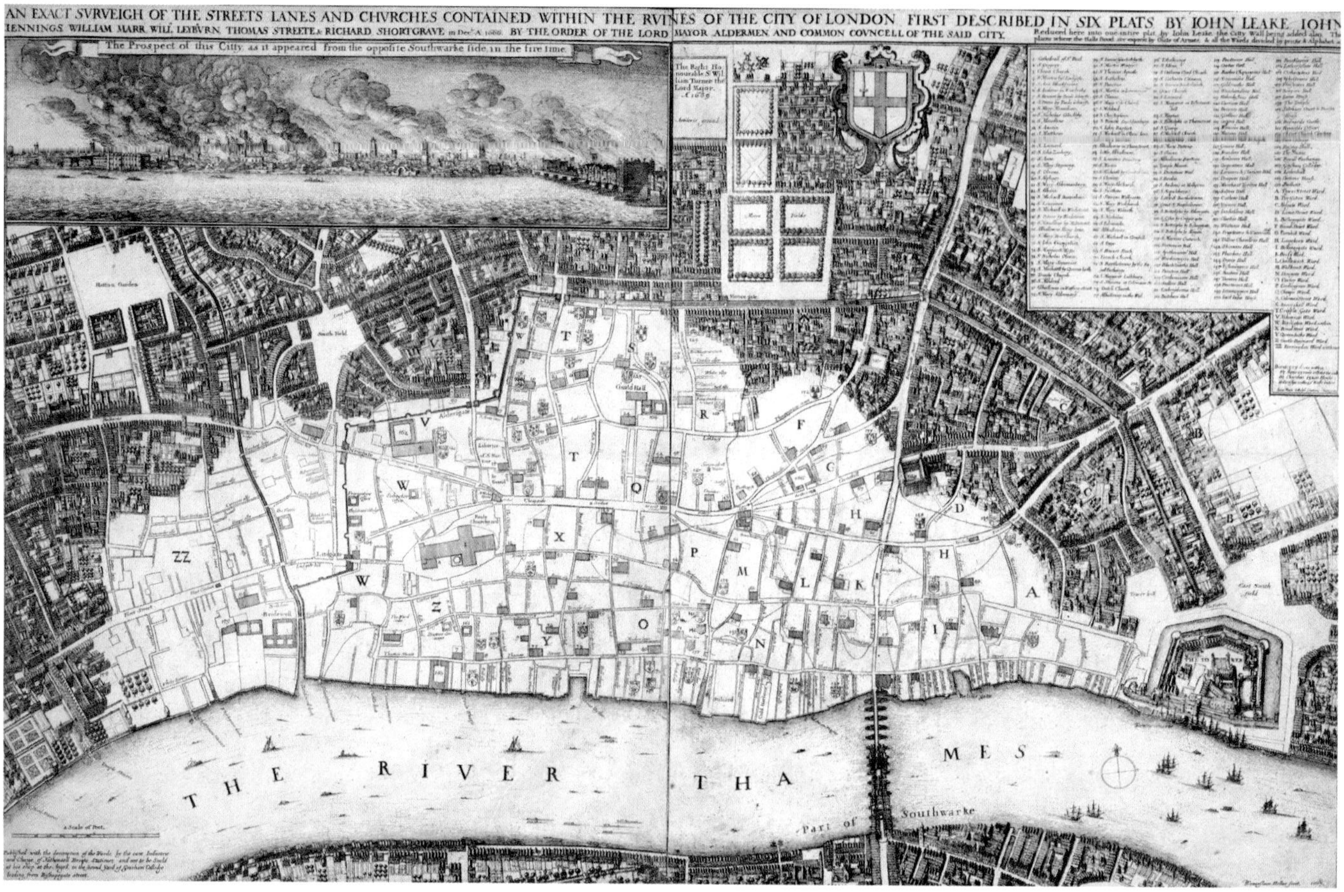

Wenceslaus Hollar's map of London after the Great Fire of 1666 [Maps Crace Port. 1.50]

The 'Great Southern Continent' as it appears on the 'Dauphin' or 'Harleian Map' of around 1547 [Add. MS 5413]

Jacopo de' Barbari's 1500 map of Venice [British Museum]

As images

The world can change in the blink of an eye, but maps retain what has been lost to us. For example, if you want to get an idea of how London was at the time of the Great Fire of 1666, there is probably no better place to look than the maps of Wenceslaus Hollar (1607–77). If you want to see places which were believed to exist but never have, places rather unfairly labelled as 'cartographic blunders' such as the Island of California or Lynam's Great Southern Continent, old maps are some of the few places where you will find them. The spurious Great Southern Continent, which lingered on maps up to the second half of the eighteenth century when it was emphatically established not to exist, may have been a charming 'mistake' but it shaped people's understanding of the world at the time. There is food for thought, too: couldn't this aspirational utopia of the sixteenth century be substituted for ideas about Antarctica, the moon or Mars in the twentieth?

The capacity of maps to store historical information is not limited to what they show: it is also how they show it. Maps have been called the 'first truly scientific technology',[5] and as monuments to the history of science the precision or quality of their imagery can constitute important milestones of civilisation. For example, the representational accuracy of 'portolan' sea charts produced from the thirteenth century onwards, maps of the first national trigonometrical survey, or even the earliest aerial photographs, are images of significance which, it could plausibly be argued, outweigh the purposes for which they were originally made.

But maps are not just scientific diagrams. They are also artistic images, created in such a way as to appeal to the tastes and trends of their times. After all, surveyors had to be competent artists in order to make their maps appealing to their patrons. Maps such as those in the hand-painted seventeenth-century atlas by Pedro Barreto de Resende (see pages 48–9 and cover image), or the stylish engraved maps of Romeyn de Hooghe (1645–1708, see frontispiece), are a delight to behold. Though taste in art may be subjective, quality is timeless. But can maps be too artistic? Certainly, for so highly regarded is the artistic imagery in maps such as those by Jacopo de' Barbari (1450–1516) or Grayson Perry (1960–, see pages 256–7) that they have become categorised in the public mind as works of art first, maps second.[6] This atlas considers the merits of all maps as images.

The main part of the damaged 'Aslake world map' of *c.* 1350–75 [Add. MS 63841 A]

As objects

Maps are images, but they are also objects which have been made, bought and sold as commodities, with a tangible existence bound into books with other maps, or mounted on walls. For most of their Western history maps have been predominantly ink drawings, watercolour paintings or prints on paper or animal skin, but they have also taken the form of three-dimensional objects such as coins, medals, models, globes (see pages 34–5) and jigsaws (see pages 38–9). Non-Western mapping practices have traditionally displayed far wider variety. From the sixteenth century onwards the different aspects of maps from Asia, Africa, America and Australasia meant that they were enthusiastically collected by Europeans as curious and exotic cartographic objects (see pages 72–3 and 140–1). They are the sorts of objects which would have been placed in a ruler's cabinet of curiosities or *Wunderkammer*, the sorts of spaces which gradually morphed into the modern museum. European objects might also be admitted if they were extraordinary enough, such as the abnormally large Klencke Atlas (see pages 218–9), which John Evelyn (1620-1706) noted as the 'vast book of mapps in a volume of neare 4 yards large' in the cabinet of Charles II in 1660.[7]

Most maps are not splendid objects like the Klencke Atlas. Most are scruffy pieces of paper like the *Rom Weg* (see pages 194–5), a map showing the pilgrim's route to Rome, which bear the scars of heavy usage and, as a result, have stories to tell. Some maps have survived simply due to their subsequent use as objects. For example, the only reason the fourteenth-century Aslake world map has survived is because somebody thought the vellum it was drawn on would make a durable book cover.[8]

As carriers

If they were simply images and objects, maps would not be so complicated. But maps also function in a representational capacity as carriers of messages and meanings. For example, a pink mark can represent Ipswich, and a tiny number in the water can stand for the depth in fathoms of the sea at that point. Maps are communication models which carry those messages to us. Of course, we tend to take this functionality for granted. If they did not represent space and what is in it, they would not be of much use.

But there is more to it than that. Without us realising it, maps also transmit a variety of attached meanings alongside these messages, which tell us about the circumstances and perceptions of the time. The pink mark is an abstract sign denoting an urban centre (like Ipswich).[9] On a twentieth-century map it might be larger than other pink marks on the same map, and smaller than others, indicating the size of its population relative to other urban centres. One of the most important characteristics of a town today is how many people live in it, because this can also suggest characteristics such as its economic and cultural status.

Now imagine Ipswich on a sixteenth-century county map like Christopher Saxton's (*c.*1542–1610/11, see pages 150–1). Ipswich might be represented by a more pictorial sign, with a miniature church spire. As well as indicating the location of Ipswich, the sign indicates the town's ecclesiastical status, which was crucially important in an era when the church had a powerful presence in local and national affairs. The difference between these two visual traditions, more pictorial in the earlier example, more abstract in the later, also tells us how different eras preferred to receive visual information.

Detail of Christopher Saxton's map of Suffolk (1575) showing Ipswich [Royal MS 18 D.iii]

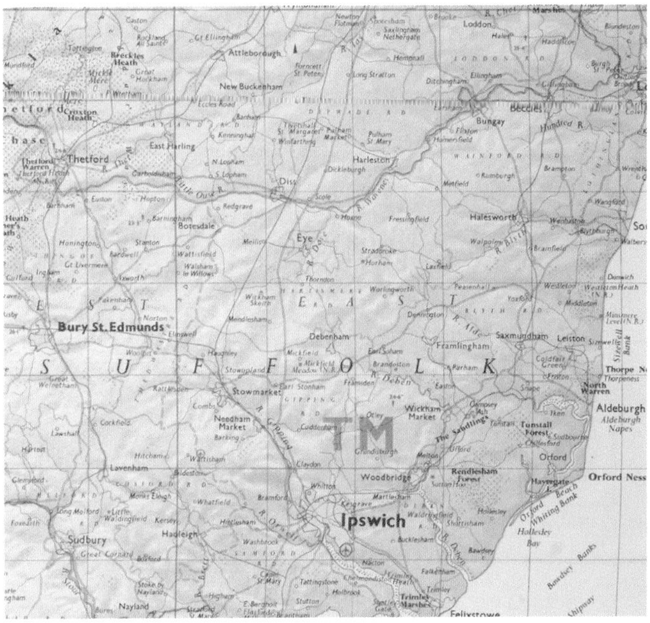

Ipswich as it appears in the 1963 'Atlas of Britain and Northern Ireland' (Clarendon Press) [Maps Ref.C.10.(3.)]

The historical significance of maps

It is not always possible to decipher the deeper meanings and messages in maps, which can be obscured and distorted by the passage of time. This is particularly true of the mysterious medieval world maps known as *mappae mundi*, of which our understanding continues to evolve. Nevertheless, the deeper meanings which underpin maps can make them valuable historical sources. By examining these associated meanings, we can appreciate why they showed things the way they did, and as a result understand more of the preoccupations of earlier times.

Some maps can be so significant as to impact on our view of the past. For example, from the British Army Command's 1917 set of Western Front relief models (see pages 204–5) we can infer that generals needed to visualise the front line to make informed strategic decisions. From the maps included in Marino Sanudo's (1260–1338) *c.*1325 treatise advocating a Christian crusade to the Holy Land (see pages 26–7) we can understand that maps had a certain potency in making places appear more tangible, and as a result increased the treatise's likelihood of success.

These are the sorts of world-changing episodes from history by which maps have acquired significance through association. They can provide privileged insights. Through them, we can get closer to what happened and attempt to understand it better, even using them to question established accounts of the events.

Maps can also increase and decrease in significance over time and between different users. For example, the SYMAP computer maps of the late 1960s (see pages 146–7) are now recognised as valuable artefacts from the early years of digital cartography. And maps can acquire altogether new meanings and significance. For example, fifteenth- and sixteenth-century maps containing early references to America, following European contact with the continent in 1492, were eagerly collected in the United States from the mid-nineteenth century because they were seen to legitimise the existence of the young nation against a backdrop of indigenous land appropriation.[10]

The meanings behind maps are complex, layered, subjective and ever-changing, and dependent on the users' assumptions and levels of understanding. They have not been called 'slippery witnesses' for no reason.[11] In the early twenty-first century they also have meanings which are particular to this time, and the accompanying text of this atlas strives to capture what fascinates us about them now.

What are maps, anyway?

Not only are the meanings behind maps subjective; the very definition of a map continues to be the subject of debate. But whether they should conform to the narrow 'diagrammatic representation of an area of land or sea'[12] or 'graphic representations which facilitate a spatial understanding of things',[13] or even 'you know one when you see one',[14] there can be no doubt from the varied maps in this atlas that 'what a map is' has changed over time.

However, the maps in this atlas are not really so different; they are virtually all, with the exception of globes and models, images of geographic or some other kind of space on two-dimensional surfaces. This is one downside of a 'library' map collection, which promotes paper-based maps over other formats. There are none of the earliest things we identify now as maps – drawings on cave walls (rock art) from tens of thousands of years ago – nor are there many coins, medals or mental maps. In fact, the main distinction between the maps in this atlas is that some of them are simple and diagrammatic, while others are complicated and pictorial.

Some are certainly more 'accurate' than others, and it is true that mathematical accuracy became a key requirement of Western cartography from the sixteenth century onwards, but we should be careful when using it to judge maps. For example, the map of the Jain universe (see pages 18–19) is as accurate a visual representation of its complexities as it is possible to be. And of course, one of the most lauded of modern maps, the 1932 London Underground map of Harry Beck (1902–74), has accuracy issues. It is topological, like many medieval maps, in that it shows the position of one place in relation to another, but not to scale nor necessarily in the right direction.[15] But what we might call 'inaccurate' maps are still maps.

Despite its relative narrowness, its Eurocentricity (see pages 266–7) and (with a few important exceptions) British focus, the development of the map collection of the British Library, the British national map collection, provides a good snapshot of the changing appreciation of maps.[16] Collections such as this have generally been seen as barometers of what is accepted as a 'map', and if we look back on the few hundred years of its existence we can see that some types of map were favoured over others, while the importance of some has only been realised long after they ceased to be contemporary.

The evolution of maps in the British Library's collection

When the British Museum was founded in 1753 there were maps scattered throughout the four main private libraries which were brought together to form it. These 'founding' collections included bits which are traceable back to monastic collections of the Middle Ages and include a variety of medieval maps drawn in books such as psalters and chronicles (see pages 24–5). The bulk of these collections, however, were from the Early Modern period, reflecting the blossoming of European Renaissance learning and culture and the increasing availability of knowledge in visual and printed form.

By the sixteenth century maps began to exist independent of books as stand-alone objects. They began to be collected seriously, arranged together and viewed as distinct from other types of knowledge, for example the Tudor maps held together in the 'Augustus' range of the Cotton Library (see pages 232–3). In recognition of their often unique format and in order to examine them all properly in the British Museum, a special six-by-eight-foot reading table was installed in a 'charts room' in 1759.[17]

Well before that maps had begun to be based on some form of mathematically based survey such as triangulation, and to display features such as a constant scale and grid over the face of the map. Changing tastes in style also meant the conscious avoidance of any form of pictorial or decorative quality within the geographic content: sea monsters were banished from the oceans. Yet during this time maps were also collected for their relevance to antiquarianism and the study of the past. One of the best antiquarian map collections, the Topographical Collection of George III, rich in topographical views as well as maps, reached the British Museum in 1828.[18]

It was in the nineteenth century that maps became far more powerful and potent objects. Their representational and scientific qualities were developed in order to support national and imperial agendas. The word 'cartography' came into use, and mapping became more distinct from other disciplines such as geography and history. 'National' map collections were established in the British Museum in 1867 (previously a sub-department), the Bibliothèque royale in Paris (1828) and the Library of Congress in Washington, DC (1897), and they began receiving greater quantities of maps.[19]

What is intriguing is that at this point people began to become interested in old maps again. Scholars began to look for those medieval and early modern maps in libraries, and previously unidentified ones were brought into the light. The British Museum began to purchase greater quantities of old maps, and paid good money for them, too – for example, the considerable sum of £40 was paid for Peter Apian's 1530 heart-shaped world map in 1885 (see pages 28–31). Just as up-to-date maps enabled people to understand, and thus control, territory, so the possession of historical maps enabled people to understand and control the past.

The British Library was created out of the British Museum Library collections in 1973. Today its map collection is one of the world's largest, with over four million maps dating from between 15 CE and 2018 CE. This 'banquet of maps',[20] as it was referred to by one of Lynam's most dynamic successors, Helen Wallis (whose particular specialism was early globes), has continued to reflect contemporary thought and anticipate future ideas about maps in its collecting activities.[21] Crucially, maps which had previously been shunned as non-accurate, non-mathematical 'ephemera', mapping such as postcards (see pages 136–7), posters and property plans (see pages 158–9), were added. A century from now, when people once again ponder 'what is a map?', they will have the British Library's map collection and this atlas to remind them.

How this atlas is arranged

Thanks to Mercator and his mapmaking successors the atlas became the definitive cartographic product and the principal format for maps up to the present day. Despite the successive eras in which atlases have been produced, from the scientific age to the age of empire, and even through the turbulent change of the twentieth and early twenty-first centuries, the sequencing of maps within them has remained remarkably consistent. In the introduction to *Philip's Concise Atlas of the World* it is described as 'the classical arrangement adopted by most cartographers since the 16th century',[22] whereby maps of Europe are placed at the beginning followed by those of continents successively further away from Europe. This method of organising the world is perfectly understandable: everyone has the tendency to place themselves at the start, and those furthest away or less relevant to them at the end.

The world is now a different place, and just as old maps can find themselves newly relevant in fresh circumstances, so atlases have realigned themselves with the times. Accordingly, the British Library's atlas takes the more neutral arrangement in which continents are placed in alphabetical order.[23] That this places Europe at the end seems quite apt given its overbearing role in the modern story of maps. They may be 'children of their times',[24] but not only do maps have the capacity to transport us back in time to the periods of their creation, their inclusion in this atlas in the early twenty-first century tells us a lot about ourselves, too.

Endnotes

1 The full title is *Atlas sive cosmographicae meditationes de fabrica mundi et fabricati figura.*

2 *The Times Atlas of European History* (London: Times, 1998).

3 For a guide to map collections see the International Federation of Library Associations and Institutions, Section of Geography and Map Libraries' *World Dictionary of Map Collections.*

4 Edward Lynam, *The Mapmaker's Art: Essays on the History of Maps* (London: Batchworth Press, 1953), 37.

5 Richard S. Westfall, 'Charting the Scientific Community' in Kostas Gavroglu, Jean Christianidis and Efthymios Nicolaidis, *Trends in the Historiography of Science: International Conference: Selected Papers* (Dordrecht; Boston: Kluwer Academic, 1994), 12.

6 The British Museum's Department of Prints and Drawings includes a number of maps, many of which were transferred there from the map collections because their artistic qualities were judged more important than their status as maps. There are two examples of Jacopo de' Barbari's 1500 map of Venice in the Prints and Drawings collection.

7 John Evelyn's diary, quoted in Peter Barber and Tom Harper, *Magnificent Maps: Power, Propaganda and Art* (London: British Library, 2010), 92.

8 Peter M. Barber and Michelle P. Brown, 'The Aslake World Map' in *Imago Mundi* 44:1 (1992), 24–44.

9 Catherine Delano-Smith, 'Map Signs' in Peter M. Barber (ed.), *The Map Book* (London: Weidenfeld & Nicolson, 2005), 76–77.

10 J.G. Kohl, 'Substance of a Lecture Delivered at the Smithsonian Institution on a Collection of the Charts and Maps of America' in *Smithsonian Institution. Annual Report, 1856* (1857), 93–145.

11 H.H. Parry, 'Old Maps are Slippery Witnesses' in *Harvard Magazine* (Alumni ed.), April 1976, 32-41, quoted in J.B. Harley, 'The Map and the Development of the History of Cartography' in J.B. Harley and David Woodward (eds.), *The History of Cartography Volume One: Cartography in Prehistoric, Ancient and Medieval Europe and the Mediterranean* (Chicago: University of Chicago Press, 1987), 3.

12 The Concise Oxford Dictionary (Oxford: Oxford University Press, 1999).

13 *The History of Cartography Volume One,* xvi.

14 James R. Akerman and Robert W. Karrow (eds.), *Maps: Finding Our Place in the World* (Chicago: University of Chicago Press), 2.

15 Roger J.P. Kain, and Catherine Delano-Smith, *English Maps: A History* (London: British Library, 1999), 3.

16 As might be expected, the British national map collection has historically been focused on British-produced maps and the British 'experience' in the world, which are inevitably reflected in this atlas.

17 Helen Wallis, 'The Map Collections of the British Museum Library' in Helen Wallis and Sarah Tyacke (eds.), *My Head is a Map: Essays and Memoirs in Honour of R.V. Tooley* (London: Francis Edwards, 1973), 13.

18 *Catalogue of the Maps, Prints and Drawings etc. Forming the Geographical and Topographical Collection Attached to the Library of His Late Majesty King George the Third* (London: British Museum, 1829). See Peter Barber, 'George III and his Geographical Collection' in Jonathan Marsden (ed.), *The Wisdom of George the Third. Papers from a Symposium at the Queen's Gallery, Buckingham Palace. June 2004* (London: Royal Collection, 2005), 282–93.

19 Tom Harper, 'Map Collections' in *History of Cartography Volume Five: Cartography in the Nineteenth Century* (Chicago: University of Chicago Press, forthcoming).

20 Helen Wallis, 'A Banquet of Maps' in *Map Collector* 28 (September 1989), 2–10.

21 Over the course of the twentieth century map librarians, particularly Helen Wallis and her predecessor R.A. Skelton, were instrumental in redefining the study of maps and turning the British Library's map collection into an internationally recognised centre for the discipline.

22 *Philip's Concise Atlas of the World* (London: George Philip & Son, 2008).

23 Within continents the atlas follows the sequence devised in the 1840s for the arrangement of the map collection's sheet map series.

24 *English Maps: A History,* 1.

The Universe

(1830)

Some of the most profound maps we know of are those which show belief systems: places, people and processes associated with religion and spirituality. These maps, which include many of the medieval European Christian *mappae mundi*, served as important educational tools for helping people to visualise the invisible and to lead lives consubstantial with their beliefs.

Among the most extraordinary of these are the cosmographical diagrams showing the structure of the Jain universe. Jainism is a Śramara religious system founded in northern India in the sixth or seventh century BCE which adheres to the belief in a cycle of life and death (*samsara*) and eventual liberation from that cycle (*moksha*). The soul takes a spiritual journey through the lands of the 'middle' or human world and then the sacred world in order to achieve enlightenment or *nirvana*.

The specifications of the Jain universe were contained in ancient texts and refined over many centuries, and maps were occasionally drawn from them, which would have adorned the libraries attached to monasteries where the texts were composed. They were collected by Europeans during the nineteenth century, including many who were associated with the British East India Company, the archive of which is now in the British Library.

The map, which is in Sanskrit, was created using paint on cloth in around 1830 in Rajasthan. It illustrates a fusion of human and sacred geography. At the centre is the flesh-coloured world of humans (Manusya-loka), with the sacred Mount Meru in the middle. Immediately surrounding the mountain, the land of Jambu-dvipa is divided into seven zones with the lowest, Barata, divided from the others by the Hamavat (Himalayan) mountains, conforming to the Indian subcontinent.

This is the recognisable, terrestrial world of people. Surrounding it is the spiritual world: green concentric-ringed continents illustrated by lunar symbols and separated by fish-filled oceans, beyond which is the outer land of the *jinas* or prophets. This sublime paradisiacal landscape confirms itself through its colour, beauty and illustration of an array of beasts and birds, citadels and rich landscapes as the ultimate goal of the Jainist spiritual journey.

This is sacred geography based on centuries of study and refinement. But the map may also have had a contemporary dimension when it was produced. During the second quarter of the nineteenth century, as with Korean *cheonhado* world maps and Japanese Buddhist world maps, it is possible to see the Jain maps as a reaction against contemporary imperial European incursions into their spheres of existence, and evidence of the concerted desire of their makers to reaffirm themselves at the centre of the map.

Septentrio
Oceanus Deucalodonius
MARE
ATLANTICUM
Tropic: Cancri
Æquinoctialis
OCEANUS
ÆTHIOPICUS
Tropicus Capricorni
MARE ARABI
Golfo de Bengala
INDIA
MAR
TYCHONIS BRAHE
Habes hic candide Lector
signa celi accurate delineata iuxta
observantiam Tichonis Brahe et
Frederici Houtmanni

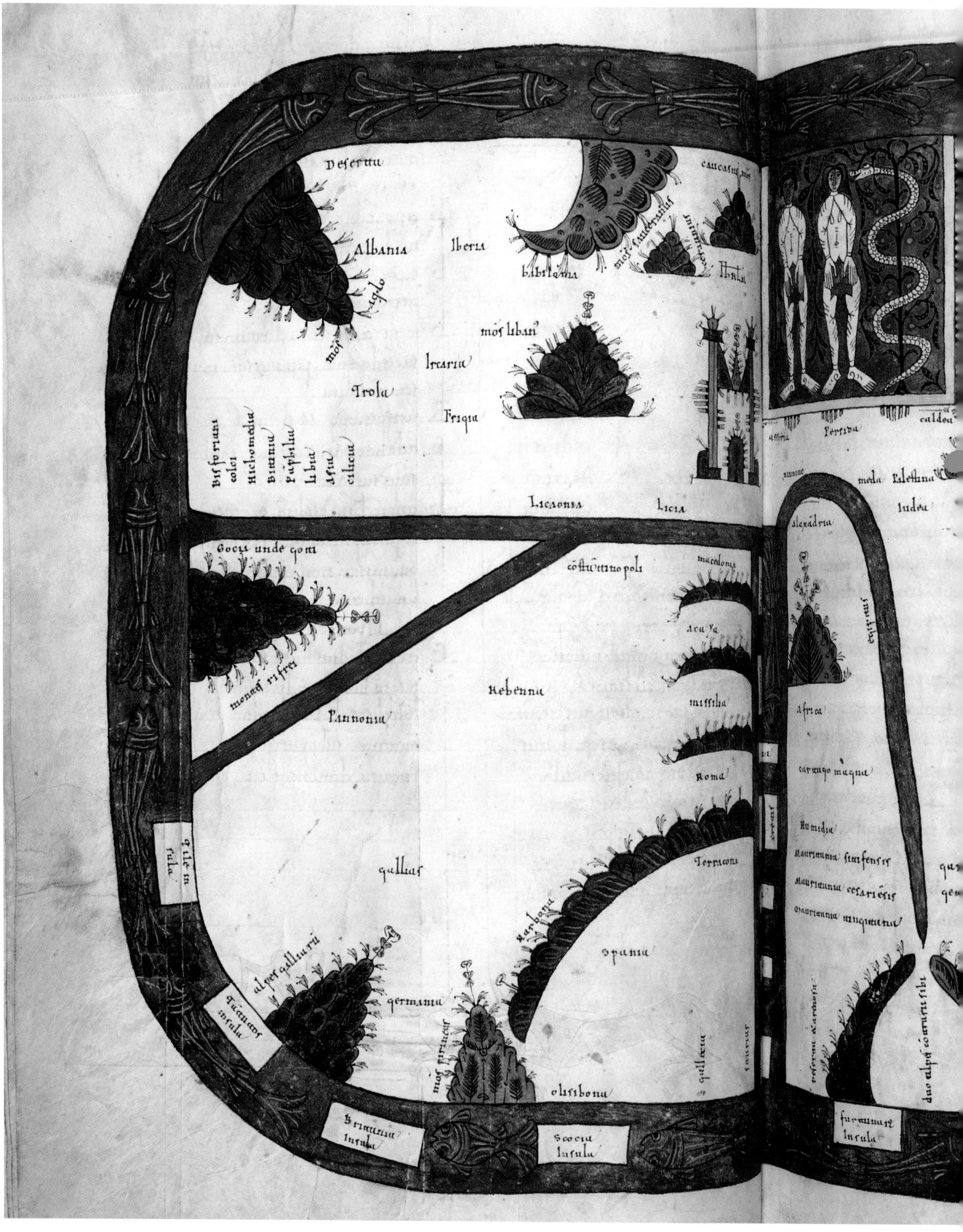
Desertu
Albania
Iberia
babilonia
Troia
Frigia
Licaonia
Licia
Persida
caldea
media
Palestina
Iudea
alexandria
Africa
cartago magna
Numidia
macedonia
Acaya
Roma
Pannonia
gallias
Spania
germania
olisibona
Scocia insula
Britannia insula

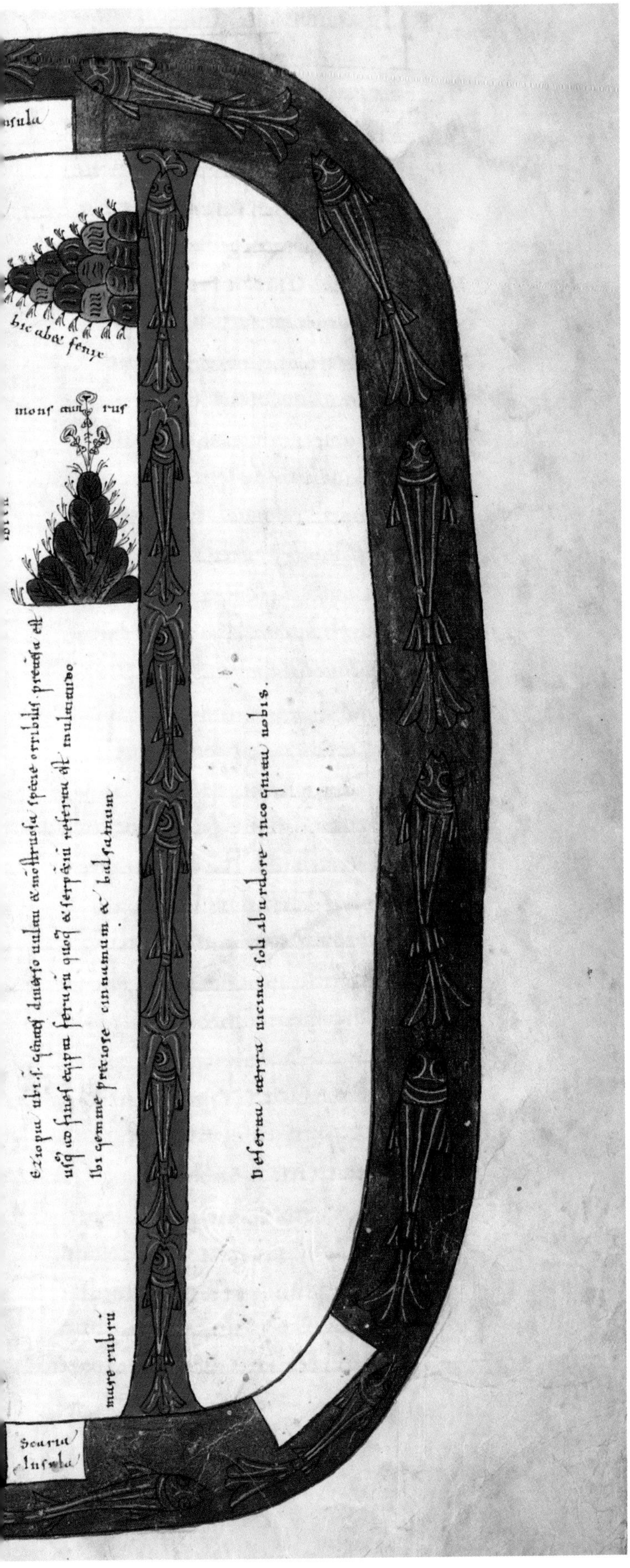

The World

(c.1109)

The 'Beatus' world maps look like nothing else in the history of cartography. The British Library's example is a diagrammatic image with powerful pictorial elements that are completely different to other medieval world maps of the time. This is because it was produced in northern Spain in around 1109, and as a result reflects Islamic pictorial influence that had spread from northern Africa. We can see the 'bright opaque colours and arabesque illustration' including the fishes swimming in the sea encircling the world, the 'molehill' mountains and the unforgettable image of the Garden of Eden at the top of the map, in the east.

The 15 surviving Beatus maps are included in textual commentaries on the Apocalypse of St John (from the New Testament Book of Revelation) by the Spanish theologian Beatus of Liébana (*fl.*776–86). The text of Beatus focuses on the ministries of the apostles in the separate parts of the world, culminating in the evangelisation of the known world which would be followed by the Apocalypse and the Last Judgement. This map shows three continents divided by seas: the Mediterranean running up through the centre with the Don River dividing Europe and Asia, and the Nile curving back on itself, roughly separating Asia from Africa. What seems to be a fourth continent in the south, the Antipodes, is separated from the rest by the Red Sea, which is coloured red.

This fourth continent is an uncommon and controversial feature to appear on a world map. Separated by a sea, this land of searing heat was inhabited by 'monstrous races'. Some theologians have argued that the concept of a fourth continent was heretical in that it could not be reached by the three sons of Noah or the apostles, and was as a result beyond the reach of God's word. To counter this, other scholars argued that the sea depicted on this map was intended only as an inland sea.

There is something ominous and brooding about the map, which communicates to us the fear of Christians in eleventh-century Spain at the spreading influence of Islam from the south. It is surely not incidental, given that the theme of the Apocalypse of St John was the persecution of the early Christians.

The World

(c.1265)

This tiny world map of huge significance was drawn in around 1265, and although only 15 cm in height it contains an astonishing amount of minutely observed detail of the world. This level of information is one reason why we believe it to be a derivative of a much larger *mappa mundi*, now lost, owned by King Henry III (*r*.1216–72).

As well as providing missing links with other lost examples, the 'Psalter map' is a clever piece of devotional cartography. The map's name comes from the fact that it is included in a book of prayers known as a psalter, and it would have provided visual support to prayers being recited from this. Like most *mappae mundi* it contains sacred Christian geography, among other types of knowledge. The world is shown with east at the top and the Mediterranean Sea running vertically through the centre. Jerusalem has been purposely placed at the map's centre and other Christian features are prominent, from the Garden of Eden and the four rivers emanating from it, to the Tower of Babel. Above and outside the frame of the map we see Christ triumphant, flanked by putti who swing incense burners, another visual liturgical reference that would not have been lost on the user.

The map's clever symbolism does not end there. The 'Psalter map' actually has another map drawn on the back of it. Whereas the map discussed above is largely pictorial, the map on its reverse is almost wholly textual, consisting of a sphere that has been divided into three (for the three parts of the world, or continents, which were populated by the descendants of the three sons of Noah), with each part containing descriptions. This map emphasises the power of the written word, and the power of prayer of the sort being recited from the psalter. And if the user were in any doubt, the image of Christ trampling a serpent underfoot rams the message home.

There is a lot more besides sacred geography in the 'Psalter map'. Read from top to bottom the map shows successive eras of knowledge from the Old Testament through the Classical period (the Alexander legend and the Roman writings of Pliny and Herodotus), right up to the contemporary world of the map, with European commercial centres such as Salzburg, and Henry III's lost dynastic possessions in France included.

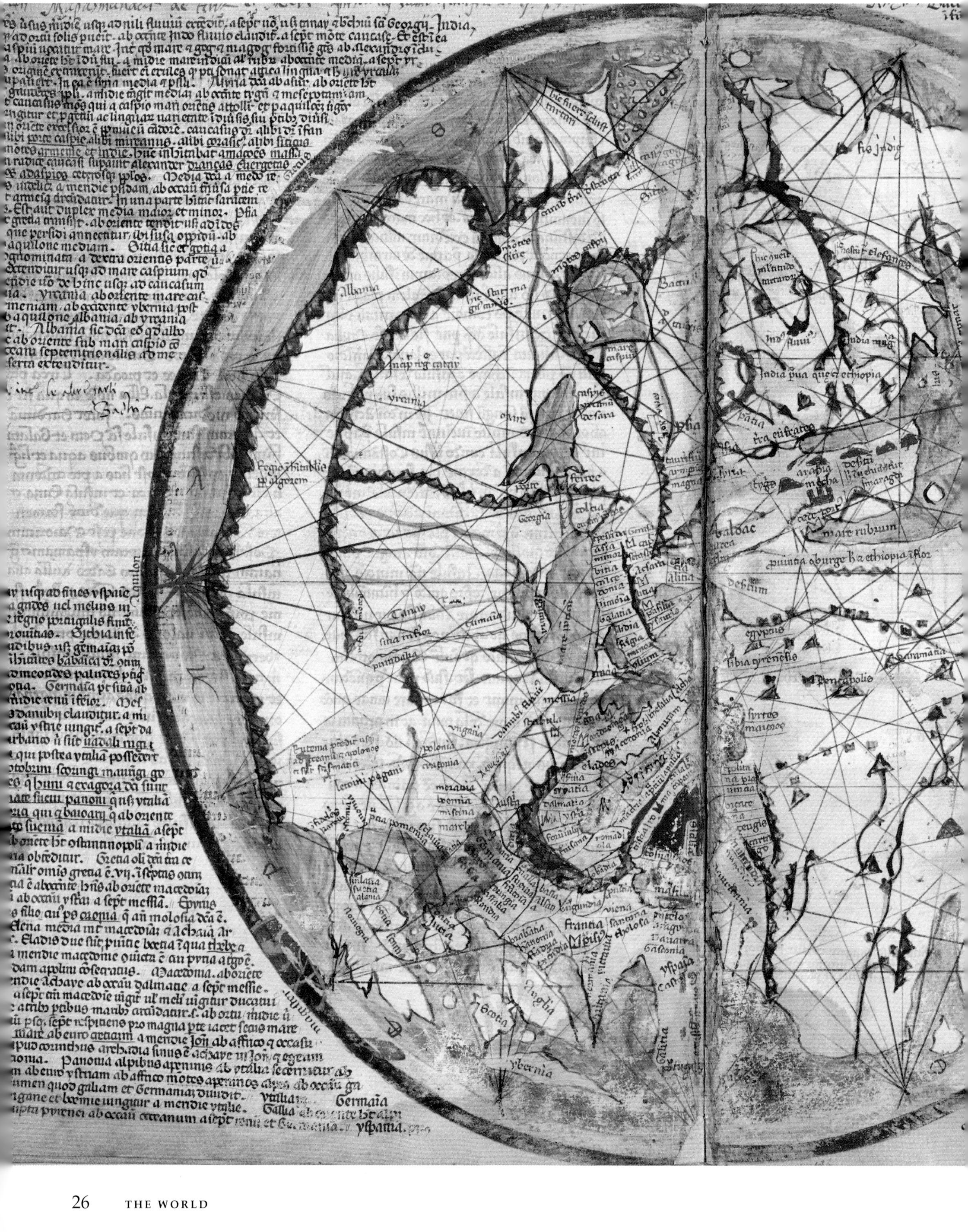

Albania
Georgia
Tanay
mare rubrum
egyptus
Pentapolis
Scotia
Anglia
ybernia
Francia
Aquilon

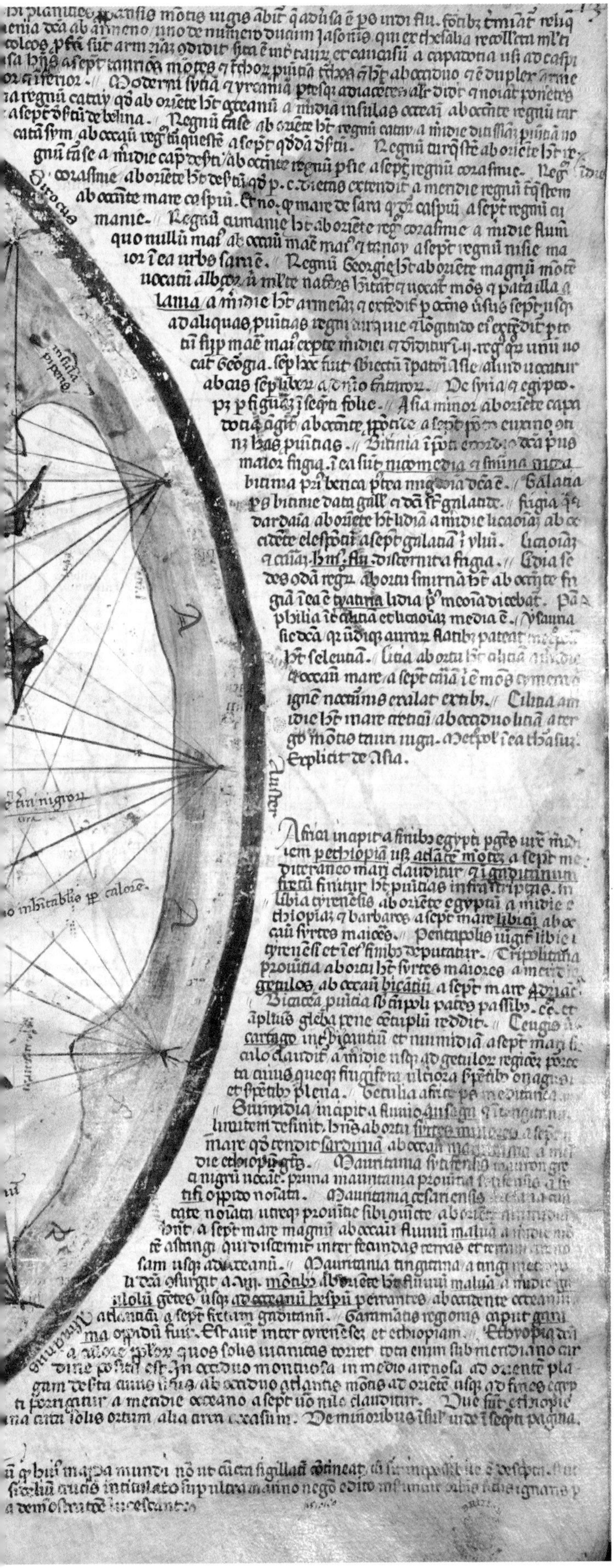

The World

(c.1325)

With its vaguely organic appearance, this early world map is one of the most unusual and compelling maps we know of. Its context was an Italian proposition for the launching of a crusade to the Holy Land in the early fourteenth century. The aim of this crusade was to recapture the town of Acre (in modern-day Israel) which had been taken in 1104 during the First Crusade, but had fallen to the Muslims in 1291. Any crusade required the support of the Pope, and so we come to the Venetian author and geographer Marino Sanudo (1260–1338) – 'a man with a mission', as the historian Evelyn Edson has described him.

A wealthy and devout Venetian, Sanudo was a strong advocate of the crusading spirit and keen to convince Pope Clement V (*c.*1263–1314) and his successor John XXII (1244–1334) of the merits of a holy war. To do this he wrote a book between 1306 and 1320 with the tantalising title *Liber Secretorum Fidelium Crucis*, or 'Secret Book of the Faith of the Cross'. As well as the copy Sanudo presented to John XXII in 1321 (now in the Vatican Library), others, including this one, were written for influential Christian world leaders.

The book was a masterpiece of cunning persuasion. It contained practical information in the form of a plan of action dealing with tactics, strategy and logistics, and a historical and geographical description of the Holy Land. A handful of maps drawn in the workshop of the Genoese chart maker Pietro Vesconte (*fl.*1310–30) were also included in later copies. These comprised a world map and maps of the Mediterranean Sea, Egypt (the first stop on the campaign), Acre, Jerusalem and the Holy Land itself. This is the clever bit: not only were they included in a practical capacity, to assist with the planning and strategy of the projected campaign, but they may also have been included to illustrate and thus frame the goal of the Holy Land clearly in the influential viewers' minds.

The world map is an extraordinary hybrid, combining two types of medieval map. First, it is a traditional circular world map, or *mappa mundi*, oriented with east at the top, Jerusalem (and the Holy Land) at the centre, and a variety of classical and contemporary places marked on it.

It is also drawn in the style of a 'portolan' sea chart, with its distinctive navigational criss-crossing 'rhumb' lines and an emphasis on the seas, coasts and rivers. The practical functionality of this sort of map is clear, and it was Vesconte's speciality, but it may also have served to support the ideology behind the *Liber Secretorum*. By playing down, relatively speaking, the Christian iconography of the world map (there is no Garden of Eden illustrated, for example, as was common in the *mappae mundi*), could the purpose have been to manipulate the fears of the Christian elite in order to encourage them to support action?

Sanudo's efforts at persuasion were in vain, however, and decades would pass before another Christian holy war.

SEPTENTRIO
OBSERVATIO. PTOLEM.
OBSERVATIO. VE SPI.
Septentrio
Aquilo
Chorus
Subsolanus
Priuilegium Imperiale
Pulchrũ inuẽtũ, insigne, recẽs, cui cordĩ imago ẽ
Natio nũc omnis cui studiosa fauet.
Triginta durat cui cautio Cæsaris annos,
Ne quisq̃ hoc aliis edat in orbe typis.
Aphricus
Vulturnus
ORIENS
OCEANVS OCCIDENTALIS
AMERICA
ASIA
AFRICA
MARE INDICVM MERIDIONALE
Terra Noua
Euro Aph.
Euroauster
Miliaria Germanica
50 100 150 200 250 300 350 400 450
Auster
MERIDIES
Nobiliss. simul et prudentiss. viro ac D. Do
mino LEONARDO ab Eck in Wolfs et
Randeck do: oratori et philosopho insigni / me
coenati suo cum primis humanissimo P. Api
anus de Leyßnigk Academie Ingolstadiane
Mathematicus hanc vniuersaliorem cogniti
orbis Tabulam / ex recentibus obseruationibus
confectam: Dedicat.
Anno M. D. XXX. die .9. Noa.

The World

(1530 and 1559/60)

Among the most romantic maps we know of are cordiform (heart-shaped) world maps. These maps originated in the early sixteenth century and were intended to do two things. First, they attempted a mathematical projection which could accommodate the Americas, then only recently discovered by Europeans. Second, they celebrated the symbolic potency of the image of the heart in religious iconography, as well as honouring the Holy Roman Emperor Maximilian I (*r*.1493–1519), for whom it was a favourite emblem.

The British Library has two of the most intriguing examples of this map type, and both require some explaining. The first is a woodcut produced in Bavaria by a man called Peter Apian (1495–1552) and dated 9 November 1530.

Although it was an Austrian mathematician called Johannes Stabius (1450–1522), who worked for the Emperor Maximilian, who invented the heart-shaped map, he doesn't seem to have drawn a map of it and other examples have not survived, so this is the only copy of the earliest surviving one. Apian deserves much credit, particularly for including the two images at the top of the map which explain most clearly how the projection (right, modelled by Amerigo Vespucci (1454–1512), the man after whom America is named) improved on Claudius Ptolemy's (*c*.100–170) ancient map, which is shown on the left.

In terms of its production, the map is also ground-breaking. In 1970 the map historian David Woodward noticed that some of the letters on the map were, at only 1.5 mm high, far too small for even the most skilled woodcutter to have carved out of wood. He worked out that the wooden printing block would originally have been littered with tiny metal strips containing cast letters inserted into notches. The ingenuity of this production process is only slightly more impressive than Woodward's achievement in working it out purely by looking at the printed copy.

The second heart-shaped map overleaf is, if anything, even more unusual. In 1795 six original woodblocks made in 1559 or 1560 for printing a world map were discovered in the Biblioteca Marciana in Venice. The library had maps printed from them, of which this copy is one. It is a world map with text in Ottoman Turkish, which the text describes as having been produced by a Tunisian Muslim called Hajji Ahmed. It goes on to describe how Ahmed was captured by infidels and was forced to produce the map in order to gain his freedom.

Historians have since established that the map was likely to have been commissioned from Venetian mapmakers by wealthy Ottoman customers. Not only that, but it is believed that the sorry tale of Hajji Ahmed was probably fabricated by Venetians in order to make their map more saleable to Ottoman clients. But their cunning marketing ploy seems not to have worked. The woodblocks were confiscated by the powerful Venetian Council of Ten, possibly for censorship reasons. Attempts to publish the map a decade later were scuppered by the worsening of international relations between the Ottoman Empire and Venice during the 1560s, culminating in the 1571 Battle of Lepanto. These, then, are the British Library's two map mysteries of the heart.

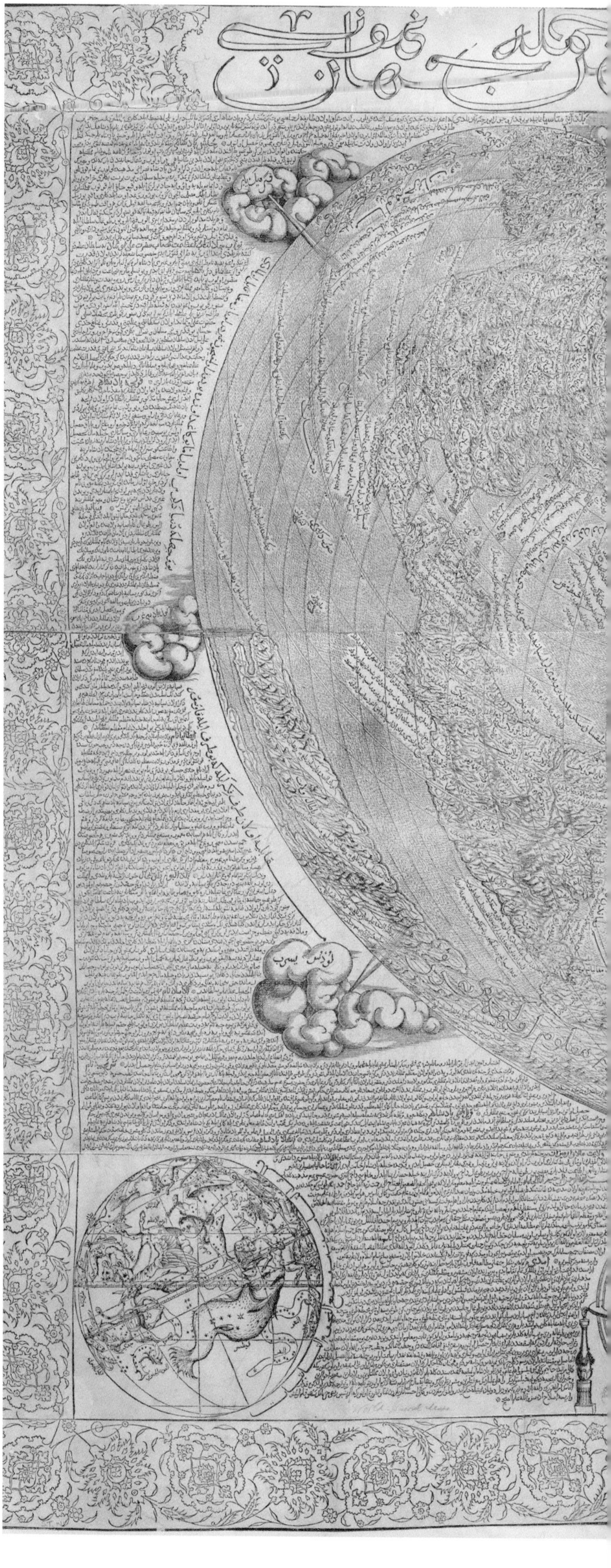

The World

(c.1617)

A genre known as 'double-hemisphere' maps emerged from Netherlands map publishing houses from the late sixteenth century. They became the archetypal Dutch map product and signature image at a time when the Netherlands was emerging as the pre-eminent commercial power in Europe, and a cultural pioneer. The world appeared within two great circles, or hemispheres, at the centre of the print. Not only did this replicate the spherical shape of the globe far better than previous maps, but it provided lots of empty space in the western hemisphere for further anticipated European discoveries of lands in the Americas and the Pacific.

From a design perspective the map format also provided gaps between each of the hemispheres where decorative elements and pictures could be inserted. This is quite an important moment in the history of maps because it was the point at which the variety of geographical, iconographic, mythical and ethnographic information, which had all been placed together in traditional cosmographical world maps, began to be moved neatly to the margins of the map. By placing the geography within the hemispheres at the centre of the map, a hierarchy of knowledge emerged. Geography thereby became the most important aspect of a map.

This world map by Claes Janszoon Visscher (1587–1652) shows how elaborate this format could become. It is a map based on an earlier map by Petrus Plancius (1552–1622) which contains complex types of information of different levels of importance, set within an architectural frame. An outer frame provides full-length ethnographic portraits, all in traditional costume, while flanking the map on either side are views of world cities. This was the world and these were the people being brought into focus by the growing Dutch empire. It was a cosmopolitan world for merchants and traders who purchased and used maps as much for intellectual stimulation as for practical use, hanging them on the walls of their homes. This was the audience upon which the 'Golden Age' of Dutch cartography was built.

The inner spaces of the map have been reserved for sacred scenes from the Old and New Testaments, the most important level of information aside from the geographical content. These have been carefully positioned in such a way that each Old Testament story corresponds with its New Testament equivalent, signifying the fulfilment of scripture. For example, the Fall of Man mirrors the Crucifixion as it would in a religious painting cycle. This iconographic awareness complements the engraving, which has assimilated the lessons and forms of southern Renaissance art. By owning this map, a merchant was able to demonstrate his piety as well as his taste and wealth.

POLONI
MOSCOVI
TARTARI SAMOIEDÆ
IAPONI
CHINENSES
SUMATRÆ MALACENSES
O IN PLURIMIS EMENDATUS, AUCTUS, ET ICUNCULIS ILLUSTRATUS
Auct: Nicolau Ioã: Visschero
AMSTERDAM
LONDON
DANTZIGK
CONSTANTINOPOLIS
MOSKOU
ORMUS
PERNABUCO
HAVANA
MEXICO
CUSCO
MAR DEL NORT
AMERICA MERIDIONALIS
PERUVIANA
Fretum Magellanicum
Rio da Plata
Oceanus Deucaledonius
MARE ATLANTICUM
Tropicus Cancri
Æquinoctialis
Tropicus Capricorni
OCEANUS ÆTHIOPICUS
MARE ARABICUM
MAR DI INDIA
MARE LANTCHIDOL
OCEANUS
TERRA AUSTRALIS INCOGNITA
Septentrio
Habes hic candide Lector signa cœli accurate delineata iuxta observantiam Tichonis Brahe et Frederici Houtmanni
Tichonis Brahe
inus homo, terræ utsoboles, sic vafra Draconis
Dicta, Dei sanis vocibus ante ferens,
que, suosq; omnes in diram præcipitavit
erniciem; et Satanæ mancipia esse facit.
At Deus humanum, quod defecisse videret,
Restituit, proprio motus amore, genus.
Umgenum mittens Natum, qui victima factus
In cruce, pro nobis debita nostra luit.
Non uno contenta malo gens impia Mundum
Cædibus, et thalamis polluit illicitis.
Aeris et Terræ, quare, iratus cataractas
Solvens, perdit aquis cuncta creata Deus.
Postremam mundi gentem haud meliora secutam
Iudicium poena non leviore manet:
Iudicis adventu Mare, Tellus, igneperibunt
Aeternumq; perit gens inimica Deo.
MAGELLANI
BRASILIENSES
BONESPEI. MADAGASCARI
GUINEENSES
ANGLI
BELGÆ

The World

(1623)

The 'Chinese Globe' of 1623 is a key cultural artefact in the history of maps and, along with a handful of other maps, it is of huge importance to our understanding of the interaction between Europe and China during the seventeenth century. It is a large 59-cm diameter globe which has been hand-painted on to plaster and wood, then varnished. It shows the latest geographical understanding of the world as shown in the European-produced atlases of Abraham Ortelius (1527–98) – but the text, including large panels explaining theories and concepts of the world, is entirely in Chinese.

Despite its unofficial name, the globe was actually constructed by Europeans working in Beijing. The Jesuit order had been based in China since the late sixteenth century. By promoting Western science through objects such as maps, they hoped to increase acceptance of Christianity in Chinese society. One of the earliest and best known of these geographical products was a large printed world map in Chinese, which was published in 1602 by the head of the Jesuit order, Matteo Ricci (1552–1610). It showed parts of the world that were entirely unfamiliar to the scholarly audience who saw it, and whose Sino-centric maps had tended to denigrate parts of the world such as Europe which were unimportant to them. Ricci's map was hugely influential, copies even reaching Japan.

However, being a flat two-dimensional image, Ricci's map was unable to explain the concept of a spherical earth. Though we know that the Chinese constructed globes prior to this, the concept was contrary to Chinese belief in the seventeenth century. This is the context of the production of the globe by Ricci's successor as head of the order, the Sicilian Nicolò Longobardo (1565–1654) and his Portuguese associate Manuel Dias (1574–1659), who have signed the globe using their Chinese names. Its three-dimensionality enabled latitude and longitude to be properly demonstrated (finely painted parallels and meridians cover the globe's surface). The text, much of which was copied from Ricci's map, discusses subjects such as terrestrial magnetism which were already familiar to Chinese scholars.

Looking at the globe today, it is impossible not to be affected by its physical presence. Its darkened surface yields tantalising glimpses – a brutish sea monster and a vast ship with billowing sails – of what must once have been a brilliant blue object. Its uneven round shape, cracks and other surface damage are the scars of an object which has witnessed much through the centuries. It has a few tales to tell us yet. The globe was donated to the British Museum by the porcelain collector Sir Percival David (1892–1964) in 1962. David had acquired it in 1939 after seeing a photograph of it when in Paris. The globe reached London from Beijing with the assistance of the French sinologist Paul Pelliot (1878–1945).

Majorca
Algiers
I. Madera
C. Cantin
Tropic of Cancer
SAHARA
C. Blanco
Cape Verd Iflands
Equator
I. S. Thome
C. Lopo Gonfalve
A T L A N T I C

AFRICA
in its
PRINCIPAL DIVISIONS
By J. Spilsbury.
1767.
MEDITERRANEAN SEA
Candia
Cyprus
Jerusalem
Damieta
Alexandria
CAIRO
Kalaat-el Acaba
EGYPT
Girge
Asna
MEDINA
ARABIA
Mecca
RED SEA
TURKISH NUBIA
Ibrim
Aidab
Napata
Dungalla
NUBIA
Talac
Meroe
KOGA
Sennar
Kᵐ OF TIGRE
Moka
Aden
Babelmandel
I. Socotra
C. Guadafui
Kᵐ OF DANCALA
Dobas
ABISSINIA
Zeila
Barbora
WESTERN GALLES
EASTERN GALLES
Ausa Gurel
COAST OF AJAN
Dry & Desert
Ommo Zaidi
GINGER BOMBA or ZENDERO
Machidas
Magadoxa
Kᵐ of Brava
Maricatos
MACOKO or ANZICO
Monfol
UNKNOWN
MONUMUGI
Pato
Lamo
Melinda
Mombaza
Pemba I.
Zanguebar
Monfia I.
Quiloa
C. Delgado
COAST OF ZANGUEBAR
Iˢ. of Komoro
C. Natal
MOZAMBIQUE
Angocha
Fungeno
Casangi
MUJAC
I. de l'Amirante
Banks of Nazareth
INDIAN OCEAN
BUTUA

Longit. West frm Ferro
TURKEY IN EUROPE
ITALY
Corsica
Sardinia
Minorca
Majorca
Ivica
PART OF SPAIN
Str: of Gibraltar
Algiers
KREr of ALGIERS
Sicily
Malta
C. Bon
REP. OF TUNIS
Candia
Cyprus
MEDITERRANEAN SEA
I. Madera
C. Cantin
Sale
Fez
Kd. OF FEZ
MOROCCO
Bessara
Tegorarin
Tuegurt
Guergela
Cafsa
Capes Bay
Tripoly
C. Rasat
Gulf of Sidra
Derne
REP. OF TRIPOLY
Alexandria
Damieta
BARBARY
DESERT OF TARGA
HAYR
Murfouk
Fatsan
Zala
Siwah
Augila
Santrich
CAIRO
EGYPT
I. Ferro or I. de Fer
I. Canaries
C. Bajador
Tegelmelse
Dara
Tafilet
Tropic of Cancer
Ludaya
Tefeez
DESERT OF BARBARY
DESERT OF LEMTA
Zawila
Gherma
OF BERDOA
Girge
Afna
EL WAH
SAHARA OR DESERT
ZANHAGA called the Sandy Sea
Tagazarael
DESERT OF ZUENZIGA
KINGDOM OF AGADES
Mt. Tatanel
Kouko
TURKISH NUBIA
Ibrim
Dungalla
Napata
C. Blanco
TOMBUT
Tocrur
Kd. OF TOMBUT
Desert
Gana
BOURNOU
Karna
Lake of Cayar
Timbi
NIGRITIA
Cape Verde Islands
I. S. Jago
Rybovra Grand
C. Verd
Goree I.
Ft. James
Bissago I.
R. Senaga or Senegal
Gambia R.
Kantor
State of Conche
King of the Sulos
Lamlen
Wangara
KOGA
Semegonda
Sennar
NUBIA
Nubia the Antient Meroe
Desert of Zeu
Reghill
NEGROLAND
KINGDOM OF MADONGA
Songo
Desert
Isago Gabon
Ulcuma
Jahou
BIAFARA
Medra
Courourfa
ABISSINIA
MALAGUETE or GRAIN COAST
GUINEA
GOLD COAST
TOOTH CST.
Aquamba
KINGDOM OF BENIN
Kalbongos
Oweri
MUJAC
GINGER BOMBA OR ZENDERO
WESTERN GALLES
Bosham
Cambet
C. Palmas
C. 3. Points
St. George de la mina
C. Formoso
GULF OF GUINEA
LAND MACOKO or ANZICO
Baki-bakee
Majomba
Equator
I. St. Thome
Meridian of Ferro
C. Lopo Gonsalve
Monsol
UNKNOWN
MONUMUGI
KINGDOM OF CONGO
St. Salvador
Fungeno
Cafsangi
Ascension
Loando
DONGOS
S. Philipp
Kd. OF BENGUELA
Gumbandos
Jago Coconda
C. Negro
BUTUA
Cimbeba or Mataman
Chicova
Munhay
Zimba
Massapa
MANOMOTAPA
MANICA
SOFALA
SABIA
Sofala
ATLANTIC OCEAN
I. St. Helen
Desert of Basso
LAND OF THE CAFFRES
Desert of Conerian
BIRI
Inhamban
Tropic of Capricorn
Corrientes
Desert of Curco
Brigudis
Cabonas
Hensaquas
C. Voltas
Goriquas
Land of Natal
Odiquas
OF THE HOTENTOTS
Spilsbury ENGRAVER MAP & PRINT Seller in Russel Court, Covent Garden LONDON, 1767.
Cape of Good Hope
C. des Aiguilles
Needles Cape
Longitude West from London

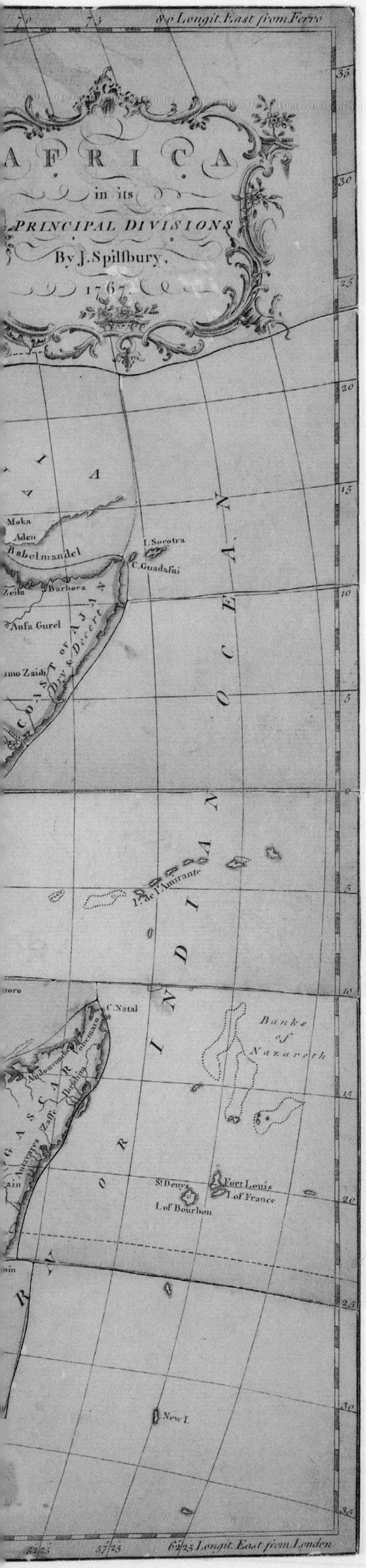

Africa

(1767)

John Spilsbury (1739–69) was a mapmaker with a good idea. In order to cater to the increasing numbers of upper- and middle-class parents wishing their children to learn about geography and be entertained while doing so, he designed and manufactured the first commercially produced jigsaws. These 'dissected puzzles', of which the first was published in 1766, were maps mounted on card or wood which had been cut along the national borders. By assembling them, following the principles of 'learning through play', the idea was that the child would become familiar with the world's political divisions.

Spilsbury's games were produced during a trend in Georgian Britain that has been called the 'commercialisation of childhood' because of the increasing number and variety of products, including books, toys and clothes, being manufactured for children. Other map publishers were producing cartographic games at the same time, such as Spilsbury's former mentor Thomas Jefferys (1719–71) with his 'Royal Geographical Pastime' board game. Spilsbury, who described himself on his business card as an 'engraver and map dissector in wood in order to teach geography', was smart enough to see the opportunity, and he milked it, producing a variety of puzzles of particular geographical areas which the curriculum required children to know about. For example, in addition to maps of the continents and of Britain there was a map of the ancient world to support the study of Classics and one of the Holy Land to support the study of the Bible.

Whether Spilsbury was the first to come up with the jigsaw idea is difficult to say. It certainly is not hard to imagine home-made bespoke map puzzles being produced earlier, and French educators have also been credited with the invention. Whatever the case, Spilsbury's puzzles were a roaring success, so much so that the governess to the children of George III (*r.*1760–1820) and Queen Charlotte (1744–1818), Lady Charlotte Finch (1725–1813), used them along with her own hand-made ones to educate her young charges.

This puzzle is one of the four continental maps that Spilsbury created, published in 1767. It shows the political divisions a century prior to the development of complex European imperial borders which by then were spreading across the continent. The Africa of 1890 would have been a difficult jigsaw to complete, but by that time 'physical' geography had supplanted the political world as the essential study of Britain's future inheritors of empire.

A label on the inside of the box reads: 'A gift of Lady Cecilia Johnston, May 17 1792'. Johnston was a socialite who was caricatured by James Gillray (1756–1815).

A MAPP of the CITTY of TANGER; with the STRAIT
The Bay of Tanger
Part of the Bay of
The New Haven of Tanger
THE
MOLE
Parade

Tangier, Morocco

(1664)

The marriage of Charles II (*r.*1660–85) to Catherine of Braganza (1638–1705) in 1662 brought with it the added bonus of the North African coastal town of Tangier as part of Catherine's dowry. Britain had acquired a strategic port and a further foothold, along with Gibraltar, in an area of Iberian influence, and quickly set about fortifying and improving it. In 1663 a group of surveyors and military architects visited the town to plan for the construction of a mole, a sort of pier and breakwater, in order to improve the harbour and make it suitable for British warships. One of the surveyors was Sir Jonas Moore (1617–79).

Moore had been instrumental in the 4th Earl of Bedford's (1593–1641) engineering project to drain the English Fenlands. This project was completed during the 1650s, and Moore created a large, impressive map in 1658 to commemorate it. His appreciation of the importance of maps to both planning and commemoration carried over to his work in Tangier. Returning to England after 'setting out the bounds of the mole', he produced a map showing what the finished and improved harbour would look like, selecting the best graphic artist then working in Britain, Wenceslaus Hollar, to engrave it. Hollar later visited Tangier and produced views of the town.

The large printed map which was published in 1664 is a spectacular bird's-eye perspective view of Tangier, and a piece of realism which takes the breath away. Light and shade, together with skilfully contrasting engraved lines to describe the smooth constructed surfaces and broken rough crags, make the image appear to sit above the flat surface of the paper it has been printed on. We can see the projected mole on the new harbour's southern side, with sailing vessels nestling in the angle of the bulwark. The depth of the sea in fathoms is given along it.

Moore's map brought the mole to life before people's eyes, and actual construction followed, costing £340,000. Its usefulness proved short-lived, however. Attacked by the Moroccan king Ismail ibn Sharif (*r.*1672–1727), the British abandoned Tangier in 1684, but not before they had blown up the mole to prevent others from benefiting from it.

Egypt

(1604–08)

In 1606 Sir Walter Raleigh (1554–1618) was a prisoner in the Tower of London. Following the death of his patron Queen Elizabeth I (*r.*1558–1603), the great explorer and courtier had become a *persona non grata* and, through his association with a plot against James I (*r.*1603–25) was imprisoned, though his life was spared. In order to alleviate the boredom of 16 years behind bars (though not too much boredom, since his son was sired during this time) he took to writing no less a work than a complete *History of the World*, compiled as a learning aid for the benefit of James's son Prince Henry (1594–1612). This *magnum opus* was unluckily curtailed by the death of the prince, the appended work being published first in 1614. This is his preparatory notebook compiled between the years 1604 and 1608.

Unlike finished printed books, which may give away little of their inspiration or method of compilation, this book shows the workings of Raleigh's mind and how Early Modern authors read, assimilated and ordered their knowledge of the world. It is essentially a geographical dictionary containing 175 pages, lettered at the top from A to Z, into which Raleigh added place names together with descriptions, the source of information and even the odd map. Clearly Raleigh was not short of reading matter, for as well as biblical and classical sources (a list of the books he had while in the Tower takes up a large part of the notebook) he had access to some of the great contemporary atlases, such as those by Abraham Ortelius, Jan Huygen van Linschoten (1563–1611) and Gerhard Mercator. These probably provided the sources for the handful of maps of parts of North Africa, including this map of the Nile Delta in Egypt, and the Middle East. They are in varied states of completion, often coloured in blues and pinks.

Raleigh's swashbuckling reputation, his looting of Spanish towns and attacks on Spanish ships (which eventually cost him his head in 1618), contrast with the studious side to his character which is evidenced by the notebook.

Raleigh began his *History* with the 'Old World' of the ancients and the Bible. The Old World was filled with promise for Raleigh, and he engaged in its study with customary zeal. Compared to Raleigh's search for the mythical El Dorado in South America, his quest to find the location of the Garden of Eden (then thought to lie somewhere in Persia) was no less passionate, but waged through written texts, geographical descriptions and maps rather than across forests and rivers. The geographical parts of the notebook demonstrate how he used maps as a way of understanding history, in line with contemporary theorists who promoted maps in their writings.

stoned to death, & with the hebrews call Soan. & hath also the name
Melr: gnil:
of Bais, & now Sibnit.

...sium. the scrip=
...s call Sin, & Lib=
...aith Montanus.
...s take it for
...tor. Castaldus &
...lerus think it is
...iata. Ang: Curio
... yt it is now Bil=
... Ortelius Tenes=
...thers, Belbais.

...ilon, the Arabians
... Mazar. the Chal=
...s Alchaby &. Josep=
... spolin, the Hebrews
...aim. Cairo stood
...e west side of it &
...now become one
..., saith Brochard.

...opolis, ther are too
... of ye name, the
... the edg of the
... or Egypt, the other
...amed metropolis
...eth farther north,
...iptures call it On. gen. 41. Esai. 19.
...la l. 63. c. 9. & pliny
...9. call it Solis
...um. Melr: Guilandinus,
... it Bethsemes,
...us, Malber. the
...beans, Bahalbeth.
...eon Sethi, Solis fons.
...emes. in Josua c. 15. 19. 22.
..., 1. 6. kings. 4. 14. par. 1. J. 2. 25. 28.
...phis built by Apis saith Aristippus
...i books of the Arcadien history, &
...ors Aristeus argiuus called it
...pidis. & Apis was the third from
...cus.

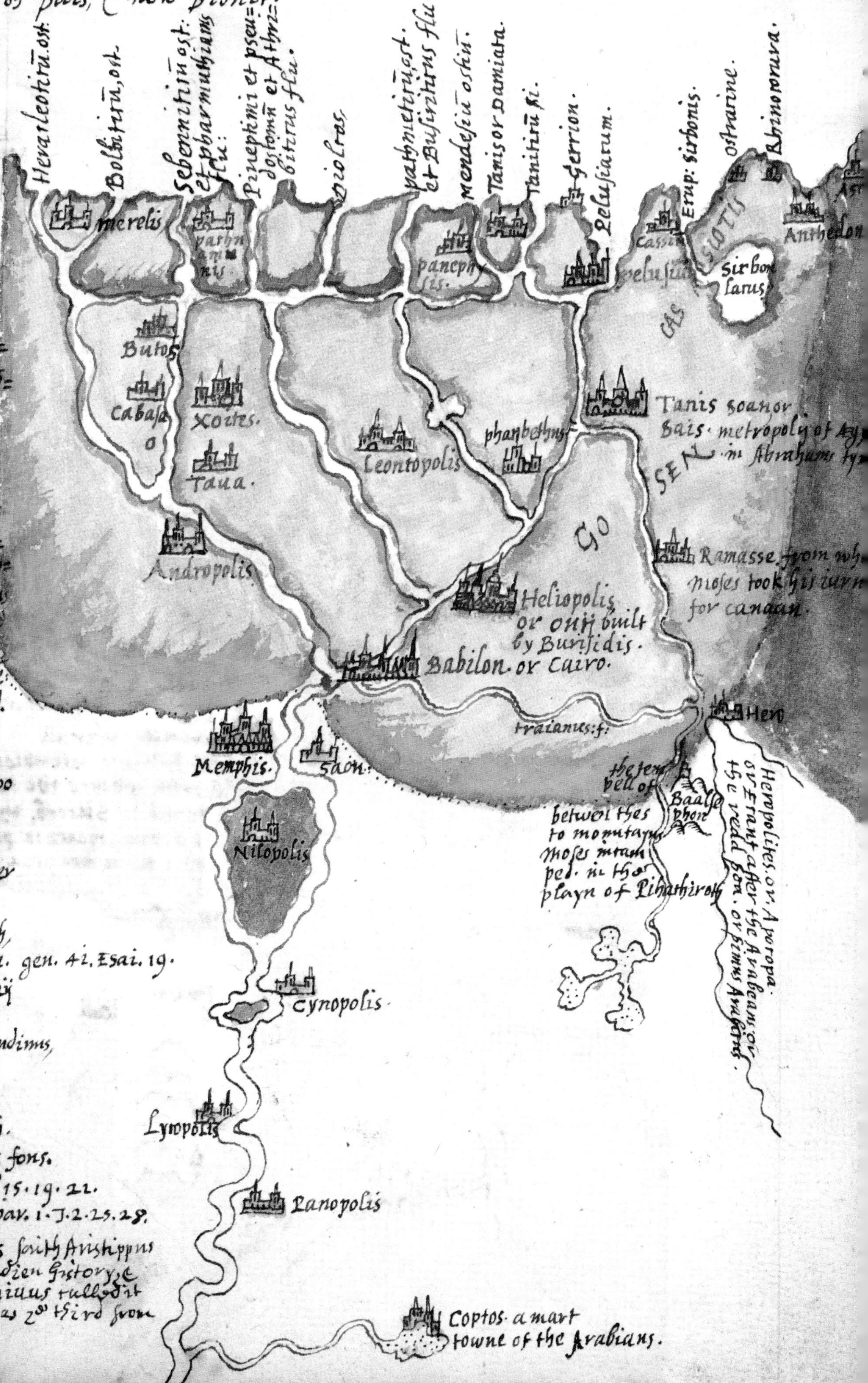

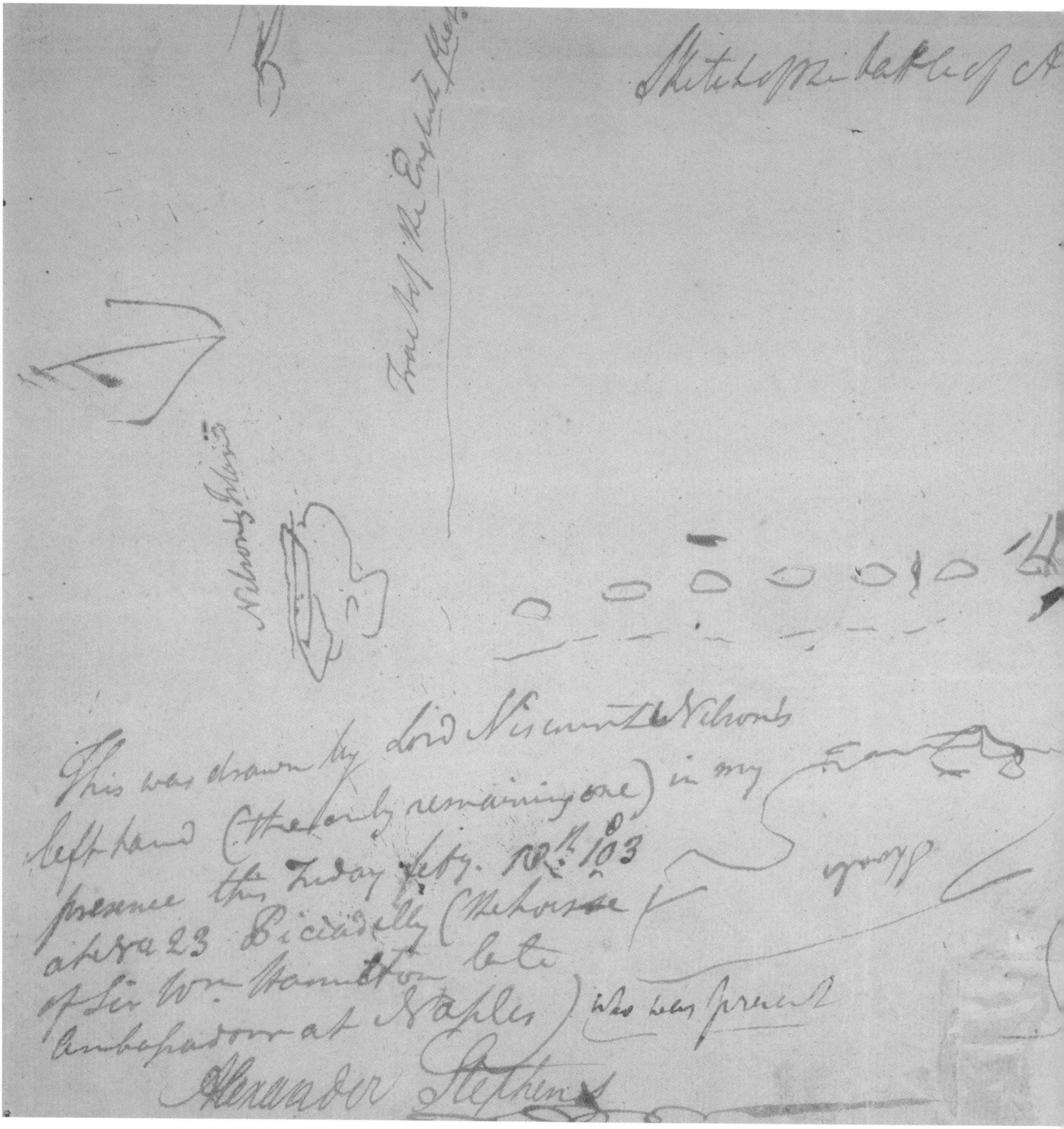
Sketch of the battle of A
Nelson's Island
This was drawn by Lord Viscount Nelson's
left hand (the only remaining one) in my
presence this Friday Feby. 18th 1803
at No. 23 Piccadilly (the house
of Sir Wm. Hamilton late
Ambassador at Naples) who was present
Alexander Stephens

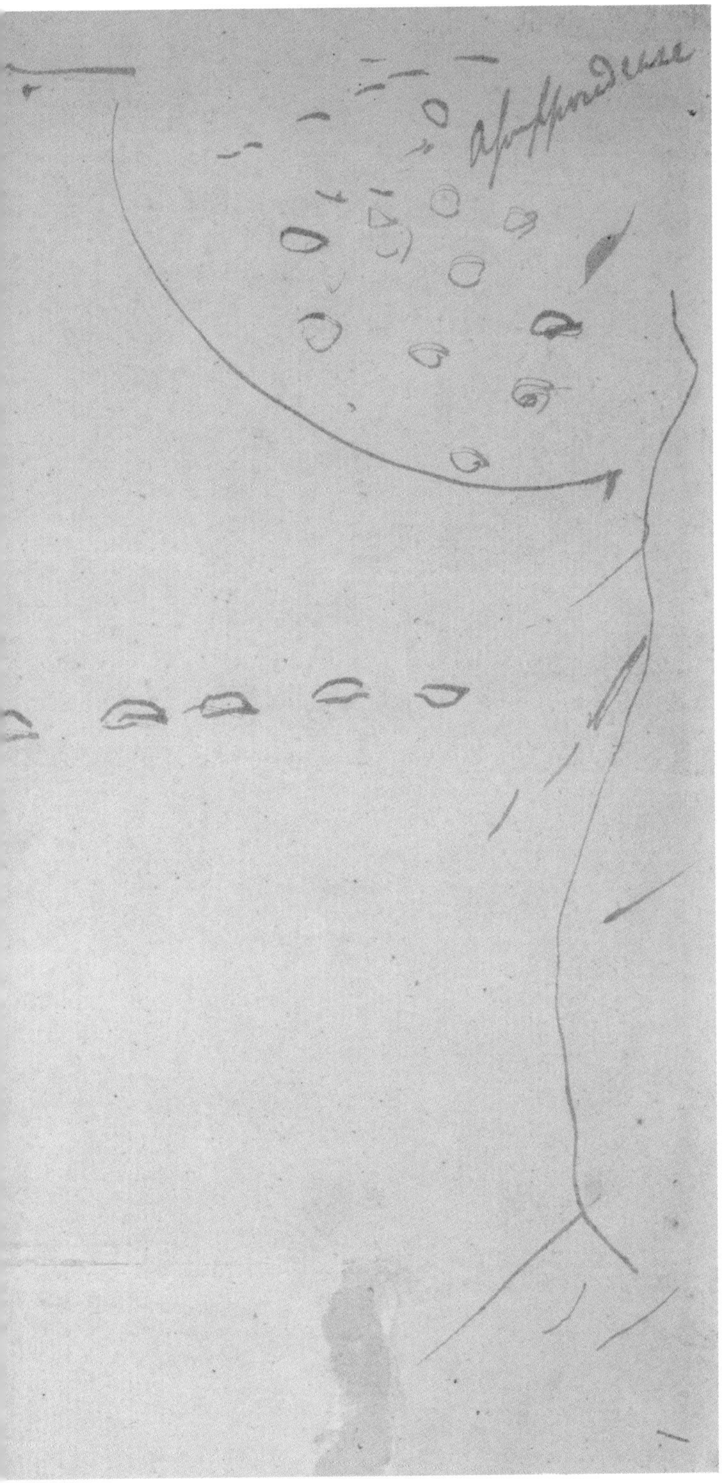

Abū Qīr Bay, Egypt

(1803)

This scruffy-looking sketch was drawn on 18 February 1803 by the British naval commander Horatio Nelson (1758–1805). We know this because a large annotation below the map reads: 'This was drawn by Lord Viscount Nelson's left hand (the only remaining one) in my presence this Friday Febr. 18th 1803… 23 Piccadilly (the house of Sir William Hamilton late ambassador at Naples) who was present.' The annotation is signed 'Alexander Stephens'.

Thankfully, Stephens also added a title which tells us that it is a plan of the Battle of Abū Qīr (here Aboukir) Bay. The battle took place on 1–3 August 1798 and was one of Nelson's greatest victories over the French navy. Its context was Napoleon Bonaparte's (1769–1821) planned French invasion of Egypt in 1798. Nelson was recuperating from injuries sustained in the Battle of Santa Cruz de Tenerife in 1797 (in which he had lost an arm), but he sailed to the Mediterranean to track down the invading French fleet. At first Nelson struggled to find it, and the French successfully disembarked their troops at Alexandria on 1 July. But on 1 August the fleet was finally discovered moored in Abū Qīr Bay, 20 km east.

One reason why Nelson was such a hero was because of his audacious and daring battle tactics, and Abū Qīr Bay was no exception. We can relive the battle through his sketch. The French fleet (the horizontal line of ovals) was moored and chained together in battle formation near shoals. Attacking at night, Nelson's fleet (the vertical line running from the top edge) split into two. HMS *Goliath* was able to pass through a gap between two French ships and attack along the French line on their ships' undefended side (the dashed line running under the line of ovals) with Nelson simultaneously attacking their other side. Only four out of a total of 17 French ships escaped, and *L'Orient*, the French flagship, crossed through on the map, exploded.

The victory further embellished Nelson's reputation as a celebrity. His relationship with Sir William Hamilton's (1730–1803) young wife Emma, Lady Hamilton (1765–1815), also began to attract attention at this time. We can just imagine the delight of Alexander Stephens, who was a contributor to the journal *Public Characters*, at being in the presence of the great man, in Hamilton's house, being able to speak with him, and better still to receive a souvenir, this map, into the bargain.

East Africa

(1558)

The Queen Mary Atlas is so called because it was commissioned by Queen Mary (*r.*1553–58) as a gift for her husband, Philip II of Spain (*r.*1556–98). It is certainly an atlas fit for a king: a jaw-dropping collection of eight hand-painted sea charts of the world and its regions, with elegant miniature illustrations added into the redundant spaces of land.

The mapmaker chosen for the commission was the Portuguese Diogo Homem (1521–76). Homem had fled to England from Lisbon in 1545 after being implicated in a murder. There he found ready employment, first under Mary's father Henry VIII (*r.*1509–47), who, like Philip, saw the value in maps for rule. Homem later worked in Venice. He was prolific, and an unusually large quantity of his work has survived, but the Queen Mary Atlas, though now incomplete, is undoubtedly his greatest in scale and conception.

To produce it Homem would have drawn in the coastal outlines, taking care to highlight islands in striking colours and prevent the place names from obscuring any of the coasts. Navigational use, though, was not the purpose. Miniature artists then added illustrations of towns, people, animals and sea monsters, banderoles (long text-filled ribbons) and the heraldic devices of imperial powers, placed over territories to which they laid claim.

This chart shows eastern Africa and the coastline of the western Indian Ocean, then an area dominated by Portugal. How strange then for the arms of Portugal to be so small and unassuming, certainly in comparison to the vast Spanish arms in places of Spanish dominance. We can only assume that Homem, despite being Portuguese himself, was attempting to gratify Philip and Mary. Another significant illustration refers to one of the main motivations for Iberian intervention in Africa. The king sitting on a throne is the mythical Christian monarch Prester John, with whom Portugal and Spain – in their Christianising zeal – planned to rendezvous and together repel the threat of Islam (though the accompanying inscription suggests doubts as to whether he existed).

The atlas did not reach Philip, and Mary died in 1558. In considering the motivation behind the atlas's production, the historian Peter Barber has suggested that 'Mary may have thought that a handsome atlas by a leading chart maker would please her husband, and remind him of their shared dominions and perhaps also of her'.

Siria.
India prima caisar.
Mediteraniu
Arabia petrea.
Persarũ Imperium.
Persia :-
Terreste mare.
EGI TVS
Arabia sterilis
Arabia felix
sinus persicu
Mare rubru
Barnacais.r.
Aethiopia sub egitu.
Abeschi.r.
India maior ethiopi
preste
sinus arabic
Adel.r.
Mare Indicum.
mero et saba
Media thiopia.
Coiame .R.
Azama.r.
Damate.r.
EQVINO TIALIS
AFRI CA
Melin dan.r.
Linomiera
Aeth iopia Interior
Quiloa.r.
Tibus deserti
Bona spes.
TROPICVS CAP RICORNI
Mare bone spej.
MERI DI ES
OCC I DE NS
O R I E NS
Narsinga.r.
Ceilam

MOMBACA

Mombasa, Kenya

(c.1640)

By the turn of the seventeenth century the Portuguese empire in Asia faced competition from Britain and the Netherlands through their respective East India companies. One cartographic incident which is cited as having checked Portugal's maritime dominance was the theft of restricted maps and charts from the Portuguese archbishop of Goa by his Dutch secretary Jan Huygen van Linschoten. Linschoten had maps engraved from them and published these in a bestselling book in 1596. This erosion of Portuguese power might have been overstated, however. Cartography remained adept at presenting a business-as-usual picture of Iberian power, for example in the heavily Christianised world map of 1623 by Antonio Sanches, and the great illustrated book of Portuguese possessions in the East Indies which includes this map of Mombasa, commissioned by Philip IV of Spain and III of Portugal (*r.*1621–65) and produced around 1640.

It was possibly as a consequence of foreign encroachments that Philip had ordered his viceroy of India to produce a written and pictorial description of Portuguese holdings, conforming roughly to the entire coastline of the Indian Ocean from South Africa to the Philippines. The chronicler Antonio Bocarro (*c.*1594–1642) was entrusted with the task, while work on the maps of coasts and forts was given to Pedro Barreto de Resende. It was probably Resende who drew the bird's-eye views of port towns including Mombasa, Goa, Ormuz, Bombay and Manila, using a strong dark blue for the sea, a high level of detail for architecture and vegetation, and occasionally adding descriptions of actual events. The island and port of Mombasa was a key strategic stronghold which Portugal had fortified with the construction of Fort Jesus in 1596.

A number of other charts in the volume were produced by the leading chart maker Pedro Berthelot. Berthelot had done the opposite to Linschoten, swapping from the Dutch to the Portuguese side in 1626 and eventually rising to the grand position of Cosmographer to the State of India. This volume may have portrayed a fading empire (Mombasa had been captured by the Imam of Oman in 1631, though it was recaptured afterwards), but it continued to dazzle and impress. It passed into the collection of the British minister in Portugal, Francis Parry, in 1676, possibly following a request for information by the British Committee for Trade and Plantations. By 1710 it was in the collection of the founder of the British Museum, Sir Hans Sloane (1660–1753), where its 'elegant paintings' were viewed by the German polymath Zacharias Conrad von Uffenbach (1683–1734).

Uganda

(1907)

Official maps played an important role in British colonial activities in East Africa from the late nineteenth century. Following increasing government influence in the area from the 1880s, and the assumption of direct administration of British East Africa and the Protectorate of Uganda from the 1890s, surveyors working under the auspices of the British War Office collected extensive quantities of topographical and survey data in the form of maps, views, itineraries and reports. The work was essential for the control and exploitation of the region. Material was sent to London, where it was used by the Geographical Section of the General Staff to produce printed maps.

This compilation material is now known as the War Office Archive, a collection of thousands of hand-drawn and printed maps and other documents covering areas of British influence in the world, which passed to the British Library as a place of official deposit in 1965 and 1989. The maps themselves are varied in their type and scope, from sketch maps of military tours to highly finished topographical sheets. They provide an unparalleled and unflinching view of the territories in which Britain was involved.

This map is a hand-drawn 'field' sheet from a War Office Original Survey (WOOS) carried out between 1903 and 1907, showing part of central Uganda around the River Mayanja. The map, which consists of 16 sheets and is at the scale of one inch to the mile, was surveyed by A. Richardson and E.G. Fenning using a plane table – a special drawing board, versions of which had been in use since the sixteenth century (a surveyor with a plane table appears on the title page of Saxton's 1579 atlas). There are a number of location points (the red dots) and a handful of triangulation points, the measuring of which was delayed in 1903 when Richardson's assistant, G. Woodruff, broke his leg while constructing an observation tower. The map was used for a printed War Office map (GSGS 2571) published in 1911.

It is a phenomenal display of disciplined mapwork, from the handling of the ink on the paper to the economy of description. It provides precisely what is required to be shown: where places are, what they are called and how high up they are, cultivated and swampy areas, and the locations of rivers and roads. It also illustrates just how powerfully maps can codify the world. The map is an abstract series of patterns, with the bulrushes in the river being, along with the blue of the river itself, possibly the only naturalistically portrayed feature in it. This process of abstraction and reduction is perhaps the most powerful trait of colonial mapping.

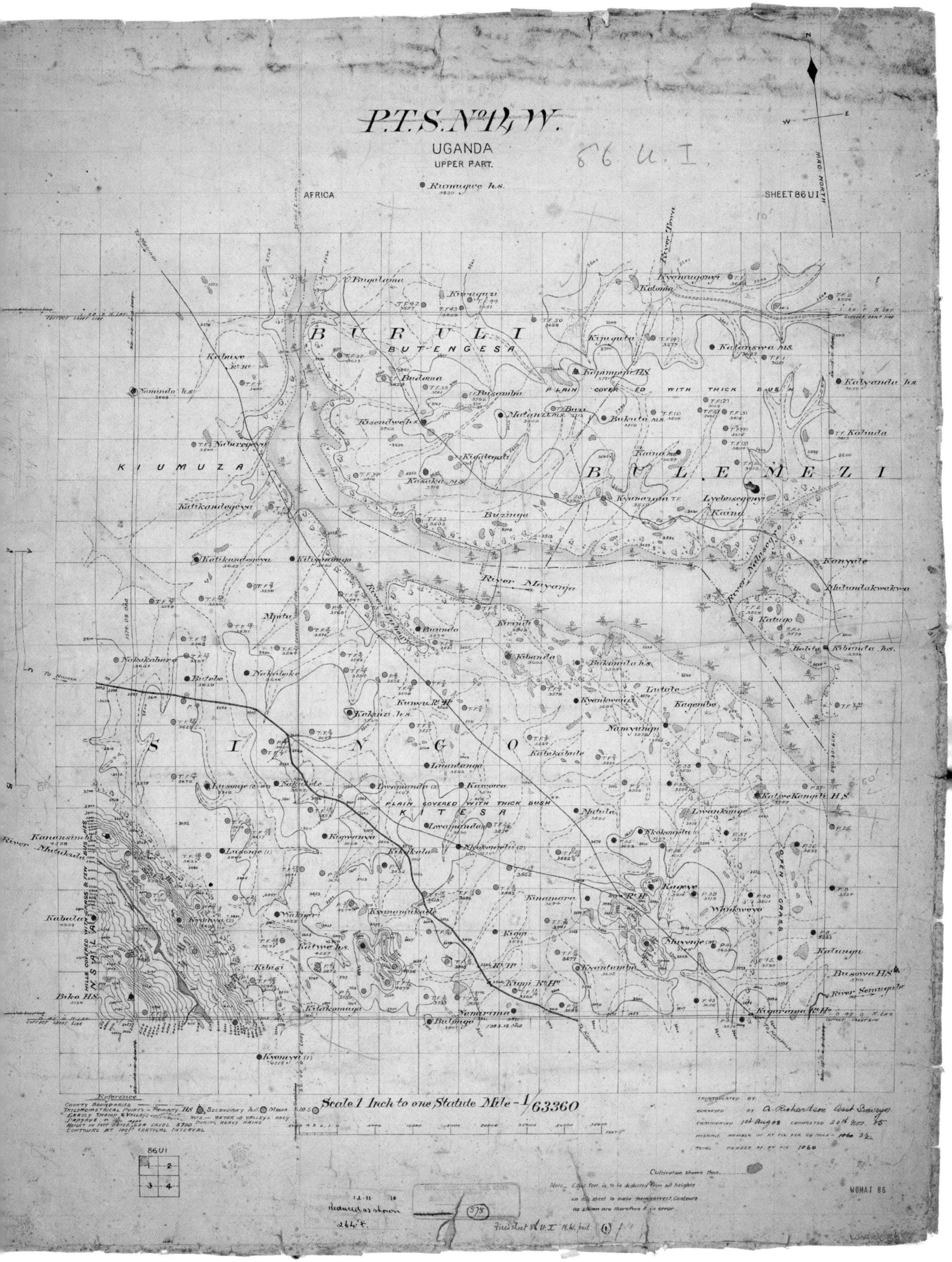

P.T.S. No 14 W.
UGANDA
UPPER PART.
86 U. I.
AFRICA
SHEET 86 U I
MAG NORTH
Kumugwe h.s.
BURULI
BUTENGESA
KIUMUZA
BULEMEZI
SINGO
KITESA
PLAIN COVERED WITH THICK BUSH
PLAIN COVERED WITH THICK BUSH
River Mayanja
River Ndrsogyo
River Towa
River Mutukula
River Semuyabo
OPEN GRASS
HILLS COVERED WITH GRASS & FEW BUSHES
Bugalama
Kiwaguzi
Kyanagonyi
Katoma
Kajuguta
Katanswa h.s.
Kabuye
Nomindo h.s.
Budama
Busamba
Kapimpini H.S.
Kalyanda h.s.
Matanzi h.s.
Bukuta h.s.
Kisendwe h.s.
Naburegeya
Kifalagali
Kalinda
Kasaka h.s.
Kaina
Katikandegeya
Kyanazam T.F.
Lyebusegenyi
Buzinga
Katikandegeya
Kilijomango
Kanyale
Mdundakwakwa
Mpitu
Buindo
Kirindi
Katugo
Nakakabara
Nakabake
Butebe
Kibanda
Bukwaida h.s.
Bobito
Kibanda h.s.
Kuwu Rt Ho
Kakaza h.s.
Kyankwanzi
Lutale
Kagembe
Namyungu
Kabukabule
Luantanga
Lusonge (2)
Nakalele
Lwagunda (2)
Kawawa
Katwe Kangili H.S.
Lwajnanda
Mdula
Lwankonge
Kanonsimbi
Kigwanya
Kikakala
Nkokangolu (2)
Lusonje (1)
Nkokangolu (1)
Kageye
Kabula
Kyanya (2)
Wakigri
Kwanamukale
Kinamara
Wankweyo
Katwe h.s.
Kiggi
Nsuwenje (2)
Katungu
Kibisi
Kyantambo
Busowa H.S.
Biko H.S.
Kiggi Rt Ho
Kilakomaga
Namarima
Bulongo
Kigaranga Rt Ho
Kyomyu (1)
To Kapimpini
To Hoima
Reference
County Boundaries
Trigonometrical Points — Primary H.S. Secondary h.s. Minor M.S.
Grassy Swamp & Valleys
Papyrus
Height in feet above sea level 3780
Contours at 100ft vertical interval
Note. — Water in valleys only during heavy rains
Scale 1 Inch to one Statute Mile — 1/63360
Triangulated by
Surveyed by A. Richardson Asst Surveyor
Commenced 1st Aug 03 Completed 20th Nov. 05
Average number of Rt Fix per sq mile — 3½
Total number of Rt Fix 1060
86 U I
1 2
3 4
Cultivation shown thus
Note. — Eight feet is to be deducted from all heights on this sheet to make them correct. Contours as shown are therefore 8 ft in error.
12.11.10
Reduced as shown
264 F.
575
Field sheet 86 U.I. N.W. part (1)
WOMAT 86

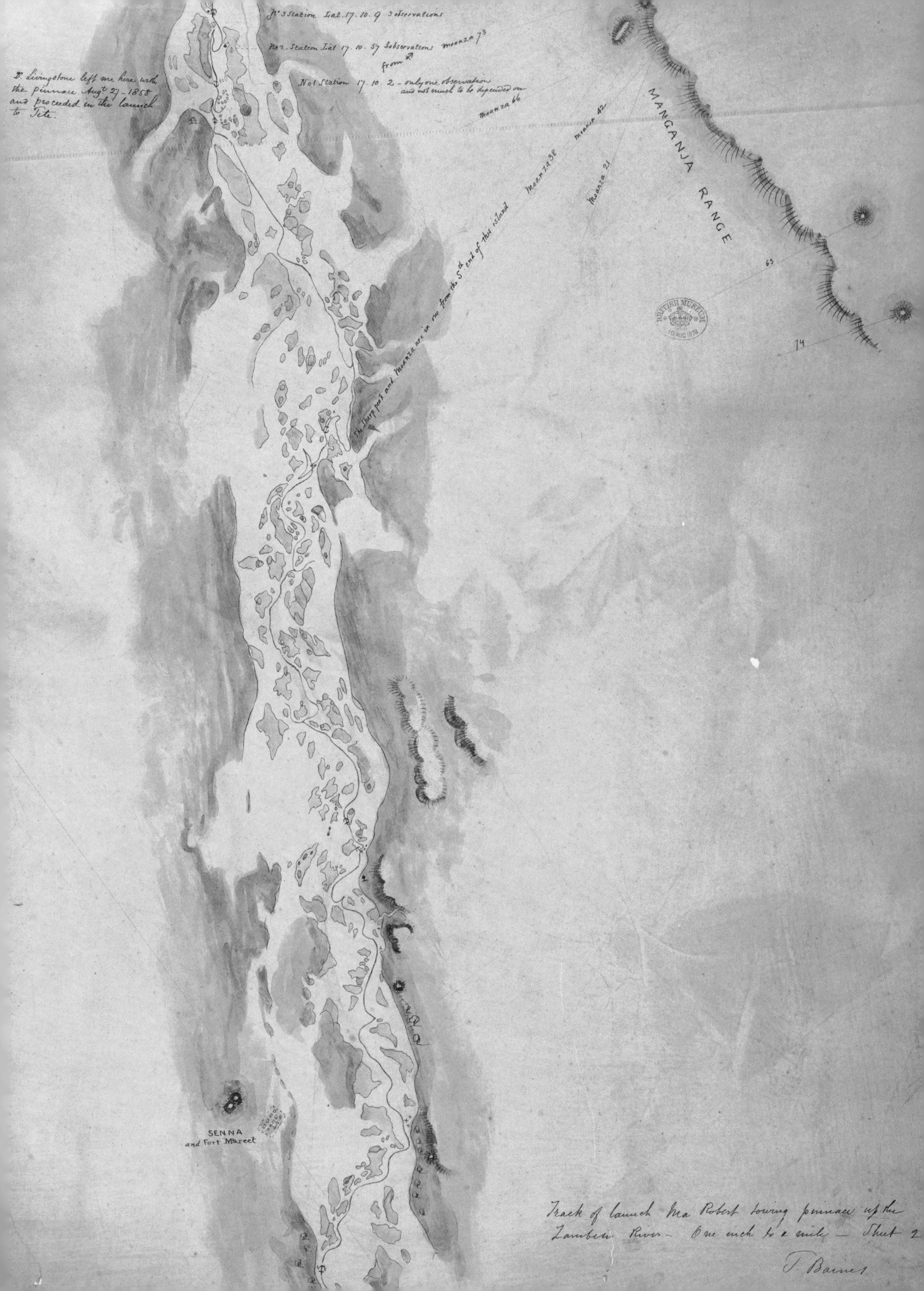

Nº 3 Station Lat. 17. 10. 9 3 observations
No 2 Station Lat 17. 10. 57 3 observations moanza 73 from 2
No 1 Station 17. 10. 2 – only one observation and not much to be depended on
Dr. Livingstone left me here with the pinnace Augt 27 – 1858 and proceeded in the launch to Tete.
moanza 66
moanza 42
moanza 38
moanza 21
MANGANJA RANGE
63
74
BRITISH MUSEUM 10 AUG 1874
The Sharp peak and Moanza are in one from the St end of this island
SENNA and Fort Mareet
Track of launch Ma Robert towing pinnace up the Zambesi River – One inch to a mile – Sheet 2
T. Baines

Zambezi River, Mozambique

(1858)

The British state-sponsored Second Zambezi Expedition was launched in March 1858. Led by the indefatigable explorer David Livingstone (1813–73), the stated aim was to 'open up' the Zambezi River so that it could be used to facilitate trade with the areas it passed through (modern-day Mozambique, Zambia, Zimbabwe, Namibia, Botswana and Angola) between Lake Victoria and the Indian Ocean. But as Livingstone discovered to his dismay, the river was unnavigable due to its rapids, rocks and gorges. The expedition did produce something of worth, however, in the form of drawings and maps by the English artist Thomas Baines (1820–75), although they were not created without some cost to the artist.

This is part of the large five-sheet map of the Zambezi River which Baines drew in October 1858. The original is held by the Royal Geographical Society, but the British Museum received this copy of it, also by Baines, along with tracings from a number of other maps of Livingstone's travels in Africa.

The map shows the river between Nyangoma Point and the town of Tete in modern-day Mozambique, and we can clearly see the complex and maze-like quality of the river with its numerous islands and inlets. To compound the difficult going, the specially constructed steam launch *Ma Robert* (which had undergone trials on the River Mersey) was difficult to steer, not unlike 'driving a London bus in the fog', as Livingstone noted. Baines has marked the route of the boat in red as it passed, according to the historian J.P.R. Wallis, 'through the tortuosities and among the dismal flats of the Zambezi'.

It did not get any better for Baines, who was repeatedly ill due to the tropical climate. On part of the map he wrote: 'I cannot answer for most corrections in this sheet as I am not well enough to be constantly up.' Even worse was to follow, when Baines was accused of misappropriating supplies by Livingstone's brother Charles and sacked from the expedition. History has, however, maintained Baines's reputation, and his work has become highly valued. Given the circumstances under which he produced this map, he has rightly earned his plaudits.

Johannesburg, South Africa

(1937)

The fire insurance maps of Charles Goad (1848–1910) are some of the most astonishingly vivid depictions of urban life ever committed to paper. To the historian they can appear too good to be true. Maps rarely show the minutiae of daily life, particularly of normal people, but these maps offer such privileged access into people's lives and businesses that one almost feels like a voyeur for examining them.

Fire insurance maps helped insurance companies to accurately assess insurance risk and calculate rates for their policyholders. To do this they needed information on the nature of their property – what it was made of and how flammable it was, neighbouring properties and their concentration, and details about fire prevention factors such as the width of streets and locations of hydrants. These are the types of map which Charles Goad's company, established in Montreal, Canada in 1875, set out to produce.

A civil engineer by training, Goad was a Londoner but moved to Canada in 1869 to work in railway construction. Having become aware that fires were a significant threat to the wooden buildings of Canada's new towns, Goad bought out the business of another fire insurance mapmaker, D.A. Sanborn (1827–83) of New York. His company would go on to map over a thousand Canadian towns. His business turned international with a move back to London in 1885, from which his surveyors travelled to towns across the globe including Copenhagen in Denmark, Buenos Aires in Argentina, and Johannesburg in South Africa, which was mapped in 1937.

This is one of several sheets covering the town of Johannesburg. It shows part of the inner-city Newtown district. Formerly an ethnically diverse area known for brickmaking (hence its former name, 'Brickfields'), in 1904, following reports of a bubonic plague outbreak, it was evacuated and burnt to the ground by the fire brigade. Seizing the opportunity presented by the disaster, the city's administration re-planned 'Newtown' as an industrial area. The map shows the power station, car factory and workshops, but also the 'compound', 'Indian dwellings' and 'native registration court' – signs of a racially segregated society.

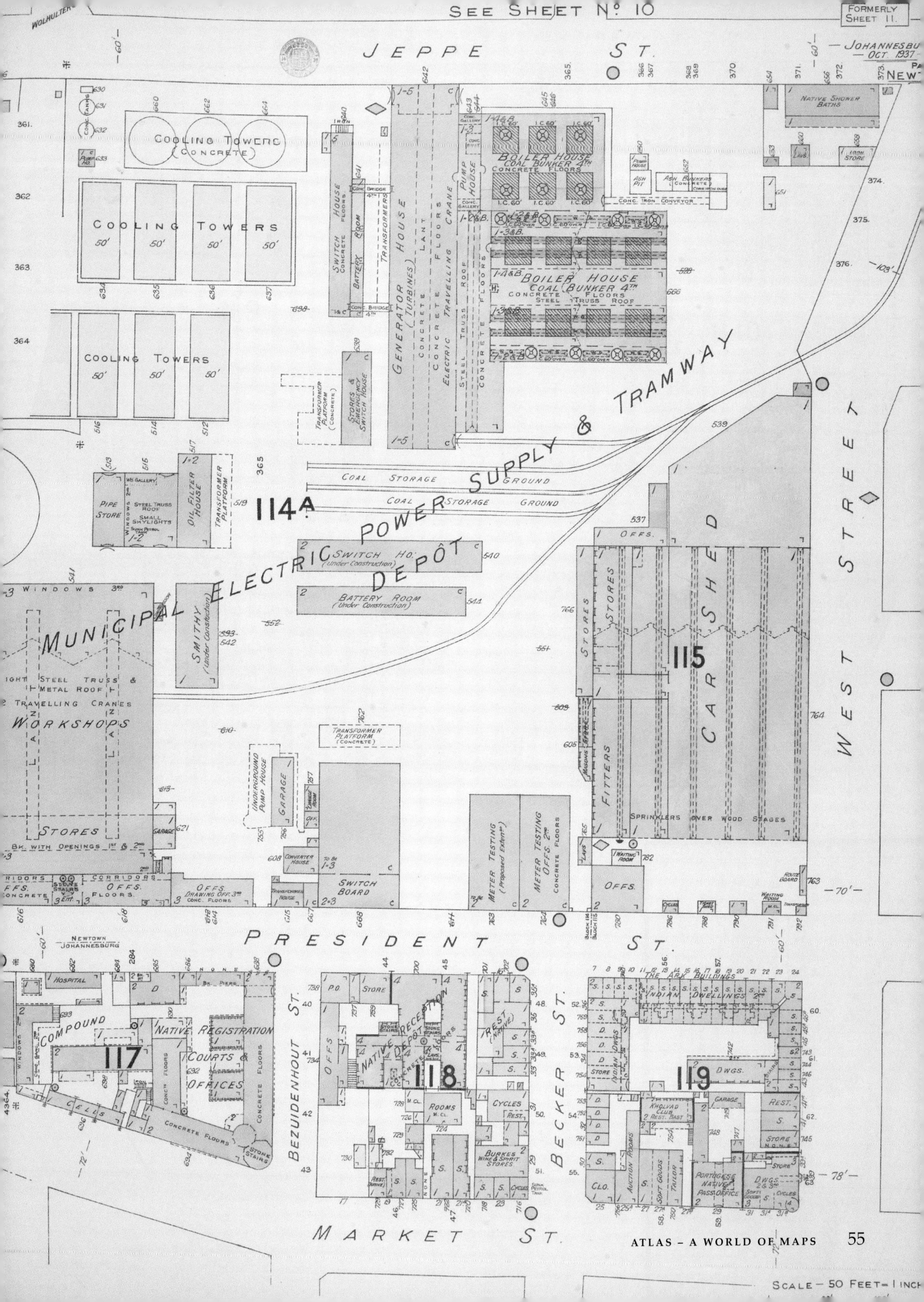

SEE SHEET No 10
FORMERLY SHEET 11.
JOHANNESBURG OCT. 1937
NEWTOWN
JEPPE ST.
WOLHUTER
COOLING TOWERS (CONCRETE)
COOLING TOWERS
COOLING TOWERS
PUMP HO.
SWITCH HOUSE
BATTERY ROOM
TRANSFORMERS
GENERATOR HOUSE (TURBINES)
CONCRETE FLOORS
ELECTRIC TRAVELLING CRANE
PUMP HOUSE
BOILER HOUSE COAL BUNKER 4TH CONCRETE FLOORS
BOILER HOUSE COAL BUNKER 4TH CONCRETE FLOORS STEEL TRUSS ROOF
ASH BUNKERS
ASH PIT
CONC. IRON CONVEYOR
NATIVE SHOWER BATHS
IRON STORE
TRANSFORMER PLATFORM
STORES & EMERGENCY SWITCH HOUSE
MUNICIPAL ELECTRIC POWER SUPPLY & TRAMWAY DEPÔT
COAL STORAGE GROUND
COAL STORAGE GROUND
114A
PIPE STORE
STEEL TRUSS ROOF SMALL SKYLIGHTS
OIL FILTER HOUSE
TRANSFORMER PLATFORM
SWITCH HO. (Under Construction)
BATTERY ROOM (Under Construction)
SMITHY (Under Construction)
LIGHT STEEL TRUSS & METAL ROOF
TRAVELLING CRANES
WORKSHOPS
STORES
BK. WITH OPENINGS 1ST & 2ND
OFFS. CONCRETE FLOORS
OFFS. DRAWING OFF. 3RD CONC. FLOORS
TRANSFORMER PLATFORM (CONCRETE)
UNDERGROUND PUMP HOUSE
GARAGE
CONVERTER HOUSE
SWITCH BOARD
METER TESTING (Proposed Extent)
METER TESTING OFFS. 2ND CONCRETE FLOORS
OFFS.
STORES
FITTERS
CAR SHED
115
SPRINKLERS OVER WOOD STAGES
WAITING ROOM
WEST STREET
PRESIDENT ST.
NEWTOWN JOHANNESBURG
HOSPITAL
COMPOUND
117
NATIVE REGISTRATION COURTS & OFFICES
CELLS
CONCRETE FLOORS
STONE STAIRS
BEZUIDENHOUT ST.
NATIVE RECEPTION DEPOT
118
P.O.
STORE
OFFS
ROOMS
REST (NATIVE)
CYCLES
BURKES WINE & SPIRIT STORES
BECKER ST.
THE ARK BUILDINGS
INDIAN DWELLINGS
INDIAN DWGS
119
DWGS.
KHOLVAD CLUB
GARAGE
REST.
AUCTION ROOMS
SOFT GOODS
TAILOR
PORTUGESE NATIVE PASS OFFICE
MARKET ST.
SCALE – 50 FEET = 1 INCH

The Indis of occident quhar the spangzartis
doith occupy
Couba
Lucata
Conde of florida

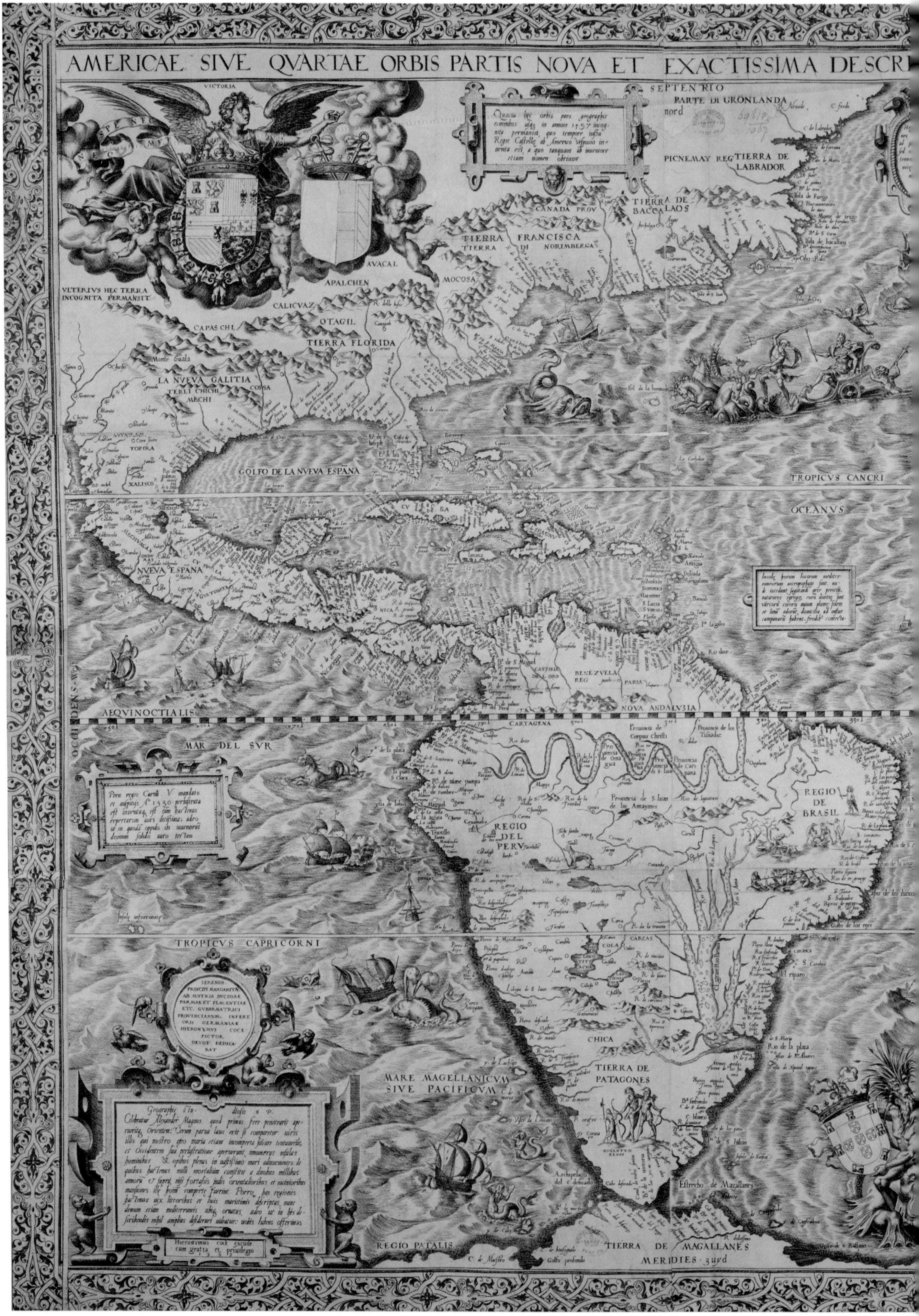
AMERICAE SIVE QVARTAE ORBIS PARTIS NOVA ET EXACTISSIMA DESCRI
VICTORIA
SEPTEN RIO
PARTE DI GRONLANDA
nord
Quævis hæc orbis pars geographis omnibus usq; in annum 1497 incognito permansit, quo tempore iussu Regis Castellæ ab Americo Vespucio inventa est, a quo tanquam ab inventore etiam nomen obtinuit
PICNEMAY REG
TIERRA DE LABRADOR
CANADA PROV
TIERRA DE BACCALAOS
TIERRA FRANCISCA
TIERRA DI NORIMBERGA
AVACAL
APALCHEN
MOCOSA
VLTERIVS HEC TERRA INCOGNITA PERMANSIT
CALICVAZ
CAPASCHI
OTAGIL
TIERRA FLORIDA
Monte Suala
LA NVEVA GALITIA
TERLI CHICHI MECHI
COSSA
TOPIRA
XALISCO
GOLFO DE LA NVEVA ESPAÑA
TROPICVS CANCRI
CV BA
OCEANVS
NVEVA ESPAÑA
GVATIMALA
NICA
Incolæ horum locorum mediterraneorum antropophagi sunt, nudi incedunt sagittandi arte peritissimi, natatores egregii, varii diuersi coloris auium plumis sese ornant, campanarum sonum ... contecta.
CASTILLA DEL ORO
BENEZVELA REG
PARIA
AEQVINOCTIALIS
NOVA ANDALVZIA
OCCIDENS
CARTAGENA
MAR DEL SVR
Peru regio Caroli V mandato et auspitiis A° 1530 perlustrata est inventaq; est cum hactenus repertarum auri ditissima; adeo ut in quodã oppido sit inuentum domum solido auro tectam
Prouincia de S. Iuan de las Amazones
REGIO DEL PERV
REGIO DE BRASIL
TROPICVS CAPRICORNI
SERENISS. PRINCIPI MARGARITÆ AB AVSTRIA DVCISSÆ PARMAE ET PLACENTIAE ETC. GVBERNATRICI PROVINCIARVM INFERIORIS GERMANIAE HIERONYMVS COCK PICTOR DEVOTE DEDICABAT
CHICA
TIERRA DE PATAGONES
MARE MAGELLANICVM SIVE PACIFICVM
GIGANTVM REGIO
Geographiæ Studiosis S.P.
Celebratur Alexander Magnus quod primus fere penetrarit aperuerit Orientem: Verum parua laus erit si comparetur viris illis qui nostro æuo maria etiam incomperta sulcare tentauerit, et Occidentem sua perlustratione aperuerunt, innumeris insulis hominibus et opibus plenis in vastissimo mari adinuentis: de quibus hactenus nulli mortalium constitit a duobus millibus annorum et supra, nisi fortassis Indis Orientalioribus et vicinioribus mansiones illæ fuerint comperte fuerint. Porro, has regiones hactenus vix littoribus et locis maritimis descriptas, nunc demum etiam mediterraneis ubiq; ornatas, adeo ut in his describendis nihil amplius desiderari videatur: vobis lubens offerimus
Hieronymus cock excude cum gratia et priuilegio
Estrecho de Magallanes
REGIO PATALIS
TIERRA DE MAGALLANES
MERIDIES zuyd

America

(1562)

By the time this map was published in 1562, over half a century had passed since the first Iberian contact with America. As it shows, they had not been idle in charting and consolidating their 'New World'. For example, the east coast of North America is spectacularly well described, the shape of South America is roughly as we recognise it today, and even the Amazon River is shown broadly correctly, snaking inland. The reason for the map's excellent geographical content is that it was based on official Spanish charts and drawn in collaboration with the senior Spanish cartographer, Diego Gutiérrez (*fl*. 1511–54). Its content contributes to the map's powerful symbolic and persuasive function. This is a map that promotes imperial Spanish power to Spain's imperial rivals.

Who were these rivals? After all, it was under the Spanish flag that Christopher Columbus (1451–1506) had sailed westwards hoping to reach the East Indies, landing on the island of Guanahani in the Bahamas in 1492. However, Portuguese expansion into America followed closely behind, and tension between the Iberian powers was only defused by a demarcation boundary, the 1494 papal-legitimised Treaty of Tordesillas, which is not shown on this map. By the second half of the sixteenth century the French had begun to explore the eastern seaboard, and before long the Dutch and English would follow suit.

To temper these rivals' ambitions, the map emphasised Spain's case with powerful cartographic force. The Spanish arms are shown at the top left, held up by Winged Victory, next to blank arms, which were planned to be filled with those of France following the marriage of the Spanish King Philip II (*r*.1556–98) to Elizabeth of Valois (1545–68) in 1559. Philip's personal arms are held aloft by Neptune in the lower right, and it is surely Philip portrayed riding Neptune-like in a chariot across the Atlantic.

This image of Spanish power was reinforced by the fact that this was then the biggest printed map of America to have been produced. It was engraved and published in Antwerp by one of the most renowned and artistically gifted artists in Europe, Hieronymus Cock (1518–70). Cock, who was working in the Habsburg-controlled Spanish Netherlands and who may have received the commission from a Spanish official, had studied in Italy and assimilated the art of the southern Renaissance. The map exhibits not only his virtuoso etching technique but also his accomplished treatment of the human form, animals and birds.The map is a tour-de-force of cartographic propaganda.

North America

(1783)

The British Library's example of John Mitchell's (1711–68) *The British and French Dominions in North America* holds one of cartography's great 'what if' moments. Had this map been known during the negotiations of the 1783 Treaty of Paris, today's inhabitants of Ontario in Canada might today be whistling the 'Star-Spangled Banner'.

Mitchell's was the most up-to-date map of North America when it was first published in 1755. It was also one of the largest, printed on eight sheets of paper which could be joined together, enabling Mitchell to include a great deal of information. Over the years the map was updated numerous times to reflect the changing borders between British, French and Spanish areas, and to incorporate information from journeys made west of the Mississippi River and in the Canadian north.

But by 1783 what was most out of date was the map's title, because in that year the British and French dominions had been joined by the newly independent United States of America after Britain's defeat in the American War of Independence (1775–83). However, before the map was retired from service it had a further job to do. Copies of the Mitchell map were used by the British and United States delegations during negotiations for the 1783 Treaty of Paris, which established the terms of the United States' independence. This is the British delegation's copy. On it are numerous annotations and lines drawn in red on the instructions of the secretary to the British delegation, Richard Oswald (1705–84), denoting the limits of fishing areas and the proposed border between the United States and Canada.

Of the many lines on the 'Red-Lined Map' drawn 'as described by Mr Oswald', one line warrants particular attention. It is the line running along the west bank of the Mississippi River, then across to Lake Michigan where it turns west–east to the St Lawrence River. The line is marked as 'the British construction according to the Treaty of Utrecht' (which had divided North America between Britain and France in 1713), and it has been contended that this line represents how much the British delegation were prepared to cede to the United States, if necessary. That is, far further north than the eventual US–Canadian border, established in 1783.

Oswald and his party got off lightly. But so scared were they at being found out that, right up until 1896, successive British governments forbade unauthorised access to the map in the British Museum, to which it had passed with the King's Topographical Collection in 1828.

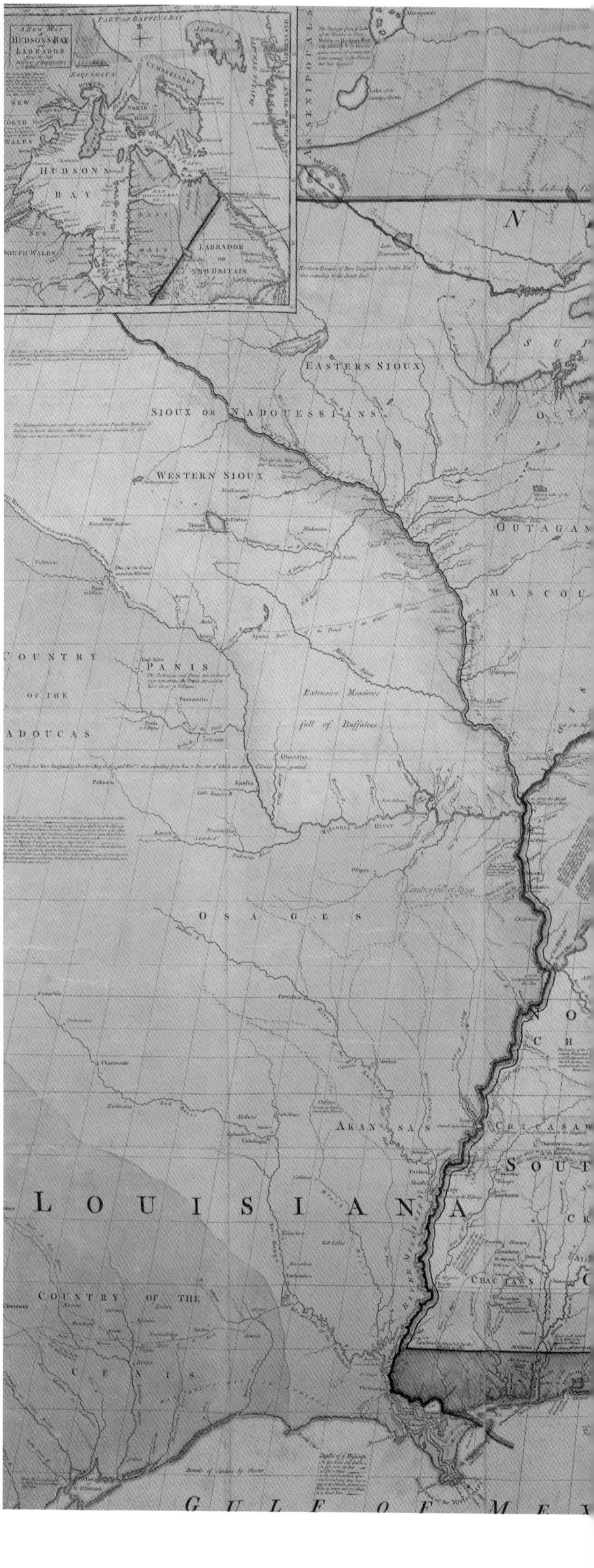

PART OF LABRADOR
OR
NEW BRITAIN
PART OF HUDSONS
ISLAND
OF
NEW FOUND LAND
GULF
FRANCE
OR
CANADA
MESSESAGUES
LAKE HURON
IROQUOIS
LAKE ONTARIO
LAKE ERIE
OKSWEGO
PENSILVANIA
MASSACHUSETTS
BAY
THE
ATLANTIC
OCEAN
CAROLINA
FLORIDA
A MAP of the
BRITISH COLONIES in
North America
WITH THE
SETTLEMENTS,
The Earl of Halifax
The Lords Commissioners for Trade & Plantations

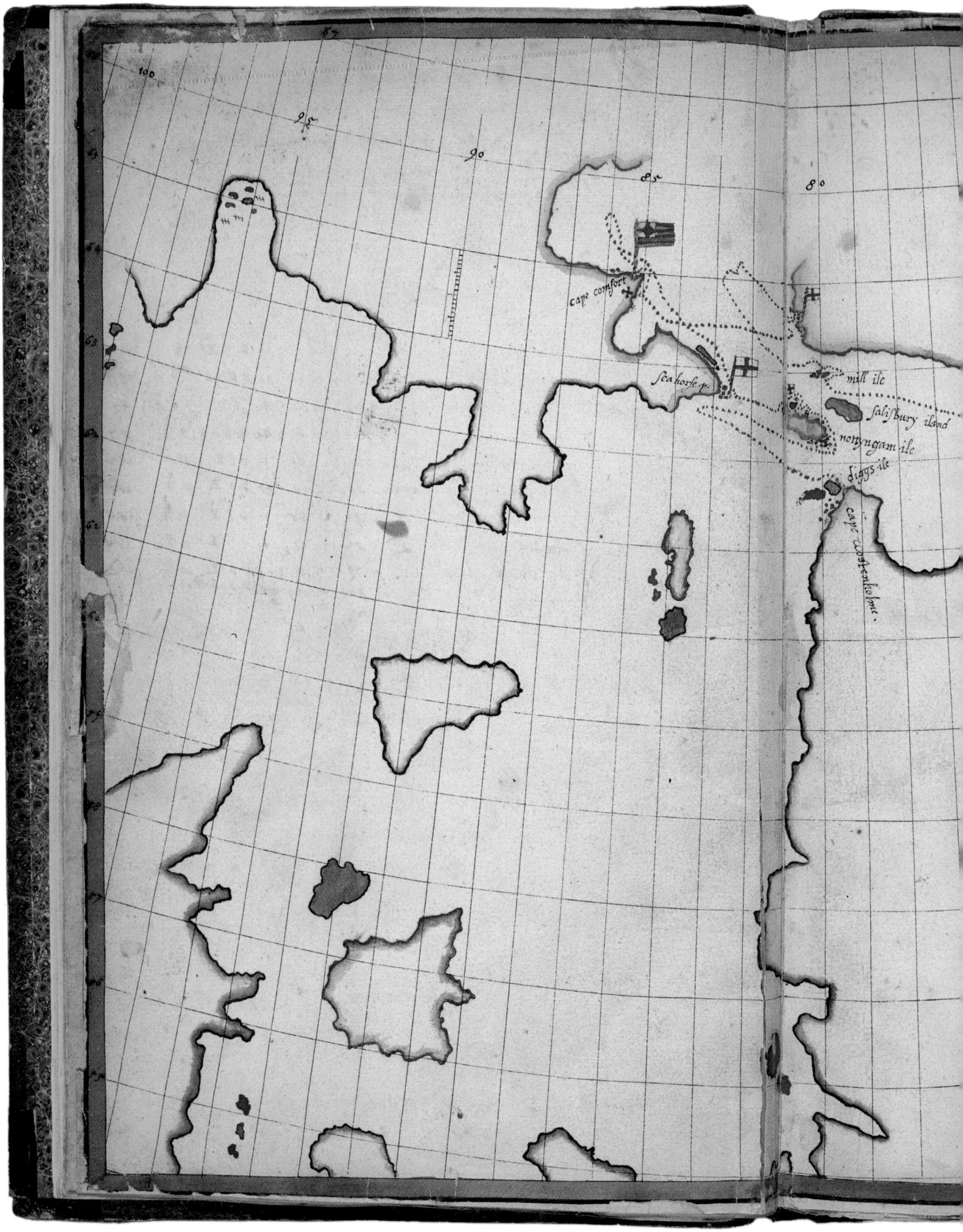

100
95
90
85
80
cape comfort
sea horse p.
mill ile
salisbury iland
nottyngam ile
diggs ile
cape wolstenholme.

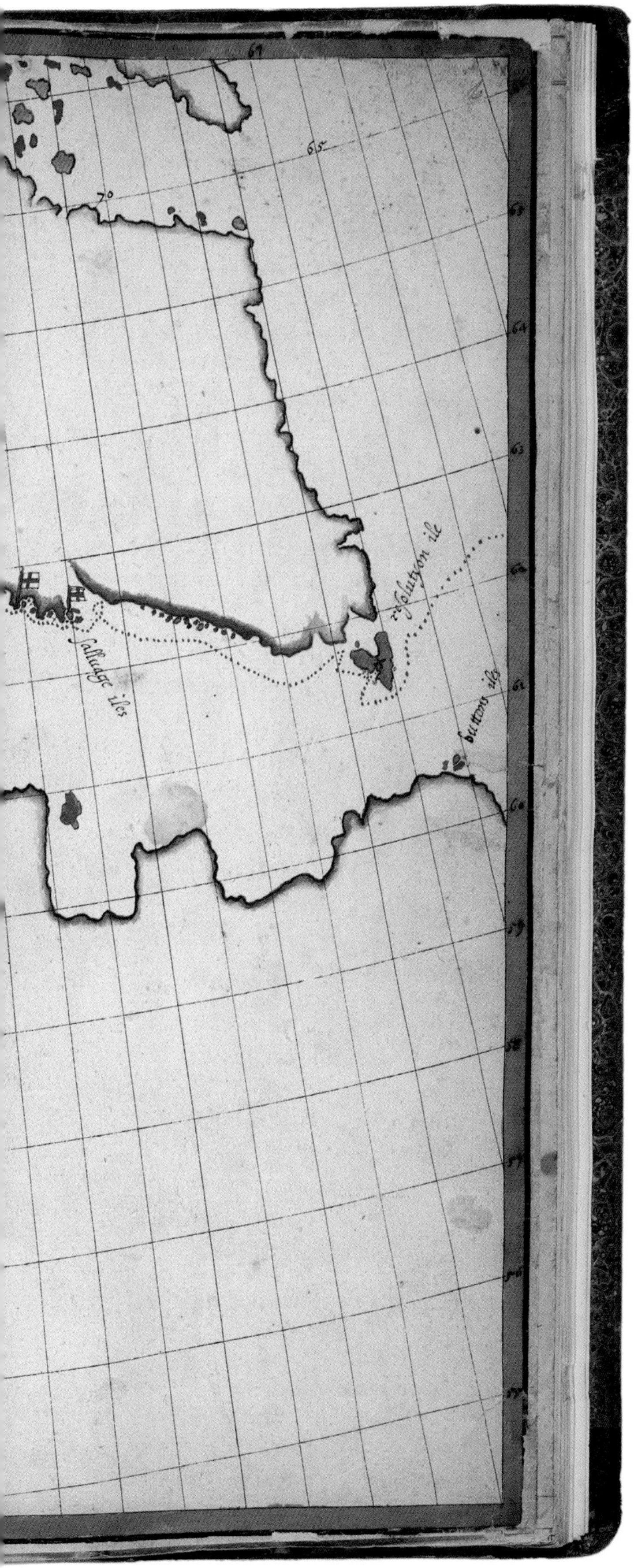

Hudson Bay

(1615)

William Baffin (1584–1622) is the man whose name is superimposed on to the vast Baffin Island and the even vaster Baffin Bay. He was not the first person to go there (indeed, people already lived there), but he was the first European to properly map it, being one of a long line of English explorers who, since the late sixteenth century, had been sailing to the Arctic in the hope of finding a northern sea route, or 'Northwest Passage', to the East Indies.

This map was hand-drawn by Baffin to accompany the journal of his fourth voyage, made in 1615. Previous voyages had only tentatively explored Canada's east coast, but in 1610 Henry Hudson (1565–1611) sailed into the huge bay which bears his name, increasing anticipation that the passage lay on the far side of it. The follow-up voyage, with Baffin as pilot, set out to build on Hudson's findings, sponsored by a group of investors called (somewhat pre-emptively) the Company of the Merchants of London, Discoverers of the North-West Passage.

On Baffin's map we can see the dotted route of Baffin's ship *Discovery* as it sailed westwards up the Hudson Strait with Baffin Island on its right, planting flags where it landed, and bestowing the names of sponsors on the places they found: Digges Isle and Cape Wolstenholme. The chart reveals that instead of heading west into the wide expanse of the bay, Baffin chose to explore further north, where he was blocked by ice. Baffin's decision supported his own opinion, as noted by the author Glyn Williams, that the chances of the Northwest Passage lying through Hudson's Bay was 'doubtfull, supposinge the contrarye'.

Baffin had nevertheless collected enough information for the most detailed chart of the region to date, information which would go towards consolidating the area through the eventual establishment of the Hudson's Bay Trading Company in 1670. He had also used his observations of the moon to calculate longitude, or how far west and east the *Discovery* was travelling, which was virtually unheard of at that time. His calculations are presented in his carefully handwritten journal. Baffin's journal was published in the collection of voyages entitled 'Purchas his Pilgrims' in 1625, but this map was not included.

St Lawrence River

(1759)

James Cook (1728–79) is best known for being the first European to chart the Pacific, New Zealand and Australia. Less well known are his charting exploits in North America during the Seven Years' War between Britain and France (1758–63). It was during this conflict that Britain secured control of Canada, and the efforts around this chart, drawn by Cook in 1759, played a role in the victory.

Following the capture of the French fort of Louisburg on the St Lawrence River, Cook was drawn into preparations for General Wolfe's naval assault on Quebec, further upstream. The 29-year-old found himself in esteemed company with the surveyor Samuel Holland (1728–1801, later Surveyor General of Quebec) and Captain John Simcoe (1710–59, father of the first governor of Upper Canada).

Cook's marine surveying skills were put to good use in mapping the treacherous river leading to Quebec, a stretch of water which Cook's subsequent biographer John Beaglehole described as having 'many islands and islets, shoals and drying banks and reefs, strong tides, whirling eddies and bewildering currents'. Of crucial importance was a section known as 'the traverse', in which ships were required to shift from a northern to a southern channel, avoiding rocks and islands, in order to continue upstream.

The French had based the survival of Quebec on this natural defence, but they reckoned without Cook and colleagues. For two days he and a surveying party mapped the soundings (depths) of the river and laid warning markers for the imminent arrival of British naval ships. In his diary Cook noted having 'ret[urne]d satisfied with being acquainted with the channel'. His map proved it by identifying the hazards to be avoided by ships transiting from right to left (Quebec lies beyond the left of the map). Three intersecting lines mark the point in the river at which the ships needed to switch banks, keeping to the deep water.

The successful traversing of the strait a week later was attributable as much to skilful sailing as high-quality mapping. Cook was only one of a number of the surveyors, but his efforts on the St Lawrence were subsequently amplified as a consequence of the fame he went on to achieve.

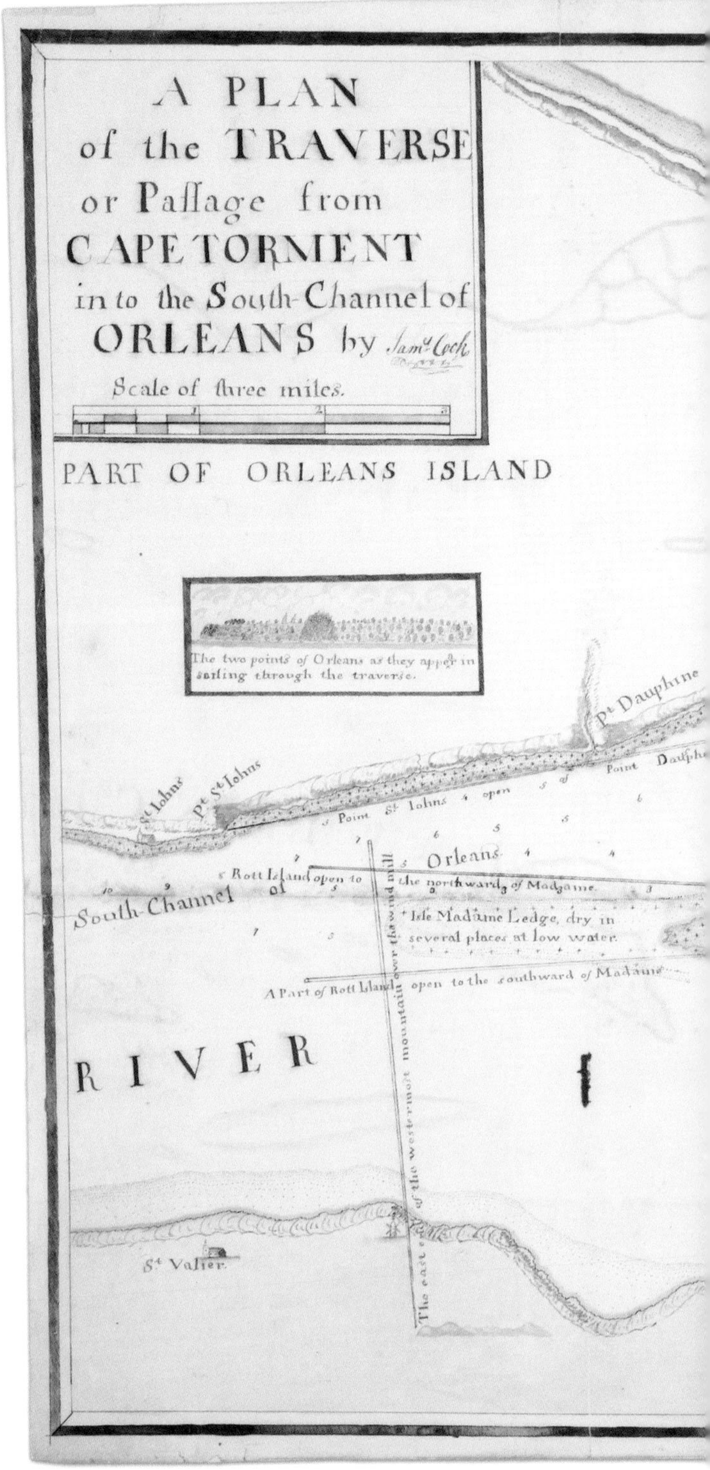

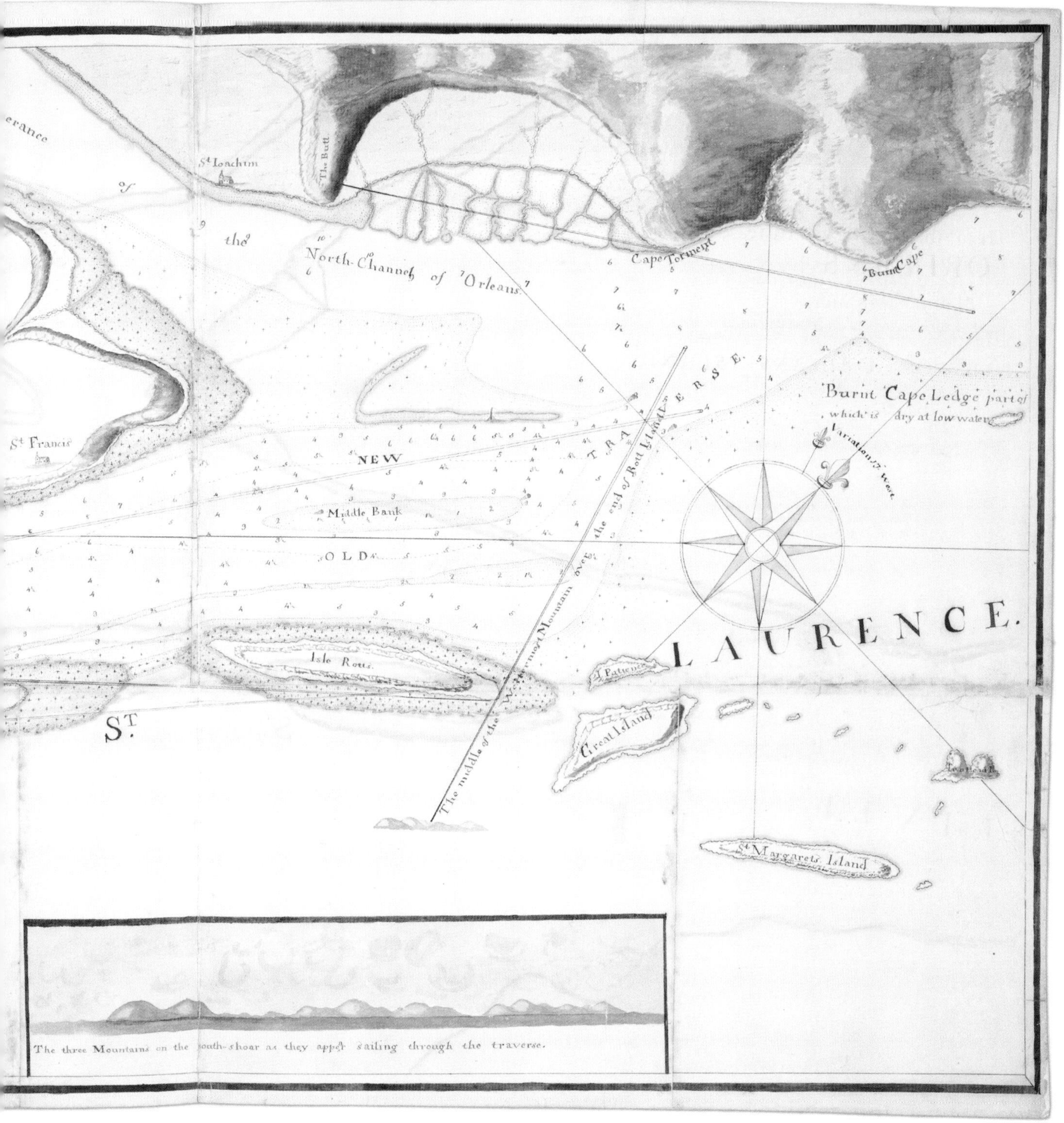

erance
of
the
St Ioachim
The Butt
North Channel of Orleans
Cape Torment
Burnt Cape
Burnt Cape Ledge part of which is dry at low water
Variation 17 West
TRAVERSE.
NEW
Middle Bank
OLD
St Francis
Isle Rous
St.
LAURENCE.
Great Island
St Margarets Island
The three Mountains on the south-shoar as they appear sailing through the traverse.

Ontario

(1790s)

Elizabeth Posthuma Simcoe (1762–1850) was an English artist and diarist who spent five years between 1791 and 1796 in Canada with her husband John Graves Simcoe (1752–1806) during his term as the first lieutenant-governor of the province of Upper Canada. During her time in the British colony Elizabeth recorded its life and scenery in her diary and in watercolour views and maps. When she returned to England she presented a special set of 32 oval watercolour views of Ontario painted on birchbark to King George III.

Ontario was a far cry from the Devon estate and polite English society in which Elizabeth had grown up. It was a frontier province that had most recently witnessed war (with the United States) less than a decade earlier. She embraced the experience, making art excursions as befitted a lady of her standing, in much the same way as she might have done in England. Some of her tours took her into rugged and wooded Ontario, where she was able to exercise her 'picturesque eye'. The wildness of nature was a popular subject and is shown to good effect in watercolours such as the one of Queenstown at the mouth of the Niagara River, where she was based between July 1792 and July 1793. In her diary Elizabeth

noted the species of trees she could see, and exclaimed how the scene reminded her of the Wye Valley on the English–Welsh border.

Another watercolour shows the Simcoes' summer house in York (now Toronto), which they named Castle Frank after their son Francis. It was built for them in a picturesque wooded area and designed on the plan of a Grecian temple. The classical columns were fashioned out of white pine logs. Elizabeth also drew maps for her husband which he occasionally included in his official reports on the progress of the colony. The map that was included with the set of views indicates forts which Governor Simcoe proposed to develop into towns, and links them together with military roads.

Painting on the bark of a birch tree was an uncommon practice and, unusually, Simcoe chose to paint on the darker brown side of the bark rather than the lighter side. However, this served to give the images an appealing copper-like quality. Because they are of a uniform size and appearance they were probably painted as a group with presentation to the king in mind, derived from Simcoe's *in situ* work. Some of them are based on sketches by the army officer and artist Robert Pilkington (1765–1810), who accompanied Elizabeth on a number of her sketching trips. The purpose of these paintings and their gifting to George III was undoubtedly to lodge a positive vision of Upper Canada in the king's mind.

Maine

(1772)

King George III's love of maps was common knowledge and consequently he was often presented with maps as gifts from his subjects, politicians, the military and fellow rulers.

This is a map which he was likely to have been given along with a few others in August 1772 by the Board of Trade, the government office responsible for Britain's colonies. It shows the coast of Maine in New England, which the Board of Trade had ordered to be mapped as part of an inventory of colonial property. This 'Northern Survey' was enacted by military surveyors such as Charles Blaskowitz (*c*.1743–1823) and the author of this map, George Sproule (*c*.1743–1817), under the direction of Surveyor General Samuel Holland, and its aim was to identify land which had not yet been developed and exploited.

The coast of Maine is not the easiest place to survey. As can be seen on the map, it is a complicated coastline with treacherous waters containing shoals, rocks and islands. Sproule's experience bore this out: his survey ship was wrecked during his reconnaissance work. Nor was it the easiest time to be mapping New England. During the 1770s the political situation between Britain and its North American colonies was deteriorating, with arguments over taxation and the 'Intolerable Acts' leading to the outbreak of hostilities in April 1775.

In this sensitive climate a deeper purpose for the map becomes clear, as the historian Alexander Johnson has demonstrated. If we look closely, beyond the details of inlets and harbours, we can see a variety of buildings and premises labelled, including meeting houses and sawmills. These locations were of interest to Britain because of their links to the illegal timber trade. Maine was the principal area where timber was sourced, and since the Royal Navy depended on it almost entirely for its ships' masts, the illegal trade had the potential to critically undermine Britain's capacity to control its colonies and even wage war against them.

The map is a spy map, to assist infiltration, espionage and countermeasures. The information was probably retained in further maps so that it did not become inaccessible when this map was presented to the king.

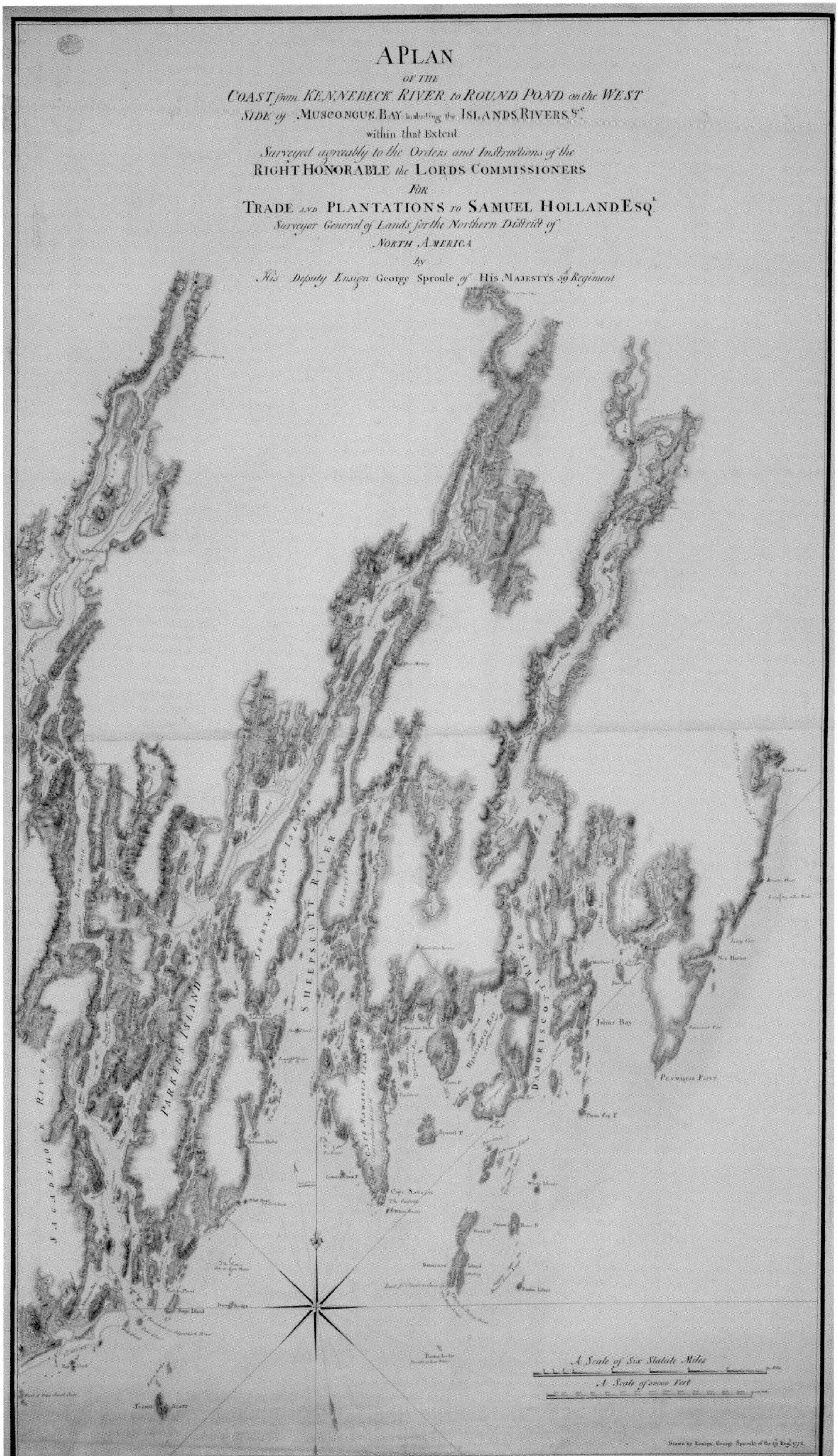
A PLAN
OF THE
COAST from KENNEBECK RIVER to ROUND POND on the WEST
SIDE of MUSCONGUE BAY including the ISLANDS, RIVERS &c.
within that Extent
Surveyed agreeably to the Orders and Instructions of the
RIGHT HONORABLE the LORDS COMMISSIONERS
FOR
TRADE AND PLANTATIONS to SAMUEL HOLLAND ESQ.R
Surveyor General of Lands for the Northern District of
NORTH AMERICA
by
His Deputy Ensign George Sproule of His MAJESTY'S 59 Regiment
SAGADEHOCK RIVER
PARKERS ISLAND
JERRYMINQUAM ISLAND
SHEEPSCUTT RIVER
CAPE NAWAGIN ISLAND
Cape Nawagin
DAMARISCOTTA RIVER
Johns Bay
PENMAQUID POINT
Round Pond
New Harbor
SEGWIN ISLAND
A Scale of Six Statute Miles
A Scale of 20000 Feet

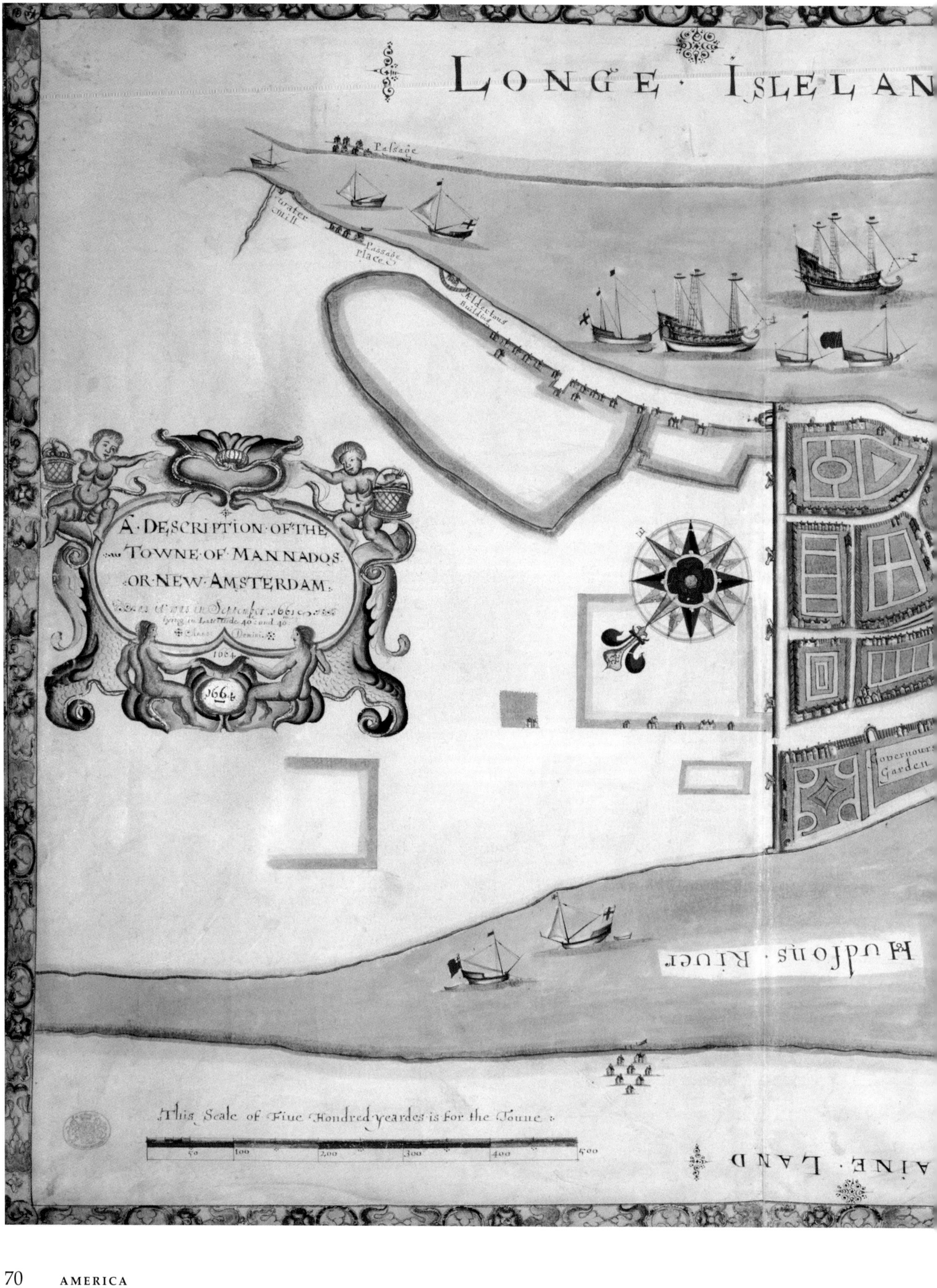
LONGE · ISLELAN
Passage
Passage Place
A·DESCRIPTION·OF·THE
TOWNE·OF·MANNADOS
OR·NEW·AMSTERDAM
1664
Governours Garden
Hudsons · Riuer
This Scale of Fiue Hondred yeardes is for the Towne
50
100
200
300
400
500

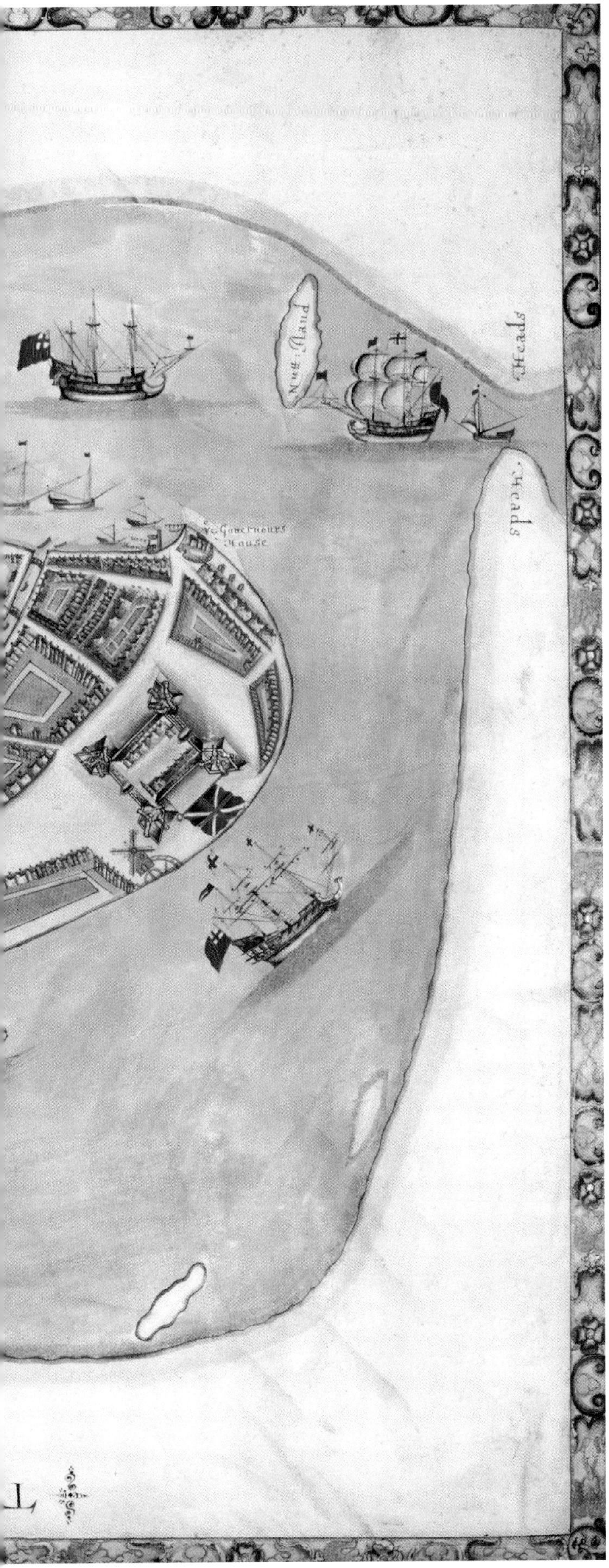

New York City

(1664)

This map, entitled 'A description of the towne of Mannados or New Amsterdam', is deemed so significant that it has been termed 'New York's birth certificate'. The reason is that it was painted in 1664, when control of the town was passed to Britain by the governor of Dutch North America, Peter Stuyvesant (1610–72). It is supposed to have been presented to James, Duke of York, the future James II (*r.*1685–88), as a way of asking his permission to rename the town in his honour. For this reason, writing about it in 1858, the librarian of the New York Historical Society, George H. Moore, named it 'The Duke's Plan'.

The map was part of the royal map collection which came to the British Museum as the Topographical Collection of George III in 1828. Given its splendid appearance, with the ornate border, decorative cartouche and remarkably fresh colours and gold finishing, it is easy to appreciate that it was intended for a royal patron. Other features, such as British sailing ships with their vast red ensigns in the East River, lend further credence to the story.

The cartographic content is derived from earlier Dutch maps of the town, particularly a 1661 map known as the 'Castello Plan' (due to its discovery in a Florentine villa in 1911) by the surveyor Jacques Cortelyou (*c.*1625–93). It shows the key features of this strategic settlement in irresistible detail. With east to the top, we can see the built-up southern tip of Manhattan with the battery, the 'governour's house', the wide thoroughfare of Broadway and the newly built wall to repel British attacks, the site of Wall Street today. The Dutch influence remains visible in the formal gardens, windmills and the canal.

Given the likely speed of the commission it is not surprising that an earlier map was copied for the Duke's Plan. Although the mapmaker is not known, it bears the unmistakeable style of the Thames School of chart makers, based in Wapping on the River Thames. Thanks to its superbly preserved state it is still possible to imagine how it would originally have been received.

South Carolina

(1721)

Precious few examples of historical Native American cartography survive today. In part this is to do with a more ephemeral mapmaking tradition in which maps were not intended to be kept. It is also surely a consequence of the dominant, eradicating effect of European mapping on other traditions. The maps which do survive tend to be those created by Native Americans at the behest of colonial authorities. Even at one remove, however, the Catawba deerskin map is an extraordinary survivor.

Around 1721 a 'Map describing the situation of the several nations of Indians in the N.W. of South Carolina', drawn on the skin of a deer, was produced for the British governor of South Carolina, Francis Nicholson (1655–1728). The original map is lost, but we know about it from two copies. One was made for the British government and is now in the UK National Archives, and the British Library's copy was made for the future George II (*r.*1727–60). The identity of the original's author, now believed to be a Cherokee rather than a Catawba Indian, is unknown.

As its title suggests, the map shows an area of South Carolina, in the southeastern United States. It is a schematic map, oriented roughly with south at the top. The town of Charleston on the left, shown as a series of rigid lines representing streets and boundaries, gives way to 13 circled areas which are linked by roads. These circles represent the Indian communities positioned between British (the square plot represents the colony of Virginia) and French colonies. The Nassaw (Catawba) tribe is the most prominent circle at the centre.

The map is an incredibly clever piece of persuasive cartography, even, according to the historian Ian Chambers, 'an up-to-date Indian statement concerning geopolitical relations'. It is believed to have been produced shortly after Governor Nicholson arrived in Carolina. Top of his 'to do' list was finding a solution to problems with the Indian skin and fur trade caused by rival colonies trading illegally. This meant meeting with representatives of each of the communities.

The maker of the map sensed his opportunity to present his own community in the best light, and to get one up on his rivals. By drawing a road directly from Charleston to the Cherokee and Chickasaw communities, avoiding and circumventing the communities at the centre (from which a road leads to rival Virginia), the map may be subtly suggesting that the Cherokee and Chickasaw were the tribes in whom Nicholson and Carolina should place their trust.

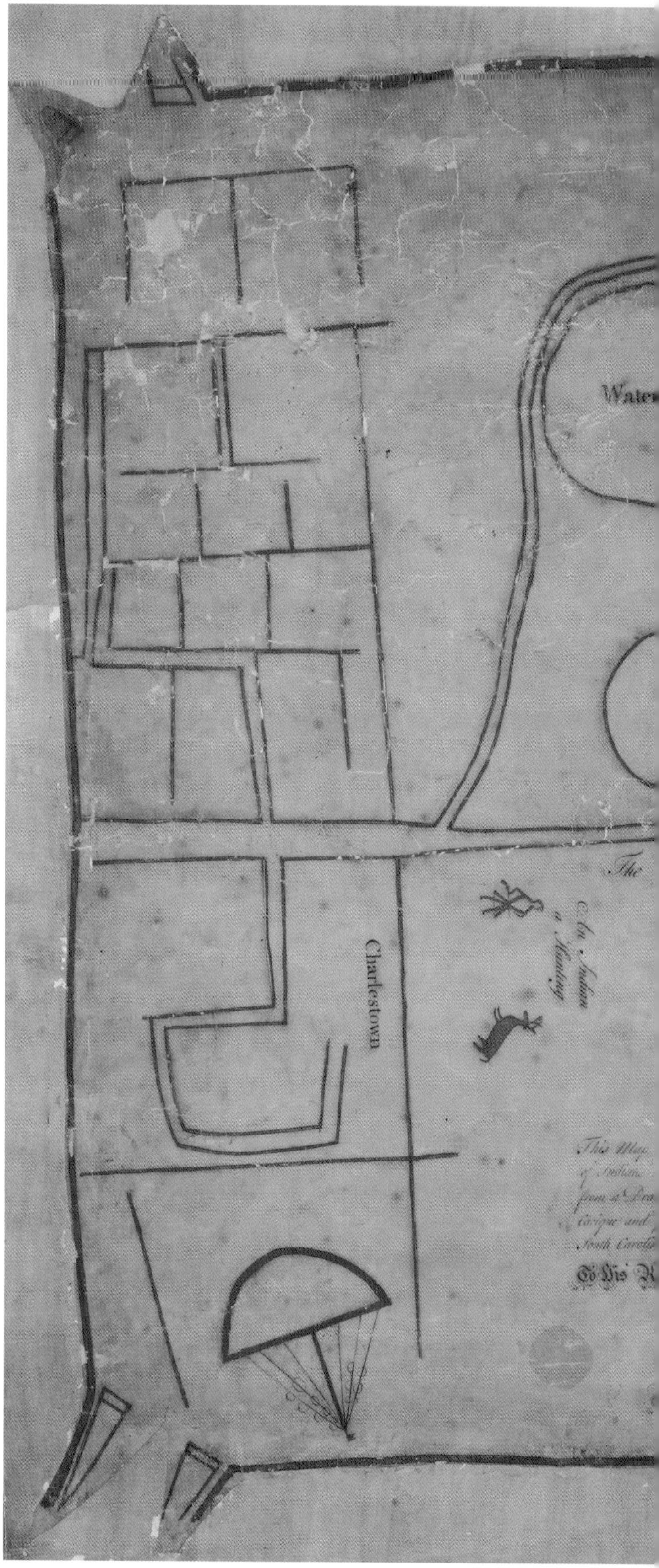

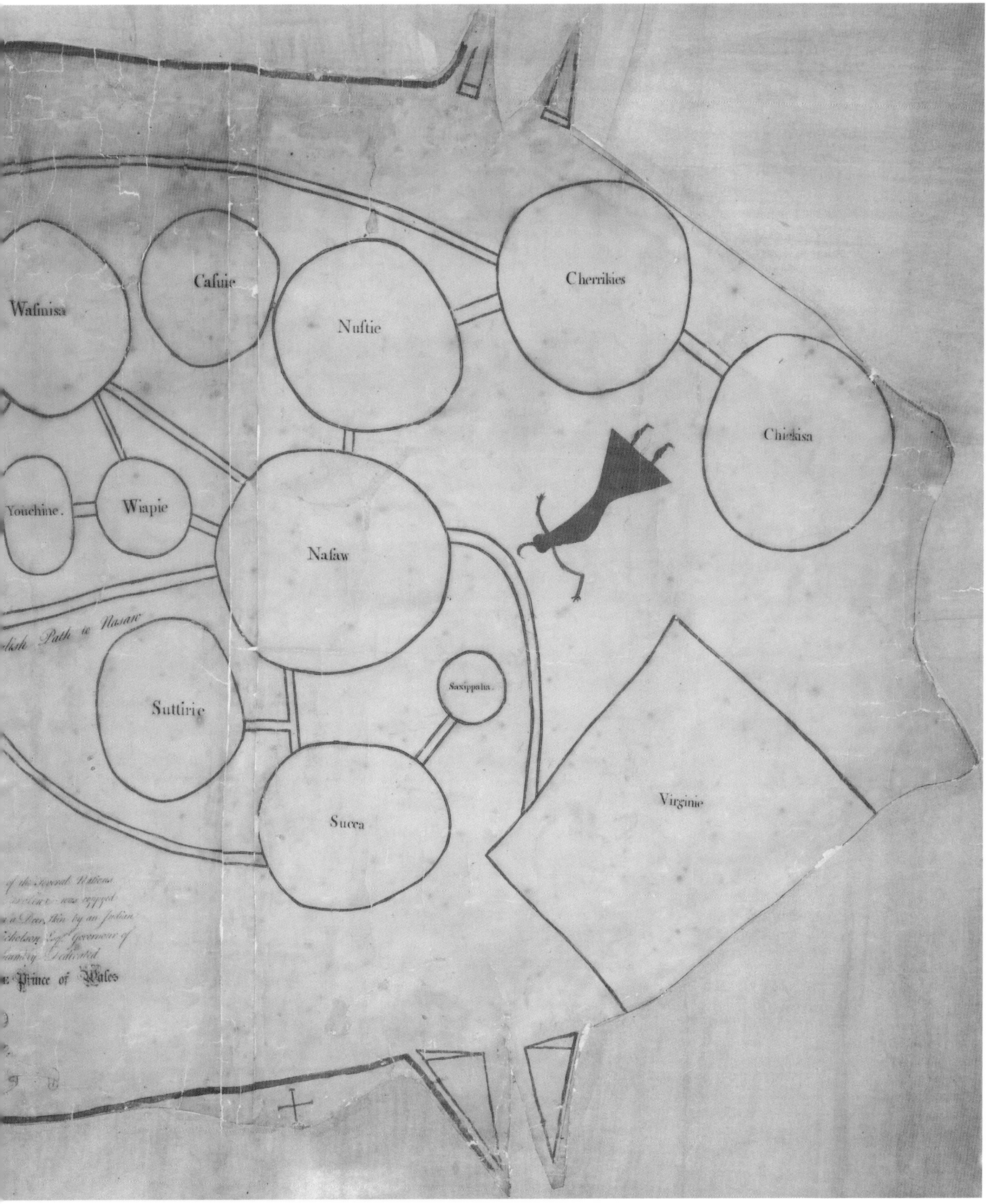
Caſuie
Waſmisa
Nuſtie
Cherrikies
Chickisa
Youchine.
Wiapie
Naſaw
Saxippaha.
Suttirie
Succa
Virginie
Prince of Wales

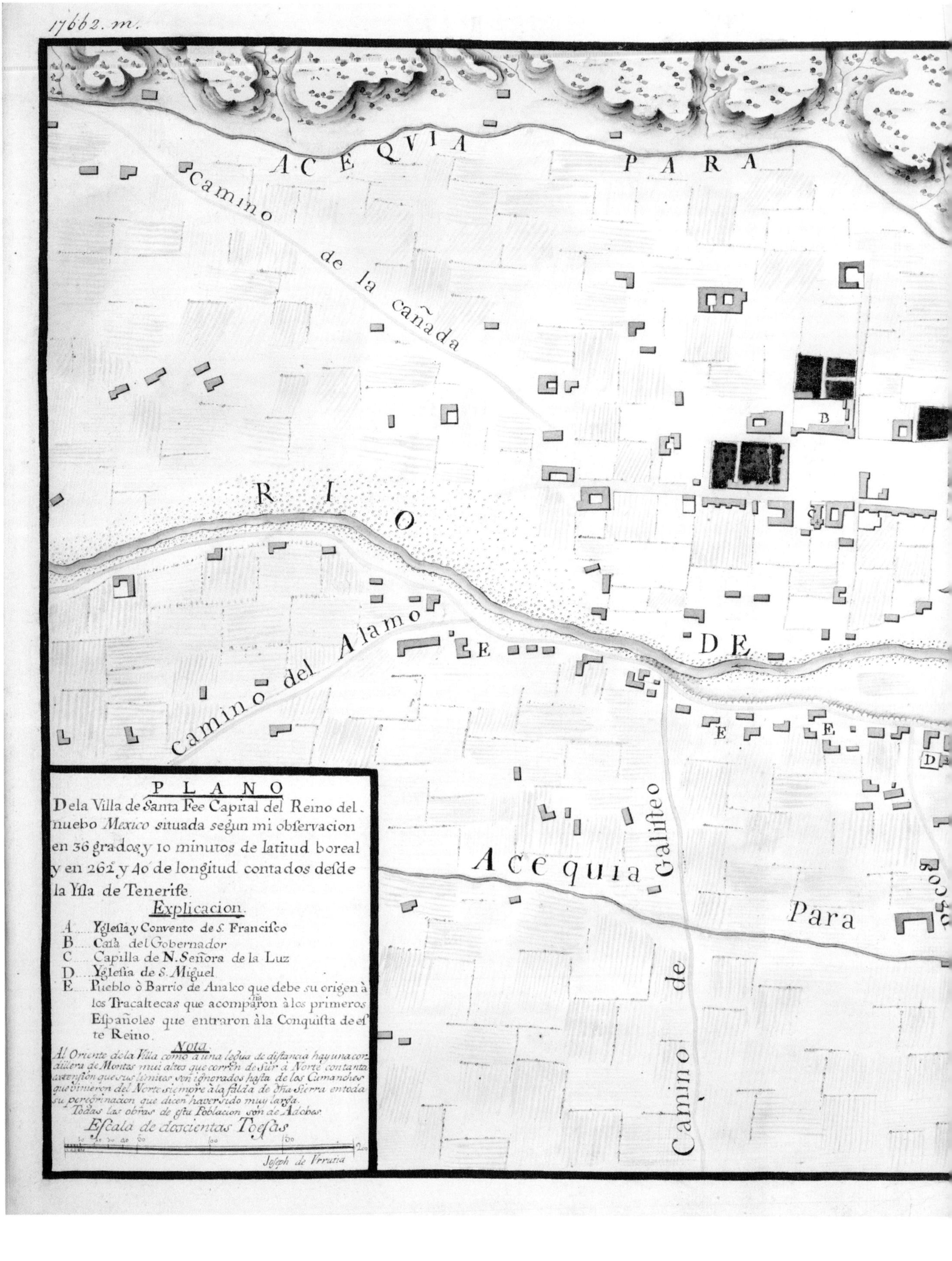

17662. m.
ACEQVIA PARA
Camino de la cañada
RIO DE
Camino del Alamo
Acequia
Para
Camino de Galisteo
B
E
D
PLANO
Dela Villa de Santa Fee Capital del Reino del nuebo Mexico situada segun mi observacion en 36 grados y 10 minutos de latitud boreal y en 262 y 40 de longitud contados desde la Ysla de Tenerife.
Explicacion.
A ... Yglesia y Convento de S. Francisco
B ... Casa del Gobernador
C ... Capilla de N. Señora de la Luz
D ... Yglesia de S. Miguel
E ... Pueblo ò Barrio de Analco que debe su origen à los Tracaltecas que acompañaron à los primeros Españoles que entraron à la Conquista de este Reino.
Nota.
Al Oriente de la Villa como à una legua de distancia hay una cordillera de Montes mui altos que corren de Sur à Norte con tanta extension que sus limites son ignorados hasta de los Cumanches que vinieron del Norte siempre à la falda de dha Sierra en toda su peregrinacion que dicen haver sido muy larga.
Todas las obras de esta Poblacion son de Adobes.
Escala de doscientas Toesas
10 20 30 40 50 100 150 200
Joseph de Vrrutia

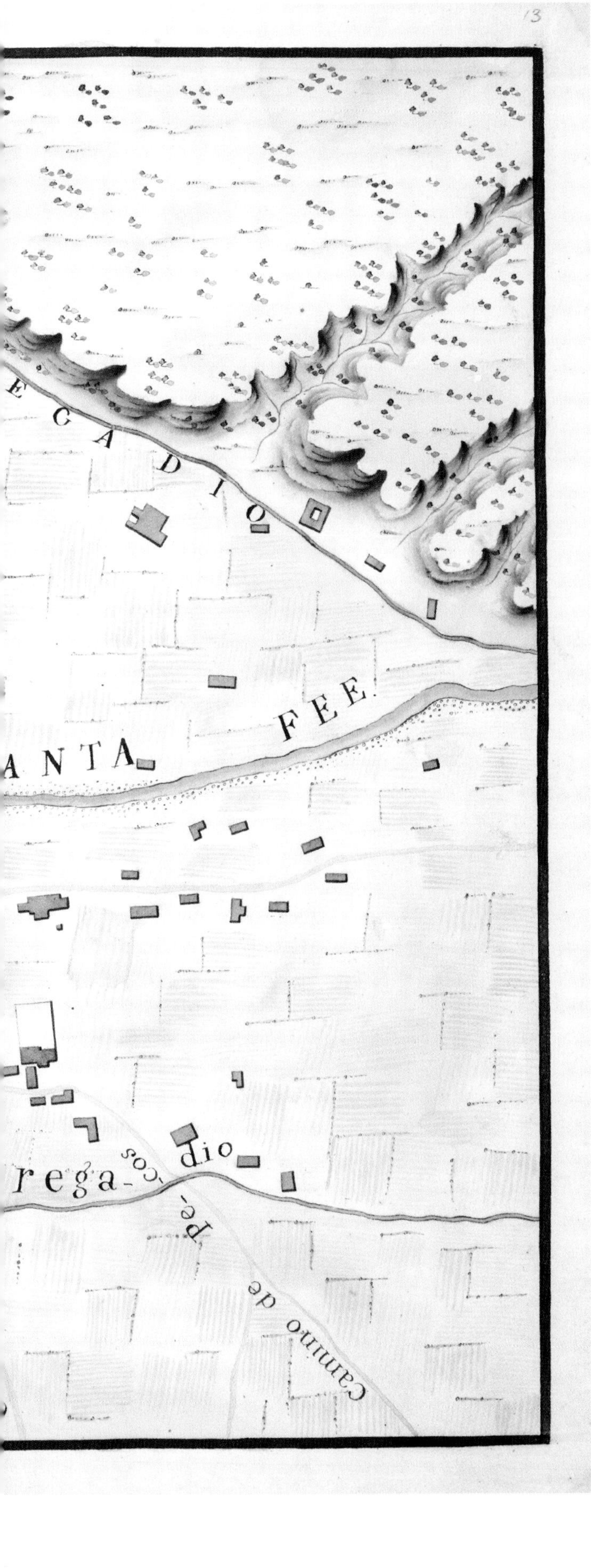

Santa Fe, New Mexico

(1768)

This, the earliest map of Santa Fe and its environs, is part of a set of maps of key presidios and towns in the north of Mexico. These were situated not far from the northern frontier of New Spain (the Spanish Empire in America). Following the Seven Years' War (1756–63) and years of neglect of its northern border, there was resolve from the Spanish administration to modernise and strengthen its positions. It was for this reason that Cayetano Pignatelli, 3rd Marqués of Rubí (b. 1730) was sent to conduct an inspection between 1766 and 1768. In attendance was the military surveyor Joseph de Urrutia (1739–1803), who produced this set of maps.

We can only hazard a guess at the possible purpose of the maps. Given how precisely Santa Fe has been drawn, with key attention to principal buildings and defences and consideration of the surrounding area, it is possible to presume a strategic use. The artistic way in which it has been created would not necessarily discount this, since high-ranking officials would have expected their maps to come well presented.

What we do know is that sometime in the following century the maps were collected as compilation material for an ambitious 'atlas' project for the Spanish Empire. This project was the brainchild of Felipe Bauzá (1764–1834), a naval officer and cartographer who had studied under the great Spanish chart maker Vicente Tofiño (1732–95) and who had been official mapmaker on the 1789–94 Malaspina expedition of scientific discovery. Bauzá felt it his national duty to 'demonstrate the truth of the geography of America' and to show the Spanish Empire in, as he saw it, its proper cartographic form for all to see.

Although Bauzá collected a huge quantity of maps and charts for his project (spending his wife's dowry in the process), the project would never become a reality. As a Liberal he was forced to flee Spain in 1822. He reached London with his maps, though not his wife and daughters, and attempted to use the maps as leverage for securing safe passage for his family. Bauzá died in 1834 and in 1847 the bulk of his maps, including this map of Santa Fe, were sold, after painfully drawn-out negotiations, to the British Museum.

Culiacán, Mexico

(1935)

The biggest mapping phenomenon of the twentieth century was the officially produced series sheet map. These behemoths were detailed military-based maps of a territory which were at a large enough scale to require printing on a number (sometimes a large number) of bordering sheets.

Multi-sheet maps were not exclusive to the twentieth century – the Cassini family's vast *Carte de France* of between 1756 and 1815 was printed on 181 sheets of paper. But hundreds of sheets were the norm for its twentieth-century descendants. It was not simply the scale of these maps that was phenomenal; it was their relentless and unflinching coverage which made them such powerful tools for the national and imperial agencies who used them.

The 'International Map of the World' was slightly different. It was a series mapping project, first suggested (by a German geographer named Albrecht Penck, 1858–1945) in 1891 during a rare period of utopian international co-operation, which aimed to create a single multi-sheet world map at the scale of 1:1,000,000 on 974 sheets. Co-operating states would map their own territories using a uniform sheet numbering sequence and mapping conventions. The principles were agreed upon in 1909. Could maps bring the world together? Unsurprisingly, given the twentieth-century climate of international hostility, they could not. But by the time UNESCO closed the project down in 1989, thousands upon thousands of updated editions of the sheets had been produced.

The cynical view is that the International Map of the World was doomed to failure. Maps and the information they contain have historically been jealously guarded, not shared, due to the sensitive and valuable information they can contain. The United States isolated itself from the IMW during the project's formative years. Between the world wars, under the auspices of the American Geographical Society, the US government created a multi-sheet Map of Hispanic America, which used the same conventions and sheet numbering sequence as the IMW. Latin America had been claimed by the USA as its legitimate sphere of interest through the Monroe Doctrine of 1823, and although mapping other states' territory ran counter to the spirit of mapping espoused by the IMW, the Hispanic America map circumvented this problem by adding a 'provisional edition' statement to the sheets' top right corners.

This map, showing the area of Culiacán in western Mexico, gives a good idea of the quality of the Hispanic map of America. The topographical content is full and precise, and this has been overlaid with a mathematical grid, comprehensive margin data dealing with scale, co-ordinates, an index to sheets, a 'reliability index' and a key to altitude shading. This sophisticated colour 'hypsometric' tinting was expensive to develop, illustrating the enormous financial resources that went into the maps and the similarly vast benefits it was hoped they would yield.

CULIACAN

PROVISIONAL EDITION N.G-13

From surveys and other data listed in the pamphlet which accompanies this sheet

1935

Scale (Escala) 1:1,000,000

Kilometers 10 5 0 10 20 30 40 50 60 70 80 90 100 110 120 Kilómetros

1 Millimeter - 1 Kilometer

Nautical miles 10 5 0 10 20 30 40 50 60 Millas maritimas

1 Mile - 1852 Meters
(Average value of one minute of arc of meridian)

English miles 10 5 0 10 20 30 40 50 60 70 Millas inglesas

1 Mile - 1609 Meters

Scale 1 Inch to 15.78 Miles or 1.014 Inches to 16 Miles

PRONUNCIATION AND TRANSCRIPTION

Spanish (in America) Vowels as in all Romance Languages.	English
b and v	identical, non explosive, almost like English v.
c	before e and i soft; before a, o, u, or another consonant, hard.
ch	as in 'church'.
d	like th in 'that'.
g	before e and i like aspirated h; before a, o, u, hard.
h	always silent.
j	like aspirated h.
ll	like lli in 'brilliant'. (In Chile pronounced as y.)
ñ	like ny in 'canyon'.
qu	like k.
rr	strongly trilled.
s	always sharp.
z	like sharp s.

Accent falls on the penult of names ending in a vowel, or n or s; on the last syllable of other words. Names varying from this rule carry a written accent to indicate the syllable to be stressed.

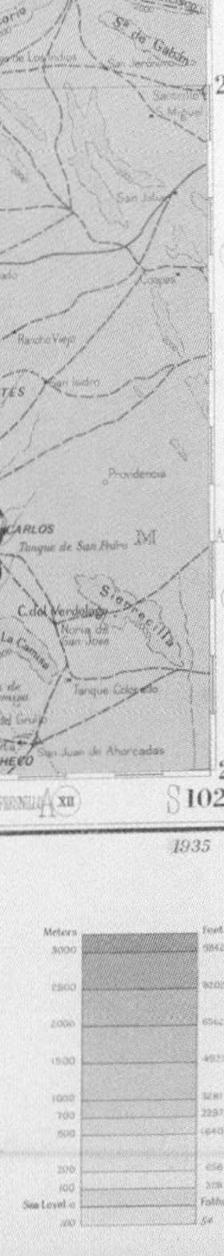

DEFINITIONS AND ABBREVIATIONS

height | La., laguna, pond

SYNOPTICAL INDEX

RELATIVE RELIABILITY

ADJOINING SHEETS

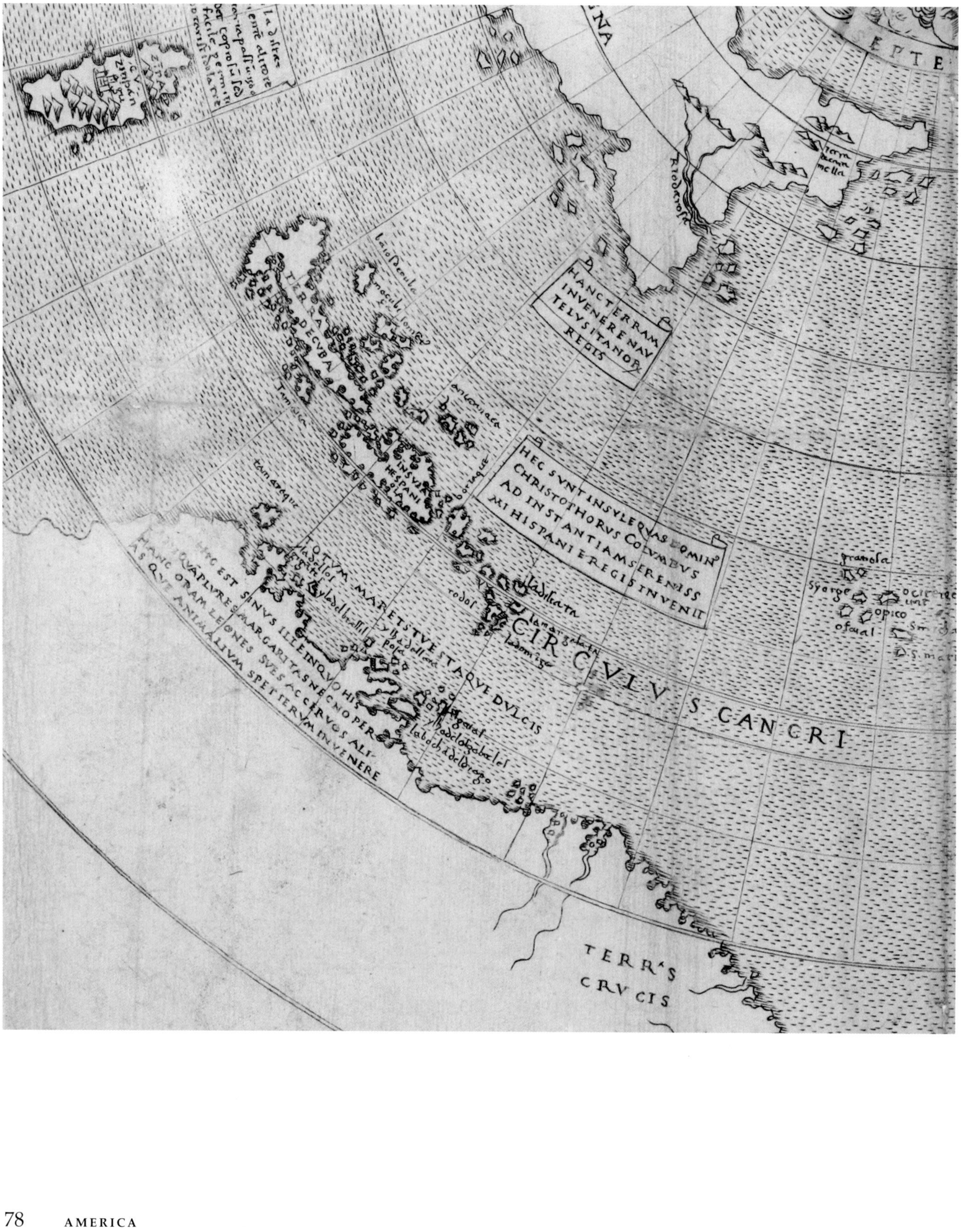
HANCTERRAM
INVENERENAV
TELVSITANOR
REGIS
HEC SVNT INSVLE QVAS DOMIN
CHRISTOTHORVS COLVMBVS
AD INSTANTIAM SERENISS
MI HISPANIE REGIS INVENIT
TERRA DE CVBA
CIRCVLVS CANCRI
TERRA S
CRVCIS

West Indies

(1506)

This is the earliest surviving printed map to show any part of the Americas. It was published in Florence in 1506, only a decade or so after Christopher Columbus had landed on Guanahani in the Bahamas (illustrated in this detail of the West Indies) during his first voyage in 1492. Because of this it reflects the contemporary perception that Columbus's 'New World' was in fact still the 'Old World'. Columbus believed he had reached China, and the map reflects this in a legend, roughly translated as 'Christopher Columbus reached the Spanish islands and then sailed to the province of Ciamba [China or Vietnam]'. The map, which is by the Venetian Giovanni Matteo Contarini (d.1507), has been celebrated for its American content ever since this only known copy was purchased by the British Museum in 1922. But there is far more of interest to it than that.

The map (shown in full overleaf) is one of the earliest pieces of cartography in which the traditional European view of the world, as developed by Claudius Ptolemy – no America, a landlocked Indian Ocean – began to be questioned. Extraordinary things appear on the map. America creeps into view with Newfoundland and Labrador cemented on to Kamchatka, Cuba and Hispaniola (which Columbus visited on his 1492 voyage) are floating next to Japan, and South America and the vast Southern Continent are joined together.

The map was a product of the Italian map trade and its maker, the engraver and seller Francesco Rosselli (1445–1513), was an early and important practitioner. Rosselli was the brother of the Florentine painter Cosimo (1439–1507) and possibly worked for Sandro Botticelli (1445–1510). He was responsible for engraving a number of important maps including the printed version of Henricus Martellus's (*fl.*1480–96) map, the first to show the Cape of Good Hope following Bartolomeu Dias's (1450–1500) journey around it in 1488. He may also have engraved the maps for the 1482 edition of Ptolemy's *Geographia*.

These were early days of the European map trade, and the Italians, with Rosselli at the helm, were instrumental in making maps available to a wider audience of merchants and professionals. Mapmaking centres would develop in Venice and Rome, reaching a high point in the 1560s, before Dutch mapmakers gained the impetus. An inventory of Rosselli's stock from 1527 survives. Among the maps is one described as '*amappamondo a mantellino*', probably this world map, shaped like a little cloak.

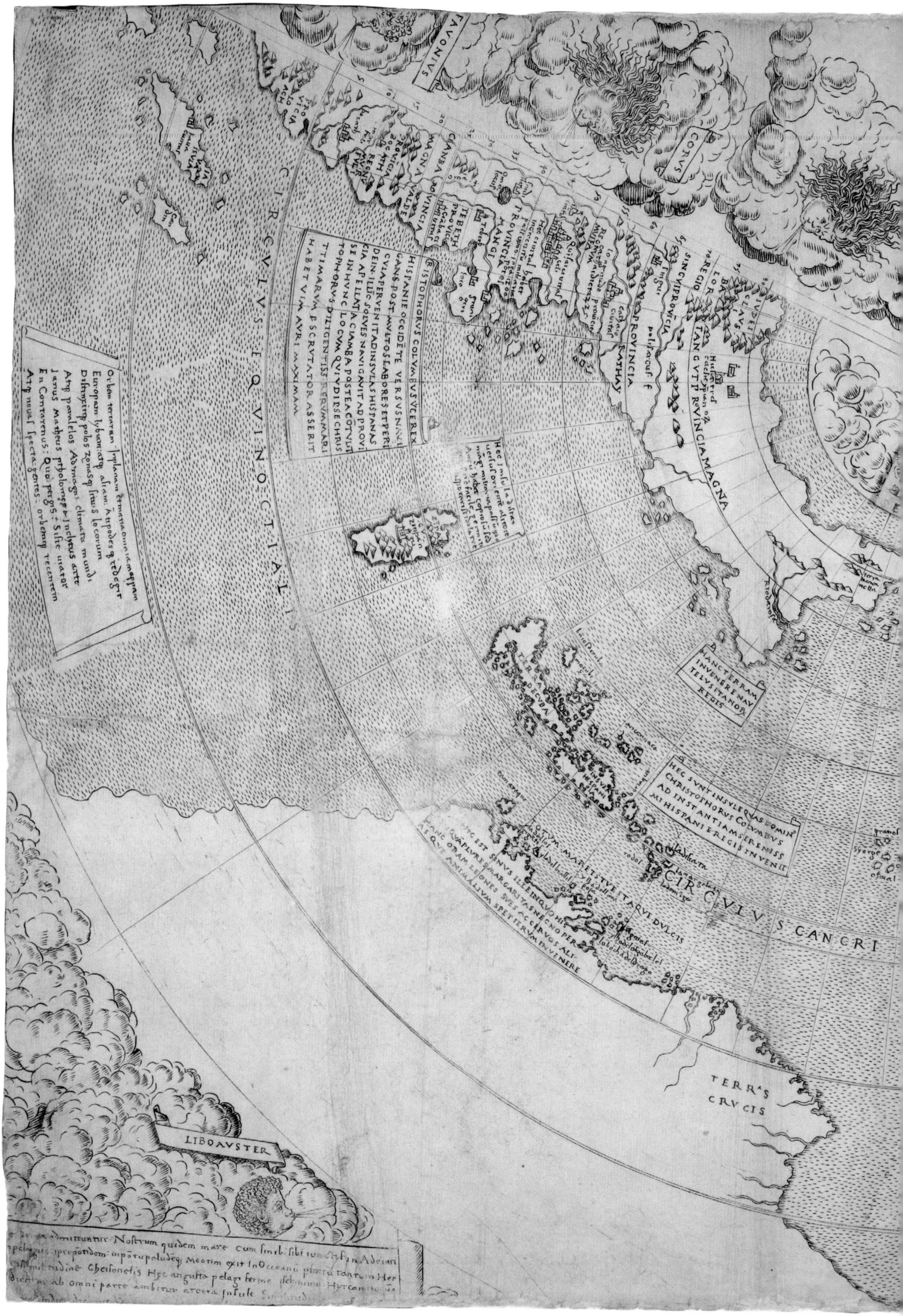
FAVONIVS
CORVS
CIRCVLVS EQVINOCTIALIS
CIRCVLVS CANCRI
CATHAY PROVINCIA
TANGVT PROVINCIA MAGNA
MANGI PROVINCIA
TEBETH PROVINCIA
CIAMBA PROVINCIA MAGNA VALDE
HANC TERRAM INVENERE NAVTE LVSITANORV REGIS
HEC SVNT INSVLE QVAS DOMINVS CHRISTOPHORVS COLVMBVS AD INSTANTIAM SERENISSIMI HISPANIE REGIS INVENIT
TERRA S CRVCIS
LIBO AVSTER

VVLTVRNVS
SVB SOL
SINVS GETICVS
MARE INDICVM
ANTE TAPROBANAM
MVLTITVDO INSVLA
RV QVAS DICVNT ESSE
NVMERO MCCCCCCLXXVIII
QVARV TAMEN NOMINA
TRADVVNTVR HAE SVNT
MARE MEDITERRANEV
MARE AFRICV
ETHIOPES
CAPRICORNI
EVRO AVSTER

West Indies

(1542)

Jean Rotz's (*c*.1505–*c*.1560) *Boke of Idrography* of 1542 has long been regarded as one of the British Library's greatest map treasures. The atlas is so highly regarded that the 1981 facsimile version published by the Roxburghe Club was presented by Her Majesty Queen Elizabeth II (*r*.1952–) to US President Ronald Reagan (1911–2004) in 1982. The original had been presented by the mapmaker to Henry VIII in 1542 (though Rotz originally intended it for the king of France), and as part of the Old Royal Library it reached the British Museum in 1757. This royal provenance is merely one of a number of important aspects of the *Boke*.

The most noticeable feature of the 12 hand-painted vellum charts of the world and its regions is the quality and quantity of the colours – golds, blues and greens – that have been used in their creation. This chart of what is now the southern United States and the West Indies is typical of the rest, being a carefully executed coastal map, with the south to the top, filled with skilful miniature illustrations flanked by a floral-patterned motif which incorporates naturalistic depictions of birds.

The *Boke* is the earliest dated example of work by the Dieppe school of northern France. Its chart makers, who included Pierre Desceliers (*fl*.1537–53) and Guillaume Le Testu (*c*.1509–73) are best known for their luscious cartography produced for an elite audience. This was not to go on a ship, but a device to help a ruler to conceptualise their world. During the 1540s the French were developing their territory in North America thanks to the exploits of Jacques Cartier (1491–1557), and information based on his efforts features in this map for almost the first time.

Rotz was a more international figure. For Jean Rotz read John Ross, a Scottish chart maker whose father, Daniel Ross, had moved his family to Dieppe some years previously. After years of voyaging, including visits to Sumatra and in 1539 to Guinea and Brazil, during which he would have honed his chart-making skills, Rotz junior was one of a number of chart makers brought to England by Henry VIII for their mapmaking capabilities, and perhaps also for their insider knowledge of England's Continental rivals.

Rotz furnished Henry with what he needed, a fabulous book of maps. But in the fallout following the king's death in 1547, the Catholic émigré Rotz became a secret agent in order to buy safe passage to France for himself and his family. Subsequently he was involved in the 'Auld Alliance' intrigue between Catholic France and Scotland, and he even played a role in a planned French invasion of Scotland.

the cost of peron
of the entillas
The Indis of occident quhar the spangartis doith occupy
Couba
Londe of florida
espagnolla
Jamaica

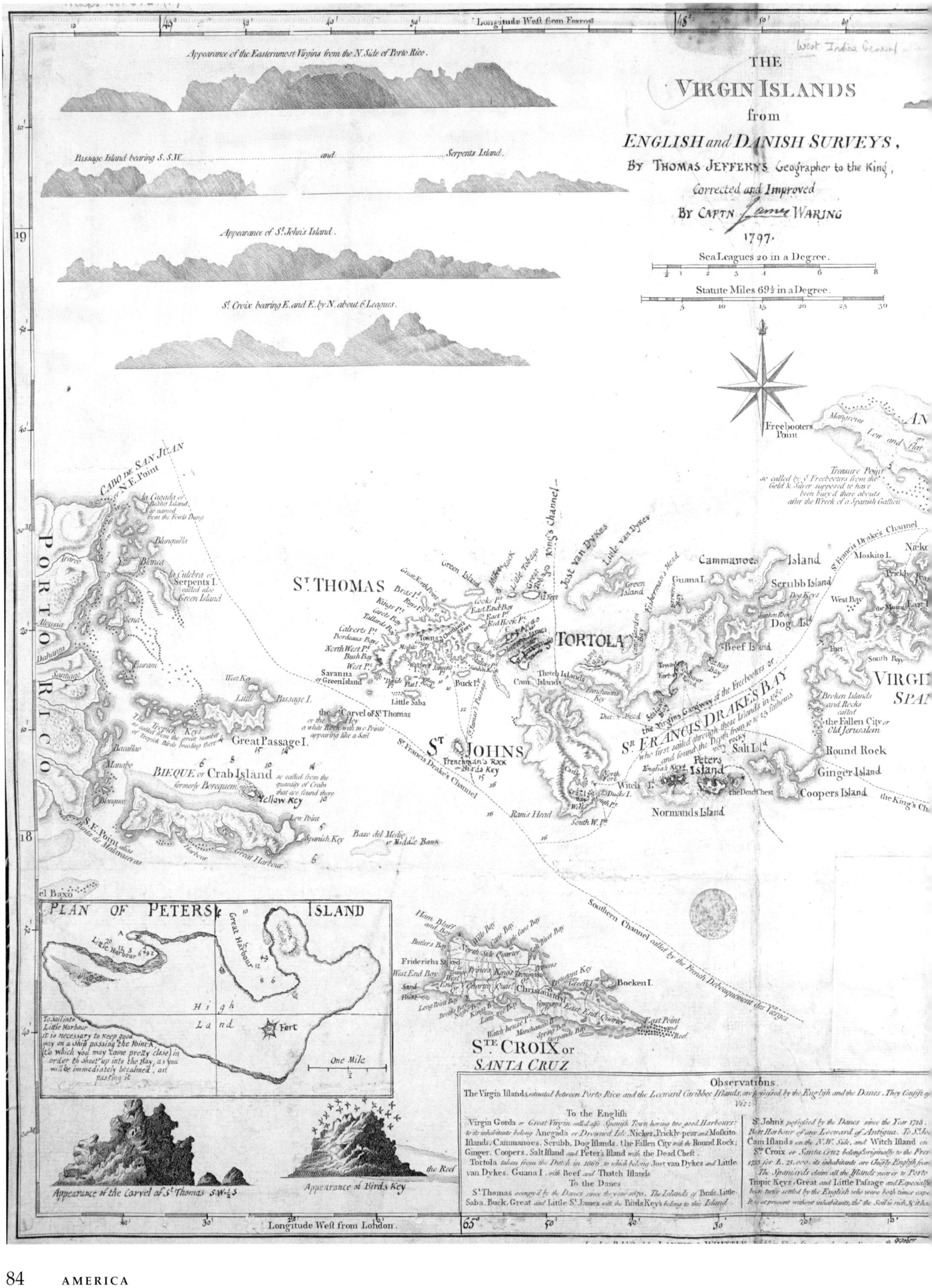

THE
VIRGIN ISLANDS
from
ENGLISH and DANISH SURVEYS,
By Thomas Jefferys Geographer to the King,
Corrected and Improved
By Captn James Waring
1797.
Sea Leagues 20 in a Degree.
Statute Miles 69½ in a Degree.
Longitude West from Ferro
Appearance of the Easternmost Virgins from the N. Side of Porto Rico.
Passage Island bearing S. S.W. and Serpents Island.
Appearance of St. John's Island.
St. Croix bearing E. and E. by N. about 6 Leagues.
Freebooters Point
Treasure Point
so called by ye Freebooters from the Gold & Silver supposed to have been bury'd there abouts after the Wreck of a Spanish Gallion
CABO DE SAN JUAN or N.E. Point
PORTO RICO
Blanquilla
la Culebra or Serpents I. called also Green Island
Passage I.
Great Passage I.
The Tropick Keys so called from the great number of Tropick Birds breeding there
BIEQUE or Crab Island
Yellow Key
Spanish Key
Great Harbour
S.E. Point
Baxo del Medio or Middle Bank
St. THOMAS
Savanna or Green Island
Little Saba
Buck Id.
the Carvel of St. Thomas
St. Francis Drake's Channel
St. JOHNS
Frenchman's Rock
Birds Key
Rams Head
South W. Pt.
Green Island
Little Tobago
Great Tobago
King's Channel
Jost van Dykes
Little van Dykes
TORTOLA
Thatch Islands
Cam Islands
Guana I.
Cammanoe Island
Scrubb Island
Dog Isl.
Beef Island
St. Francis Drake's Channel
Moskito I.
West Bay
South Bay
VIRGIN
SPAN
St. FRANCIS DRAKE'S BAY
the Virgins Gangway of the Freebooters or
who first sailed through these Islands in 1580 and found the Depth from 10 to 25 fathoms very rocky
Salt Isld.
Peters Island
the Dead Chest
Normands Island
Witch I.
Broken Islands and Rocks called the Fallen City or Old Jerusalem
Round Rock
Ginger Island
Coopers Island
the King's Ch
Southern Channel called by the French Debouquement des Vierges
PLAN OF PETERS ISLAND
Little Harbour
Great Harbour
High Land
Fort
One Mile
To Sail into Little Harbour it is necessary to keep good way on a Ship passing the Point A, (to which you may come pretty close) in order to shoot up into the Bay, as you will be immediately becalmed, on passing it
el Baxo
Appearance of the Carvel of St. Thomas S.W.½S.
Appearance of Birds Key
the Reef
St. CROIX or SANTA CRUZ
Christiansted
East End Quarter
East Point
Bocken I.
Longitude West from London.
Observations.
The Virgin Islands situated between Porto Rico and the Leeward Caribbee Islands, are possessed by the English and the Danes. They Consist of
To the English
Virgin Gorda or Great Virgin called also Spanish Town having two good Harbours: to its inhabitants belong Anegada or Drowned Isle, Nicker, Prickly pear and Moskito Islands, Cammanoes, Scrubb, Dog Islands, the Fallen City with the Round Rock; Ginger, Coopers, Salt Island and Peter's Island with the Dead Chest.
Tortola taken from the Dutch in 1666 to which belong Jost van Dykes and Little van Dykes, Guana I. with Beef and Thatch Islands.
To the Danes
St. Thomas occupy'd by the Danes since the year 1670. The Islands of Brass, Little Saba, Buck, Great and Little St. James with the Birds Keys belong to this Island
St. John's possessed by the Danes since the Year 1718,
Cam Islands on the N.W. Side, and Witch Island on
Ste. Croix or Santa Cruz belong'd originally to the Fre
The Spaniards claim all the Islands nearer to Porto
Tropic Keys, Great and Little Passage and Especially

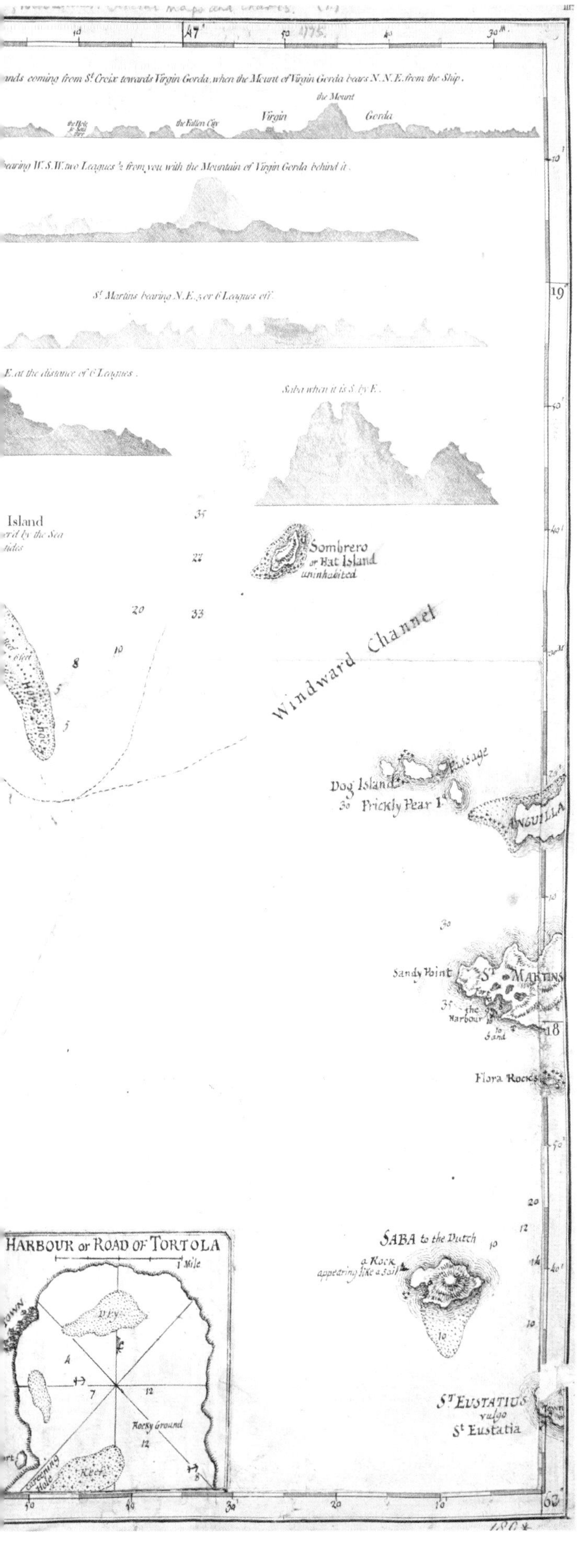

Virgin Islands

(1797)

This map of the Virgin Islands was included in Thomas Jefferys's *West India Atlas* of 1775, published after his death by his associate Robert Sayer (1725–94). It shows the collection of small islands, three of them then part of a Danish slave colony, lying west of Puerto Rico. The map provides a number of coastal profiles to aid navigation and a great quantity of information on shoals, anchorages and channels which Jefferys collated from earlier maps.

This practical information is interspersed with observations on wildlife, the origins of place names, and historical information, all of it extensively researched in typical Jefferys fashion. The most important of these, for the English viewer anyway, is the identification of 'Sir Francis Drake's Bay', the harbour from which Sir Francis Drake (1540–96) attacked the Spanish colony in Puerto Rico (in the Battle of San Juan, 1595), dying shortly afterwards. Far from being incidental, such information was seen as critical to the appreciation of place that cartography was meant to provide.

The 40 maps of the *West India Atlas* cover other islands in a similarly rich and descriptive way. Along with its companion production, the *North American Atlas*, which was published the same year, it was a milestone of European cartography of the Americas. Such was its popularity that it was reissued repeatedly for over four decades. Its success is ironic given that Jefferys, who was official geographer to George III and a prolific and versatile mapmaker, died penniless in 1771, bankrupted by the sheer cost of producing large and impressive maps.

The maps in the *West India Atlas* were updated and altered numerous times. This example is a rare survivor of that updating process. It has been extensively annotated in red ink to act as a guide for the engraver who was charged with making the changes to the copper printing plate. Numerous alterations have been made in the centre of the map, and two harbour insets added to the bottom. To the right a section of paper has been pasted on to obscure the islands of St Martin and Anguilla, which must have been too incorrect to update with ink. The new date is given as 1797 and the corrections attributed to a Captain James Waring.

Guatemala

(1682)

This is a pirate map, produced during the age of English privateering in the Atlantic and the South Sea (Pacific Ocean) during the final quarter of the seventeenth century. It shows part of the coast of Guatemala in Central America on two profile strips with bays, river inlets and a spectacular erupting volcano. This was typical of the coast patrolled by English pirates, or 'buccaneers', who pestered Spanish traders and participated in the slave trade from their base in Jamaica. They operated illegally because they did not have permission from the English Crown in the form of a Royal Navy commission. Here, however, the definition of legality was a broad one. One governor of Jamaica, which had been captured in 1660, was the notorious pirate Henry Morgan (*c.*1635–88).

The map is one of a number included in an atlas or 'Wagoner of the Great South Sea' drawn in 1682 by William Hack (*fl.*1682–1706). Hack was the most prolific of the Thames School of English chart makers, a line of dozens of masters and apprentices stretching through the seventeenth century and into the eighteenth, so-called because of the location of their workshops in Wapping on the banks of the River Thames. Significant mapmakers of this group included John Thornton (1641–1708), chart maker to the Hudson's Bay Company, and Andrew Welch, to whom Hack was apprenticed. Hack's 'brilliant but crude' charts, as Lynam described them, contain many of the typical Thames School traits, with large directional wind roses and intriguing details, yet they are often bolder and less elegant than those of his contemporaries.

Simplification, as seen in these coastal profiles, is often helpful in a map. Here a pilot would quickly be able to make out the exaggerated bays and river inlets. Yet although simple, what we see is in fact a highly sophisticated image blending coast with profile, in which the angle of viewpoint bends upwards from the coast to show the general profile of the land as seen from the sea.

Hack was drawing on a long tradition of chart-making conventions. But his maps were not drawn from information he collected himself while at sea; the cartography was itself pirate booty. In 1680 a buccaneer called Bartholomew Sharpe (*c.*1650–1702) had captured a Spanish ship which contained a collection of Spanish charts. They were taken to England and formed the basis of many of Hack's charts, which he drew for a variety of patrons. This example was made for Charles II.

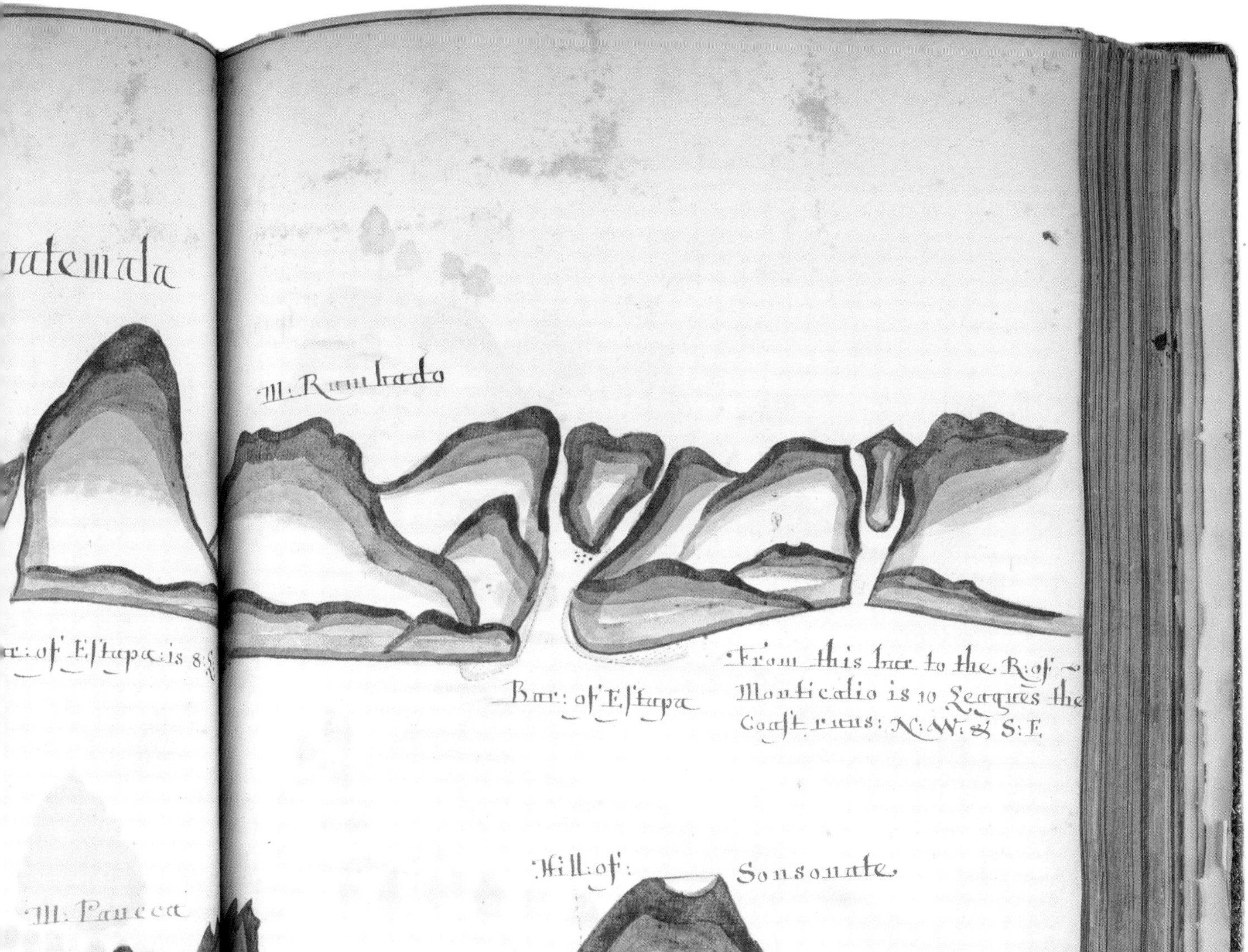
M: Rombado
Bar: of Estapa
From this bar to the R: of Monticalio is 10 Leagues the Coast runs: N: W: & S: E.
Hill: of: Sonsonate
R: Salado
Sonsonate R:
This Land apears thus when you com To this port of Sonsonate.
R: Monticaleo

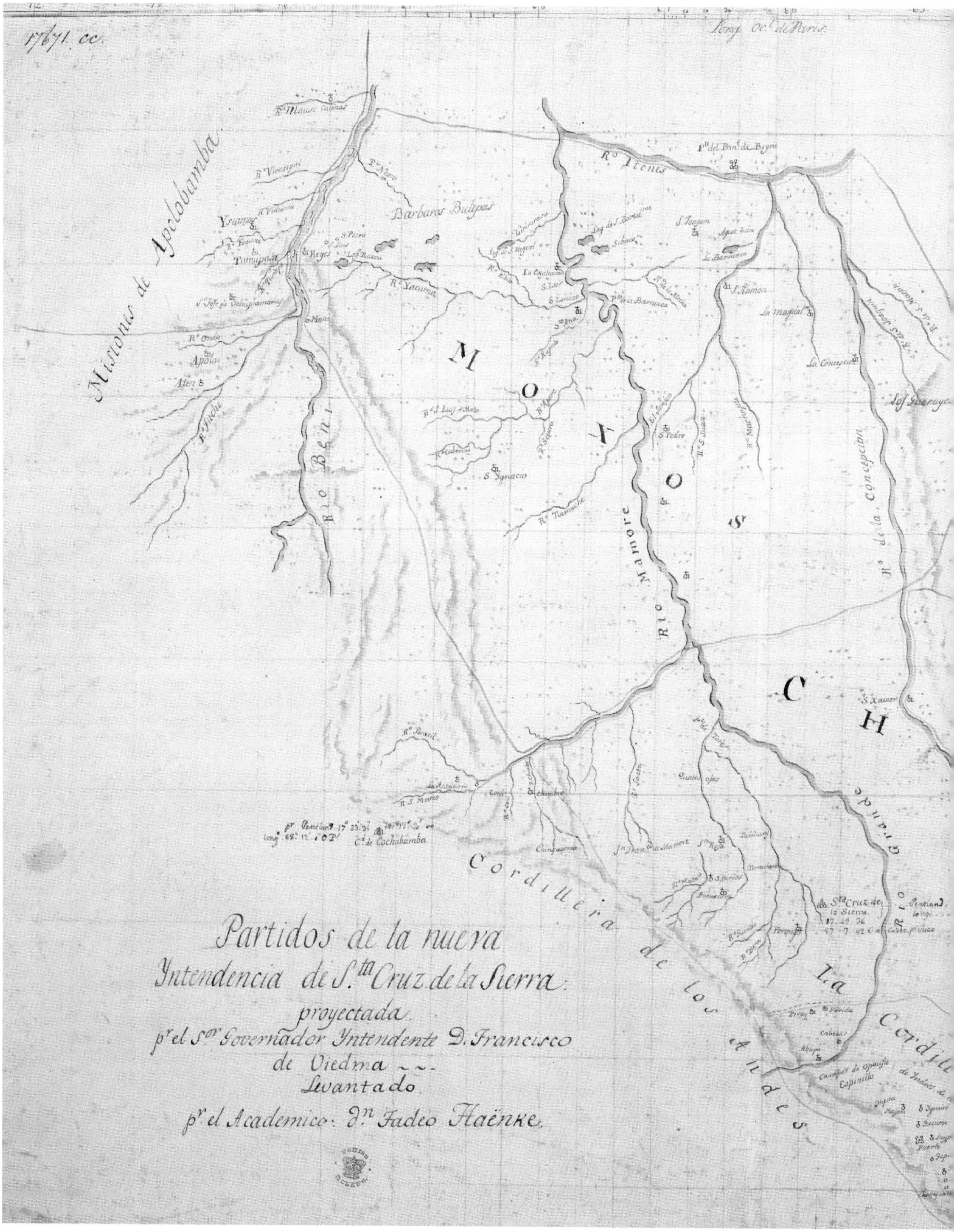
17671. cc.
Long. Oc.l de Paris.
Misiones de Apolobamba
Barbaros Bulipas
Rº Itenes
MOXOS
Rio Beni
Rio Mamore
Rº de la Concepcion
Rio Grande
CH
Cordillera de los Andes
La Cordill
S. Ignacio
S. Pedro
S. Ramon
Reyes
Apolo
Ysiamas
Tumupaza
Cd. de Cochabamba
S.ta Cruz de la Sierra
Partidos de la nueva
Yntendencia de S.ta Cruz de la Sierra:
proyectada
p.r el S.or Governador Yntendente D. Francisco
de Viedma
Levantado
p.r el Academico: D.n Tadeo Haënke.

Cochabamba, Bolivia

(c.1800)

The life of Thaddaus Hänke (1761–1816) is worthy of a film script. A naturalist from Bohemia, Hänke was one of those driven, indefatigable scientists of the late eighteenth century. He made a wide range of contributions to the fields of botany (a giant Amazonian lily is named after him), geology, anthropology, linguistics, physics and geography. This is one of his maps of an area in central Bolivia, then part of the Viceroyalty of Peru, where Hänke lived for 20 years until his death, after he was accidentally poisoned by his maid.

As a young man Hänke got a lucky break when he was selected for the official scientific and political expedition led by Alessandro Malaspina (1754–1810) to study and catalogue plants in Spanish territories in the Americas, Asia and Australasia. Unfortunately, Hänke had missed Malaspina's boat by the time he arrived at Cádiz in 1789. Undeterred, he raced across the Atlantic on another ship, hoping to catch the *Descubierta*, but he was shipwrecked, swimming ashore near Montevideo in Uruguay only to find that he had missed the boat again. Hänke then made his way west across the interior of South America, working as he went, and finally caught up with the expedition in Chile in spring 1790.

With Hänke now on board the expedition travelled up the American Pacific coast to Alaska, then across to the Philippines, visiting New Zealand and Australia, and crossing back to Peru in 1793, where Hänke disembarked. He was to travel back across the continent and rendezvous with the boat in Buenos Aires. Given his previous luck, this was surely a plan doomed to failure. South America had left a deep impression on him, and so there he remained.

The hand-drawn map shows the area where Hänke lived and studied, a remote, rural and forested region rich in wildlife, bounded in the west by the Andes. Rivers are the most prominently marked features, and numerous settlements appear on a map for the first time. After Hänke's death, his collection of maps passed to one of his colleagues on the Malaspina expedition, the mapmaker Felipe Bauzá. Bauzá, who might have taught Hänke a thing or two about mapping, annotated this map with ink to show the latitude and longitude co-ordinates of a number of the settlements.

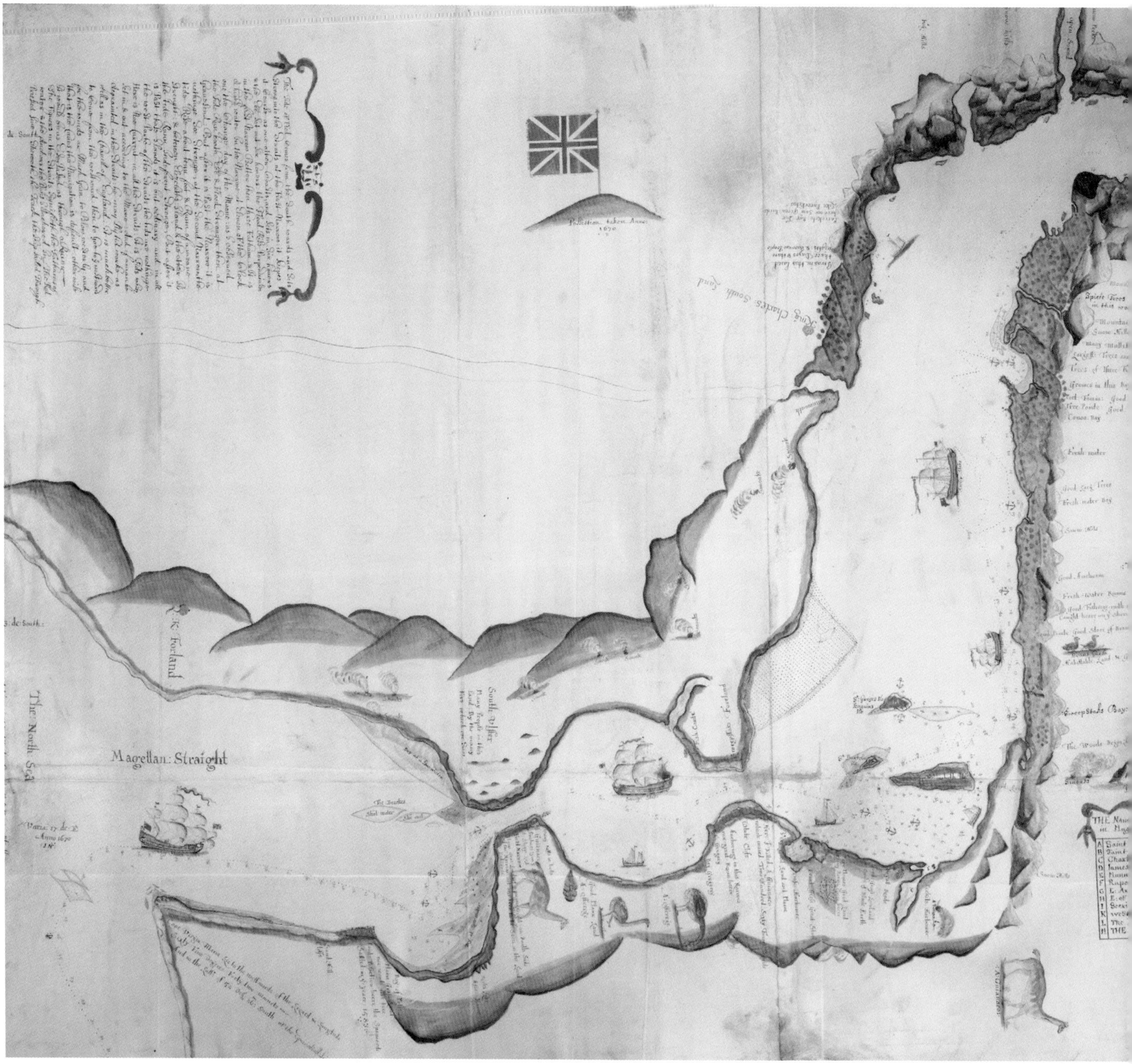

Magellan Strait, Chile

(1671 or 1672)

This map shows the Magellan Strait, a treacherous channel running through the southern tip of South America, which was the main sea route linking the Atlantic and Pacific oceans while avoiding Cape Horn. It was first sailed through by a European in 1520 – the Portuguese navigator in Spanish service Ferdinand Magellan (1480–1521) – and became a strategically important passage during the decades of imperial maritime activity.

It was only during the second half of the seventeenth century that British ships ventured into Iberian waters in the 'South Sea' with any degree of confidence, but in 1670 the strait was first navigated by an Englishman. This was naval commander Sir John Narbrough (*c.*1640–88), who had set sail in 1669 from Deptford on his ship *Sweepstakes* with the intention of establishing British trade links in the Pacific. Narbrough travelled across the Atlantic Ocean, sailed through the strait and then landed at Valdivia on the Chilean coast. His mission fell foul of the Spanish authorities and he was unable to obtain any trade agreement. Under orders not to provoke Spain, *Sweepstakes* passed back through the strait, returning to London in 1671.

In order to promote his exploits, Narbrough commissioned this hand-drawn vellum map and presented it to the Duke of York, the

future James II, the following year. It is a large and impressive image, with south at the top and *Sweepstakes* shown travelling one way and then back again through the strait. We can see the complex maze of channels, rivers and dead-ends running off the main strait and the snowy jagged peaks rising up in profile on either side. The union flag is proudly planted on dry land.

The hand is clearly that of a Thames School chart maker, but there is a great deal of other information in the form of words and images. There are small animals such as penguins and ostriches, and there is a group of indigenous people shown next to their 'habit of living'. These are in Narbrough's own hand and are decidedly more amateurish in their artistic quality. In his journal of the journey, which is now in the British Library, Narbrough notes having seen many of the things which are illustrated on the map.

Narbrough's mission demonstrated the possibilities of trade in the Pacific, even though he had been unsuccessful. The map illustrated new-found confidence, and over the following half-century there was increased British commercial activity which would culminate in the 1720 financial crash known as the 'South Sea Bubble'. The map was the definitive depiction of the strait for the following century, and it was even used in the compilation of the Magellan Strait map published in the 1773 account of the voyages of James Cook.

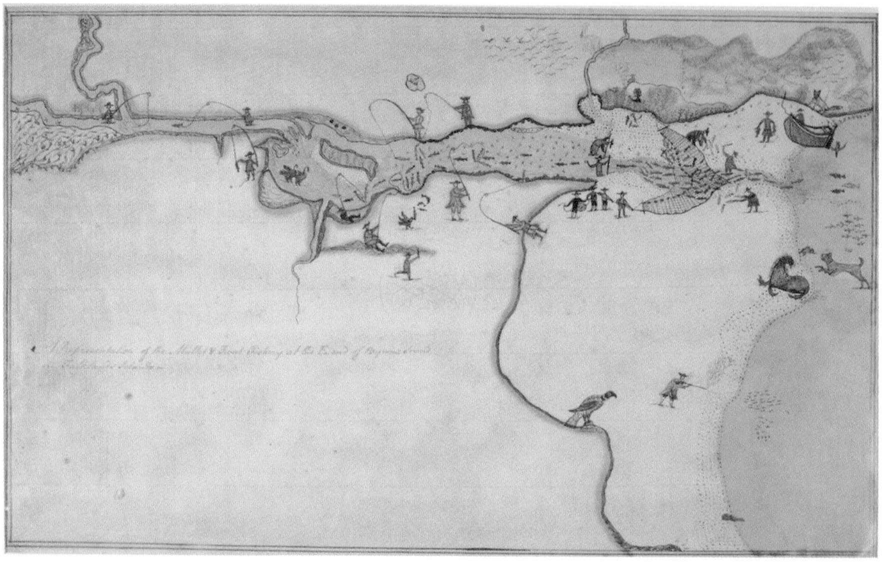

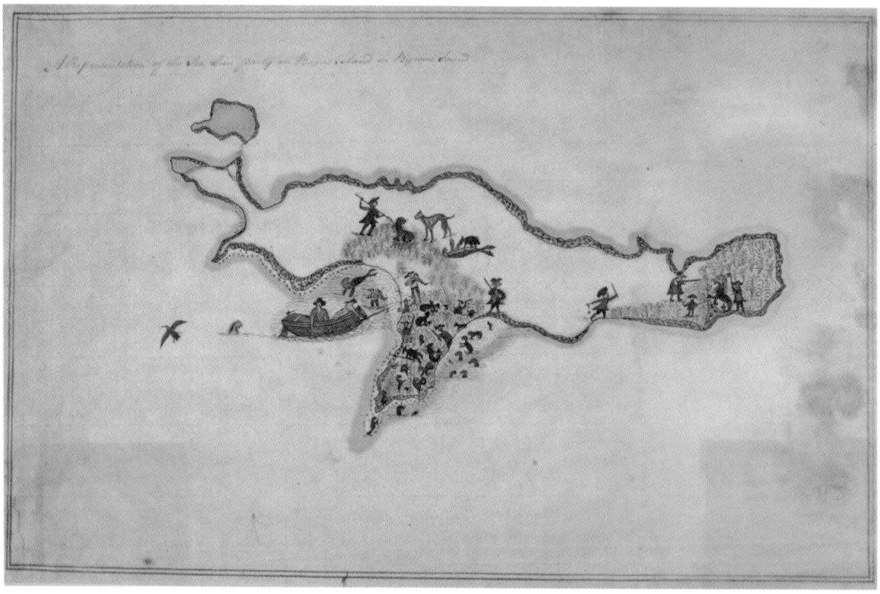

Falkland Islands

(1768)

The British settlement on West Falkland lasted from 1766 until 1774. At around the same time (1764) a French settlement had been founded on East Falkland, but two years later France sold it to Spain. The British government finally decided to withdraw its claim on economic grounds after less than a decade. None of this early colonial history paints the Falkland Islands as a particularly desirable imperial possession. These maps, which were drawn by an English mapmaker on West Falkland in 1768, do nothing to counter that impression.

Their maker was a Newcastle carpenter named Thomas Boutflower (1732–75), who sailed to the Falklands as part of Captain John McBride's (*c*.1735–1800) mission to claim the islands, arriving at Port Egmont in January 1766. We do not know why he created the maps, though they remained in his family's possession until 1978. Given their unconventional appearance and indistinct geographical content, it does not appear that they were for any navigational or administrative use. His general 'Draught of Falkland Islands' gives us only a vague impression of the layout and shape of the island, and shows the British island as far larger than the French island, though they are in fact similar in size.

These four maps are concerned less with the geography of the

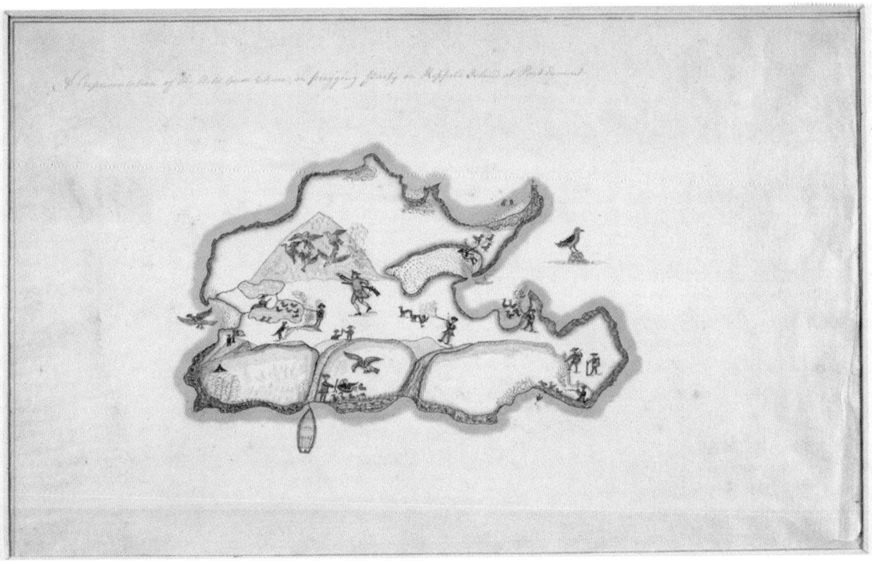

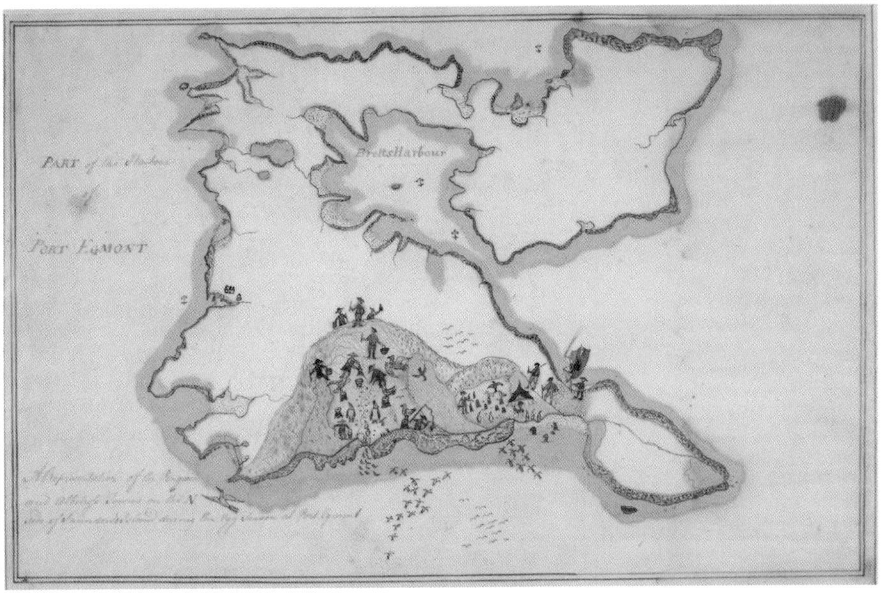

island and more with the way of life of the islanders, particularly their hunting of wildlife. The titles include 'The mullet and trout fishery', 'The wild geese chace [sic]', 'The pengwin and albitrose towns [sic]' and 'The sea lion party'. In them we see the islanders wearing wide-brimmed hats to keep off the rain and fishing with nets, lines and spears. In one of them they have clubs. In another we can see birds being shot under the watchful eye of albatrosses and eggs being collected.

Boutflower may have had good cause to present the islands as a haven for wildlife and therefore for hunting. Indeed, we can begin to appreciate why hunting is such a strong feature of the maps if we see it as an expression of Boutflower's reality. One of the reasons for the abandonment of the colony was that it struggled to become economically viable. Efforts to crow crops unsurprisingly failed, given the poor cultivation soil of the islands, leaving the hardy inhabitants to hunt in order to survive. Given the literally hand-to-mouth nature of such a way of life, perhaps hunting did dominate most days, with the rest of the time spent wondering where the next meal was coming from. Boutflower returned to England with the last of the colonists and settled in Devon.

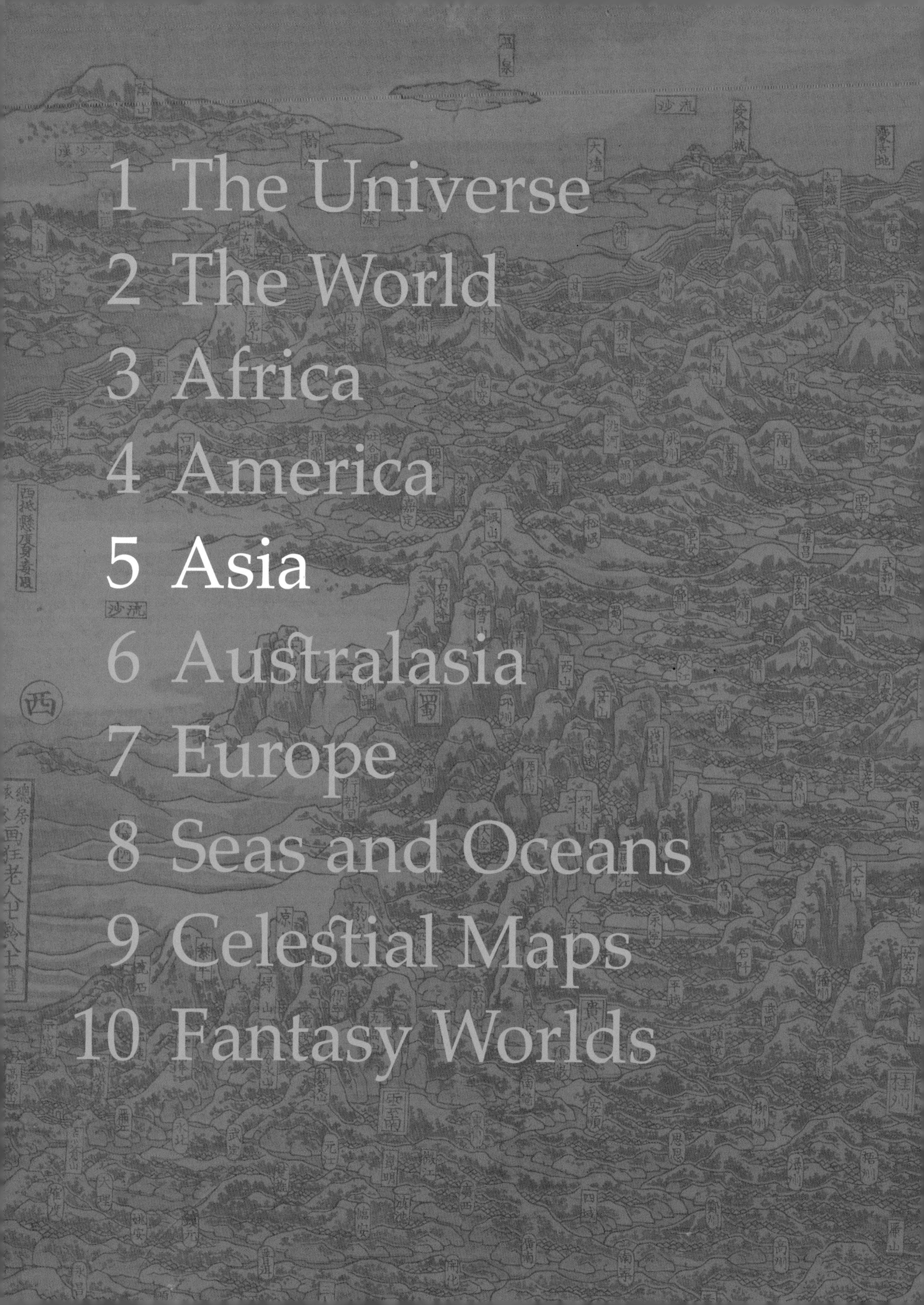

北京
山西
恒山
華山
嵩山
南陽
大梁
山東
江南
湖廣
江西
衡山
黄河
會稽山
天台山
四明
温州
台州
松江
大海洋
定海
福州
東

Asia

(c.1190)

You are looking at a map of Asia with east at the top. At the bottom we can make out Greece, the Mediterranean Sea and a crowned Constantinople (now Istanbul). This gives way to the rectangular shape of modern-day Turkey, which occupies a dominant position on the map and has been divided into provinces. Above it we can make out a variety of details of places in central, southern and eastern Asia such as the Indus and Ganges rivers, and the Red Sea (which is coloured red). Rounded tooth-like rows represent mountains, and interspersed around them are the names of provinces and towns including Babylon, Persia, India and Armenia.

It is not easy for modern eyes to relate to the geography of this complex and unusual map, bound into a volume of works of St Jerome (347–420 CE) and drawn towards the end of the twelfth century in a Benedictine abbey in Tournai, Belgium. Quite apart from the fact that many of the places on the map do not exist today (and are oddly irrelevant to the works of St Jerome), the legibility of the map is uneven. This has something do with the fact that the map has been redrawn, erased and amended over time. This identifies it as a 'palimpsest' – something which bears traces of its earlier form.

The earlier map lying underneath this one required the help of multi-spectral imaging techniques in order to be identified, but it can just be made out. There are a large number of faded dark smudges and areas of very faded writing across the map. There is also a faint large circle roughly in its centre. These are the remains of a map of the Holy Land, with a circular Jerusalem in the middle, which was erased to make way for this map. And that is not all. There seems to have been a circular hole in the vellum to the bottom right of the map, but it has been effectively filled in by a small replacement vellum patch. This has rather cleverly been adapted as the shape of the island of Crete.

We can only guess why the original map of the Holy Land was erased, but the volume provides other clues. Another map also shows the Holy Land, and this is also drawn over another earlier map of the same subject. Perhaps this is a perfectionist mapmaker (the historian P.D.A. Harvey believes a single author was responsible for all of them) practising and repeating his work in order to get it right. This repetitive process suggests that the mapmaker was copying another map in order to improve it. Judging by the considerable detail present in the map of Asia, we think that the prototype must have been a large world map which is now lost. Lost, but thanks to the not-altogether-successful efforts of a Belgian mapmaking monk, not completely forgotten.

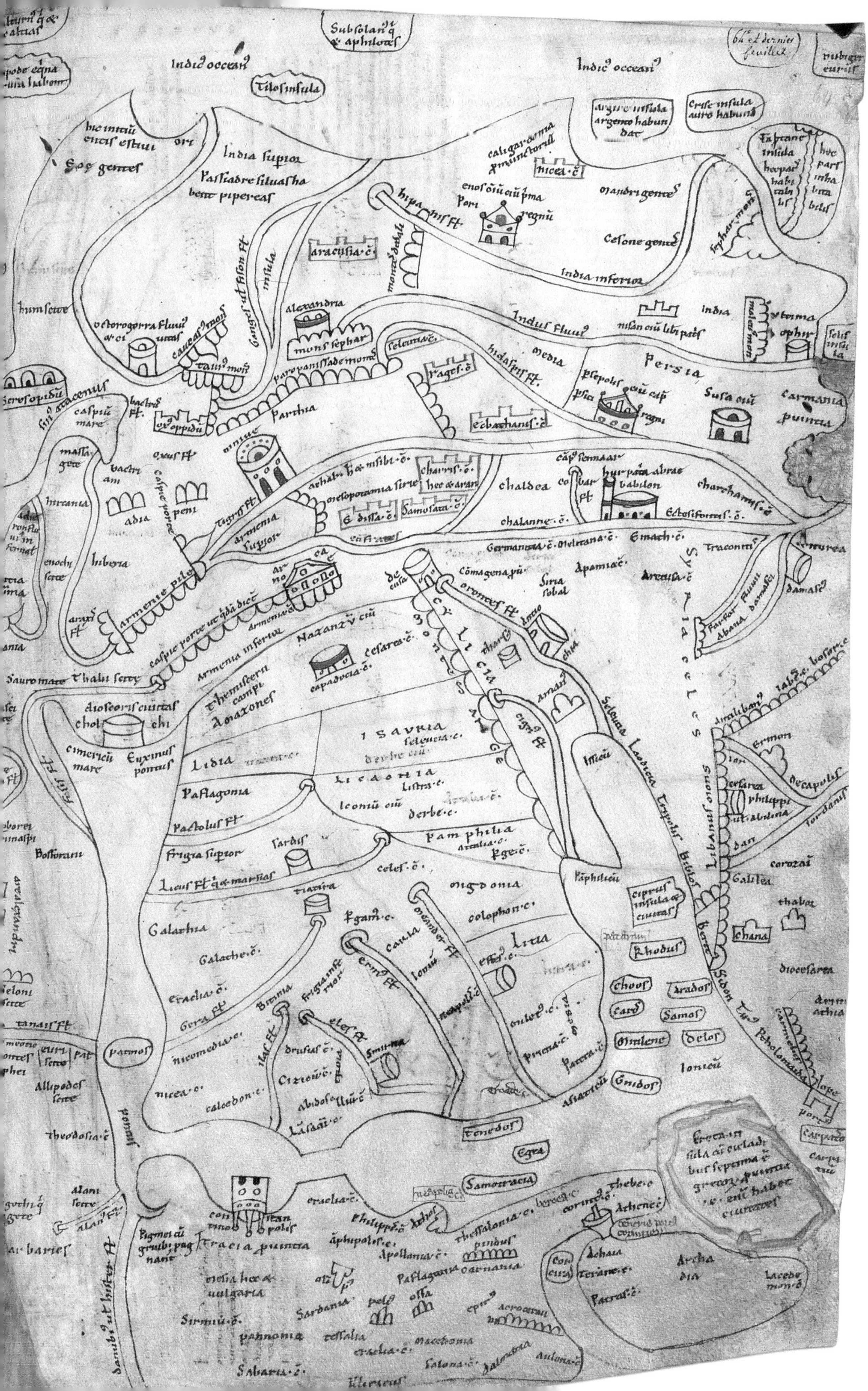

64e et dernier feuillet
Indic occean
Tilos insula
Argire insula argento habundat
Crise insula auro habunda
India superior
Gog gentes
Nicea c.
Porus regnum
Persia
Susa ciu.
Carmania provincia
Media
Parthia
Chaldea
Babilon
Caspiu mare
Hircania
Ibera
Armenia superior
Armenia inferior
Capadocia c.
Isauria
Licaonia
Lidia
Paflagonia
Pamphilia
Frigia superior
Galathia
Bitinia
Cilicia
Siria
Syria celes
Galilea
Decapolis
Damasco
Libanus mons
Laodicea
Tripolis
Biblos
Sidon
Tyrus
Thabor
Ciprus insula et civitas
Rhodus
Samos
Delos
Cnidos
Tenedos
Egea
Samotracia
Thebe c.
Athene c.
Creta insula
Achaia
Archadia
Lacedemon c.
Patras c.
Tracia provincia
Pannonia
Macedonia
Tessalia
Sirmiu c.
Constantinopolis
Euxinus pontus
Patmos
Alani
Barbares
Thessalonica c.
Apolonia c.
Epirus
Acroceraunia
Salona c.
Aulona c.

MAP OF EASTERN TURKEY IN ASIA, SYRIA

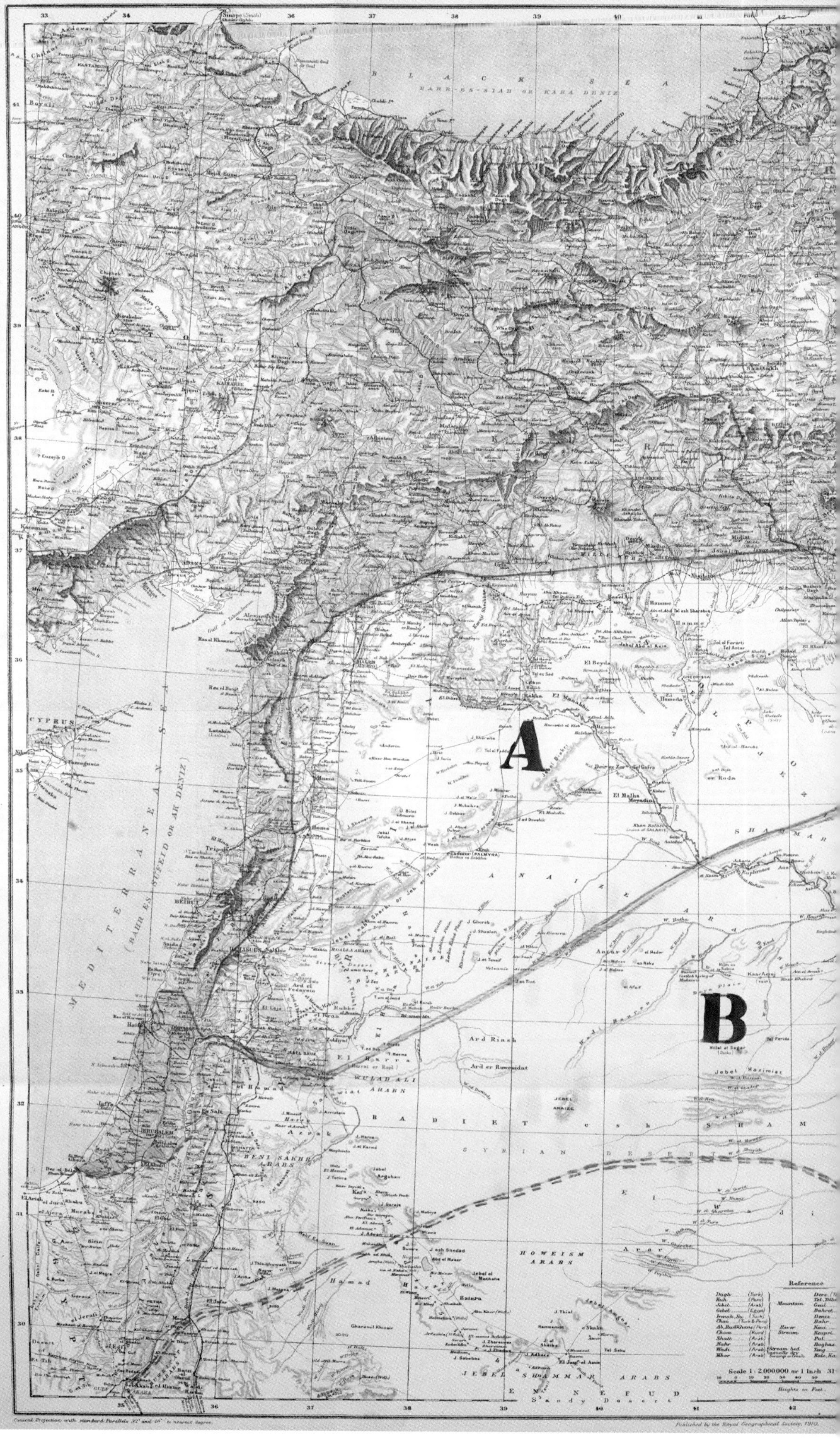

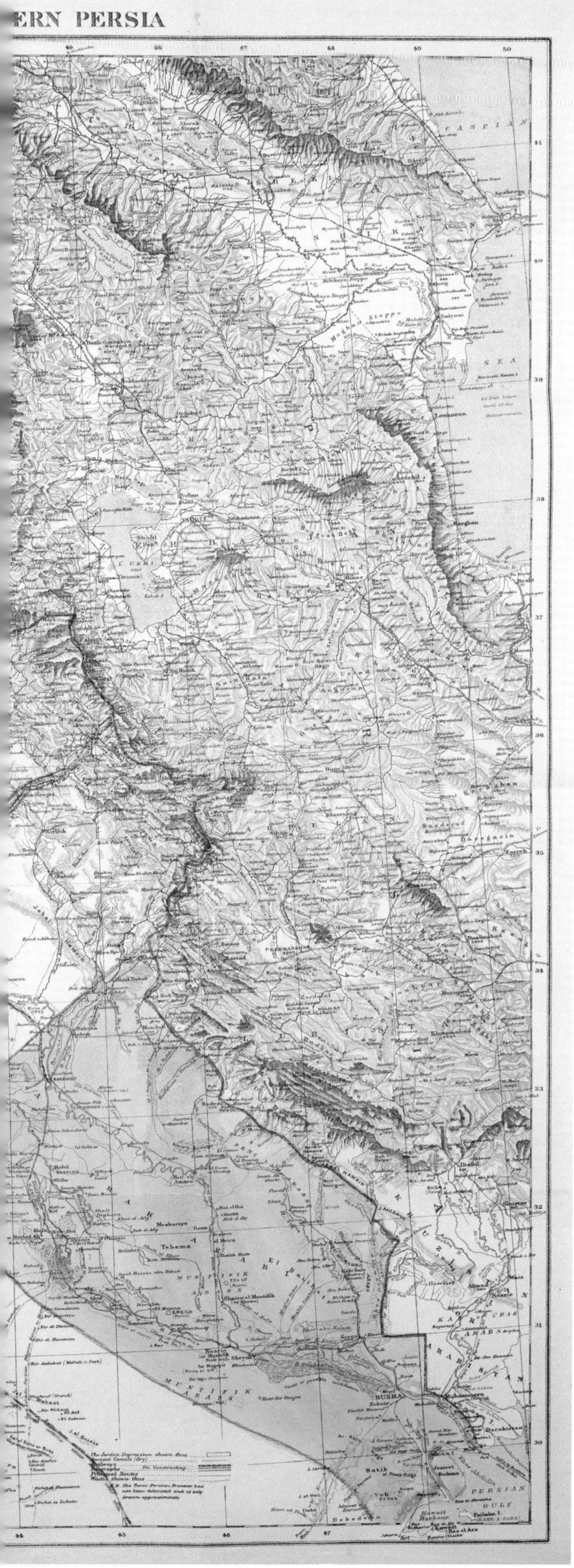

The Middle East

(1916)

Maps were heavily used during the nineteenth century to illustrate the partitioning of territory. These drawn lines on them were particularly associated with the colonial ambitions of European powers in parts of Africa and Asia. As this map shows, that function continued into the twentieth century.

The red and blue pencil were added to this printed map of the Middle East either in late 1915 or early 1916, during the secret diplomatic talks which led to the Sykes–Picot Agreement (officially known as the Asia Minor Agreement) between Britain and France. Named after the British diplomat Mark Sykes (1879–1919) and the French diplomat François Georges-Picot (1870–1951), the two main representatives, whose names have been added to another example of the map in the UK National Archives, the talks discussed the post-war division of the fragmenting and unstable Ottoman Empire into British, French and Russian (and later Italian) spheres of influence.

This copy of the map, which comes from the papers of the British statesman Lord Lansdowne (1845–1927), shows the proposed division of the area into spheres of influence, a line drawn 'from the second "K" in Kirkuk to the "E" in Acre'. The northern area including Syria and Lebanon was to be under French control, the southern part including Iran and Iraq British, while Palestine was to become an international zone under joint control.

However, Britain's diplomatic activities complicated the terms of the Sykes–Picot Agreement. For example, Britain had promised to recognise Arab independence in the region in return for an Arab revolt against Ottoman rule. Subsequently, Britain expressed support for Jewish immigration to a Palestinian homeland, in a statement known today as the Balfour Declaration (named after the British prime minister who signed the letter, Arthur Balfour, 1848–1930) on 2 November 1917.

Shortly after the Balfour Declaration, the existence of the Sykes–Picot Agreement became public, when details obtained by the Bolsheviks following the October Revolution were published in the Russian newspapers *Izvestia* and *Pravda*. This was then used in German wartime propaganda as evidence of the Allies' imperial intentions.

The Holy Land

(c.1600)

The Benedictine monastery of St Albans was dissolved in 1539 along with numerous other religious houses during Henry VIII's reign. Their libraries were dispersed, and many works found their way into private collections. This is the case with the 'Historia Anglorum' of around 1255, containing Matthew Paris's (*c.*1200–59) itinerary maps illustrating a journey from London to southern Italy and the Holy Land. This volume eventually found its way into the royal collection via Henry, Prince of Wales (1594–1612) in around 1609, where it would have been available for study by scholars who were becoming freshly interested in the history of Britain.

Among them was William Camden (1551–1623), a historian, teacher and herald, correspondent of Abraham Ortelius and author of the first published history of Britain, the *Britannia* of 1586 and later. Camden, who was mentor to the Elizabethan statesman Sir Robert Cotton (1571–1631), studied and sifted all of the works he could find (including Cotton's important library) for information to support his studies. Not only that, he occasionally copied out bits from them, especially if it helped him to refer back to it later.

This is Camden's hand-drawn copy of the final map in Matthew Paris's itinerary, the map of the Holy Land. It would be unsurprising if Camden marvelled at it when he saw it, because nothing quite like it had ever been produced in England. Like the original, Camden's redrawing showed the Holy Land with east at the top and the Mediterranean Sea at the bottom and right of the map. Various intriguing features include the mountains of Armenia in the top left, the Jordan River top right, the town of Bethlehem with a star emerging from the clouds above it, and a square, walled Jerusalem in the upper right.

However, it is the town of Acre which dominates the drawing, as it does in the original. Acre was the main crusader town in the Holy Land during the second Christian Kingdom of 1191–1291. This explains its importance on the map, which is reflected in its abnormal size – far larger than Jerusalem, which remained in Muslim hands. Within the walls of Acre we can make out a large number of features including the Genoese tower and the German hospital. The cemetery protrudes northwards from the city walls.

When Matthew Paris created his itinerary during the thirteenth century this map was placed at the end as the culmination of a journey, and Christian Acre was still a tangible reality. By the sixteenth century that reality had gone. But for Camden it captured something essential about Britain's past, and so he copied it, giving the towns and buildings a sixteenth-century makeover and modernising the French text. The crusades were part of English history in its widest context, which Camden and his contemporaries set out to retell.

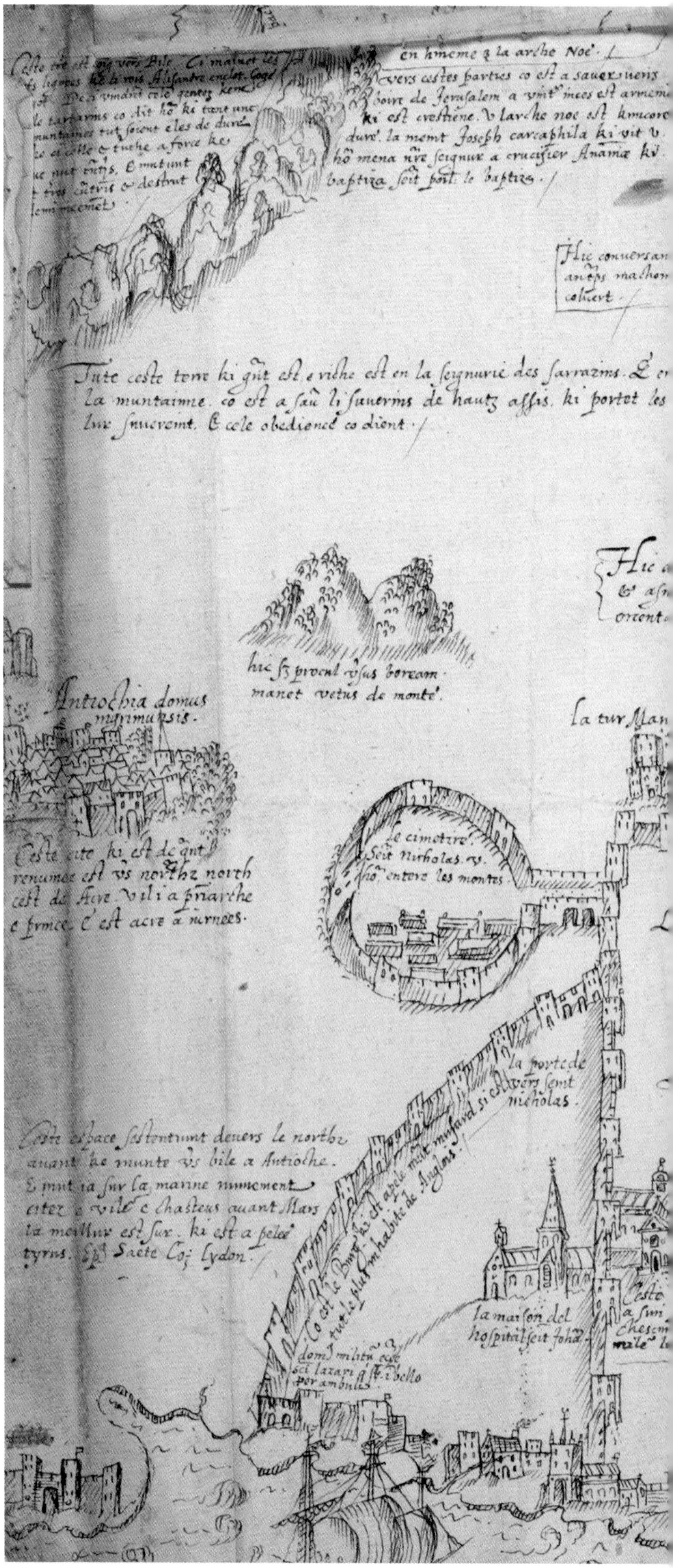

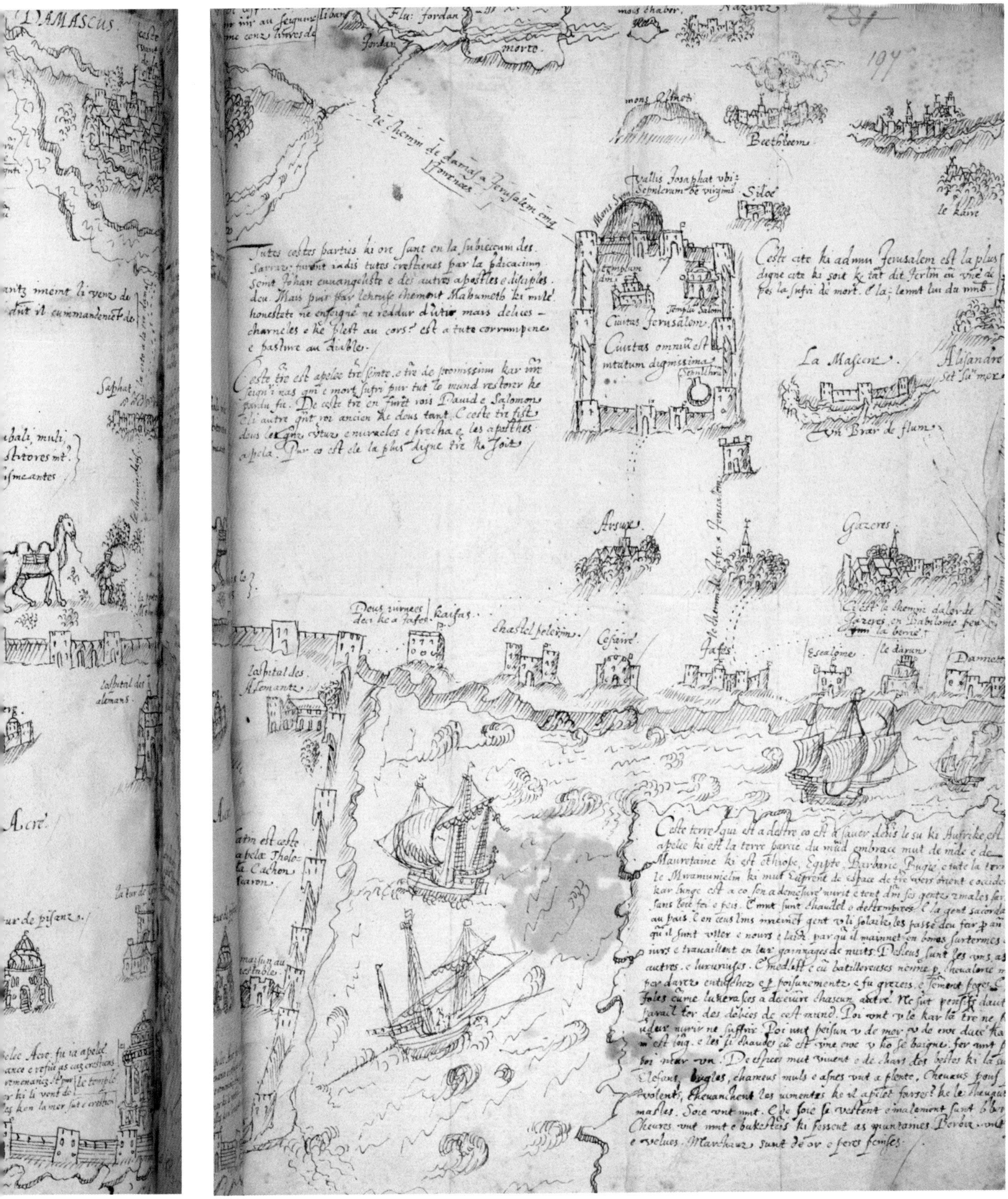
DAMASCUS
Flu: Jordan
mons thabor
Beethleem
Siloé
Civitas Jerusalem
Arsur
Gazeres
Cesaire
Jafes
Escalone
le daron

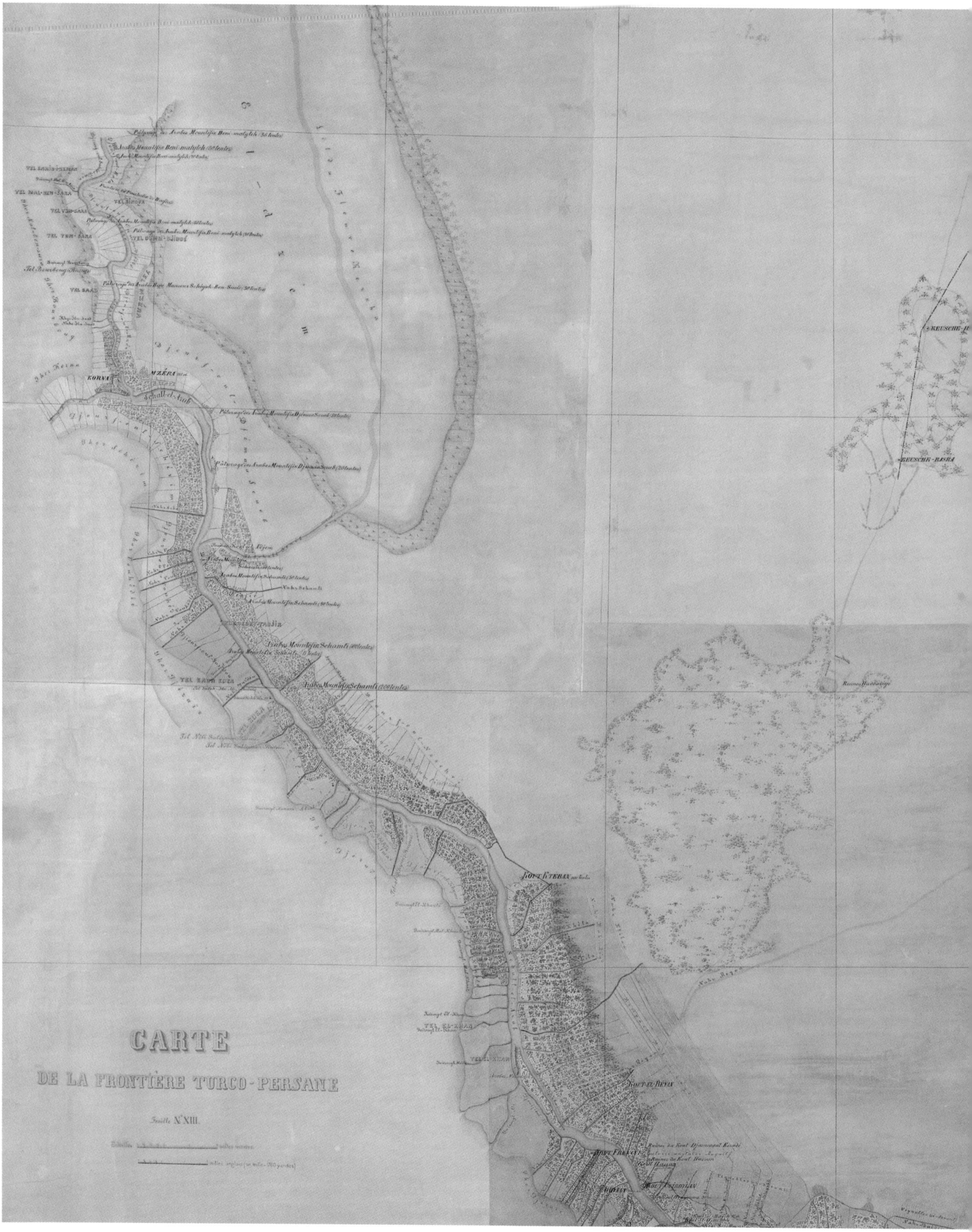
CARTE
DE LA FRONTIÈRE TURCO-PERSANE
Feuille Nº XIII.

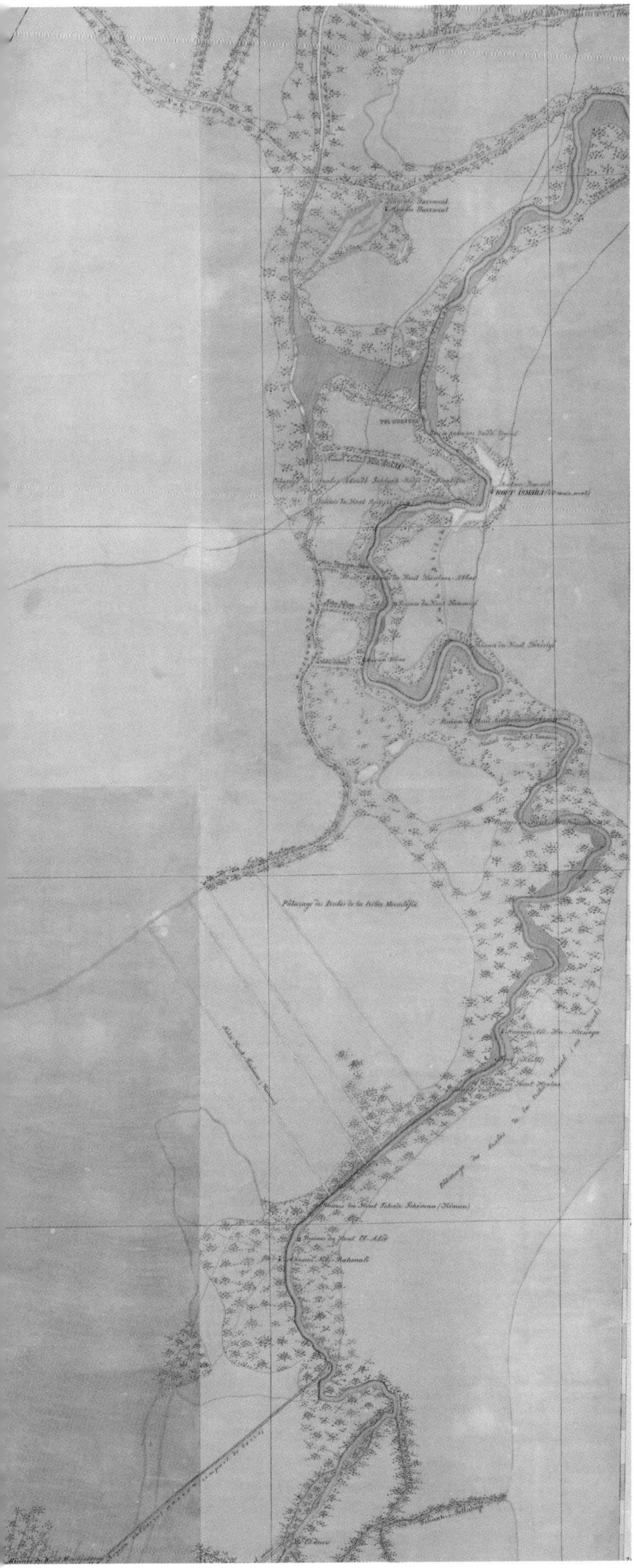

Southern Iraq

(1869)

It is fair to say that Britain and Russia did not exactly see eye to eye over the course of the nineteenth century. They faced each other down in Asia in a confrontation known as 'The Great Game', and their mutual dislike erupted into conflict in the Crimean War (1854–56). Yet this jointly produced map of 1869 shows that where their interests dove-tailed, they could work together. However, even imperial co-operation was not always enough.

By the 1840s both Britain and Russia needed stability in Central Asia in order to safeguard and develop their imperial holdings (Russia in the Caucasus region, the British in India). Their problem was conflict between the Ottoman Empire and Qajar Persia, whose 700-mile-long border was the site of increasing antagonism between the two neighbours. At the Treaty of Erzurum in 1847 Britain and Russia agreed to act as mediators in establishing a definitive border in the hope that such a line would pacify the region. With this in mind a commission was set up to map the region and establish the border, headed by the British Colonel Fenwick Williams (1800–83) and the Russian Colonel Igor Ivanovich Chirikov with Ottoman and Persian representatives.

It is worth explaining that this border area runs through the modern states of Armenia, Azerbaijan, Turkey, Iran and Iraq, and includes some of the most inhospitable terrain on the planet. It is also worth noting that many of the tribes living in the region were nomadic, and a narrow borderline, as opposed to a frontier zone, was utterly alien to their way of life. Perhaps the project was doomed to failure, or so it must have seemed when Williams lost his surveying work overboard in 1853.

When it all finally came together in 1869, the 14-sheet, 60-foot-long 'Carte Identique' must have brought hope of a solution. It was published in St Petersburg and shows the entire border zone to a width of between 20 and 50 miles, from Mount Ararat in the north to Basra and the Persian Gulf in the south. Pink-veined mountains, grey barren desert and a luscious green strip running along the Shatt al-Arab River provide a wonderfully contrasting topographical picture.

The idea was that each delegation would draw their own interpretation of the borderline on the map. But the Ottoman delegation refused to do so, arguing that the border was nowhere near the area that had been so exhaustively mapped. Neither the British nor the Russians could do anything more, since they were only mediators and not arbitrators. The border would not be finally concluded until 1912.

Delhi, India

(1850s)

Among the thousands of maps in the India Office map collection are a small number by non-European mapmakers. These could be worth their weight in gold to the colonial administration if they held valuable local intelligence not available elsewhere. This large unfinished map of Shahjahanabad, or Old Delhi, was one of these. It was probably painted in the 1850s and had arrived in the India Office collection in London by 1878. It was drawn in the European 'plan' format but was produced by a local Indian draftsman. This is not only suggested by the use of Persian script for the place names, but also by the unparalleled detail it provides of the intricate streets, alleyways and semi-private spaces of this capital of the Mughal Empire.

Shahjahanabad was constructed between 1628 and 1658 as the capital city of the Mughal Emperor Shah Jahan (1592–1666). Built as a planned city, its layout conformed to Persian principles and therefore it functioned not only as an administrative and commercial centre, but as a symbol of Mughal culture and power based on Hindu and Islamic traditions. By the beginning of the nineteenth century the influence of the British East India Company had come to the city. The British Resident became its effective ruler, with the Mughal emperor occupying the Red Fort with merely symbolic status.

We can see the Red Fort in the bottom right-hand corner of the town, with the citadel beyond it, and the river beyond that. Streets emanate from it to the north and west, signifying its focus for the town, which is divided up into zones or administrative *thanas*, differentiated on the map using colour. Beyond the general plan, and the gardens and mosques, the town was permitted to develop piecemeal, leading to the incredible maze of alleyways, courtyards and dead-ends.

This urban geography constituted a nightmare for a military force looking to suppress any revolt, as occurred in 1857 when the impetus of the Indian rebellion moved from the surrounding countryside to the capital, rallying around the Mughal emperor as the true ruler of India. Although we cannot be sure of the map's exact purpose, its detail would have come in useful for the British in suppressing the rebellion during the Siege of Delhi, which caused wholesale damage to the fabric of the city. Today the map is a valuable record of what was lost.

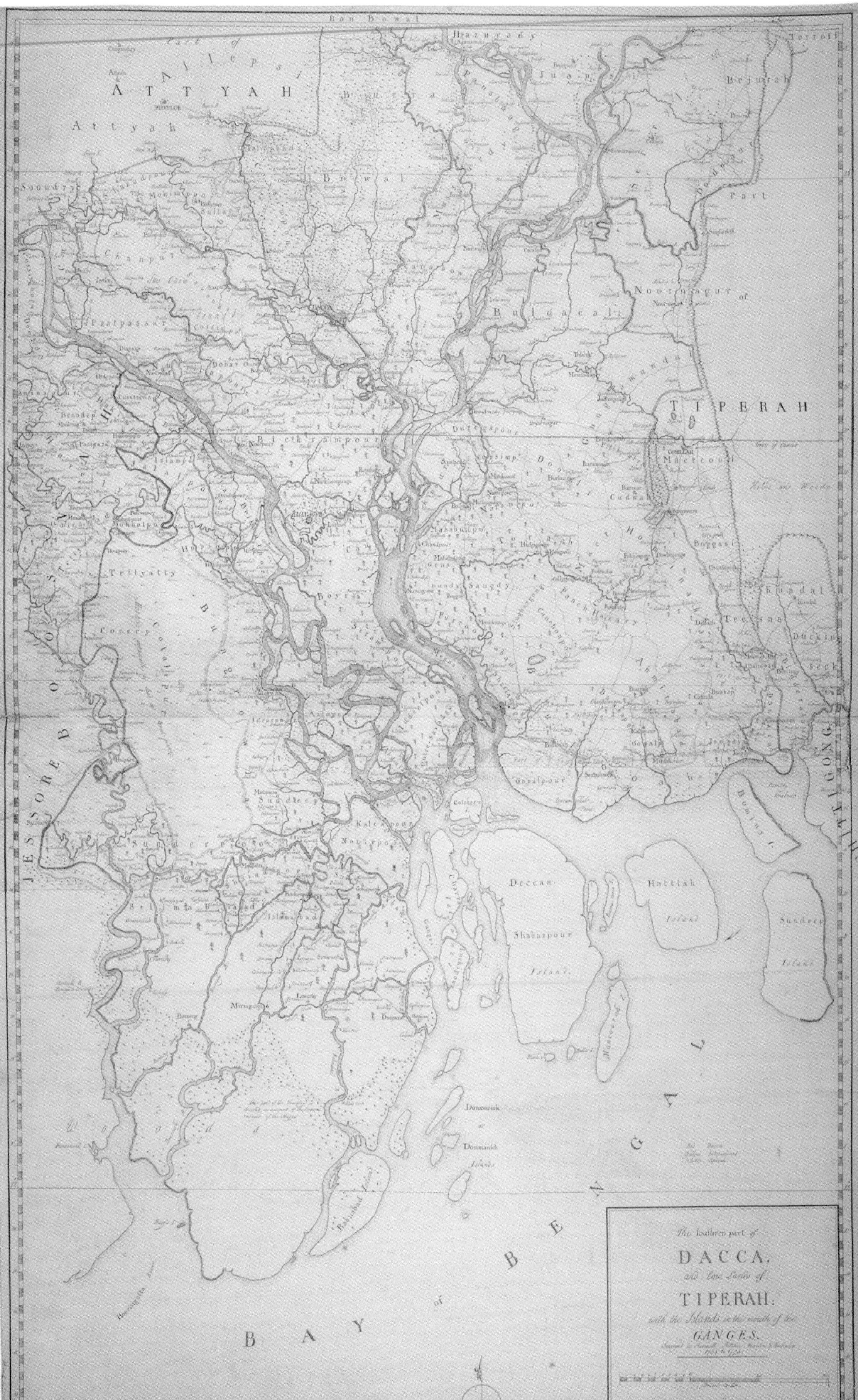
The southern part of
DACCA.
and low Lands of
TIPERAH;
with the Islands in the mouth of the
GANGES.
Ban Bowal
Hazurady
ATTYAH
Attyah
Bowal
Buldacal
TIPERAH
Bicktrampour
Noornagur
Bejurah
Soondry
Paatpassar
Tettyatty
Cocery
Deccan Shabazpour Island
Hattiah Island
Sundeep Island
Dommanick Islands
Rabnabad Island
Hills and Woods
BAY of BENGAL
JESSORE
CHITTIGONG

Bangladesh

(1773)

The mapping of the Indian subcontinent under the British East India Company is one of the most powerful and successful imperial mapping projects the world has ever seen. Beginning in earnest in the middle of the eighteenth century, this vast area was surveyed and mapped in minute detail, with the maps used to administer rule from the headquarters of the Company in London.

One of the key figures in this cartographic consolidation was British India's first surveyor general, Major James Rennell (1742–1830). Rennell's maps would go on to provide 'the definitive image of India for the British and European public'. A marine surveyor by training, Rennell was appointed by the chief administrator in India, Robert Clive (1725–74), following the British victory over the Nawab of Bengal and the French at Plassey in 1757. This victory presented Britain with large swathes of Bengal to survey and map.

Rennell set about it. He collected together existing geographical information on Bengal (such as soldier itineraries) and spent over a decade surveying the surrounding area from his base in Dacca, in modern-day Bangladesh. Surveying involved laborious and time-consuming field work, measuring land using a variety of instruments and calculations. It relied on continuing financial support, which was not always forthcoming for later surveying projects. From this variety of data, manuscript maps were drawn and sent to London for the scrutiny of Company officials.

This map is from a collection that was brought to London for the Company by Rennell when he returned home in 1778. The collection shows parts of Bengal in exhaustive detail. In the preface Rennell apologises to the Company directors for the 'tedious delay' in getting the maps to them, explaining that it was the result of '500 original surveys and the work of 10 gentlemen'. This map shows the mouth of the Ganges River north to Dacca and beyond, drawn at the scale of five miles to the inch. The scale enabled Rennell to show geographical features such as rivers, places and roads at a level of detail which, according to the historian Andrew Cook, 'delighted his employers'.

Also astonishing is how carefully, neatly and precisely every dab of ink has been applied to the paper. However, this level of information was not achieved without cost. Rennell was attacked and severely injured while surveying in February 1766, receiving a cut from a tribesman's sabre through his right shoulder. He nevertheless lived until he was 87, and during that time he saw his manuscript maps, which had originally been drawn for the express use of his employers, turned into printed maps for a wider audience.

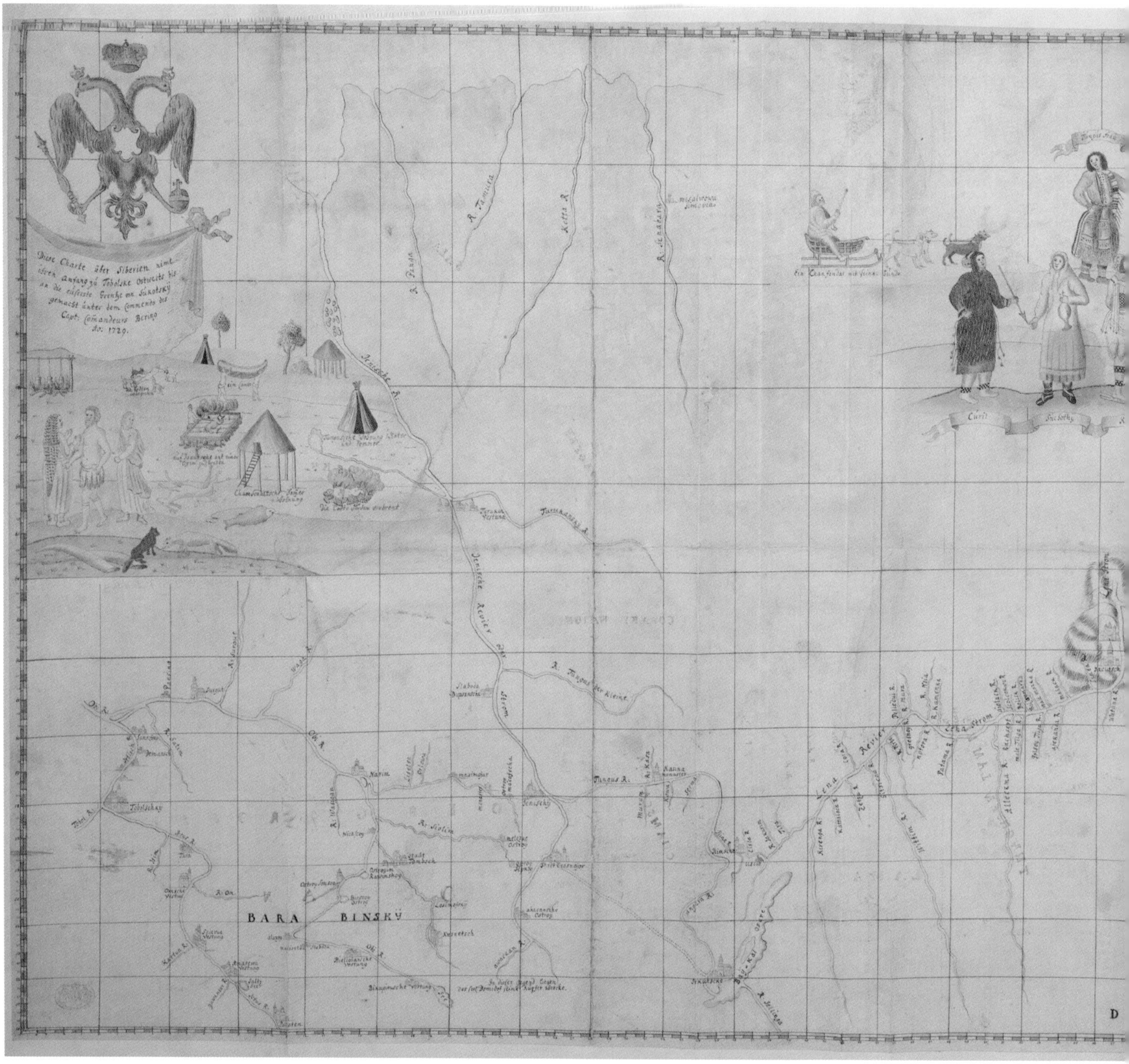

Siberia

(1729)

Vitus Bering (1681–1741) explored his way well and truly on to the map. A Danish cartographer, traveller and naval captain, Bering led two Russian expeditions, the first in 1725, to discover whether Russia and America were joined together in their respective eastern and western extremities. The success of this First Kamchatka Expedition is proven by the 'Bering Strait' separating the two continents, which bears his name. This map is a summary of Bering's team's exploits. It shows the territory through which he and his party travelled eastwards from St Petersburg – over the Ural Mountains, crossing the vastness of Siberia by navigating numerous rivers, and finally reaching Okhotsk on the Pacific coast in January 1727, two years after departure.

The party then explored the coast of the Kamchatka Peninsula in a boat, surveying the coastline, taking measurements and recording the customs of the people they met, some of whom are illustrated on the map. They sailed up the east coast until Bering pronounced that he could not see land either to the east or west, proving that Russia and America were not connected. On the map we can see their open boat *Archangel Gabriel* with Bering and his party inside. They returned to St Petersburg by 1730 and Bering was praised for his efforts.

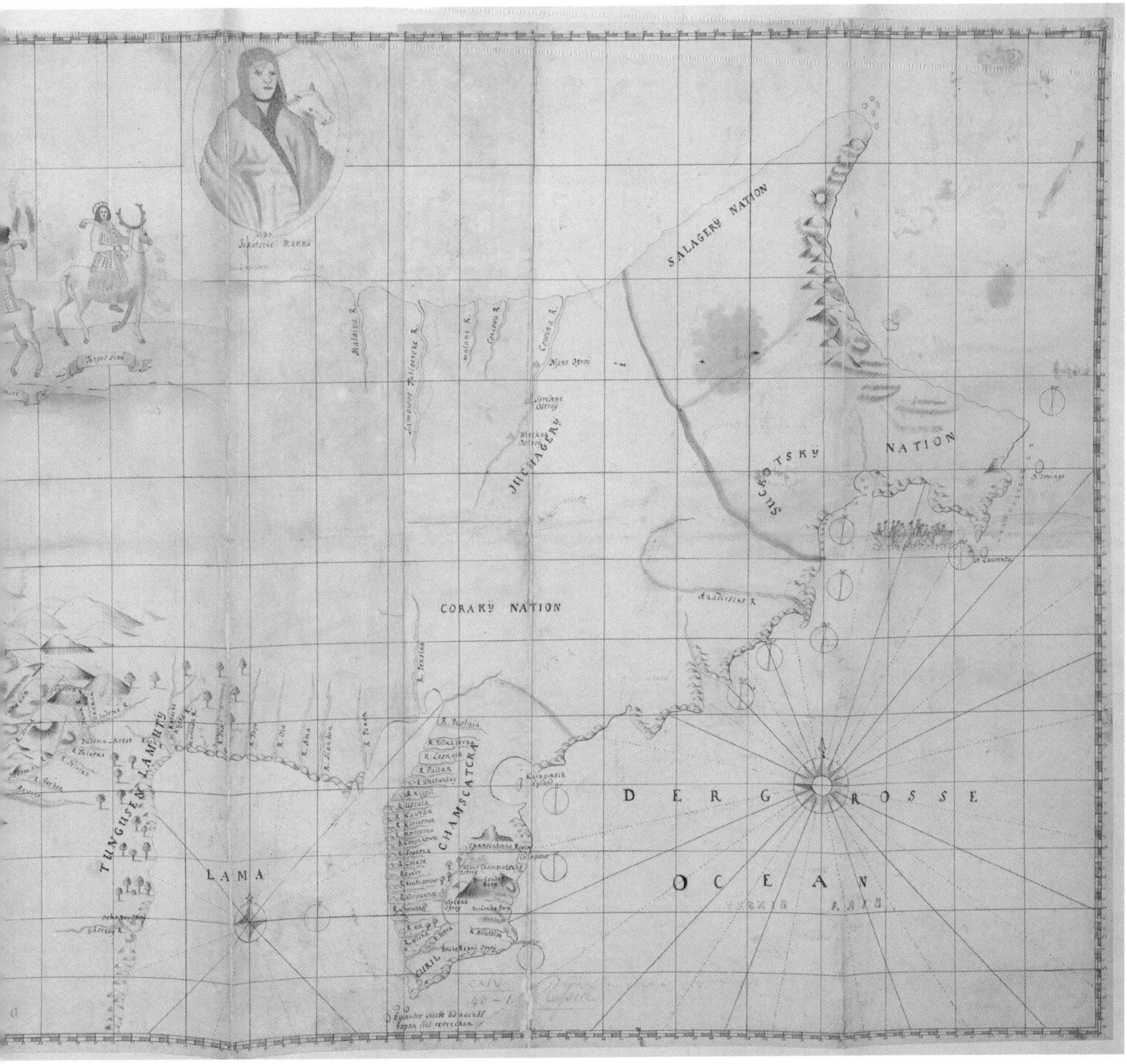

Bering's expedition was launched in the context of the age of Russian science and discovery and the emergence of the modern European state of Russia under Peter the Great (1672–1725). The St Petersburg Academy of Sciences was established in 1725 to promote, among other things, geodesy, survey and mapping in the service of the Russian state. Bering had done just that by extending Russia's control over its vast eastern territories – discovering, mapping and claiming it.

The success of Bering's expedition brought international recognition for Russia, but this compromised any potential secrecy of the mission and confidentiality of its findings. The map, by an anonymous mapmaker and in German, is one of a number of contemporary hand-drawn maps of the expedition which exist in various collections in Russia, Sweden, France and elsewhere. It is possible that the maps were purpose-made at the instigation of the Russian emperor for circulation to his fellow European monarchs, though the poor quality of the map's execution argues against this. However, the map historian Leo Bagrow noted that another copy of the map found its way into the hands of the king of Poland, who passed it to the mapmaker Jean-Philippe du Halde (1674-1743), who published it in 1735.

北
西
南
西安
蜀
貴州
雲南
桂州
廣東
萬里長城
流沙
蒙古地
華山
衡山
大昆侖
九度河
安南国地界
畫狂老人卍齡八十
彫刻 江川仙太郎
書肆 青雲堂梓

China and Korea

(1840 or 1841)

At first glance this printed map appears to be a bird's-eye view of a particularly mountainous local area. It is only when we look closer that we can see it shows an area of over nine and a half million square kilometres. Looking closer still, the map begins to align with the appearance of China: the shape of the east coast, the Tibetan Plateau in the west, the snaking Yellow River, and the Great Wall peeping out from between the hills.

This is a bird's-eye view of China, a woodcut made by Egawa Sentarô from an original drawing by the visionary Japanese artist Katsushika Hokusai (1760–1849). Responsible for one of the most famous images of the nineteenth century, *The Great Wave off Kanagawa*, Hokusai was one of the first Japanese artistic figures to gain an international reputation. The end of his career coincided with the opening up of Japanese society to the world.

As his map shows, Hokusai was a great innovator. Looking at this map is like looking at two images as the mind switches between its geographical representation and its gloriously patterned, textural quality. This latter feature is down to the lack of depth in the image. Hokusai drew it using a traditional parallel projection. Notice how the features at the far north are the same size as those at the bottom: they do not diminish in size or clarity as they would if they had been drawn using the Western convention of perspective.

It is easy to see why this map is lauded by twenty-first-century professional mapmakers. Its expansive vision of the world from above is perhaps best matched by the global map views of the American Richard Edes Harrison (1901–94), who was working a century after Hokusai. Harrison used a giant three-dimensional globe to copy his map views from, but Hokusai didn't have a model of China to copy. He created it from his imagination, and this is partly why his creative brilliance confounds and amazes those who perceive mapmaking as a purely scientific pursuit. This achievement, assimilating both generalities and specifics in a single image, takes years of craft. But Hokusai had time to hone his vision. He was 81 when he produced the map and as enthusiastic as ever, signing it 'Old man mad about painting'.

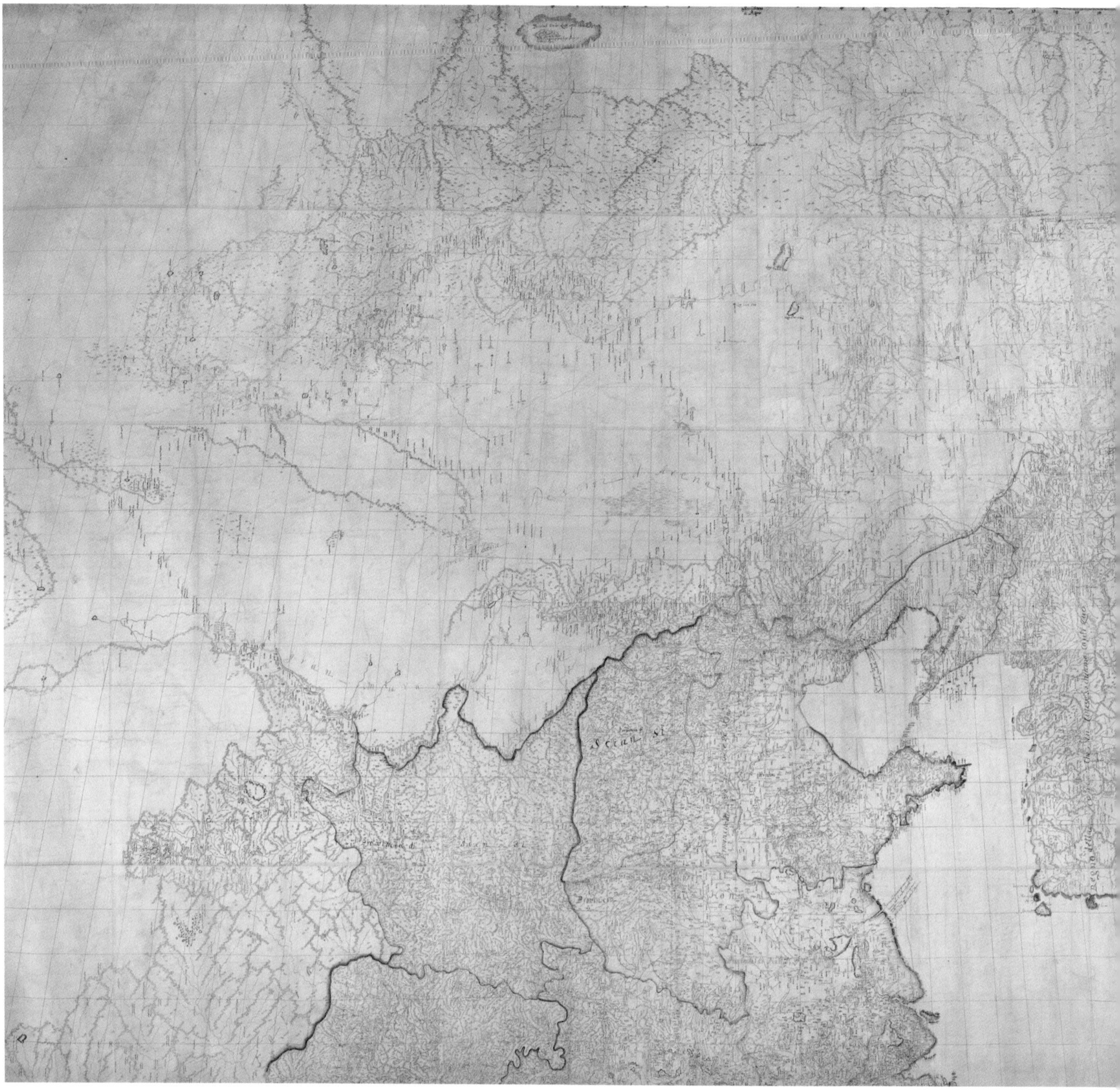

China and Korea

(1719)

Jesuit missionaries promoted Western science in China from the beginning of the seventeenth century. Their maps, instruments and texts, Trojan horses for the spread of Christianity, were often spectacular in themselves. One of these was produced by an Italian Jesuit called Matteo Ripa (1682–1746). It is a map of the entire Chinese Empire, based on survey work produced by French Jesuits for the Kangxi Emperor (1654–1722) between 1708 and 1718. It is entirely in the Chinese language, drawn on a spherical mathematical projection, at a scale of 1:1,390,000, based largely on an original survey, and engraved onto 41 sheets of paper which, when placed together, measure seven metres in width.

It is worth stepping back and appreciating the achievement: this is a map of an area the size of Europe, with coastal and interior information mapped at a larger scale than on any other map of a state then in existence, created in little over a decade. For comparison, France's national map, the Cassini family's *Carte de France*, would take over a century to complete.

Once produced, the map would have had a variety of uses. For example, drainage and engineering projects would have been served well by the large scale and utility it offered. It had, in fact, been the

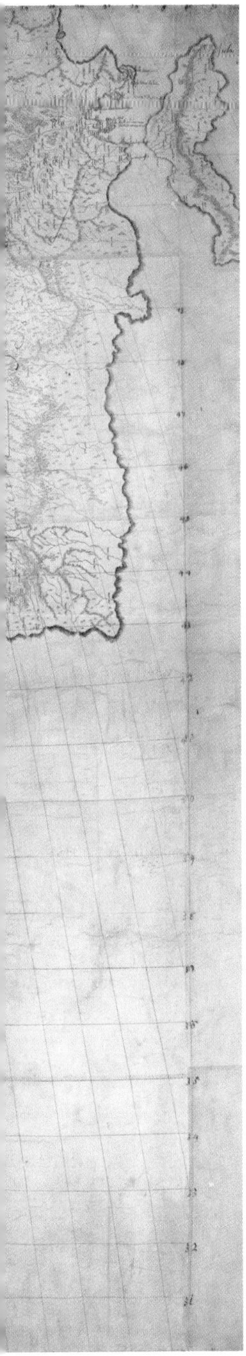

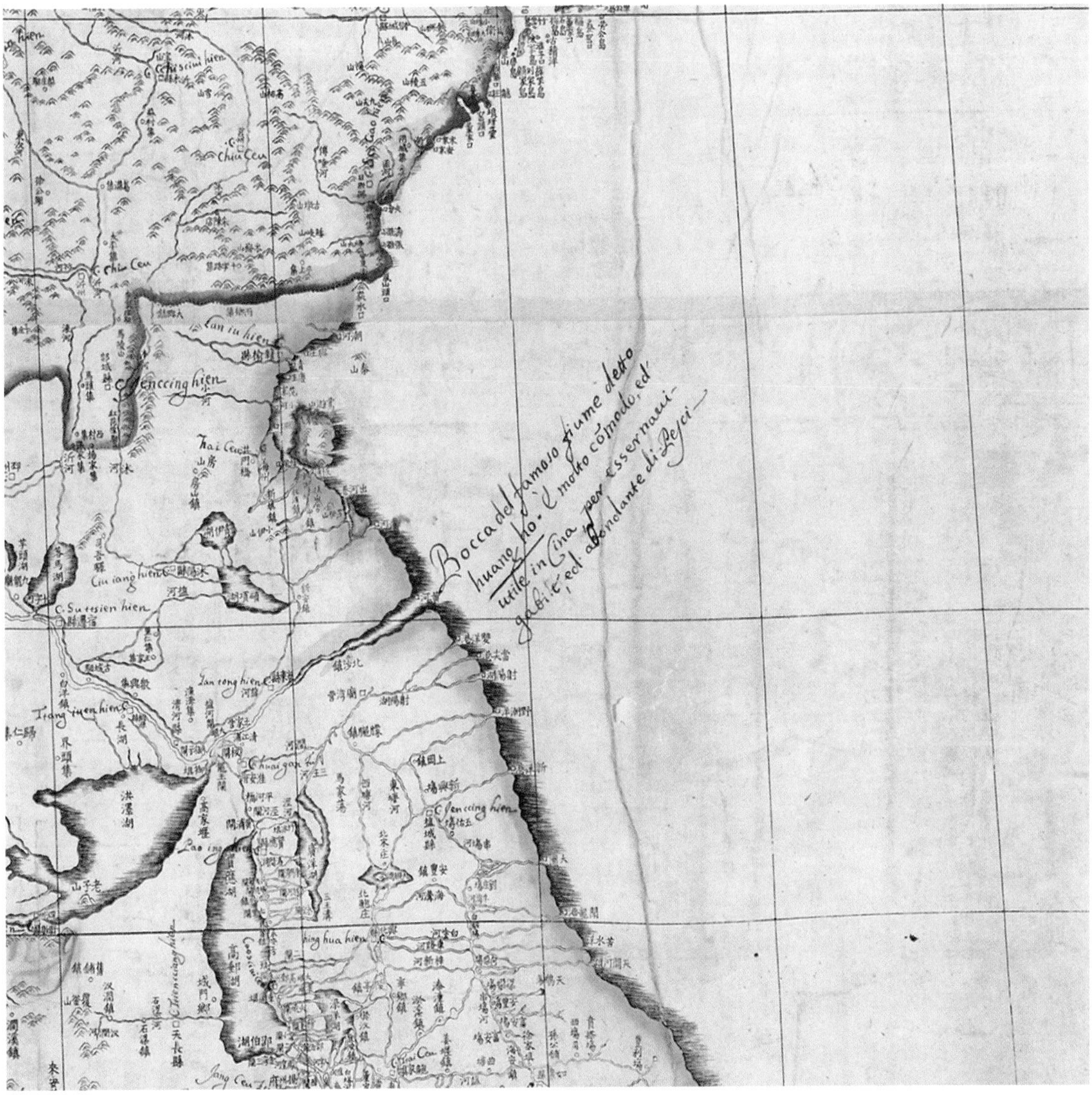

Jesuits' work on mapping the flooded agricultural region of Tianjin in 1705 that first roused the interest of the emperor. It would also have helped to centralise control by the dynasty over its vast territory, not merely through the persuasive picture of a uniform, measured and subjected empire it presented to the governing elite, but by nature of the fact that it was printed. This meant that multiple copies of the map were available, and actions could be co-ordinated.

The medium of copper engraving caught the emperor's imagination, and in 1711 he ordered Ripa to make engravings of paintings of his favourite palaces to accompany poems he himself had composed. Ripa had done well in earning the emperor's favour. He would also please others because, by retaining his map's copper engraving plates, he was able to print off additional copies and make the geography of secret and insular China available to the courts and palaces of Europe.

Ripa returned to Europe in 1724 on a British East India Company ship, arriving in England where he presented this copy of the map to King George I (*r.*1714–27) on 9 September. Ripa annotated the map in red ink, translating key place names from Chinese for the benefit of the king. This marked the beginning of Britain's serious interest in China.

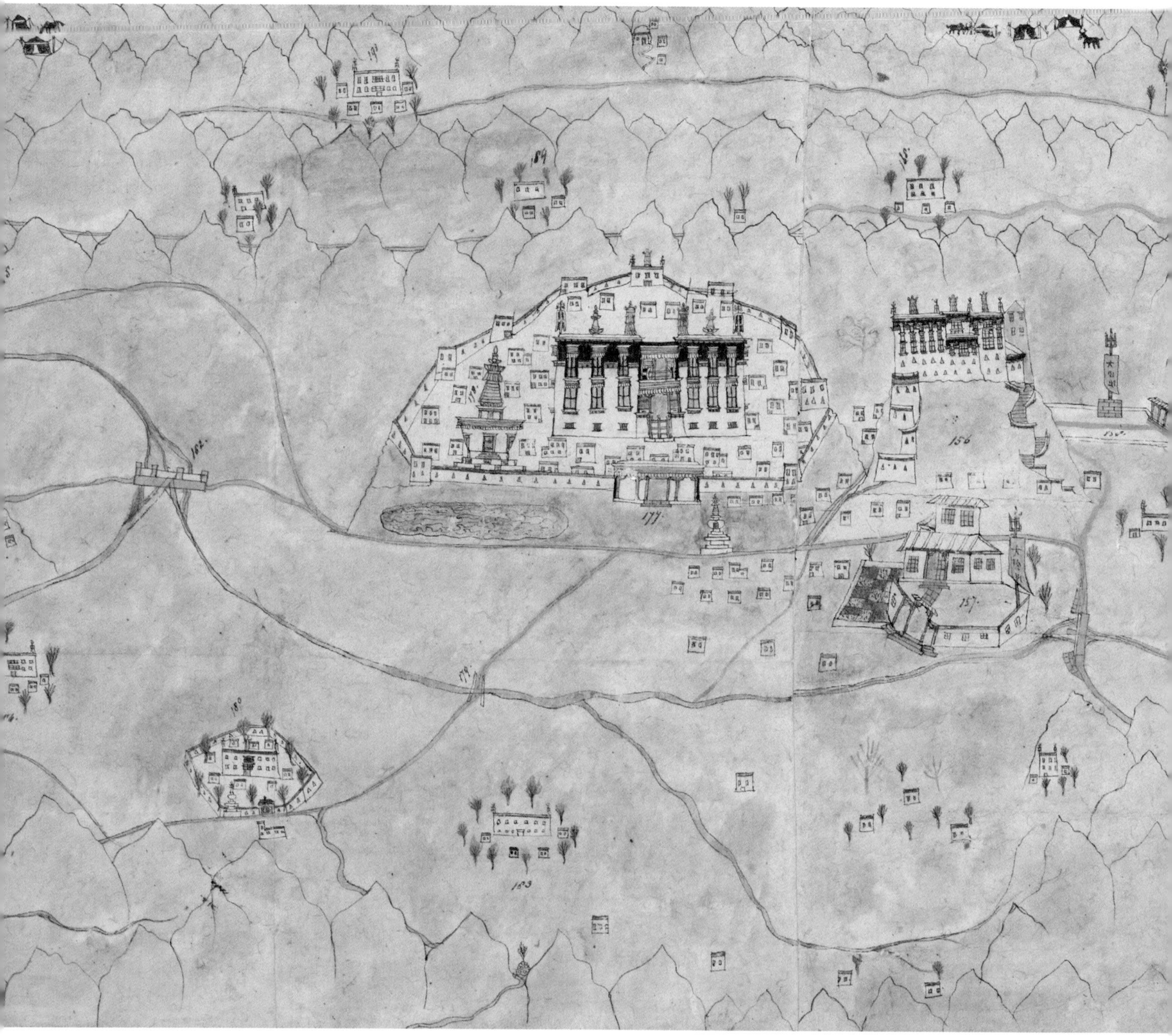

Tibet, China

(1857 or 1858)

This expansive map of part of mountainous Central Tibet was produced in either 1857 or 1858 and shows an area just southeast of Lhasa: the town of Gyantse, in the centre left of the image, with the sacred Yamdrok Lake filled with ducks. To the north we see the Yarlung River with a bridge across it and boats representing the Chaksam ferry. Scattered across the mountainous landscape are a variety of settlements, nomad camps and roads. The map is part of a vast 15-metre-long picture map covering over 1,000 square miles of Tibet. Its style is highly pictorial and overwhelmingly different to the objective scientific mapping which was at that time being practised by the Survey of India on the other side of the Himalayas, to the south. Nevertheless, it provides us with a clear and informative vision of the area which is every bit as useful.

Useful for what? A lot about this map is shrouded in mystery, but the historian Diana Lange believes that it was produced by a lama or Buddhist teacher. There may have been more than one hand at work. It was commissioned by a British India government official named William Edmund Hay (1805–79). Britain had invested heavily in mapping much of the Indian subcontinent, but until this point Tibet had remained out of reach to the north. However, just at this time, specially selected British spies known as 'pundits' were infiltrating this

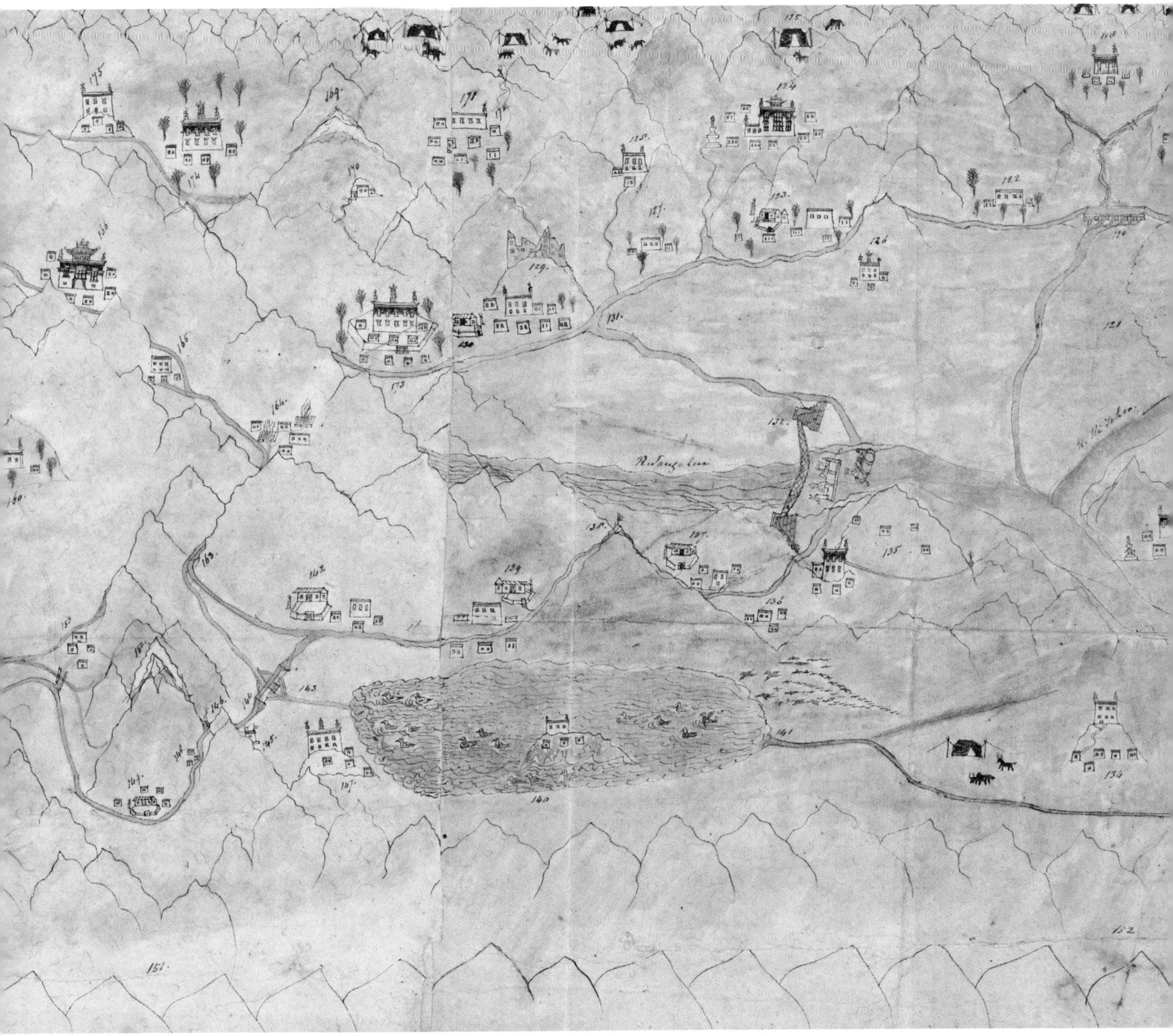

border region and obtaining intelligence for trade and influence. With Tibet now in the British administration's sights, we can perceive Hay setting out to find someone with local knowledge and ordering it in as useful a format as possible.

The map fits the description of an intelligence map drawn from local first-hand experience. It is strongly 'un-European' in its pictorial format, in the way that features such as mountains and rivers have been shown, and in its hierarchical structure (whereby more important features are exaggerated in size). Yet it pays strong attention to linear features such as roads, passes and crossings, all important for military movement and trade. The hesitant hand suggests that the artist was being guided, and this is supported by the peculiar way in which the panorama has been made up of sheets of paper that have been joined together in an ad hoc manner. All of this points to the creator of the map being supervised, and we can almost imagine Hay standing at his shoulder, making suggestions, and later annotating them with captions.

Whatever this extraordinary map's original purpose, it was passed to an associate of Hay's, Thomas Alexander Wise (1802–89), and reached the India Office Library, where it has been preserved as a unique visual record of a place at a critical point in time.

Jiangsu, China

(1793)

Britain's first official diplomatic mission to China took place between 1792 and 1794. Its leader, Lord Macartney (1737–1806), headed an entourage of officials, artists, scientists and diarists primed to record cultural information and pass on Western knowledge to their hosts. The embassy failed to extract any trade concessions that would have enabled the British East India Company to increase its influence ahead of its European competitors. The failure has often been blamed on Macartney's refusal to kowtow or show deference to the emperor, but the truth is probably more complex than a simple slight. However, the cultural capital which resulted from the mission was enough for it to be judged an overall success.

One of the artists employed for the journey was the painter William Alexander (1767–1816). His neat, colourful and descriptive watercolours covered a variety of subjects as the embassy arrived in Guangzhou and sailed up the Bey River to Beijing, and then, when dismissed by the emperor a month later, travelled west along the Grand Canal and then back to Guangzhou. In Alexander's paintings we see landscapes filled with people – ethnographic portraits, Chinese customs, even the odd piece of agricultural machinery. In one watercolour a fleet of Chinese boats carrying Macartney along the Sanhe River have attracted a considerable crowd of onlookers. The town walls of Pao-Yin Hsien are in the background.

On returning to England Alexander's original watercolours, together with others by Henry Parish and maps by the future Lord of the Admiralty John Barrow (1764–1848), were presented by Macartney's deputy Sir George Staunton (1737–1801) to King George III. Alexander also had a number of his watercolours engraved and published. This was in direct contravention of Macartney's stipulation that a single official account of the voyage was to be published (it was authored by Staunton and published in 1799). A number of Alexander's original sketches, which were probably produced for the engravings, were purchased by the British East India Company, and Alexander became Assistant Keeper of Antiquities at the British Museum in 1808.

五老峰
香爐峰
湖口
上鍾山
下鍾山
水師營
南湖
鎖江樓
琵琶亭

Jiangxi, China

(1682–91)

There's something about the effect of paint on silk that makes it appear to shimmer before the eyes, which we can appreciate by looking at examples from this set of 14 paintings of Jiangxi province in eastern China from the late seventeenth century. They have been coloured using generous amounts of aquamarine, turquoise and gold heightening for added effect. Such is the artistry deployed that it is difficult to appreciate that this was a practical map produced for administrative purposes.

The notion that practical maps have to be unadorned, unattractive and robust is a modern Western perception. In Europe, as well as in China, maps for high-level administrators once had to be pleasing on the eye. This set comprises a map of Jiangxi and 13 maps of its individual prefectures, mounted concertina-like in an album. What is immediately noticeable is how many rivers and mountains there are in this part of the world, with the mountains coloured in shades of blue and turquoise and the rivers in turquoise, covered with an intricate pattern which looks rather like fish scales.

The prominence of these natural features provides the key to understanding the purpose of the map. Jiangxi is situated across the main route between northern and southern China, with the Yangtze River in the north and its tributaries (including the Gan River) facilitating transit towards the south coast. This map was for the use of administrators running the region, who were required to travel across and through it, to the many towns and settlements which are marked. If we look closely we can see that key river crossing points are shown as well as details of beaches, dunes and sandbars.

The settlements themselves are described in detail. This includes the identification of government offices and schools, in which were taught the future members of China's vast and complex administrative class, its civil service – the users of such maps as this one.

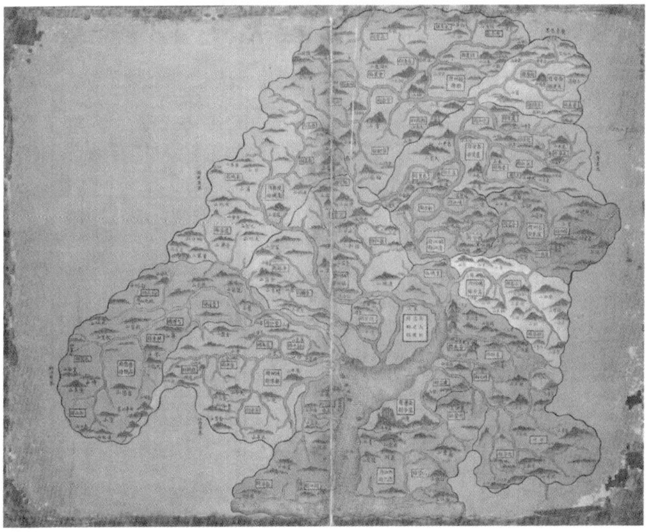

Guangzhou, China

(1760s)

During the eighteenth century Chinese artists developed a type of landscape painting for foreign tourists in the form of beautiful and colourful gouache panoramas of the bustling Canton (now Guangzhou) harbour front. These were made for the steady stream of Western merchants who wanted souvenirs to take home with them.

This example, from the Topographical Collection of George III, is a particularly impressive example over eight metres in length. It was painted by an unknown Chinese artist during the 1760s and not only exhibits a greater-than-usual skill in rendering buildings but an aptitude for adapting the style to conform to Western pictorial modes – specifically, perspective and convincing recession into space. The view also contains an endlessly interesting series of scenes of everyday life. People are on boats, on foot, conversing, lifting, carrying, buying and selling – everything you would expect to see in one of the world's great ports.

Canton had become the principal trading post for European companies engaging with China at a time when the rest of the country remained closed to foreigners. In 1793 the first British delegation to China, led by Lord Macartney, failed to extract any further concessions for Britain. Business in trading tea, porcelain and other commodities remained strictly limited to this harbour front. The view shows the Swedish, Dutch, French, British East India Company and others' premises, called factories, built in the self-

consciously civilised neo-classical style with white colonnades. Their ships were moored several miles downstream.

The view has been dated by the historian Paul Van Dyke to between 1764 and 1770 on account of the presence of a Chinese ship or 'junk' called the *Samjeck*, which is moored in front of the French factory. Records for the *Samjeck* show that it sailed from Canton to Cambodia and Vietnam each year during this time. The artist has captured with exactitude the city, its people and even individual sailing vessels, placing this view at the very peak of topographical description. Canton is frozen in time, but the panorama's vivid quality suggests that at any moment it might burst into life once more.

Part of Singapore Island
Plantations
High ground
Uncleared ground generally low and marshy
Malay Village
Brick Kiln
Bugis Town
Dry at Low Water Spring Tides
Low Swampy Ground
Western hill
Low Sandy ground
Flag Staff
Fresh water River
Battery
Rocky point
Brick Kiln
Gambier Plantation
High grounds
Tanjong Malang
Tanjong Pagar
Rocky point
Sandy beach
Pooloo Hantoo
New Harbour
Mount Harris
Passage to the New Harbour
Mud Bank
Sandy Bay
18th June 1825.
500 1000 1500 2000 2500 3000
Scale of 400 Yards to 1 Inch. 1760 Yards to 1 Mile.

Singapore

(c.1823)

A group of British soldiers and administrators landed at the southern tip of the Malay Peninsula in 1819, taking over the small settlement of Singapura. British Singapore was created by the then governor of Bencoolen in Sumatra, Sir Stamford Raffles (1781–1826), against his government's orders and in the face of rival Dutch claims. Due to its strategic location, its free port status (meaning that no restrictions or charges were imposed on trade) and the efforts of Raffles and his associate William Farquhar (1774–1839), it quickly became a powerful trading centre.

These two sea charts of Singapore and Singapore Island, 'the new British Settlement', were produced within the first decade of the town's establishment and were sent to London for the eyes of the British East India Company board of directors in 1825. They constitute the earliest detailed charts of the area, incorporating coastal surveys that had been initiated in order to consolidate British control of the island.

This included work by the official hydrographer to the East India Company, James Horsburgh (1762–1836), James Franklin (1783–1834), elder brother of the British explorer Sir John Franklin, and Farquhar, Raffles's right-hand man, who was in charge of Singapore from 1819 when Raffles left to continue his governorship.

These charts are large final versions which collect together all of the surveying work, mathematical data, topographical details and toponyms (place names). Coastal information and soundings (water depths) were particularly crucial for Company ships. The latter are given as numbers in fathoms, and we can see them marking off the main sailing track which was to be followed into the river and harbour. Key coastal features are shown topographically and symbolically according to well-established custom. One such 'Rocky Point', standing at the mouth of the Singapore River, would be blown up by dynamite in 1843 in order to make it more easily navigable.

Farquhar's time in charge of Singapore would prove controversial. Although Raffles charged him with developing the town in a particular European style, for example by employing a European-style urban development 'grid' pattern and racially segregating its residents, Farquhar appears to have been content to let the settlement develop of its own accord. It continued to prosper, but when Raffles returned in 1822 he removed Farquhar from his post and initiated his own 'Jackson plan' for Singapore, which included straight roads and the indigenous areas of 'Bugis Town', 'Chinese Town' and 'Malay Town', which began to appear by 1825.

The Philippines and Manila

(1734 and c.1739)

A time-honoured propaganda method by which states demonstrate their influence is through maps. By mapping somewhere you lay claim to it, but by producing an extravagant map you can emphasise your patronage. These extraordinary printed maps of the Philippines and its capital city, Manila (overleaf), give a powerful message about the commercial status of the eighteenth-century Spanish colony.

Pedro Murillo Velarde's (1696–1753) engraved map of the Philippines was published in 1734. As well as Spanish use, it would have been available to international traders, and in this way its message would have been transmitted across the globe. The islands are positioned at the centre of the map, the navigational rhumb lines and coastal emphasis indicating that it has been derived from a sea chart (the Spanish knew comparatively little about the islands' interiors, despite having claimed possession of them a century and a half earlier).

Around the edge of the map are town plans, views and street scenes. The latter are particularly interesting because they illustrate trade between people whose ethnicity is emphasised – Chinese, Mongolian, African, Moluccan, Japanese, Indian, Persian and 'Mestizo' (Spanish–Filipino) – as if to demonstrate the multicultural trading facilitated by the Philippines' ideal location.

The map of the Philippines' chief town of Manila (overleaf), published first in 1717 and here in around 1739, is another symbol of Spanish patronage. Indeed, in the upper portion of the map we can see the Governer General of the Philippines, Fernando Valdés y Tamón (b.1700), presenting a miniature version to the Spanish King Philip V (*r.*1700–24). It is a superbly detailed vision of a bustling commercial centre. Looking closely we can see the streets teeming with people and the quayside packed full of boats.

Once again the printed map enabled the image to be transmitted far and wide. But was this a mistake? In 1762 the British besieged Manila capturing and looting it, and holding it for two years before returning it to Spain. George III authorised the plan of attack, and on this, his copy of the map, words like 'breach', 'batteries' and 'guns' have been added in ink, so it is tempting to believe that he used this map when planning or following the siege. Given the value to Spain's enemies of the map's excellent portrayal of the town's defences, perhaps producing such a public printed map had not been the best idea.

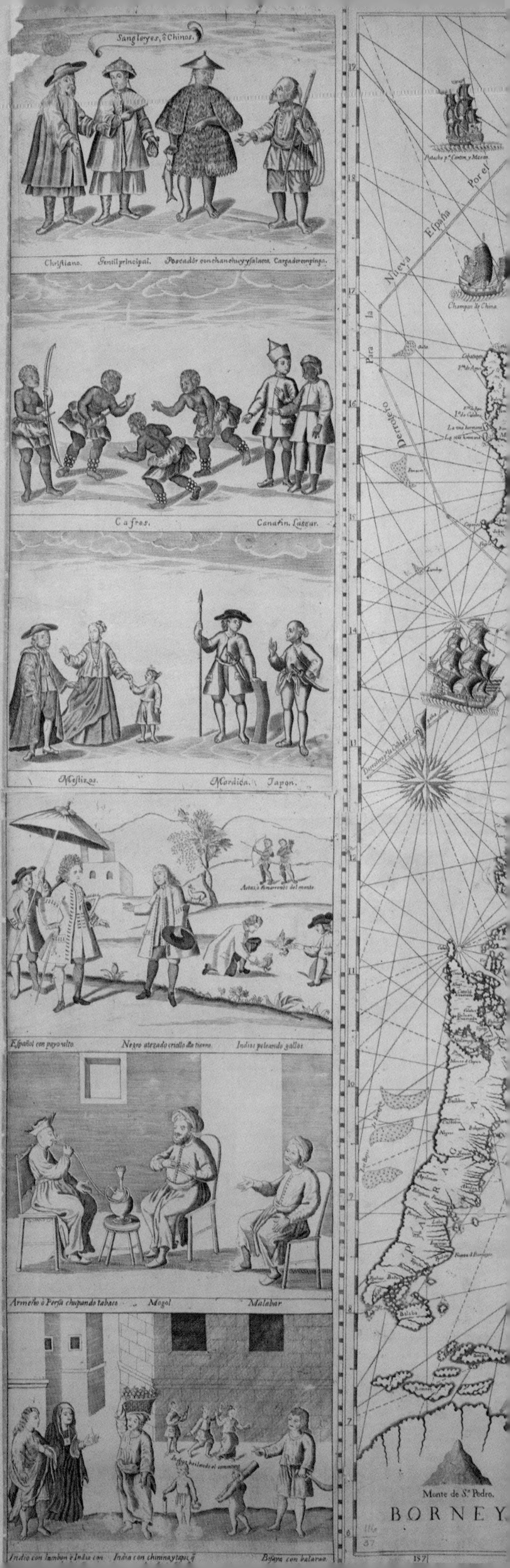

CARTA HYDROGRAPHICA
Y CHOROGRAPHICA
DELAS YSLAS FILIPINAS
DEDICADA
AL REY NUESTRO SEÑOR
CASTILLA
ZON
YSLA DEGUAJAN.
RIODEPASIG
MANILA
Por el Embocadero de Sn. Bernardino
YBABAO Ó SAMAR
PANAY
LEYTE
BOJOL
SAMBOANGAN
PUERTO DECAVITE
YSLA DE MINDANAO

TOPOGRAPHIA
DELA CIUDAD DE MANILA, CAPITAL
delas Yslas Philipinas. Fundada en la de Luzon
Nuevo Reyno de Castilla,
DEDICADA AL REY NUESTRO SEÑOR
D. FELIPE V. (que Dios gu.de)
Por el Mariscal de Campo D. Fernando Valdes Ta-
mon su Governador y Capitan Genl. de dhas Yslas,
y Presidente dla Rl. Audiencia y Chancria. d ellas.
Delineada de orden de su Magd. por D. Antonio Fernandez
de Roxas: y esculpida por Fr. Hipolito
Ximenez dl Orden dla Hospitd.
dl Glor.o S. Juan d Dios.

EXPLICACION.
A Cathedral.
B Palacio delos Governadores.
C Real Audiencia.
D Collegio de S. Phelipe.
E Contadutia, y quarteles d Solda.
F Almasenes Nuevos.
G Capilla Real.
H Almasenes Viejos demolidos.
Y Sta Clara.
J Hospital Real.
K Cassa de Cabildo
L Collegio de Sto Thomas Vniv.
LL Yglesia y Convento d Sto Domgo
M Beato de Sta Chatarina de Cena.
N Collegio de Sn Juan de Letran.
Ñ Yglesia y Hospl de S. Iuan de Dios
O Yglesia y Convento de S Francisco, y Capilla de la tercera Orden.
P Yglesia y Convento de Agust. descal.
Q Sta Potenciana.
R Compañia de Iesus.
S Collegio de S. Joseph.
T Casa dela Fundicion.
V Yglesia y Convento de S. Agustin.
X Collegio de Sta Ysabel.
Z Solar end se fabricaba el Censnario
A A Palacio Arzobispal.
Sementeras
Sepulturas d Sangleys
Pueblo de Dilao
Ygla Y Convto d S. Fr
Principio del pueblo de Bagumbaya
Puerta de Sta Lucia
Sta Ysabel
S. Joseph
S. Eugenio
S. Diego

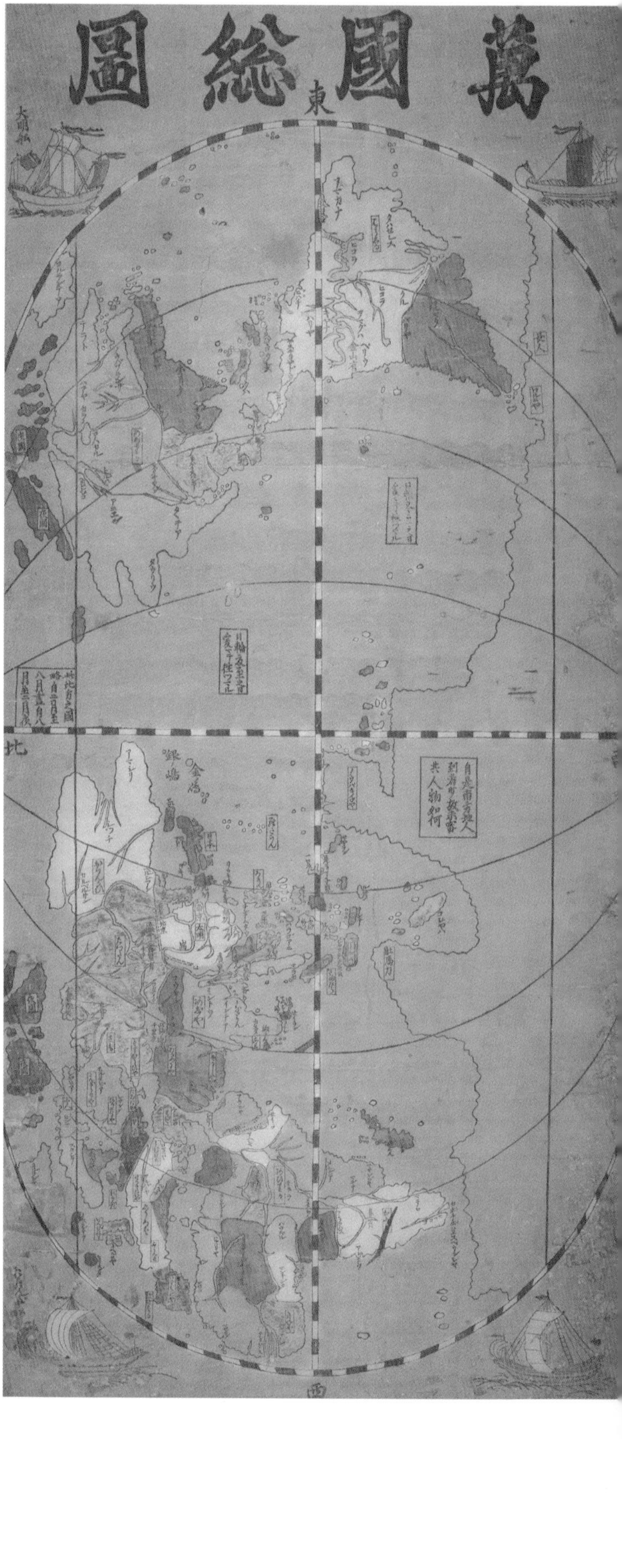
萬國總圖
東
大明
北
西

Japan

(1645)

This world map is one of a handful of surviving Japanese world maps from the seventeenth century known as a *bankoku sōzu*. What is interesting about these maps is that they are European-style hybrid maps representing the influx of European tastes and traditions into Japan during the Tokugawa era of Japanese isolation from the outside world (1600–1858).

A lot of research has gone into deciphering the European sources of the *bankoku sōzu*, principally the cartographic work of the Jesuits in China, and particularly the world map of 1602 by Matteo Ricci. This oval-shaped world map contrasted with traditional Eastern and Buddhist map traditions in the way it was drawn and in the proportion of space given to non-Eastern parts of the world. Copies of it were in use in the Jesuit academy in Kyoto in 1605, where its Chinese characters would have been readable by educated Japanese.

There were further European influences on the *bankoku sōzu*, and these came via Dutch merchants who were permitted (along with the Chinese and Portuguese) to trade with Japan under strict conditions from 1639. But these conditions were not so strict as to preclude the circulation of Dutch prints, such as maps and ethnic portraits.

In the British Library's *bankoku sōzu*, a woodblock print of 1645 published in Kyoto by Hyashi Jizaemon, we can see how these principal traits have been assimilated and adapted into a new and dynamic product. The oval-shaped world map follows the Western style and includes features derived from these maps, such as a reference to South American cannibals. However, it is oriented with east to the top, with the central meridian passing through the Pacific rather than the Atlantic Ocean. Ships in each of the four corners are representative of Japanese, Chinese and European vessels.

The *bankoku sōzu* has collected the 40 ethnic portraits together as a second woodblock print called a *jimbutsuzi*. This was designed to hang, scroll-like, on a wall next to the world map, not placed in the margins as on Dutch *carte à figure* maps. The portraits were of equal importance to the world map, and their ethnographic, traditional and cultural messages were as significant for Japanese viewers as scientific qualities were important to Europeans.

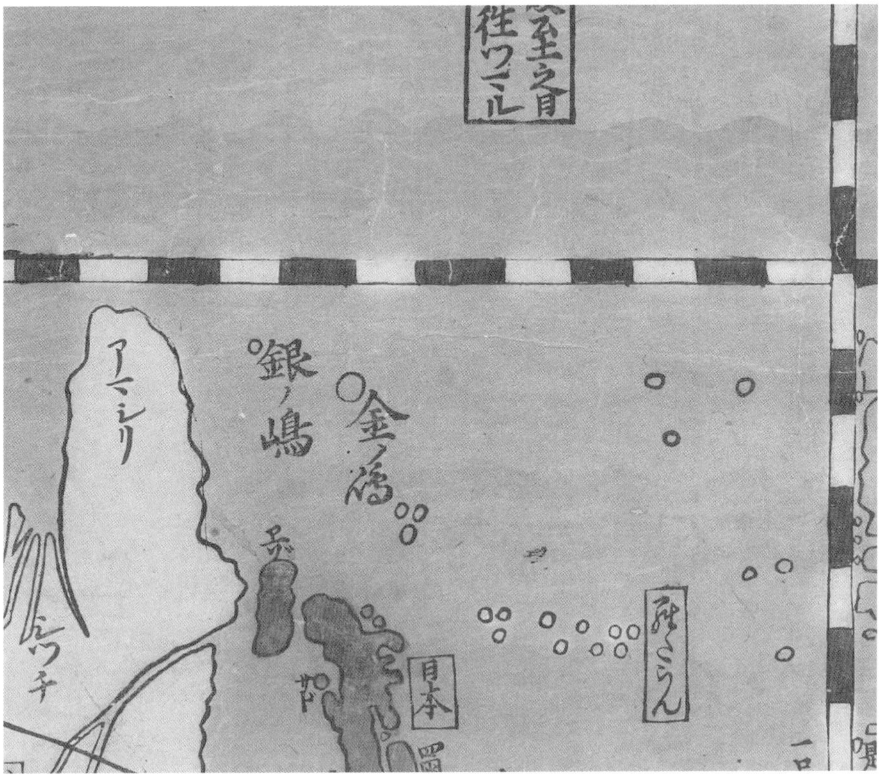

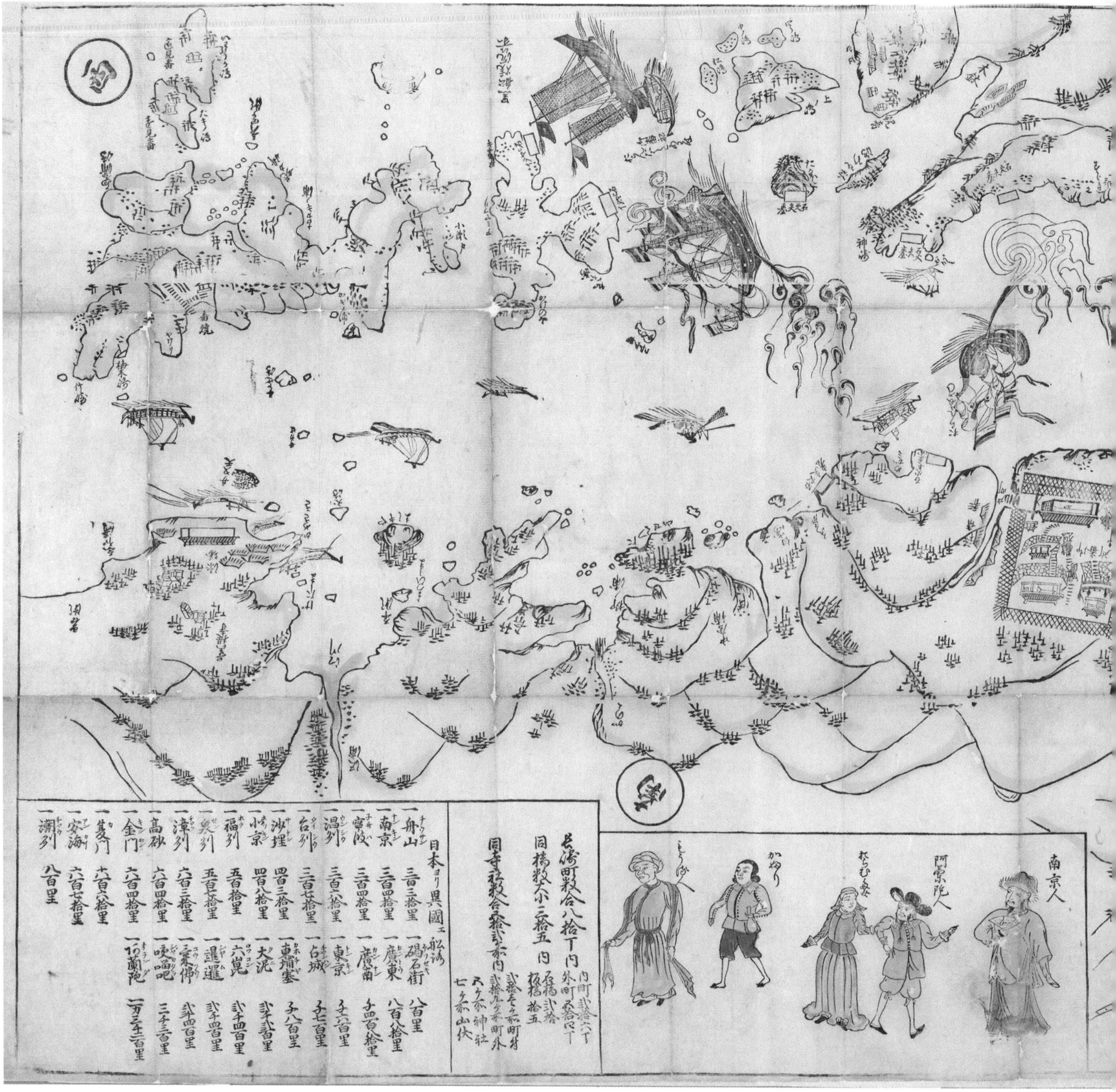

Nagasaki, Japan

(c.1680)

This map of the Japanese town of Nagasaki was printed there in around 1680. It was collected at the end of the seventeenth century by the German author Engelbert Kaempfer (1651–1716) while he was in Japan working as a medic for the Dutch East India Company between 1690 and 1692. The map is important not only because it provides early and virtually unique information on the layout and topography of one of the world's great trading cities, but also because it presents, along with its accompanying texts and images, an unparalleled snapshot of urban Japanese culture and society at a time when this information was severely limited for Europeans.

Japanese isolation from world affairs had been self-imposed in 1600 and was only repealed in the mid-nineteenth century. Until that point the only European traders permitted to visit were the Dutch, who were stationed on an island in Nagasaki harbour called Deshima. The island is the fan-shaped area to the centre-right of this map, connected to the mainland by a bridge that was drawn up at night, so that Kaempfer and his associates were, in his words, 'sealed off and guarded like thieves'.

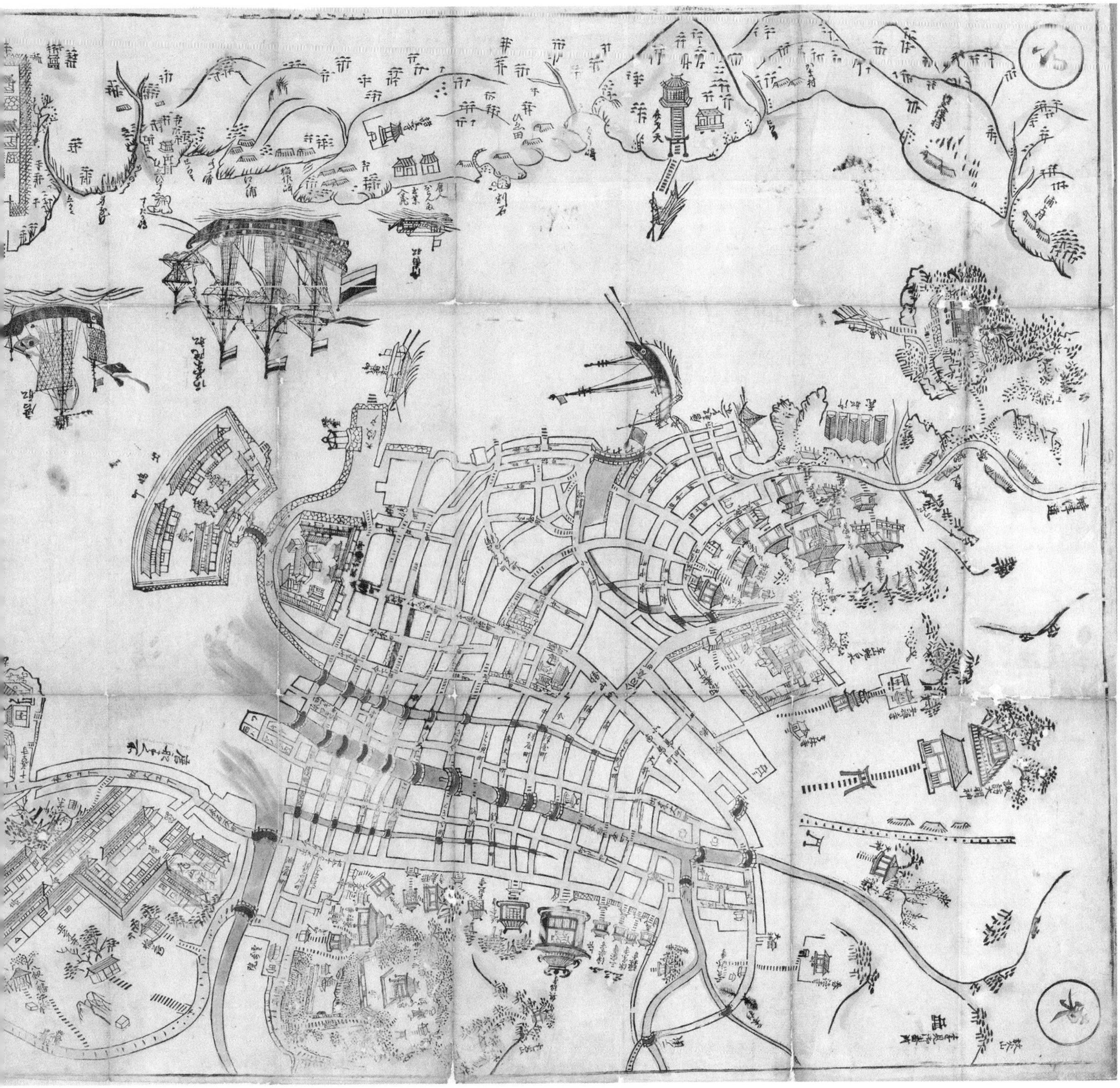

Restrictions were tight, but not so tight that Kaempfer wasn't able to acquire his printed map, which showed the area of the bay, the layout of the streets, some principal buildings, images of Dutch and Chinese ships, and full-length ethnographic portraits. In actual fact, Kaempfer enjoyed substantial access to Japan and twice travelled with a Dutch contingent to the capital city of Edo (modern-day Tokyo) to pay tribute to the Tokugawa shogun. Kaempfer recorded everything on the journey, from being offered a snack of 'shellfish fried over a fire of pine cones' to observing suicides swinging by the roadside near Mount Fuji – 'the most beautiful mountain in the world'.

Kaempfer returned to Europe with vast quantities of books and prints on a variety of aspects of Japanese culture, from everyday customs to natural history, and a considerable quantity of his own writings and drawings. These were purchased by Sir Hans Sloane between 1723 and 1725, who used them for his 'History of Japan', published in 1729, and then donated them with the rest of his collections to the British Museum in 1753.

1 The Universe
2 The World
3 Africa
4 America
5 Asia

6 Australasia

7 Europe
8 Seas and Oceans
9 Celestial Maps
10 Fantasy Worlds

March 1956

Australia and New Zealand

(1956)

The twentieth century was a period in which map production was increasingly affected by mechanical and digital processes. However, maps continued to be made using traditional methods, and in examples such as this watercolour relief map (indicating elevations and depressions in the landscape) of Australia and New Zealand we can appreciate the skill and virtuosity of their practitioners.

This is the preparatory artwork for a map which was included in an atlas of 1957 entitled *Odham's New Illustrated Atlas of the World*. It is one of a set of physical maps which were positioned at the beginning of continental 'chapters'. (In twenty-first-century atlases it is more common to find satellite images fulfilling this function.) After completion the map was photo-reproduced and the image was then amended, with names, places and a graticule (co-ordinate grid) added, before being reproduced, printed, and bound up with the rest of the atlas.

Looking at the original painting, it is impossible not to marvel at the sensitive and intricate patterns which form the map's topography. The vivid and exaggerated colours successfully communicate areas of fertile land, vegetation and barren desert, all of which are well represented in this part of the world. It is worth remembering that satellite images tend to have their colours exaggerated in order to increase their visual effect. By contrast, the organic nature of the colour pigments used in this painting lend it even greater authenticity.

The artist was designer H.T. (Bert) Hawes (d.2008). Working to a brief set by George Philip & Son's cartographic director, Harold Fullard (1915–2001), Hawes worked for 21 months on the eight relief maps required for *Odham's Atlas*, taking the outlines from other maps, then filling them in, with little room for error (watercolours are notoriously difficult to amend). Reminiscing about the project with a former colleague in 2000, Hawes remembered his 'quiet desperation' at the cost-cutting imposed on him as he worked, as well as experiencing difficulties with the layering and copying process. However, he described it as one of George Philip's 'better efforts'.

Due to the fact that they were essentially preparatory maps, artwork like this tends not to survive. However, these remained in the possession of Philip's until 2014, when they were donated to the British Library along with the business archive of the mapmaking company. In 2016 the British Library was able to celebrate Bert's skills by displaying two of the maps in the first major exhibition of the mapping of the twentieth century.

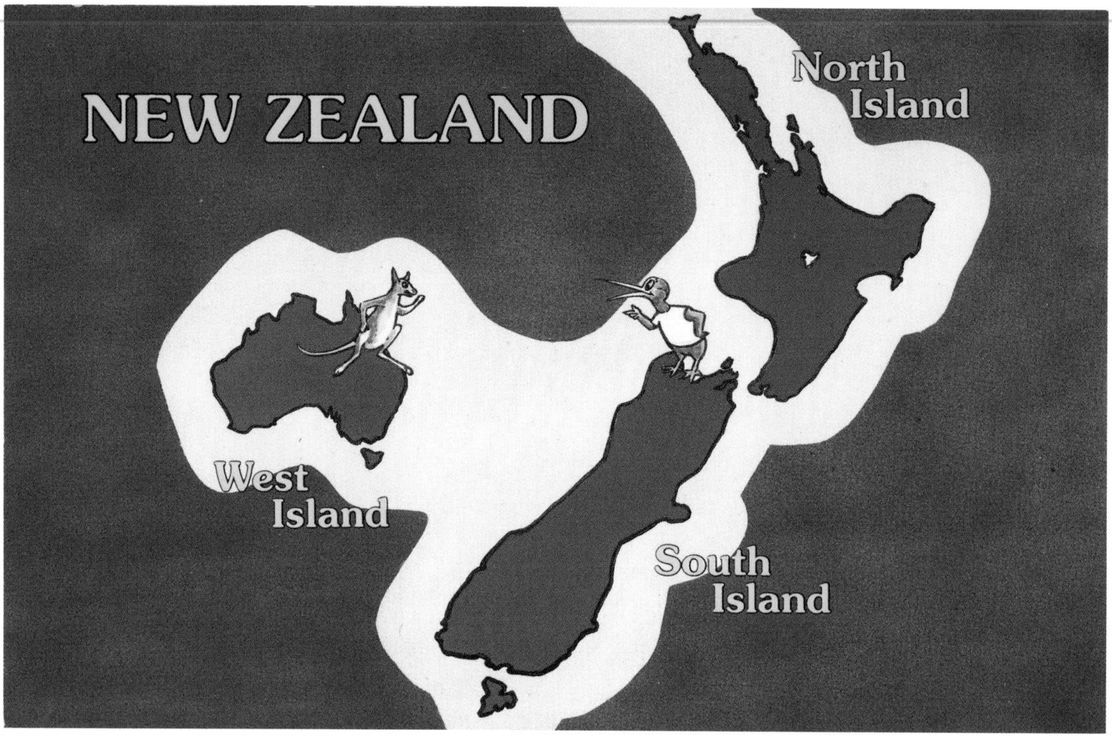
NEW ZEALAND
North Island
West Island
South Island

NELSON
CHRISTCHURCH
DUNEDIN

Western Australia
MAINLY UNEXPLORED DESERT

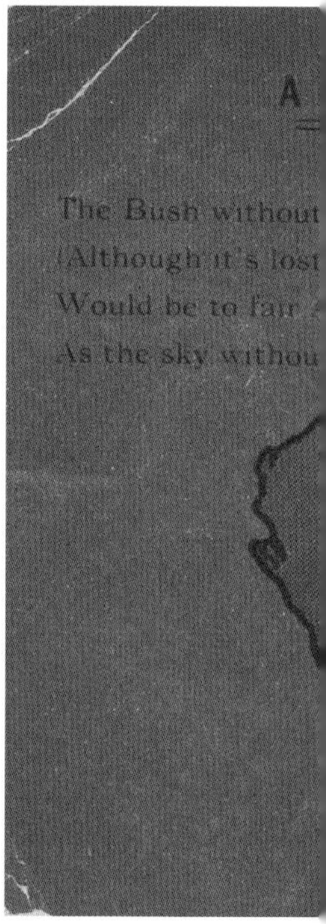
The Bush without
(Although it's lost
Would be to fair
As the sky withou

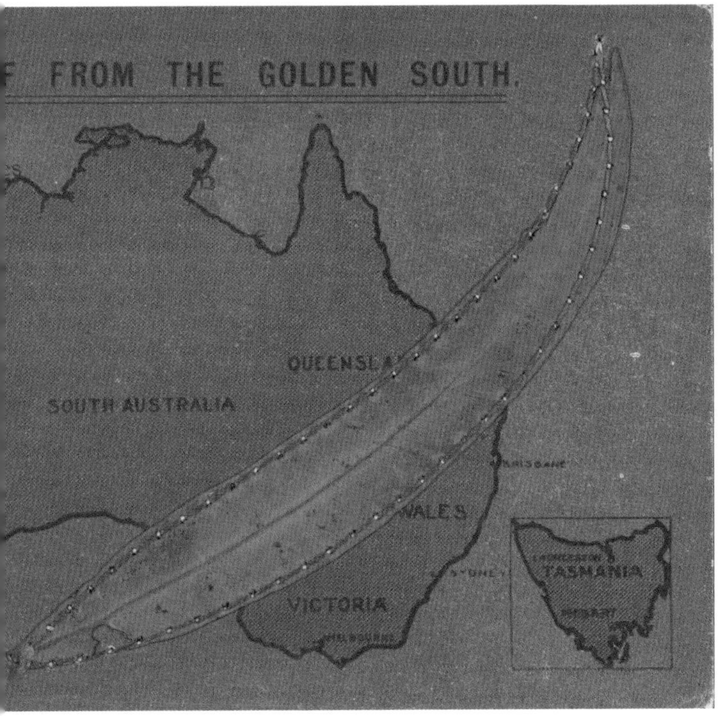

Australia and New Zealand

(1906–c.2000)

Postcards are some of the most ephemeral and discardable objects we have, yet their continuing popularity, particularly in the age of digital communication, emphasises their enduring importance to us. The earliest produced postcard is thought to date from the middle of the nineteenth century, but it was during the decades around the turn of the twentieth century that they first became a phenomenon. As many as ten UK postal deliveries a day made them a major mode of mass communication at a time when people were finding themselves increasing distances away from their loved ones, whether as a result of holidays, migration or war.

Among the varied types of image included on postcards are maps. Often appearing alongside other pieces of information such as views, poems, portraits and slogans, maps were the principal way of signifying a place. The immediately recognisable shape of Australia, for example, made it an essential component of postcards from that country.

This selection of postcards of Australia and New Zealand demonstrate the versatility of the map image. One of the earliest (lower right) is a gold-tinted postcard of 1906 from Victoria in southeastern Australia. It has a gum leaf sewn on to it, together with a poem equating gum leaves and 'The Bush' with Australia and the sun. At that time the British government was actively encouraging migration to Australia, and postcards captured the attraction of a golden paradise on the other side of the world.

Other postcards from the final quarter of the twentieth century show how the map plays a part in competitive banter. In the lower left postcard, Australia has been drawn in order to demonstrate the attraction (for tourists) of Western Australia compared to the more heavily populated, wealthier east, which the card describes as 'mainly unexplored desert'. In another (upper left), vast Australia ('West Island') is mockingly shrunk in size alongside its close neighbour New Zealand. The distortion is obvious and unsubtle, but it is also a device which 'serious' maps have deployed throughout the history of cartography.

The British Library's cartographic postcard collection was begun in the 1980s when it received the map postcards of Sir Richard Cave (1912–88), a former clerk of the House of Commons. The collection's subsequent growth reflects the increasing relevance of map postcards to the study of social history and cartography. In the introduction to the map postcard catalogue of 1995 they are described as 'the modern successors of the medieval *mappae mundi*' because of their inclusion of non-geographical information and their capacity to 'convey the mentality and perceptions of their age'.

Sydney, Australia

(1793)

Today this area is covered by the main harbour front of Sydney, with the Harbour Bridge to the right and Sydney Opera House just beyond the left edge of the painting. In April 1793 when it was painted, however, it showed the British penal colony that had been established just a few years earlier, in 1788. Rather curiously for a penal colony, there are no convicts shown in the watercolour. But as the historian Peter Barber has demonstrated, this is a key to understanding its meaning.

It was painted by an Italian artist, Fernando Brambila (1763–1834), and is one of three paintings which constitute the earliest artistic representations of what was to become Sydney by an academically trained artist. Brambila had been a painter in the Spanish court and was a contemporary of Goya's, but in 1791 he found himself one of the artists on board the famous Spanish expedition of scientific discovery led by Alessandro Malaspina. The voyage, which took in much of the Americas, the Pacific and Southeast Asia, reached Sydney on 12 March 1793.

The purpose of the expedition may ostensibly have been scientific, but it was also one of political and military discovery (or, put another way, spying). Malaspina wished to learn the nature of the British

colony. Could it be a naval base from which Britain planned to attack Spanish possessions? His artists and mapmakers were ready to record and capture this intelligence.

Brambila's watercolours were subterfuge, created as cultural gifts in order to disguise the true purpose of the mission. The Spanish were welcomed by the British, who extended the greatest hospitality, and which was reciprocated. The watercolours were presented to Francis Grose (*c.*1758–1814), Lieutenant Governor of New South Wales, and later found their way into the collection of George III. This painting shows the colony with Grose's recently constructed Governor's House on the left and its hospital buildings on the right. A boat, possibly containing Grose and Malaspina themselves, is being rowed ashore.

In this view there is no place for criminals, convicts, or anything else unsightly or likely to constitute social comment on Britain's reprehensible treatment of convicts (though Malaspina commented on it in his diary). It is particularly ironic, then, that the group of Aboriginal figures in the foreground were copied from an earlier image by a Scottish convict artist, Thomas Watling (1762–1814).

Pacific Islands

(1769)

It is fair to say that Tupaia's Map has intrigued and confounded as much as any map in the history of cartography. It shows islands in the South Pacific Ocean and was probably copied by the explorer James Cook from an earlier lost map of 1769. It captured on paper the remarkable geographical knowledge of the ocean of a Tahitian priest named Tupaia (*c*.1725–70). The significance of the map is that apart from being one of the earliest detailed maps of this part of the world, containing 74 separate islands spread over more than 1,000 square miles of sea, it is a Western encapsulation of indigenous geographical knowledge, an artefact bearing the weight of the European encounter.

Cook reached the island of Tahiti during his first voyage in 1769, with orders to observe the transit of Venus (a celestial event of importance for determining longitude at sea). While there, he and his chief scientist Sir Joseph Banks (1743–1820) spoke with the local people about their knowledge of the area, and quizzed them on their astonishing skill of navigating over huge distances with only the sun, moon and stars to guide them. Tupaia, one of the leading figures in Tahiti, dictated an extensive list of islands including the Society, Marquesas and Austral islands from which the lost original map was created.

Unfortunately, as historians found when studying this copy of the map from the library of Joseph Banks (and a 1774 printed version of a second copy, also lost), there was more than a hint of what the historian Gordon Lewthwaite has called 'trans-cultural confusion'. First, only just over half of the islands shown here have been identified. This may have something to do with problems Cook and Banks had in understanding the Tahitian language. Second, this language barrier probably also affected the Europeans' grasp of Tahitian terms for north and south, meaning that a number of the islands are in the wrong place. Third, Tupaia's knowledge of the area naturally decreased for islands further away from Tahiti, and some are considerably inaccurate.

The map is a relic of this early, significant exchange. Tupaia agreed to return with Banks to London, but he died en route in Jakarta.

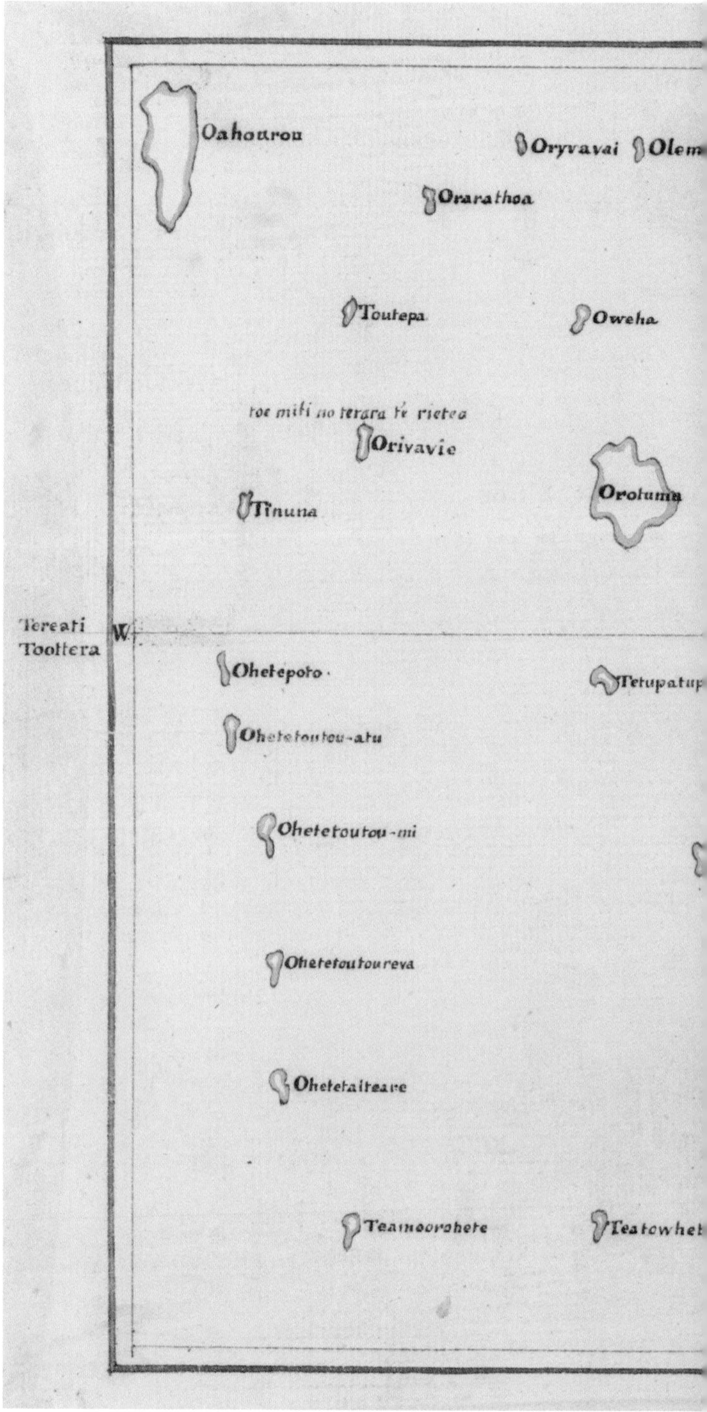

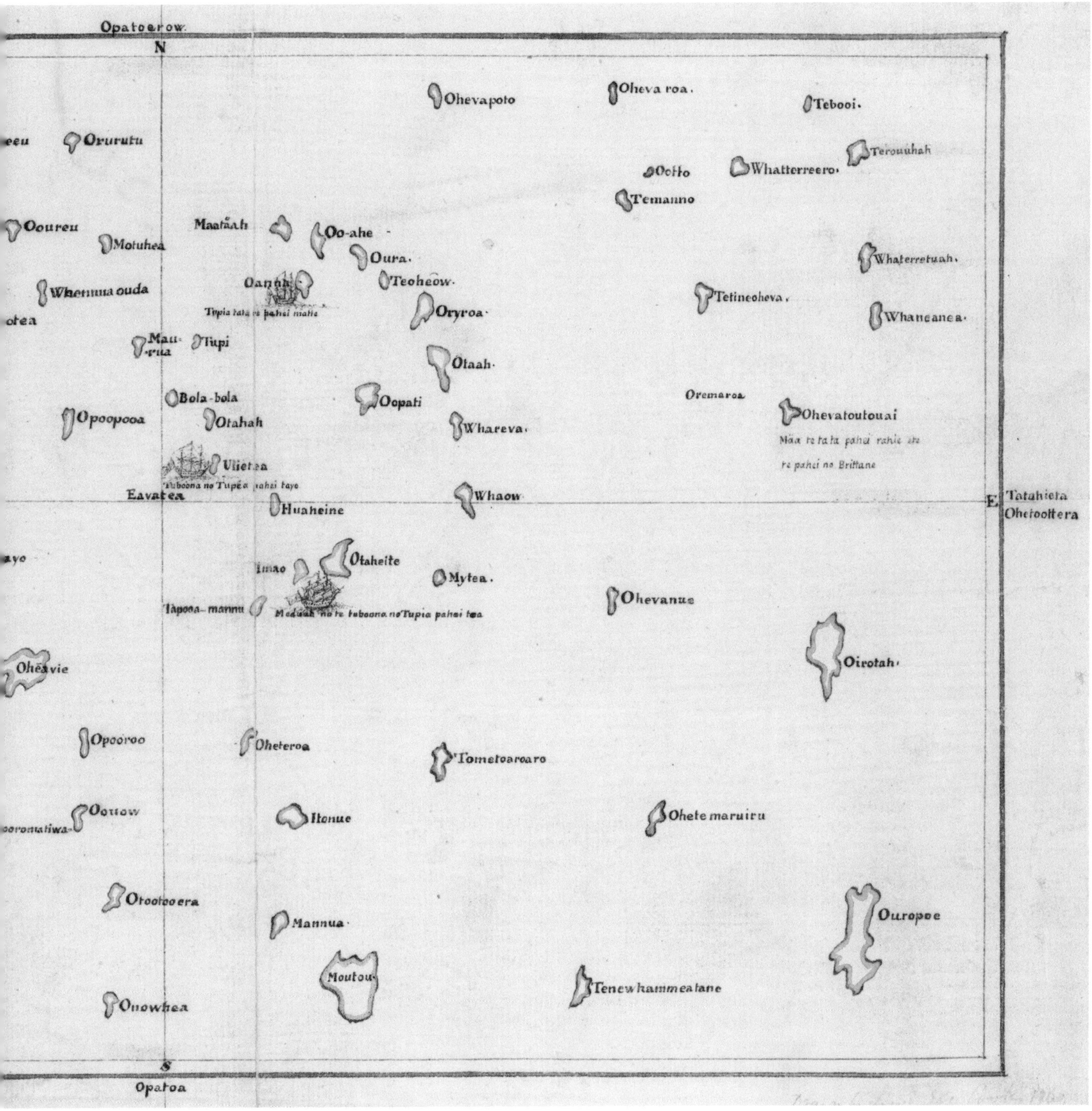

Opatoerow
N
Ohevapoto
Oheva roa
Tebooi
Ororutu
Terouuhah
Ootto
Whatterreero
Temanno
Ooureu
Maatáah
Oo-ahe
Motuhea
Oura
Whaterretuah
Teoheow
Whennua ouda
Tetineoheva
Oryroa
Whaneanea
otea
Mau-rua
Tupi
Otaah
Bola-bola
Oopati
Oremaroa
Ohevatoutouai
Opoopooa
Otahah
Whareva
Ulietea
Eavatea
Huaheine
Whaow
E
Tatahieta
Oheiooltera
Otaheite
Imao
Mytea
Tapooa-mannu
Ohevanue
Oirotah
Oheavie
Opooroo
Oheteroa
Tometoaroaro
Oouow
Itonue
Ohete maruiru
Otootooera
Ouropoe
Mannua
Moutou
Tenewhammeatane
Onowhea
S
Opatoa

1 The Universe

2 The World

3 Africa

4 America

5 Asia

6 Australasia

7 Europe

8 Seas and Oceans

9 Celestial Maps

10 Fantasy Worlds

Lagnes promont
Farre in sulę
Scetlant in sulę
Hebrides, Ebo nię vel Meuanię in sulę
Hirta
Sco tia
Irla
An glia
Londen
Edinburg
Lapp en lant
Fin marc
Scrikfinnia
Suedia
Nor rue gia
Bergen
Da
Go tia
Finlan
Bod dicus sinus
Liuonia
Die oftzee
Samogitia
Mosco
Nowgorod
Germa nia
EU RO
PA
Polonia
Hun garia
Gal lia
Hisp an ia
Corsica
Sardinia
Sicilia
Mare Me diterra
Bulgaria
Grecia
Morea
Pontus Euxi
Tunis
Creta insula

Europe

(1570–72)

There is something peculiar about this map of Europe. Do you notice how some parts of Europe, particularly those furthest north, are proportionally far bigger than they should be? For example, the British Isles are considerably larger than Italy (although fairly similar in size), while Scandinavia dwarfs the whole of Western Europe (it is somewhat smaller). This distortion is down to the fact that the parallels (the horizontal lines of latitude with numbers near the left margin of the map) become further apart the further north they are positioned. This was the ingenious calculation behind Gerhard Mercator's map projection, which first appeared in his world map of 1569. The world map is significant because its projection enabled navigators to plot straight long-distance courses on a map for the first time (without Mercator's calculation, such a line would take the disastrous real-life form of a spiral). The map revolutionised European maritime navigation.

This map of Europe is actually a piece taken from that world map and forms part of another important project Mercator was working on in 1570 while at the court of the Duchy of Jülich (now in western Germany and the Netherlands). Mercator was commissioned to produce maps of Europe for a projected journey by the crown prince Johann Wilhelm (1562–1609) and so set about crafting a sequence of maps in book form. To create it he used parts of larger maps and amended them (in this map he has drawn a new border around it). He included maps which had just been published by his friend Abraham Ortelius in his 1570 *Theatrum Orbis Terrarum*. He also drew two maps of the regions of Lombardy and Trieste, the only two maps in his hand that survive today.

What Mercator did was to create a sort of bespoke prototype 'atlas', and when we look through it, despite extensive alterations by a Cistercian monk during the eighteenth century, we can witness his thought process at work as he added, removed, cut, pasted, annotated and amended it, striving to find the perfect order and balance for his patron. The map of Europe is placed at the beginning, with a map of Turkey and the eastern Mediterranean at the end. The atlas reveals the mind and approach of a perfectionist, finding answers to cartographic quandaries which we take for granted today.

Britain

(1969)

These computer print-outs were produced on 7 October 1969. They are IBM computer-drawn maps of Britain and represent one of the most important shifts in the history of maps and mapping. Drawing statistical maps from data has always been difficult. Creating a visual image of an area which simultaneously shows how many people live where and how relatively wealthy they are, for example, has taxed the most brilliant cartographic brains. This sort of social information became far more relevant in Europe, particularly after World War Two (1939–45) when the new social contract increased the involvement of the state in people's lives. Computers helped to map it.

What might take a human brain many hours or even days could in theory be done by a machine in seconds. One such computer mapping program called SYMAP (from 'synagraphic map') was developed by computer scientists in the US academic institutions of Northwestern and Harvard universities during the 1960s. Written in a computer language called FORTRAN IV, SYMAP used algorithms to turn statistical data, which had to be laboriously typed into the program, into a thematic map which could then be printed out on paper. SYMAP's maps were constructed using keyboard symbols such as + and 0, where each key was given a value and also an x and y co-ordinate to locate it. Different types of thematic map such as contour maps were also possible.

These particular maps visualise the historical land-use statistics provided in Sir Dudley Stamp's (1898–1966) 'Great Britain Land Use Survey' published in 1962, specifically the percentage of arable land available in Britain in 1874. There are five different key values, with the darker ones (such as zeros) representing the areas with most arable land and lighter ones (full stops) the fewest. Stamp could certainly have done with the automatic qualities of SYMAP when having his original land-use map painstakingly hand-coloured.

SYMAP went further with its 'conformant' map feature, which was able to provide a three-dimensional perspective view of the same arable land-use statistics. Here the arable land appears raised up, with the less arable (usually mountainous) areas such as the Scottish Highlands shown as flat regions. It was counter-intuitive and so did not really work. However, in this early and time-consuming yet technically impressive computer-assisted mapping program, we can see the dawn of the digital age.

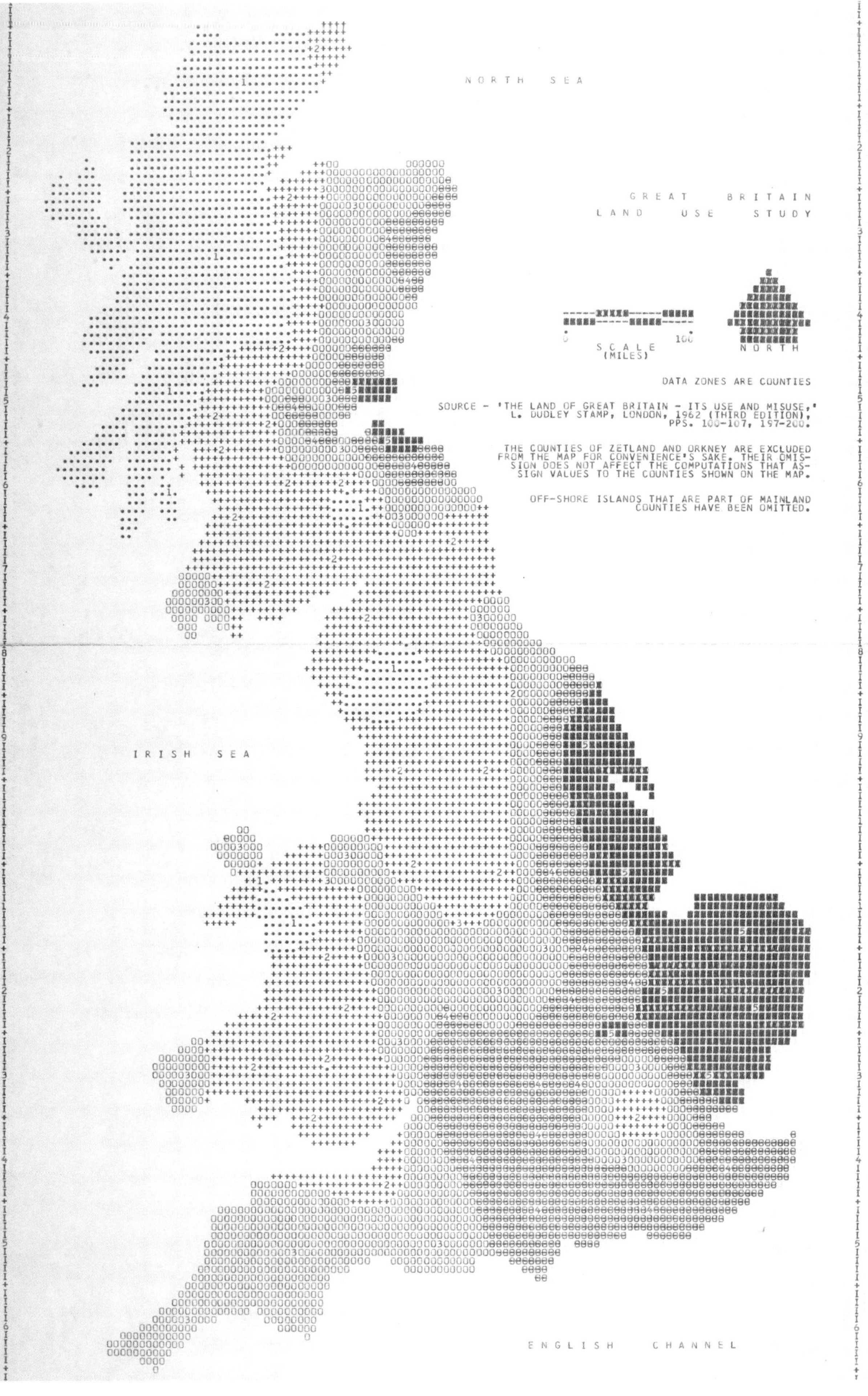
N O R T H   S E A
G R E A T   B R I T A I N
L A N D   U S E   S T U D Y
0
100
S C A L E
(MILES)
N O R T H
DATA ZONES ARE COUNTIES
SOURCE - 'THE LAND OF GREAT BRITAIN - ITS USE AND MISUSE,'
L. DUDLEY STAMP, LONDON, 1962 (THIRD EDITION),
PPS. 100-107, 197-200.
THE COUNTIES OF ZETLAND AND ORKNEY ARE EXCLUDED
FROM THE MAP FOR CONVENIENCE'S SAKE. THEIR OMIS-
SION DOES NOT AFFECT THE COMPUTATIONS THAT AS-
SIGN VALUES TO THE COUNTIES SHOWN ON THE MAP.
OFF-SHORE ISLANDS THAT ARE PART OF MAINLAND
COUNTIES HAVE BEEN OMITTED.
I R I S H   S E A
E N G L I S H   C H A N N E L

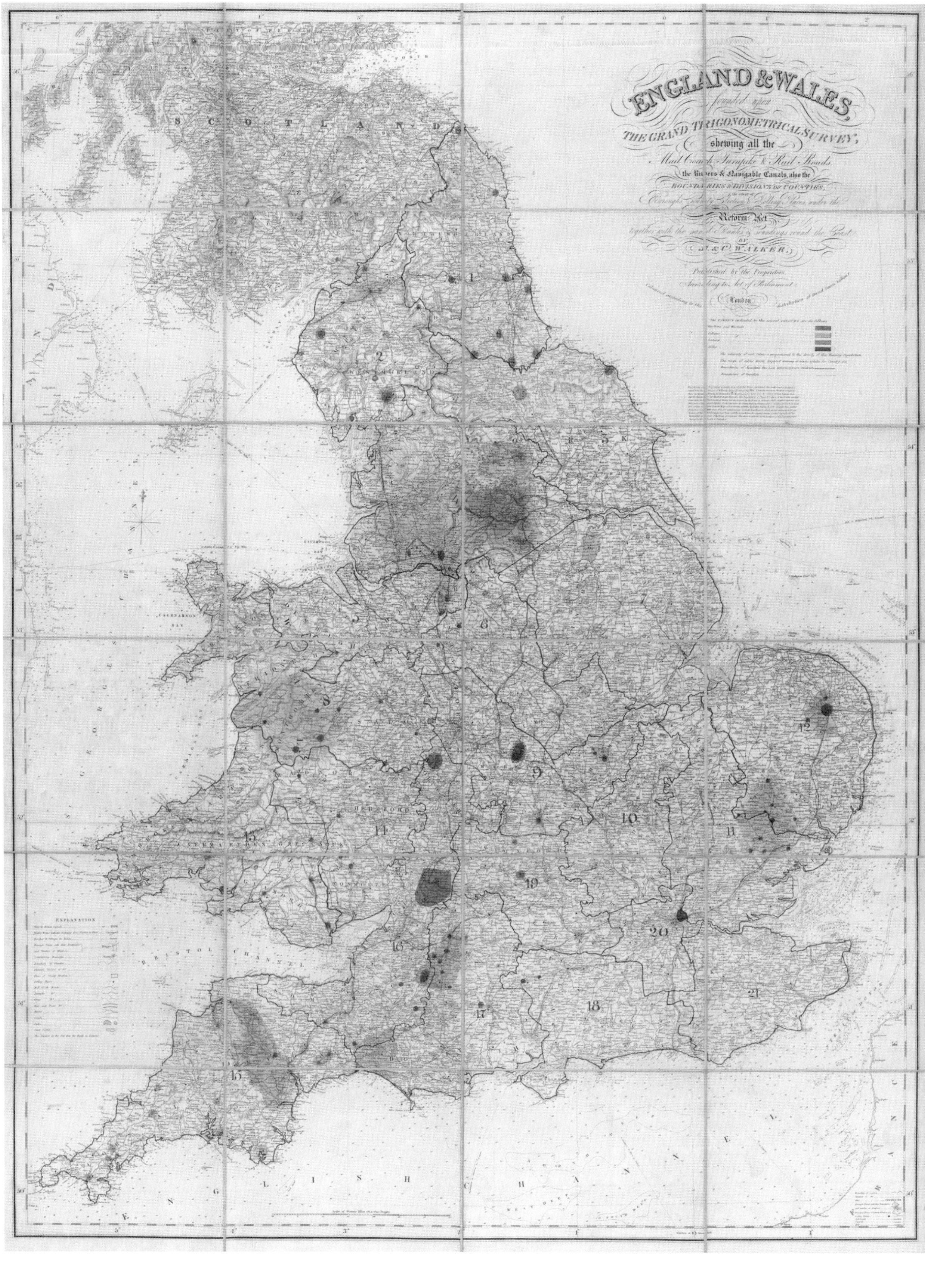
ENGLAND & WALES,
founded upon
THE GRAND TRIGONOMETRICAL SURVEY,
shewing all the
Mail Coach Turnpike & Rail Roads
the Rivers & Navigable Canals, also the
BOUNDARIES & DIVISIONS OF COUNTIES,
Reform Act
BY
J. & C. WALKER.
Published by the Proprietors
According to Act of Parliament
London
SCOTLAND
CAERNARVON BAY
BRISTOL CHANNEL
ENGLISH CHANNEL
EXPLANATION

England and Wales

(1841)

In 1837 a Royal Commission (a type of public enquiry) was set up to investigate poverty within the hand-loom weaving industry. This is the trade in making a diverse range of cotton, silk, linen and wool products such as stockings or carpets using a hand-operated loom. The precarious state of weavers was due to complex factors, which included the end of a boom in business following the Napoleonic Wars (and the resumption of foreign competition) and the introduction of mechanised machinery such as the power loom, with which hand-loom weaving could not compete. This in turn led to low wages, longer hours, unemployment and consequently a breakdown of the structure of working communities.

More seriously for the government, anger at the destitution of hand-loom weaving communities was channelled into agitation for parliamentary reform through the Chartist movement, and this may have motivated the action. Nine assistant commissioners were appointed to investigate the trade, and their findings were published in 1840 and 1841.

This map was specially adapted for use as part of the commission. It is a large printed map of 1835 by the firm J. & C. Walker which shows England and Wales with the Scottish Lowlands, folded into a leather-backed case entitled 'Hand-loom Enquiry Commission England'. The map has been hand-coloured to show the locations, and the density within them, of hand-loom weavers, with different colours used to differentiate between cotton, linen and silk. In it we can see the large yellow swathe of Lancashire cotton manufacturing with Manchester – 'Cottonopolis' – in its south. Similarly large blue areas of wool manufacturing are in West Yorkshire, Mid Wales and Devon.

But we can also see smaller and more concentrated blue areas of wool scattered across Britain, a similar pattern to the red areas of silk weaving. These were particularly vulnerable pockets of hand-loom weavers, isolated from other weavers and susceptible to unfair or exploitative practices by their employers, for whom the 1834 Poor Law Amendment Act had removed any safety net that might previously have existed. The map may have visualised the problem for the commissioners, but it did not provide any solutions.

This density map was part of a cartographic trend during the first half of the nineteenth century, when graphics were developed to make statistics more accessible to a general audience. The earliest 'choropleth' map was a population map of France produced in 1826 by the French economist Pierre Charles François Dupin (1784–1873). Dupin's map shaded *départments* according to their level of literacy. The hand-loom weaver map shows greater subtlety in its grading of density, and it pre-empted by over a decade August Heinrich Petermann's (1822–78) more famous printed map illustrating the population density of the United Kingdom based on the 1841 census.

Westmorland and Cumbria

(1576)

The first atlas of England and Wales was published in 1579. It contains maps of the counties of England and Wales by the Yorkshire mapmaker and surveyor Christopher Saxton (1542–1610/11). The maps were put together in a remarkably short space of time during the 1570s and engraved between 1574 and 1578, leading us to believe that Saxton reused existing information alongside his own work. Wherever he got his information from, others used his in turn, and they provided the source material for new maps well into the eighteenth century. Saxton's maps were also being republished, albeit heavily revised, two centuries after their initial appearance.

The commercial sale of Saxton's atlas probably began after around 1590, when the Spanish threat to national security had passed. Prior to this the project had been official, even restricted. It was commissioned by Queen Elizabeth I's Secretary of State William Cecil, Lord Burghley (1520–98), in conjunction with Thomas Seckford (1515–87), Master of Requests, who bankrolled the project and whose arms appear on each of the maps. These were maps for security, defence and administration during a period of internal intrigue and international instability.

Burghley's own copy of the atlas is made up of pre-publication 'proof' copies of the maps. He wrote copious notes on many of them, identifying potentially troublesome families, mainly though not exclusively Catholic, and possible justices of the peace to be called upon if required. In the left margin of this map of Westmorland and Cumbria, which borders Scotland, Burghley has compiled a list of 'names of ye principall lordships in ye West Marches' together with the number of horses at their disposal. The atlas also includes 18 hand-drawn maps of areas of particular sensitivity, such as Falmouth Harbour, and a second map of Lancashire, where a substantial number of Catholics lived. This was probably drawn by Francis Walsingham's cryptographer, Thomas Phelippes (1556–1625). Burghley was one of a growing number of statesmen who were convinced of the value of maps for national security. His atlas facilitated his strategic vision.

Yet in some areas the quality of the mapping was weak, even 'improvised and inconsistent', as Peter Barber has described it. For example, the Continent-facing southeastern counties of Kent, Sussex, Surrey and Middlesex are served only by a single regional map. During the Napoleonic Wars this was where the newly created Ordnance Survey immediately set to work. The reason could be that Saxton was experiencing cash-flow problems and had to cut costs. Given the preponderance of less strategically vulnerable counties (such as Montgomeryshire in Wales) in the atlas, perhaps Saxton could have planned his work better. Circumstances, however, rarely allow for such foresight.

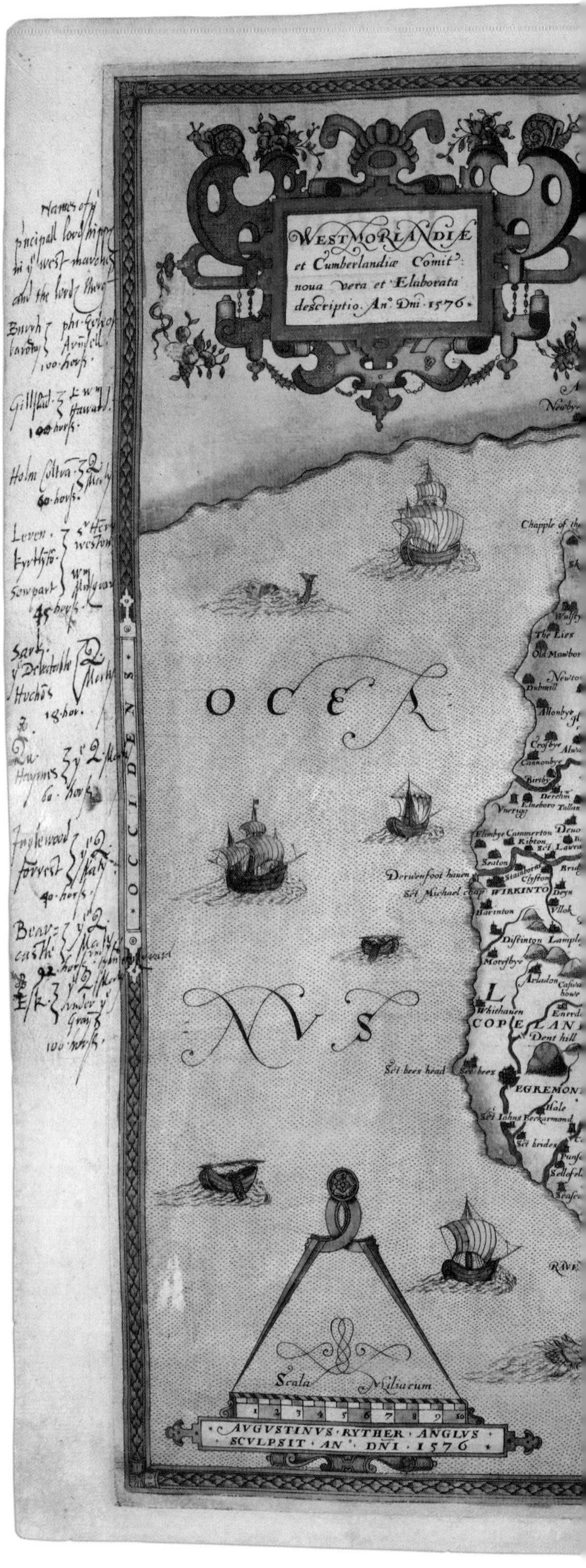

SEPTENTRIO
MERIDIES
ORIENS
NORTH VM BRIÆ PARS
Elizabeth Regina
DIEV ET MON DROYT
DVNELMENSIS EPISCOPATVS PARS
EBORACENSIS PARS
INDVSTRIA NATVRAM ORNAT
GILSLAND
CARLISLE
KESWICK
KIRKBY STEVEN
KIRKBY LAVNSDALE
Inglewood forest
Mallerstange forest
Middleton
Barnard cast
Kendall cast

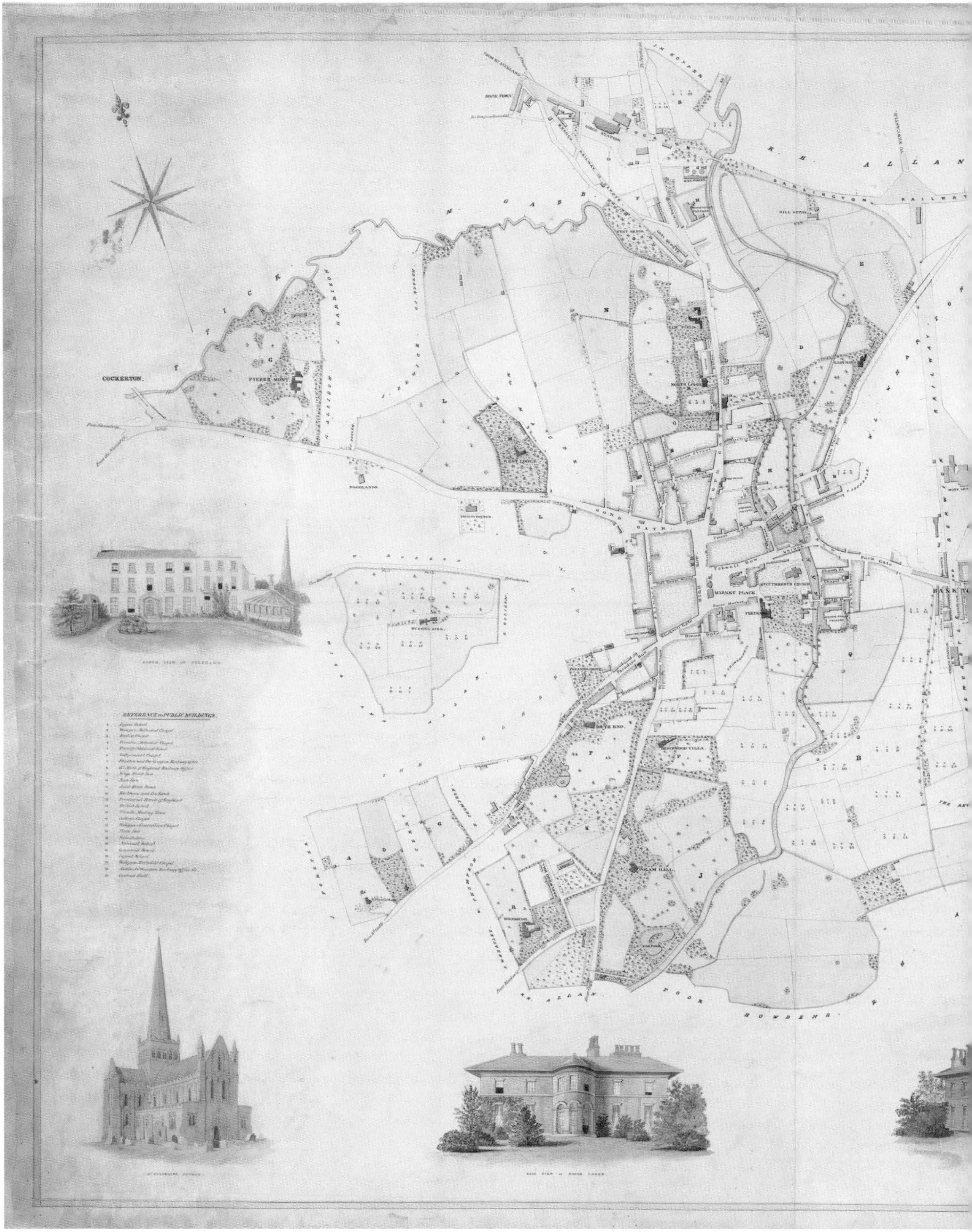
COCKERTON
PIERRE MONT
WEST LODGE
WOODLANDS
NORTH LODGE
MARKET PLACE
ST CUTHBERT'S CHURCH
SOUTH END
BEECHWOOD VILLA
POLAM HALL
REFERENCE to PUBLIC BUILDINGS

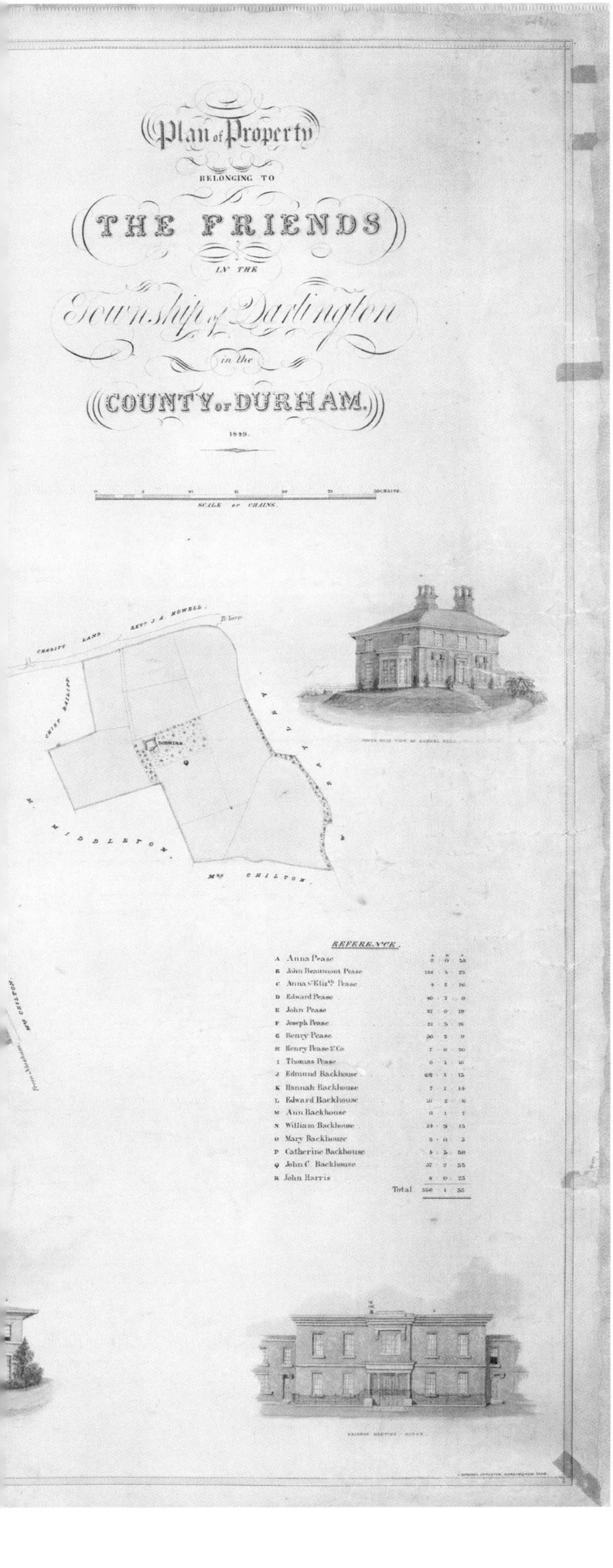

Darlington, County Durham

(1849)

This hand-painted map of 1849, entitled 'Plan of the Property belonging to the Friends in the Township of Darlington', shows the Durham town in all its local glory. It provides a plan of the town, with the principal buildings marked and some illustrated around the edge. It also marks the holdings and acreages belonging to some of the town's major landowners. These are men belonging to the Quaker fraternity, the 'Friends' referred to in the title, who almost certainly commissioned the map. The map makes a superb statement of local pride from a community whose achievements had an international impact.

Among the landowners listed, whose residences have been sensitively painted around the map's edge, are members of two of the most prominent Quaker families in Britain. The Backhouse family were bankers, horticulturalists and linen manufacturers, while the Pease family also pursued a variety of interests: in addition to banking and mining, Edward Pease was the chief promoter of the world's first steam railway, the Stockton to Darlington Railway of 1818. The port of Middlesbrough was established by Edward's son Joseph, who also became the first Quaker Member of Parliament in 1832.

The map draws on the tradition of estate mapping, which began to be commissioned by English landowners from the mid-sixteenth century and were intended as practical visual guides to assist the management of land. Acreages and land use were often included, and there was usually an accompanying estate book, or terrier. However, estate maps also functioned as status symbols which reminded the landowner and his associates of his wealth and achievements. They often contained decoration and artistry designed to demonstrate the owner's excellent taste.

The Friends' map of Darlington is conceived on the same basis, but its communal dimension also bears strong similarities with contemporary printed maps of new North American towns such as Urbana, Illinois, which were then being established along rail routes. These maps also show communities, their amenities and institutions, with the properties of their most notable residents proudly illustrated around the edges.

The impetus for the Darlington map's production may have been a visit to the town by Queen Victoria (*r.*1837–1901) on 28 September 1849 as part of her 'Royal Progress' through Britain. The Queen was presented with flowers picked from Henry Pease's garden.

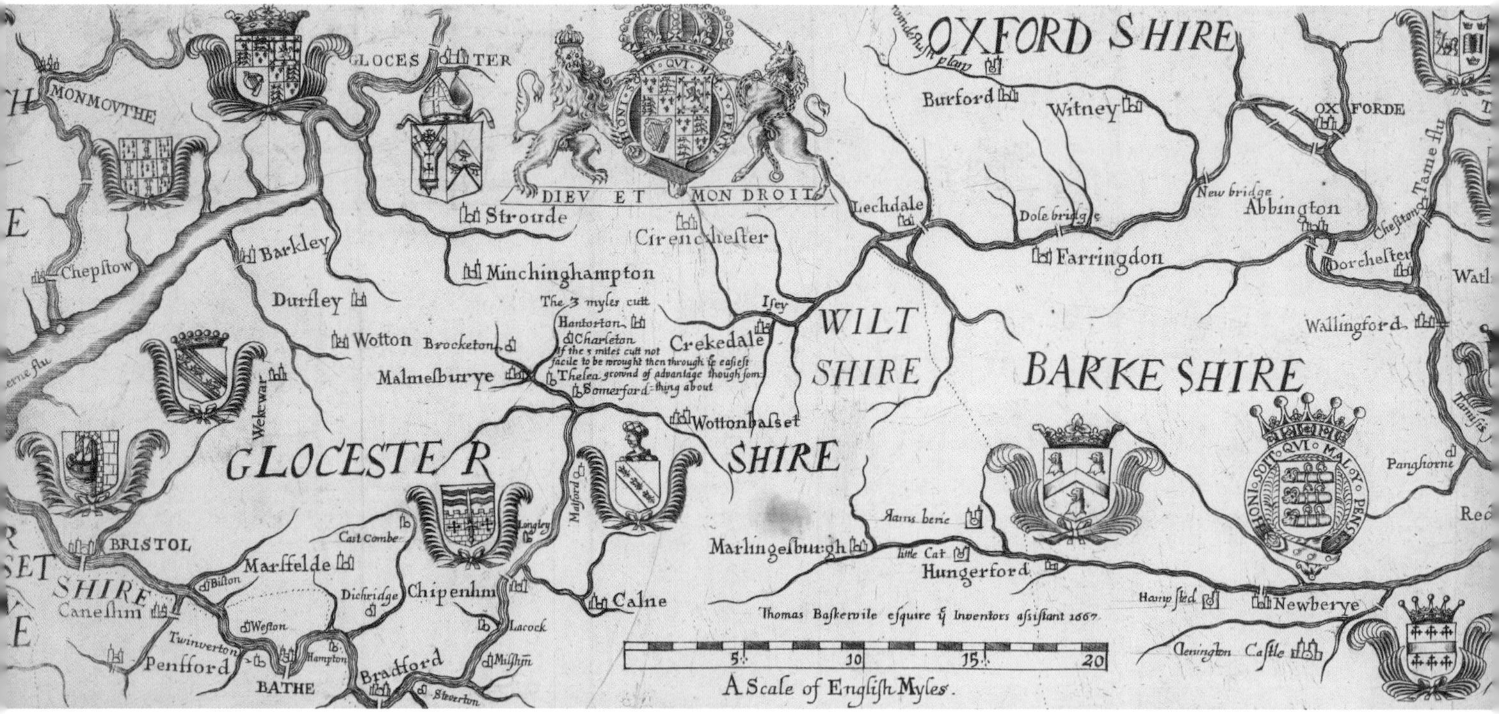

Southern England

(1668)

The great age of British canal-building began in earnest in the mid-eighteenth century. Human-constructed waterways sliced through large swathes of the country, facilitating transportation of the goods which powered the early Industrial Revolution, helping to make Britain an economic powerhouse. Canal projects had existed prior to the eighteenth century, however, as this map of an unrealised seventeenth-century scheme shows.

Three and a half centuries ago, an overland journey between Cardiff or Bristol and London was far more arduous than it typically is today. Heavy freight-loads of timber from South Wales and the Southwest were required to take the lengthy sea route around Land's End and Lizard Point, along the south coast and around the rump of Kent. What was needed, it was realised, was better communication between England's capital and its western ports and regions.

It had not escaped attention that two of southern England's main rivers – the Avon in the west and the Thames in the east – passed within around three miles of each other in North Wiltshire, and during the early seventeenth century a number of engineering projects to connect the Severn with the Thames were proposed. This was an age of emerging commercial and engineering confidence

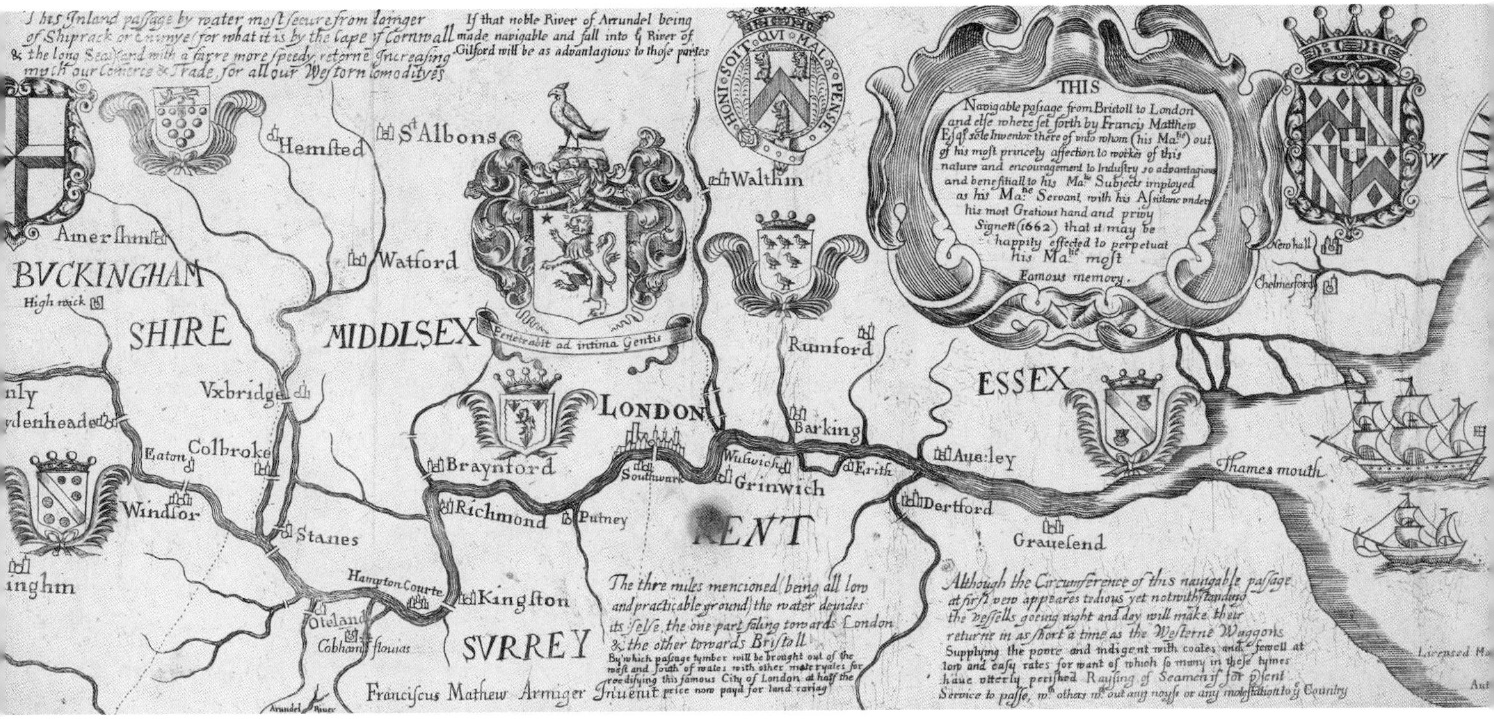

in Britain, evidenced by Francis Russell, the 4th Earl of Bedford's successful project to drain the English Fenlands from the 1630s to the 1650s. Such projects were shelved during the turbulent years of the English Civil War (1642–51), but in 1653 a former Royalist, Francis Matthew (*fl.*1653–68), first presented his plan to link the Avon and Thames to Parliament.

This map was published in 1668 to illustrate Matthew's scheme as he presented it a third time, after repeated failures to receive backing. It is a clever piece of promotion, a long map engraved by Thomas Jenner (d.1673) covering a narrow horizontal section of land between London and Newport. It shows not only rivers and towns, and the suggested three-mile cutting to join the rivers between Malmesbury and Cricklade, but also the arms of 20 influential landowners whose land the waterway would pass through and who, the map innocently suggests, might benefit in taxes and tolls from any traffic. These, of course, were the influential landowners sitting in the House of Lords who were required to give their assent to the bill. They didn't, and Matthew's scheme failed. The Kennet and Avon Canal was not completed until 1810, a century and a half after Matthew's persistent but ultimately futile quest.

Printed for H. Overton without Newgate, T. Kitchin on Holborn Hill, R. Sayer & J. Ryall in Fleet street, T. Bowles in St. Pauls Church Yard, J. Bowles & Son & Messrs. Bakewell & Parker in Cornhill

Buckinghamshire

(c.1764)

It isn't normally possible to discover exactly how maps were used centuries ago, because people didn't tend to provide commentaries on what they were looking for when poring over them. What were they thinking, and what did they hope to discover? Thankfully though, particularly given the increasing interest in historical map use, people did occasionally leave traces.

This is a printed map of the English county of Buckinghamshire, one of the 'Home Counties', lying immediately northwest of London. It was originally published alongside other maps of English and Welsh counties in *The Royal English Atlas* by Emanuel Bowen (*c*.1694–1767) and Thomas Kitchin (1718–84) of around 1764. The map has a few inked annotations on it, but on its reverse is a comprehensive list of journeys made through the country between 1775 and 1806, with the date of each journey and a brief description. Its owner, Mr R. Walsh of London, has used it with other *Royal English Atlas* maps as a travel diary.

On Sunday 13 July 1806 Walsh notes having travelled 'With Mr Fox, from Winslow through Datchette to Conbrook', while another note describes his passing through Buckingham on his journey back from Leeds. Walsh would have become familiar with Buckinghamshire, given its position as a through-route between London and the North. He was part of an increasingly mobile English society, touring for pleasure on improved roads, using the highly efficient inn and stagecoach facilities, and employing published travel guides and ribbon maps as he went.

Walsh was a fastidious recorder who was concerned with noting his movements accurately, even correcting himself on occasions. He was also keen to correct the map where its information deviated from his own direct experience. For example, he has added roads which are not marked, corrected distances between towns, crossed out incorrect factual information and amended place names. Over a description of 'Ackney Way' he has written in ink: 'They mean Ickley Way, vulgo Asckley Way'.

Walsh's criticism correlates with the general impression of late eighteenth-century English county maps as derivative and error-strewn. It was partly this which motivated the Society for the Encouragement of Arts, Manufactures and Commerce in 1762 to launch a prize for originally surveyed large-scale county maps. Despite their glaring (and not so glaring) errors, the *Royal English Atlas* county maps were conveniently sized and inexpensive enough for Walsh to use as a journal and aide-memoire of his busy life. This compulsion to document and reflect (elsewhere he records visiting his grandmother's grave in Shropshire in 1790), even more than the enjoyment in correcting the errors of others, is something to which we can relate today.

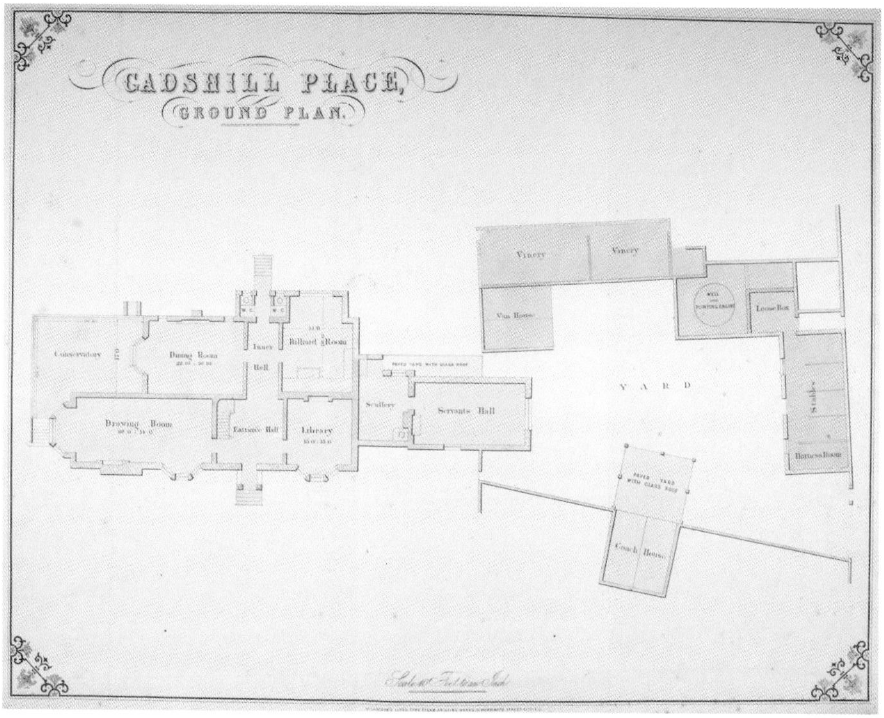

Near Higham, Kent

(1870)

Sales particulars are ephemeral booklet-like publications containing the details of properties and estates to be sold at auction. They were produced for potential buyers, and a significant number contain maps, plans and illustrations. The majority of the British Library's collection of sales particulars were produced during the later nineteenth and early twentieth centuries, a reflection of the economic decline of the landed gentry who were driven to sell their estates during this period. This prospectus of 1870 tells a different story, because it advertises the sale of a property which had belonged to one of literature's most famous figures.

According to his biographer, when Charles Dickens (1812–70) first saw Gad's Hill Place at the age of nine, his father told him that if he worked hard enough he would one day be able to afford such a house. Taking his father literally, Dickens purchased the house in March 1856 for £1,700, having by that time made a name for himself first as a journalist, then as an author with bestselling works such as *The Pickwick Papers* (1836) and *David Copperfield* (1849).

Dickens's 'little Kentish freehold' became his country house, but he had to cover the expense of it with book-reading tours. The household was run by Dickens's daughter Mary and his sister-in-law Georgina Hogarth (Dickens was estranged from his wife Catherine by 1859). In the first plan we can see the ground floor of Gad's Hill Place. These are the spaces of Dickens's life: the dining room, the drawing room, the conservatory. There is even a faint voyeurism associated with imagining him and his family and guests inhabiting them.

A second plan shows the substantial 17-acre grounds, including a croquet lawn and, tucked away among some trees, a Swiss chalet. This is the wooden cabin which was given to Dickens by his friend, the actor Charles Fechter (1824–79), and the place where, on 8 June 1870, while working on his novel *Edwin Drood*, Dickens suffered a stroke and died. Illustrating Dickens's place of death prominently on the cover of the prospectus, the auctioneers, Messrs Norton, Trist, Watney and Co., observed 'that amidst the repose and solitude of this chalet, yet in the full view of ... the highly cultivated and picturesque scenery, Charles Dickens spent his last afternoon, and it may be said that his splendid literary career was therein brought to a close'.

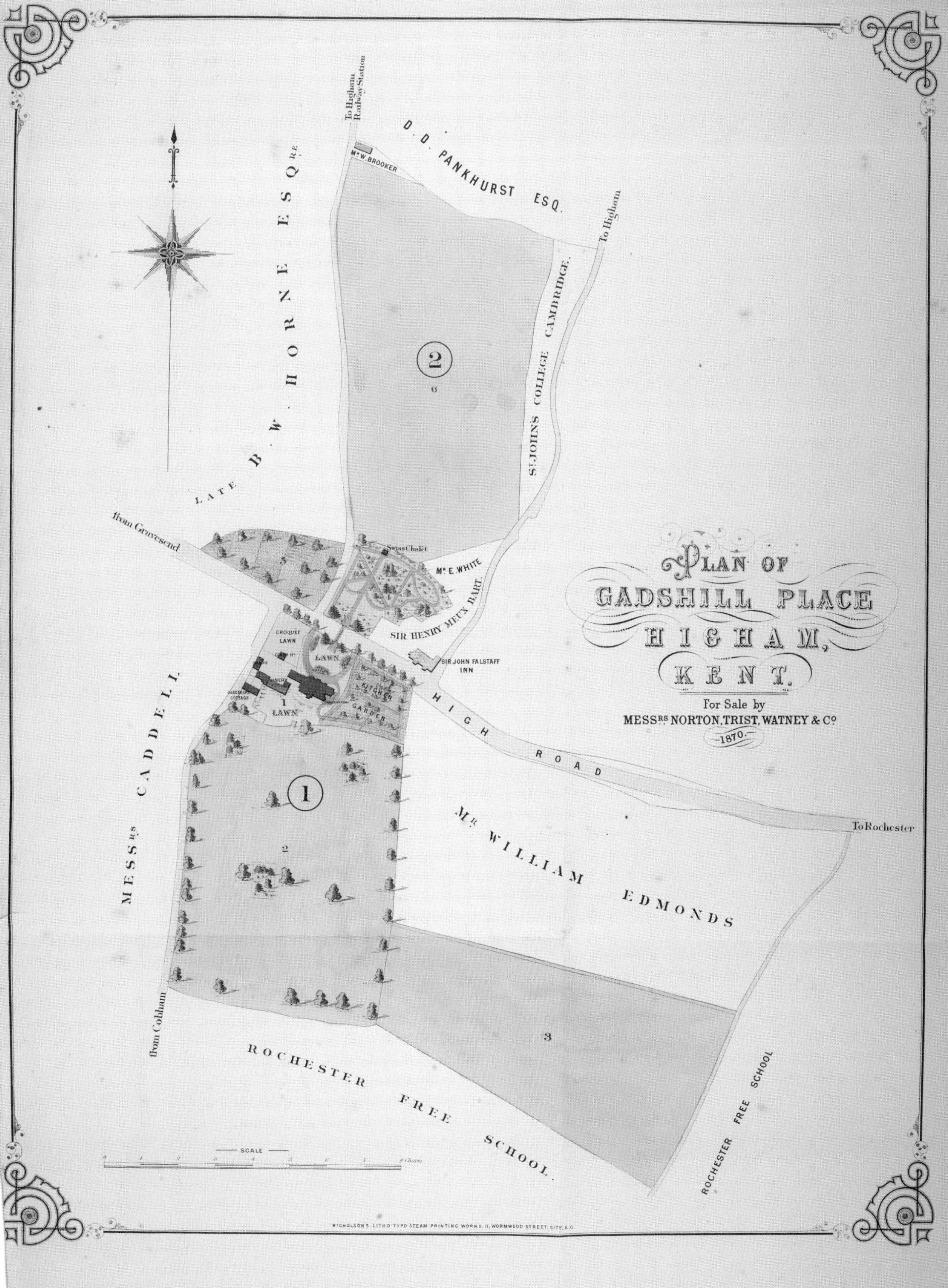
PLAN OF
GADSHILL PLACE
HIGHAM,
KENT.
For Sale by
MESSRS NORTON, TRIST, WATNEY & Co.
-1870.-
To Higham Railway Station
Mr. W. BROOKER
D. D. PANKHURST ESQ.
To Higham
LATE B. W. HORNE ESQre
St. JOHN'S COLLEGE CAMBRIDGE.
2
6
from Gravesend
Swiss Chalet
5
Mr. E. WHITE
4
SIR HENRY MEUX BART.
CROQUET LAWN
LAWN
SIR JOHN FALSTAFF INN
GARDENERS COTTAGE
1
LAWN
KITCHEN GARDEN
HIGH ROAD
MESSrs CADDELL
1
2
Mr. WILLIAM EDMONDS
To Rochester
from Cobham
3
ROCHESTER FREE SCHOOL
ROCHESTER FREE SCHOOL
SCALE
0 1 2 3 4 5 6 7 8 Chains
NICHOLSON'S LITHO-TYPO STEAM PRINTING WORKS, 11, WORMWOOD STREET, CITY, E.C.

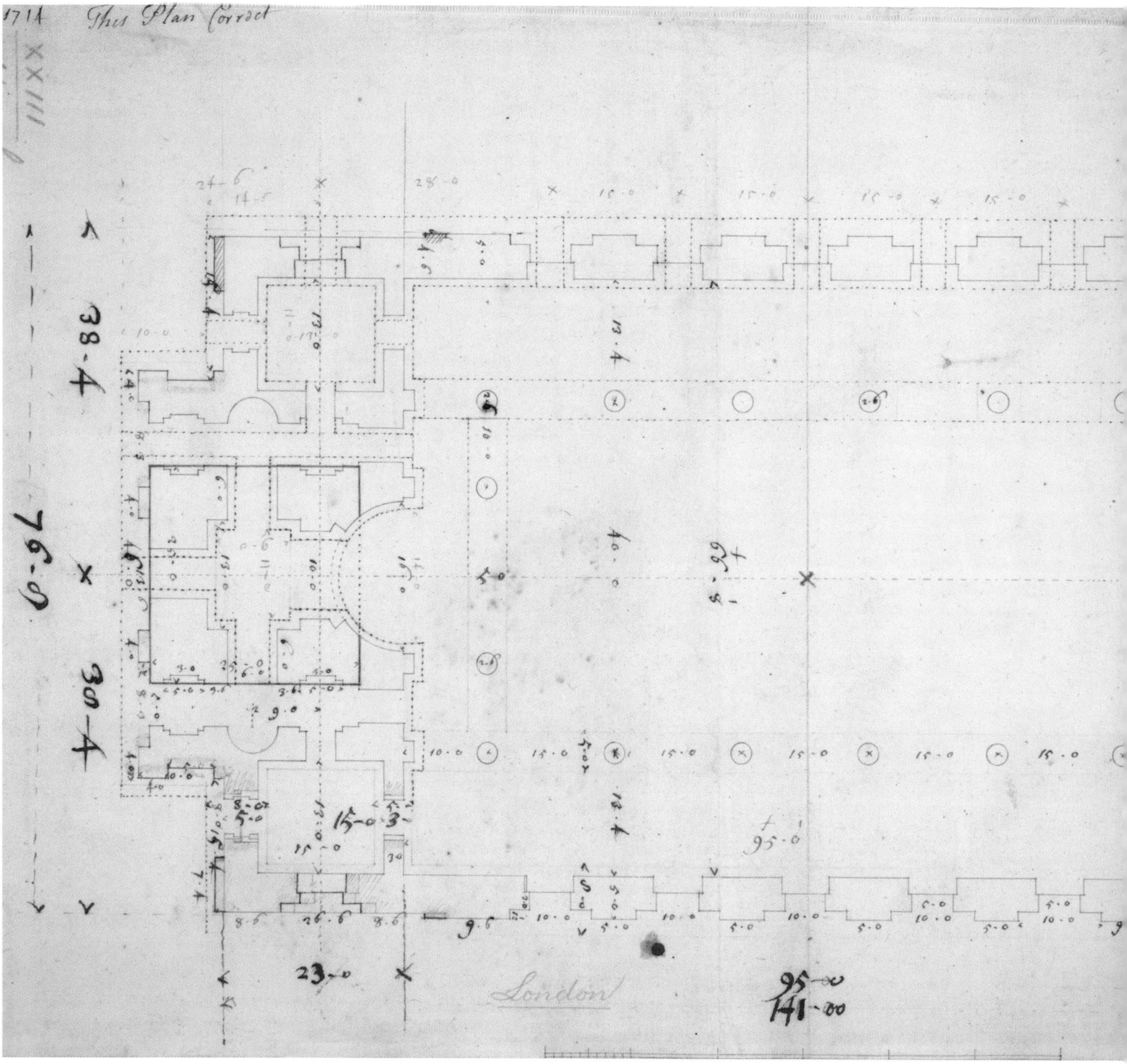

London

(1714–33)

We tend to think of building plans and elevations as distinct from maps, but actually the difference is just a question of scale. The presence of a number of architectural drawings in the British Library's map collection is important because it demonstrates that in purpose and principle they are both, crucially, manifestations of place. Included among these 'building maps' are designs for some of the most famous structures in Britain: the early eighteenth-century London churches designed by the English baroque architect Nicholas Hawksmoor (*c.*1661–1736).

Hawksmoor is regarded as one of Britain's greatest architects. His career began with involvement in some of Britain's most illustrious building projects such as St Paul's Cathedral (he was apprentice to Sir Christopher Wren, 1632–1723) and Blenheim Palace (where he worked with Sir John Vanbrugh, 1664–1726). His emergence as an architect came with the design and construction of London churches under Queen Anne (*r.*1702–14), inaugurated by the 1711 'Act of Parliament for the construction of fifty churches in London and Westminster'. Only 12 of the churches were ever built, six of them by Hawksmoor and a further two with his contributions. The Queen Anne churches were to be situated in Bloomsbury, Greenwich, the

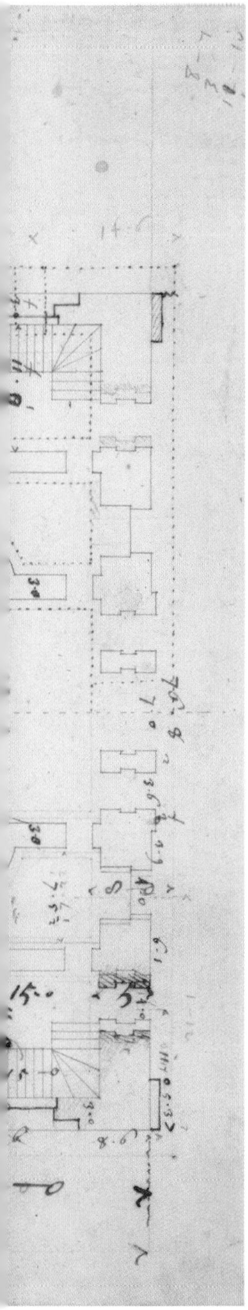

City and the East End, where new, substantial and growing urban populations were adjudged to need Anglican buildings in which to worship.

Christ Church Spitalfields (built 1714–29) is one of Hawksmoor's most famous, with its vast classical façade and Gothic spire. In the drawings we can see the architect's thought process as he expressed designs on paper, altering and changing them as the project progressed, subject to practical considerations such as cost or space as much as inspiration. We can see that originally Christ Church was to have an octagonal tower not dissimilar to that of another of his churches, St Anne's Limehouse (built 1714–30). The drawings also show us what has since been lost. Christ Church has been partially rebuilt over the centuries and the present tower is a replacement, but here we can see the original design as constructed, with windows running up it and flame-like decoration at its corners.

Finished buildings are often all we have left of an architect's work, so it is unusual and fortuitous that hundreds of Hawksmoor's working drawings survive today. They were sold off at auction after his death and found their way into collections including the Topographical Collection of George III.

Westminster

(1765)

During the 1760s Westminster, London's 'western city', increased in size at a prodigious rate. Landed estates in the rural north and west of its royal centre were developed to cater for the influx of people and business as a consequence of Britain's industrial and imperial growth.

This map by Thomas Jefferys was produced as an up-to-date guide of London construction. It is a separately issued map, printed on two sheets and updated in various editions between 1762 and 1772 to show new features of Westminster's landscape 'not extant in any other plan'. Colour coding has been used to reflect the varying stages of building works. Mayfair, part of the Grosvenor Estate, on which construction started at the beginning of the century, is almost fully developed. North of Oxford Street brown-coloured areas show the Portman Estate and Marylebone beginning to take shape.

Of course, new areas required infrastructure in the form of roads, bridges and amenities. The 'New' Road, now Euston Road, part of which was opened in 1756, has appeared in the far north of the map, while Blackfriars Bridge and planned approaches have also been added (though Jefferys rather jumped the gun, for these were amended later). Amenities such as pavements, street lights and sewers were not shown on Jefferys's map for reasons of scale, but its dedication includes the commissioners responsible for overseeing their construction and upkeep. The subsequent owner of this map would have given a wry smile at this dedication. He was Frederick Crace (1779–1859), Westminster's Commissioner of Sewers from 1818, who was left to deal with the sewage problems that were the legacy of the previous century's rapid urban development.

Crace would have had to consult old maps in order to discover more about Westminster's sewers, and he became a collector of them. Dating from between 1570 and 1880, and now split between the British Library and British Museum, his collection of maps and views is one of the most important paper collections of London and its history. It was lovingly cared for by Crace, who carefully mounted each map and view on cream card and hand-added his own inked border and title. This artistic direction reflects his career as an interior decorator during which, among other works, he designed the Chinese music room in Brighton Pavilion for the future George IV (*r.*1820–27).

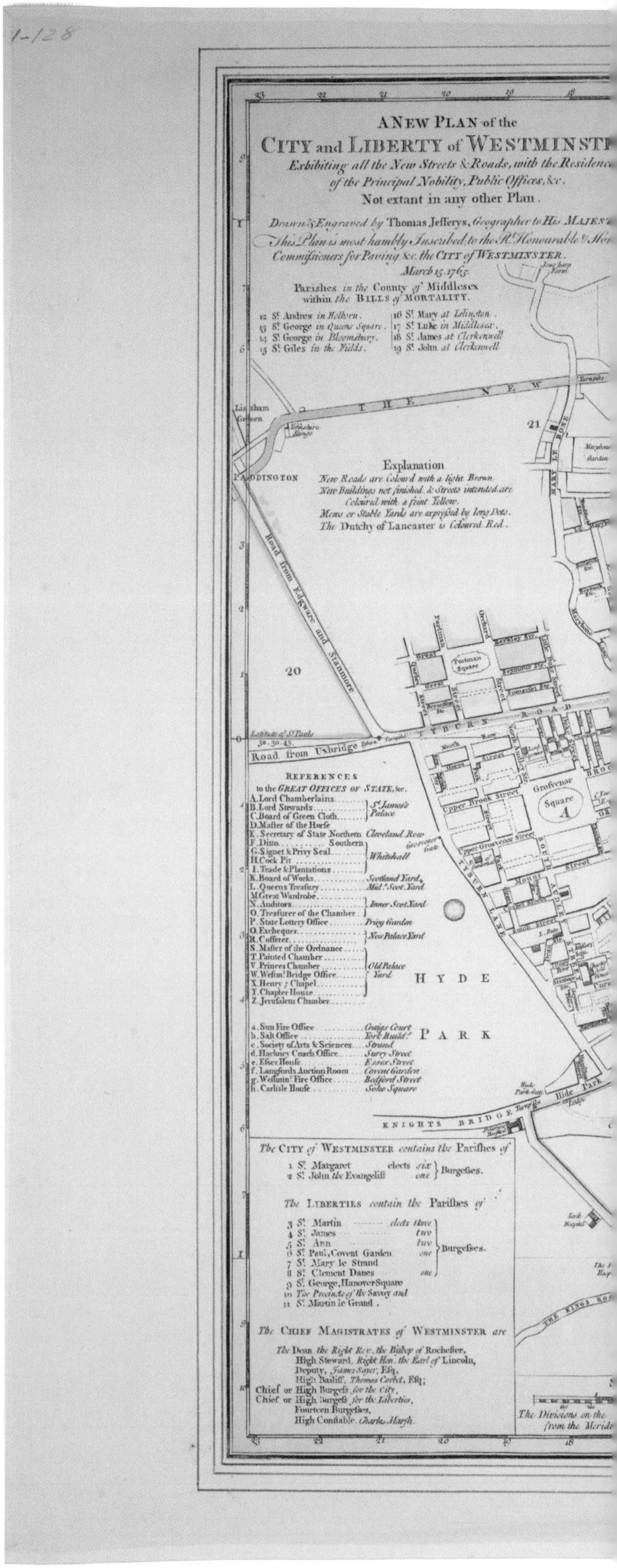

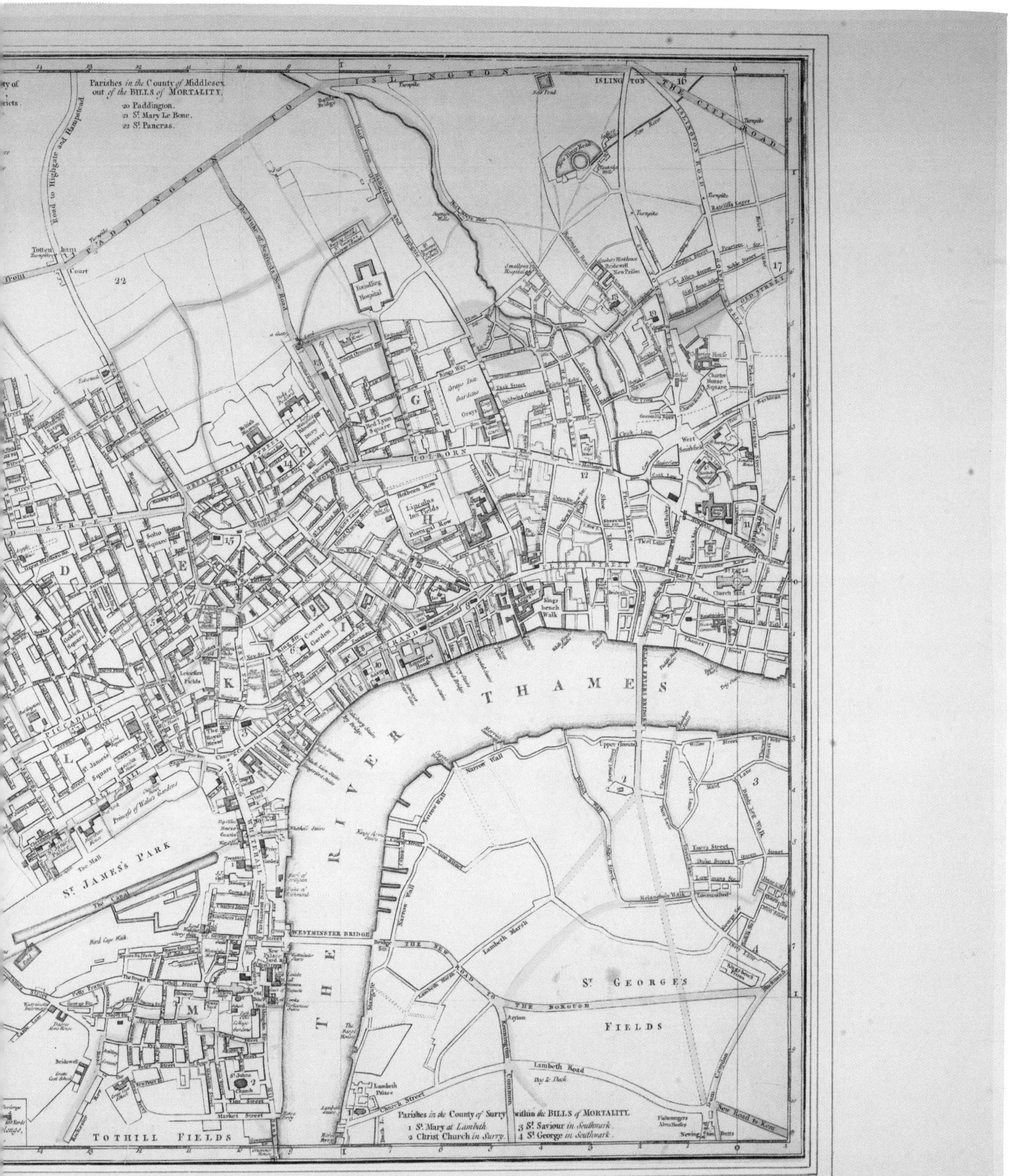
Parishes in the County of Middlesex out of the BILLS of MORTALITY.
20 Paddington.
21 St. Mary Le Bone.
22 St. Pancras.
ISLINGTON
PADDINGTON
Road to Highgate and Hampstead
Foundling Hospital
HOLBORN
Lincolns Inn Fields
Soho Square
Covent Garden
Leicester Fields
PICCADILLY
St. James's Square
Golden Square
ST. JAMES'S PARK
The Mall
Bird Cage Walk
The Canal
WESTMINSTER BRIDGE
THE RIVER THAMES
Somerset House
Kings bench Walk
Fleet Market
West Smithfield
Charter House Square
St. Pauls Church Yard
Lambeth Marsh
Lambeth Palace
Lambeth Road
ST. GEORGE'S FIELDS
THE BOROUGH
TOTHILL FIELDS
Tothill Street
Market Street
Vine Street
Petty France
Parishes in the County of Surry within the BILLS of MORTALITY.
1 St. Mary at Lambeth.
2 Christ Church in Surry.
3 St. Saviour in Southwark.
4 St. George in Southwark.
New Road to Kent
...f London the West from St. Paul's by T. Jefferys
1765.

NORTH
SOUTH
WEST
OCCIDENS
GLAMORGAN SHYRE
With the situations of the cheife towne CARDY
and ancient LANDAFFE described.
CARDYFE.
A. Smithes stret
B. Shomakers stret
C. West Stret
D. Back stret
E. Hummanbye stret
F. St. Iohns stret
G. High stret
H. North stret
K. Working stret
L. Porrag stret
M. Frogg Lane
N. St. Iohns Church
O. Castell Lane
P. Towne howse
Q. Duke Stret
R. The pootes Releife
THE SCALE OF PASES
Black fryers
Shire hall
Castell
West Gate
East Gate
The Key
PART OF BREK NOKE SH
PART OF CARMAR DEN SHEYRE
Bettus
Llaneddye
Llandilo Talabont
Istradguiles
Capel Krenant
Aberpirgum
Neath
Llanylted
Cadoxtown
Neath Abbey
Llansawled
Coidfrank Forest
Llangoyvelach
Swansey
S. Iohns
Briton Ferye
Michael church
Bagland
Aberavon
Margam
Clyncorug
Llangynewere
Bettus Chaple
Langguwid
Kenfeage Cast
The Pile
Llaleston
New castle
Bridgende
Llandydock
Mathermawre
Newton Notage
Great S. Bride
Llannyenwere
S. Kenetes Chap
The Holme
Llanmadok
Cheriton
Llangenyth
Park Brewis
Wehley
Pengwerne
Llanridien
Ilston
Pennarth
Bisshopston
Ostermouth cast
Mumbles poynt
WEST GOWRE
Rinolston
Penmayne
Rossilye
Llanddewye cast
Knolston
Pennarth point
Wormeshead poyt
Porthynon
Oxwiche
Oxwich poynt
Nashe po
The scale of English miles Anno Dom. 1610
1 2 3 4 5 6 7 8 9 10

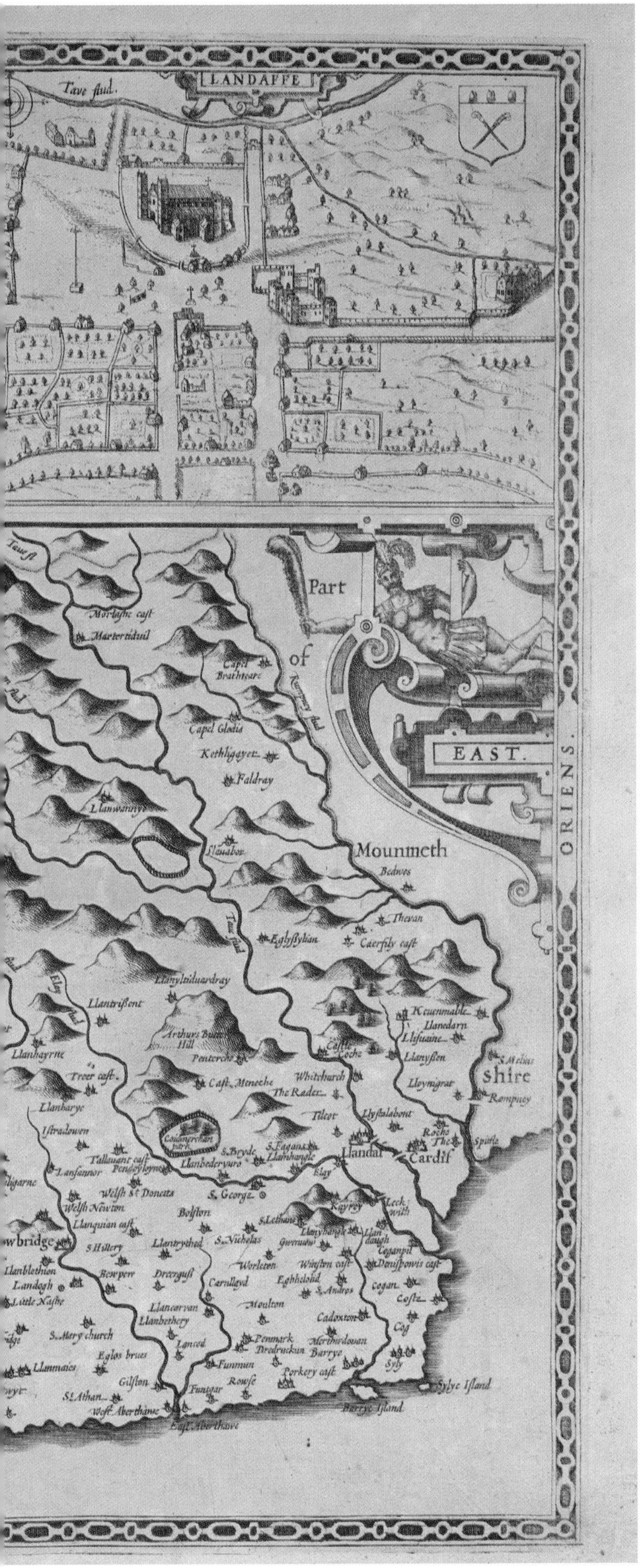

Glamorgan, Wales

(1607)

When the English historian and editor John Speed (*c*.1552–1629) admitted that he had 'dipped his sickle into other men's corne' it was a remarkably honest statement from someone who had copied and borrowed his way to producing some of the most distinctive and well-regarded English maps of the seventeenth century. His two atlases, the *Theatre of the Empire of Great Britaine* (1611–12) and *Prospect of the Most Famous Parts of the World* (1627), contain maps which are visual compendia of geography, history, heraldry, allegory, antiquity and iconography. Few of these features were the creation of Speed himself – with an exception, as we shall discover.

This map of the county of Glamorgan is from a collection of pre-publication proof copies of his county maps, first published as the *Theatre* in 1611 and 1612. The map lacks a small number of features present in the finished map, such as the zig-zagged sea pattern, indicating a late proof which the engraver Jodocus Hondius (1563–1612), working in Amsterdam, may have sent to Speed for his approval. Because the plate had not suffered much wear through printing at this stage, the freshly engraved lines on the copper plate have supplied a strong, dark print impression. This is especially noticeable when compared to the heavily worn final printing of the exhausted plate of around 1770, a century and a half later.

The content of the map, as of the others in the *Theatre*, was derived largely from the county maps produced by Christopher Saxton during the 1570s. Speed also benefited from an association with the antiquarian William Camden and the collector Sir Robert Cotton, whose library (a founding collection of the British Museum) Speed noted as having been 'set open to my free access'. Some of the town plans Speed included in each county map are based on manuscripts in Cotton's collection. Speed used other sources as well, only some of which we know. Llandaff, in the Glamorgan map, is based on an unknown prototype.

Here we must give Speed his due. Where no town plan prototype existed, he laced up his boots and went and mapped it himself. A set of hand-drawn and dated town plans in Merton College, Oxford, signed I.S., reveals that between 1606 and 1608 Speed personally mapped 33 towns. On 5 September 1606 he arrived in Cardiff and mapped it, possibly with local assistance, noting the roads and principal buildings and listing them in a key. The 'scale of pases' shown at the foot of the plan represents his strides around the town. Given that this is the first printed map of Cardiff, we shouldn't be too hard on Speed's appropriating habit.

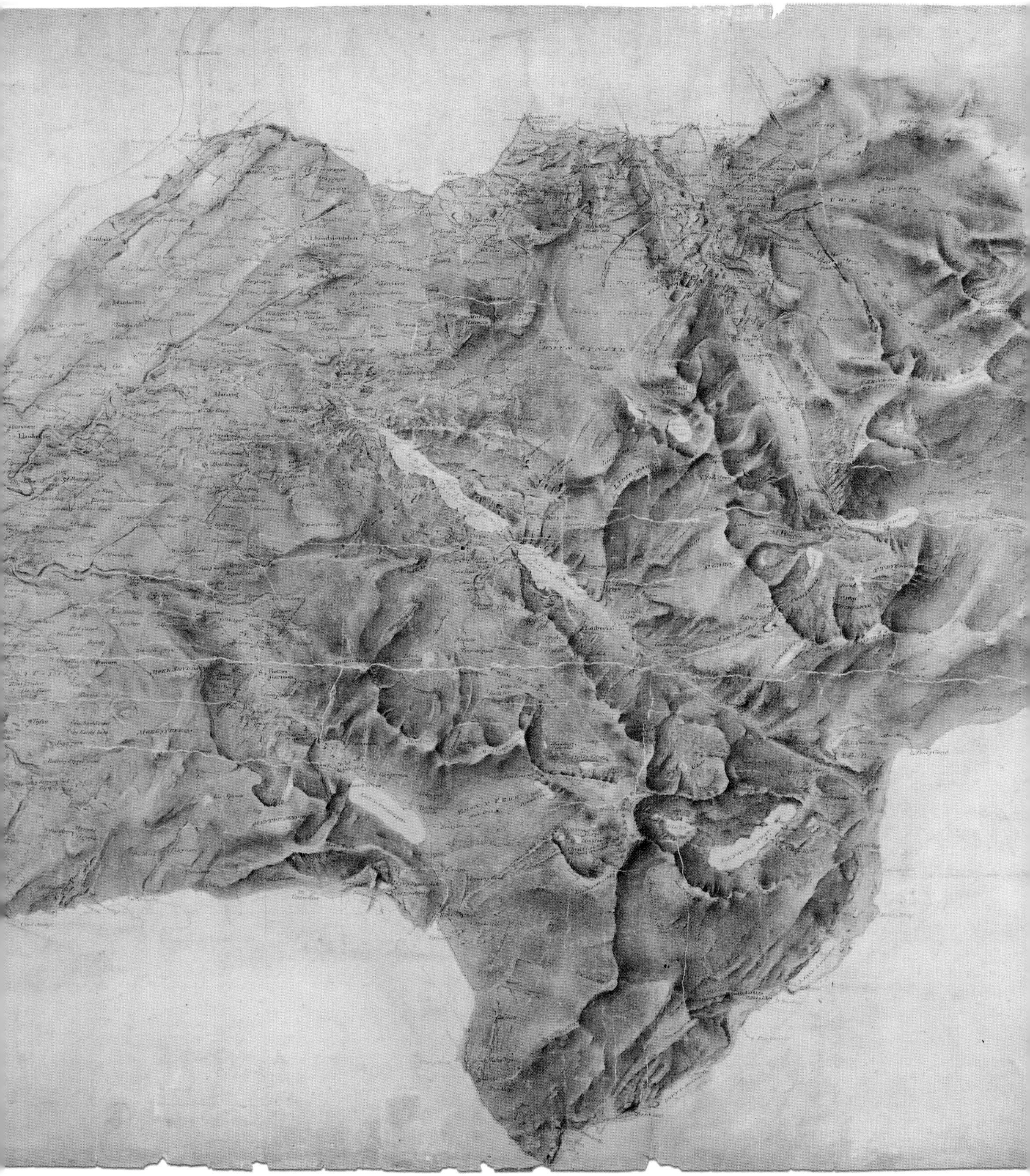

Caernarfonshire, Wales

(1816)

This large and highly finished drawing of part of Caernarfonshire in North Wales is one of the earliest productions of Britain's national mapping agency, the Ordnance Survey. Founded in 1791 but with roots stretching back to William Roy's (1726–90) military map of Scotland of 1747 to 1755, the Board of Ordnance was charged with mapping England's south coast as contingency for invasion by France during the Napoleonic Wars. The threat had passed in 1815, but the survey continued, reaching into less strategically vulnerable parts of Britain, as here.

By that time the Survey's comprehensive, topographically rich and mathematically precise large-scale mapping, which surpassed anything produced before it, was beginning to be perceived as useful for practical purposes besides defence – such as administration. A national map was also seen as a point of honour, particularly since by that time the French were well on the way to completing their own.

Over a period of half a century a team of military surveyors covered the area of England and Wales as far north as Hull (with a sojourn into Ireland between 1824 and 1846). The method by which they did it was first to measure an area by triangulation, overlaying a series of triangles using key landmarks as their corners. This gave the map its geodetic (scientifically-measured) base. Then the surveyors would 'infill' topographical detail by passing through each area drawing, sketching, measuring and calculating hills, towns, rivers, forests and roads (the latter usually formed the boundaries between mapping areas). This was the laborious part, and there were few more uncompromising places to map than mountainous Caernarfonshire.

The surveyor responsible for the map, Robert Dawson (1771–1860), was the senior surveying teacher at the Ordnance Survey and one of its best draftsmen. We can see his skill to great effect in this map in which the relief – an essential feature of any military map – has been so well crafted with hachuring, shading and wash techniques that it has a sort of three-dimensional quality. You could almost say that there is a drama to the map not dissimilar to the paintings of the same area by the artist Richard Wilson (1714–82) half a century earlier. Not all of the surveyors were as good artists as Dawson. Another surveyor working in Wales, Charles Budgen (1769–1838), was described by the head of the Ordnance Survey as 'indifferent'. Dawson, on the other hand, received criticism for his inaccuracy. Fulfilling both functions was difficult even for the best mapmakers.

These large drawings (of which 351 survive in the British Library) were used as the basis for the first printed Ordnance Survey maps – the 'Old Series' – published between 1805 and 1869. The original drawings are the superstars, and though battered and bruised, revised and amended, cut, torn and discoloured, their sublime quality shines through.

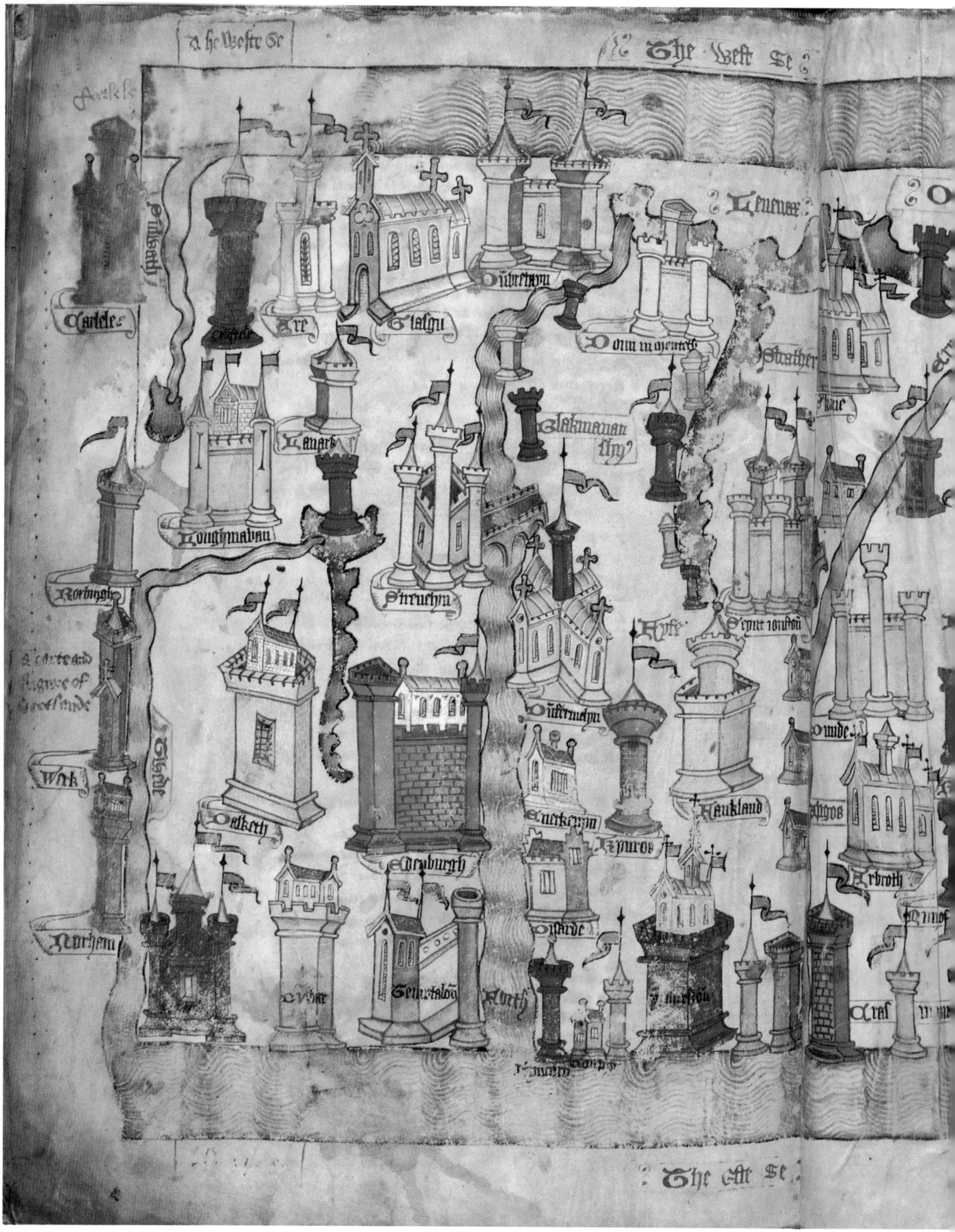
The West Se
Carlele
Are
Glasgu
Lanark
Loughmaban
Strevelyn
Dalketh
Edenburgh
Dunfermelyn
Arbroth
Norham
Werk
The Este Se

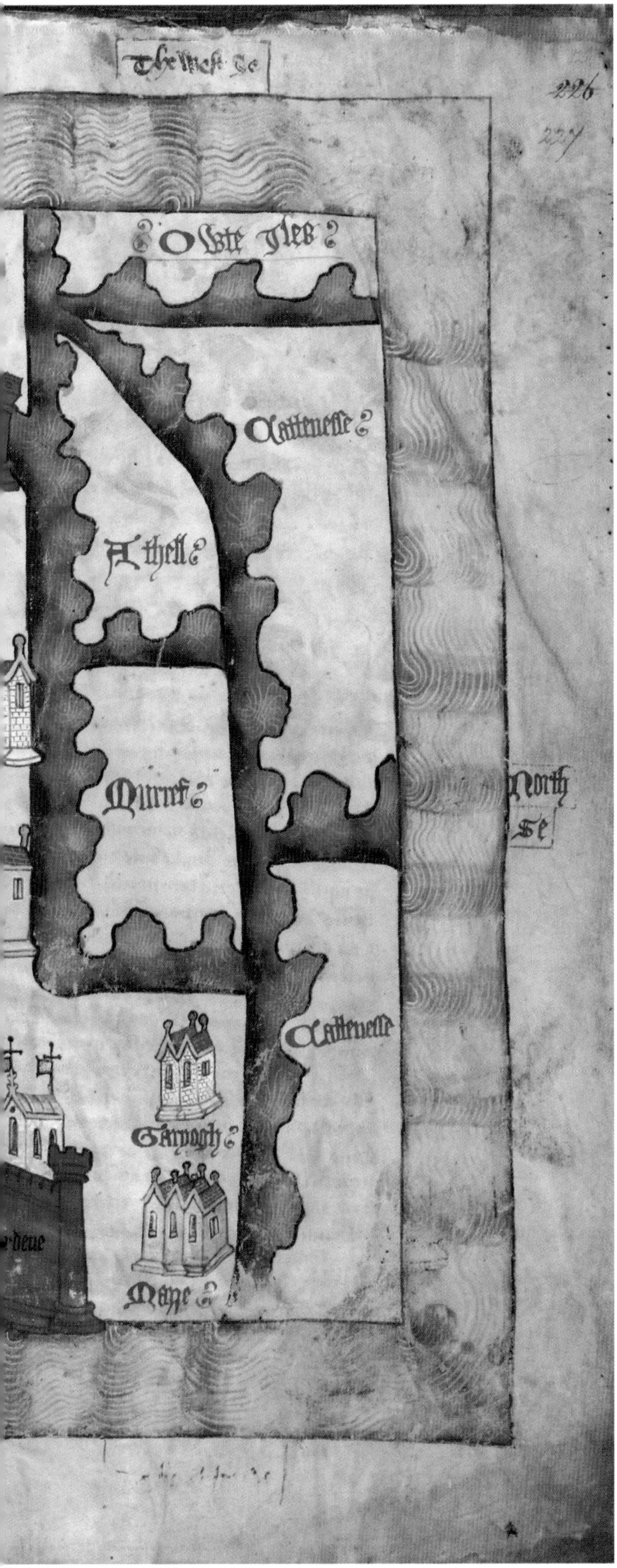

Scotland

(1437)

This squarish map could almost be mistaken for a chessboard with rather too many rooks (the castle-shaped pieces which begin a chess game in the corners of the board). This is not such a bad analogy, given the strategic aspects of both game and map. It is a map of Scotland which was drawn to illustrate an invasion plan for the country, and it was included in a chronicle of Britain which was presented by its author, John Harding (1378–1465), to Henry VI (*r.*1422–61 and 1470–71) and later in revised form to Edward IV (*r.*1461–70 and 1471–83).

The use of maps to explain and illustrate invasion planning was more common from the 1490s, so this is a particularly early example. In addition to their representational capacity, such maps have the ability to frame and visualise the territorial goal in the imaginations of would-be invaders. This is undoubtedly a purpose of Harding's Scotland map. Harding was an author who had served under various officials in the North of England and was present at the Battle of Agincourt in 1415. He appears from his writing to have been particularly preoccupied with Scotland, which was then a separate kingdom from England, but which was generally believed (in England) to be legally subject to English rule. He forged documents stating as much and presented them to the king as evidence.

The map of Scotland was another component of Harding's strategy and a classic piece of propaganda. It presents the country with west at the top, bounded to the left by the River Tweed, the large Firth of Forth to the north of it, and the green wooded mountains of the Highlands enticingly 'ffull of catell corne and prosperitie'. But it is the castles (representing towns but also themselves as the chief buildings of the towns) which catch the viewer's attention, wonderfully varied in their composition. We can recognise Edinburgh and Stirling castles among them. To the kings and princes who looked at the map, these centres of ecclesiastical and military power were incredibly desirable possessions. This was precisely the aim of the map. Not only did it frame Scotland as a place that was ripe and attractive to conquer, but it visualised Scotland as part of Britain. These associations with patriotism, identity and unity made it a persuasive and powerful picture.

Harding later produced further detailed maps to illustrate his invasion plan, but none compares in appearance to this strategic, sneaky map: checkmate.

The Trossachs, Scotland

(1755)

Maps which history has judged 'great' are usually either very large or very important. The fair copy of William Roy's military map of Scotland, produced between 1747 and 1755, is both. It is drawn on 38 long strips of paper which when put together measure around nine metres in height. It is also the first scientifically measured survey map of a British country and the precursor of the modern Ordnance Survey.

The context of the map is the English pacification of the Scottish Highlands following the Jacobite Rebellion of 1745 and the defeat of Scottish forces loyal to the pretender to the English throne, Charles Edward Stuart (1720–88), at the Battle of Culloden in 1746. He escaped to France, but retribution was exacted on his supporters which included internment, execution and land confiscation. In order to reinforce English control, a programme of road and fort construction was initiated. And at the suggestion of the influential Royal Engineer David Watson, a military survey was also authorised, led by Watson's associate Roy.

Over the following seven years Roy and his team would map the Scottish Highlands and Lowlands at a scale of two inches to the mile by a method known as 'road traverse'. Scientific instruments such as a circumferentor, plane table and chain measured distances and angles along a route, and the surrounding landscape was recorded in sketches. A drawing of 1749 by Paul Sandby (1731–1809) captured Roy's surveying party in action by the banks of Loch Rannoch in Perthshire. Sandby was a military draftsman and part of Roy's team, who were responsible for the finished Great Map.

Not for nothing was Sandby called 'the father of English watercolour art'. The map is an expansive, vivid and seductive painted impression of the often-dramatic Scottish landscape as seen from above. A careful technique has been used to describe the key roads, settlements, innumerable tiny trees, lochs and rivers, the latter painted with a fresh pale blue. This minutiae contrasts with the expressive sweeps of Sandby's brush which give form to the hills and mountains. It is a feature which places the map within the bounds of landscape art, of which Sandby would go on to become one of Britain's best-known practitioners.

The map was a product of scientific enlightenment and symbolised humanity's ability to objectively measure and master nature. Its unifying 'national' dimension became one of the key principles behind the Ordnance Survey of England and Wales established half a century later. Roy's Great Map was owned by the commander-in-chief of the English forces at Culloden, William Augustus, Duke of Cumberland (1721–65), whose collection passed to George III on his death.

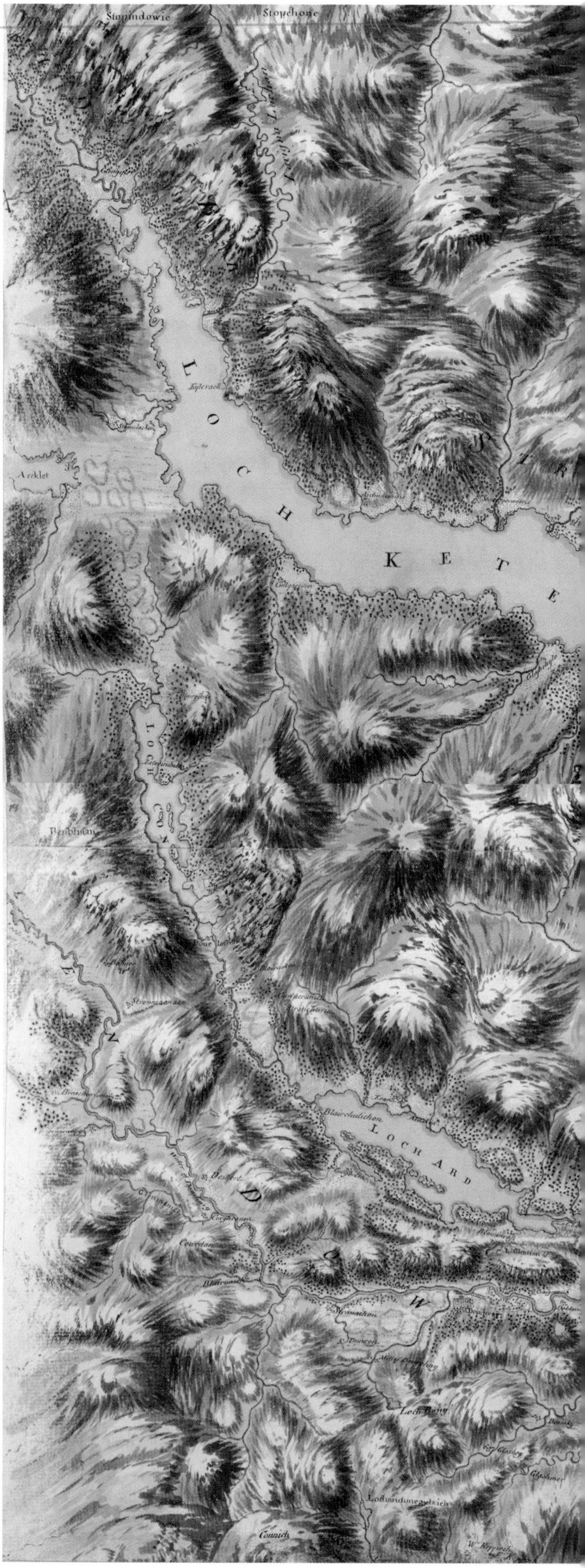

LOCH ACHRAY
LOCH VANACHAR
Bridge of Leny
CALLENDER
Bridge of Keltie
Cambusmor Castle
House of Ballochallan
River Teith
Loch Drunkie
Bridge of Aberfoil
LOCH of MONTEITH
Loch Rusky
Brendam
Sieck

THE.ENGLISHE.VICTORE.AGAYNSTE.THE.
MVSKELBROGHE. 1547.
The carters.
The englishe battell
The englishe horsemen.
The contre lothiana.
The schottishe battell.
The englishe campe.
The shurche.
THE.

Musselburgh, Scotland

(1547)

This is the only surviving copy of the earliest known map to have been engraved and printed in Britain. There is a lot we don't know about it, such as why it was produced, but thankfully there is a lot we do know about it, too, enabling us to make informed guesses. It is a plan of the Battle of Pinkie Cleugh or Musselburgh, which was fought between England and Scotland on 10 September 1547, just south of Edinburgh. The battle pitched the invading English army, led by the Duke of Somerset (*c.*1500–52), Lord Protector to the infant King Edward VI (*r.*1547–53), against a Scottish force loyal to Mary, Queen of Scots (*r.*1542–67). Somerset's attempts to unify the two countries through marriage (known as the 'rough wooing') had failed, and invasion was his plan B.

The map shows the key events of the decisive English victory. Oriented with west to the top, we look on the battlefield from the position of the North Sea. Edinburgh peeps out from behind Arthur's Seat in the top right of the image. Before us is a dynamic and swirling scene of carnage. In the middle of the page is the epicentre, with the Scottish infantry, opposed by English units, scattering across the banks of the River Esk. There are gruesome impalements and hangings. Somerset utilised naval warships to pound the Scots, which we can see in the foreground. Artillery and cavalry, visible on the left and top, completed their demoralisation and defeat.

Because of the integrated use of different methods of warfare, Pinkie Cleugh is thought to be the first modern battle of the British Isles. The involvement of maps was also innovative. This map was based on battlefield sketches by the Scotsman John Ramsay, and was likely to have been specially commissioned, maybe even by Somerset himself, to celebrate the victory. Somerset has been noted as being 'adept at the psychological use of maps', and such a map would have presented all who saw it, including foreign diplomats, with a realistic demonstration of English might over Scotland. It was probably engraved by Thomas Geminus (*fl.*1540–62) and printed by the king's printer, Reyner Wolfe (d.1573).

For the map to fulfil such a public purpose it would be expected that a significant number of them would have been produced and survived. The fact that they don't is a mystery, and the author Ashley Baynton-Williams has suggested that the map was never circulated. The ultimate goal of Somerset's campaign, the hand of Mary, eluded his grasp when she fled to France, and the victory proved a hollow one.

Ireland

(1599)

This large printed map shows Ireland with west to the top. Its near rectangular shape virtually fills the frame, and a multitude of islanded lakes and other features pattern its interior in an even and consistent manner. When it was published in London in 1599 it was the most detailed and authoritative map of Ireland in existence, so much so that Johann Baptist Vrients (1552–1612) copied it for inclusion in Abraham Ortelius's *Theatrum Orbis Terrarum* between 1608 and 1612. Ireland was no longer on the periphery of the world, as it had appeared in medieval world maps. By the end of the sixteenth century it was a place of singular importance for an English audience.

The Tudor conquest of Ireland began with Henry VIII, who proclaimed the Kingdom of Ireland in 1542, and continued with Elizabeth I. Land was confiscated from native Irish landowners and redistributed among English nobles. However, opposition led by Hugh O'Neill, Earl of Tyrone (*c.*1559–1616) and Hugh Roe O'Donnell (1572–1602) of Donegal caused a series of English defeats during the Nine Years' War (1595–1603). In 1599 one of the queen's favourites, Robert Devereux, 2nd Earl of Essex (1565–1601) landed in Ireland with 17,000 troops, then the largest force ever to leave England, to supress the Irish. Unfamiliar with the Irish terrain, they stood little chance against skilful, knowledgeable and organised opponents. Essex returned to England humiliated.

This is the background to the map's production: a timely publication which satisfied public interest. Its producer was the Italian artist Battista Boazio (*fl.*1588–1606), who had shown a taste for opportunism during the 1590s when he had produced celebratory maps for Sir Francis Drake's maritime victories over the Spanish at Cadiz (1596) and in the Azores (1597). He used various sources for his Ireland map. Maps of Northern Ireland and of the town of Kinsale, drawn in his hand, are held in the library of Elizabeth's advisor Sir Robert Cotton, indicating that he may have enjoyed privileged access to restricted official sources.

The map also included a variety of information derived from atlas maps by Jodocus Hondius and Gerhard Mercator, revealing Boazio to be more of a copyist than an original mapmaker. His map may have been larger than any of the others, but this left him with more space to fill. In the 1950s Edward Lynam noted one way in which he had done so, spotting the spurious 'Baptiste's Rock' and 'Elstrack's Isle' – Renold Elstrack (1570–after 1625) was the map's engraver. Nevertheless, these fantastical features didn't prevent the map becoming the principal source of printed maps of Ireland for future decades. The Tudor conquest of Ireland was completed in 1603.

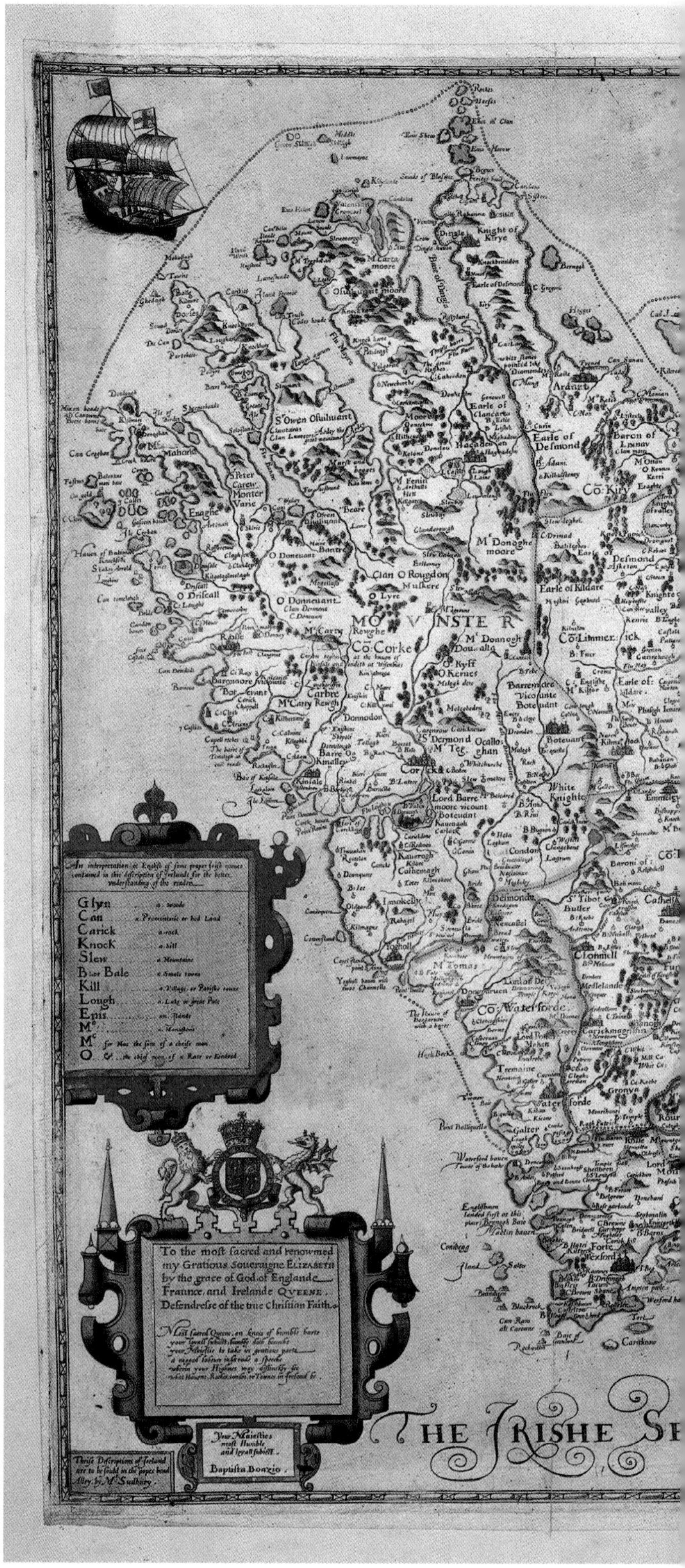

IRELANDE
In this generall discription or Chart of IRELANDE, particularlye
it showe these contentes hereafter folowinge, First by the round pricked
Lynes the division or bounds of the 4 Provinces the on from the other viz
Mounster, Conaught, Leinster and Vlster
GEORGE HIS CHANEL
Scale of 30 Common myles of Ireland
Lough Earne
Lough Eaghe
Lough Foyle
Lough Swilly
Lough Fin
Co. Knockfergus
Co. Antrim
Co. Downe
Co. Armagh
Co. Monaghan
Co. Cavan
Co. Letrim
Co. Longford
Co. Westmeathe
Co. Kildare
Co. Dublin
Co. Galway
Co. Mayo
Co. Slego
Co. Rosecomen
Co. Queenes Towne
Tirone
Tierconnell
Farmanagh

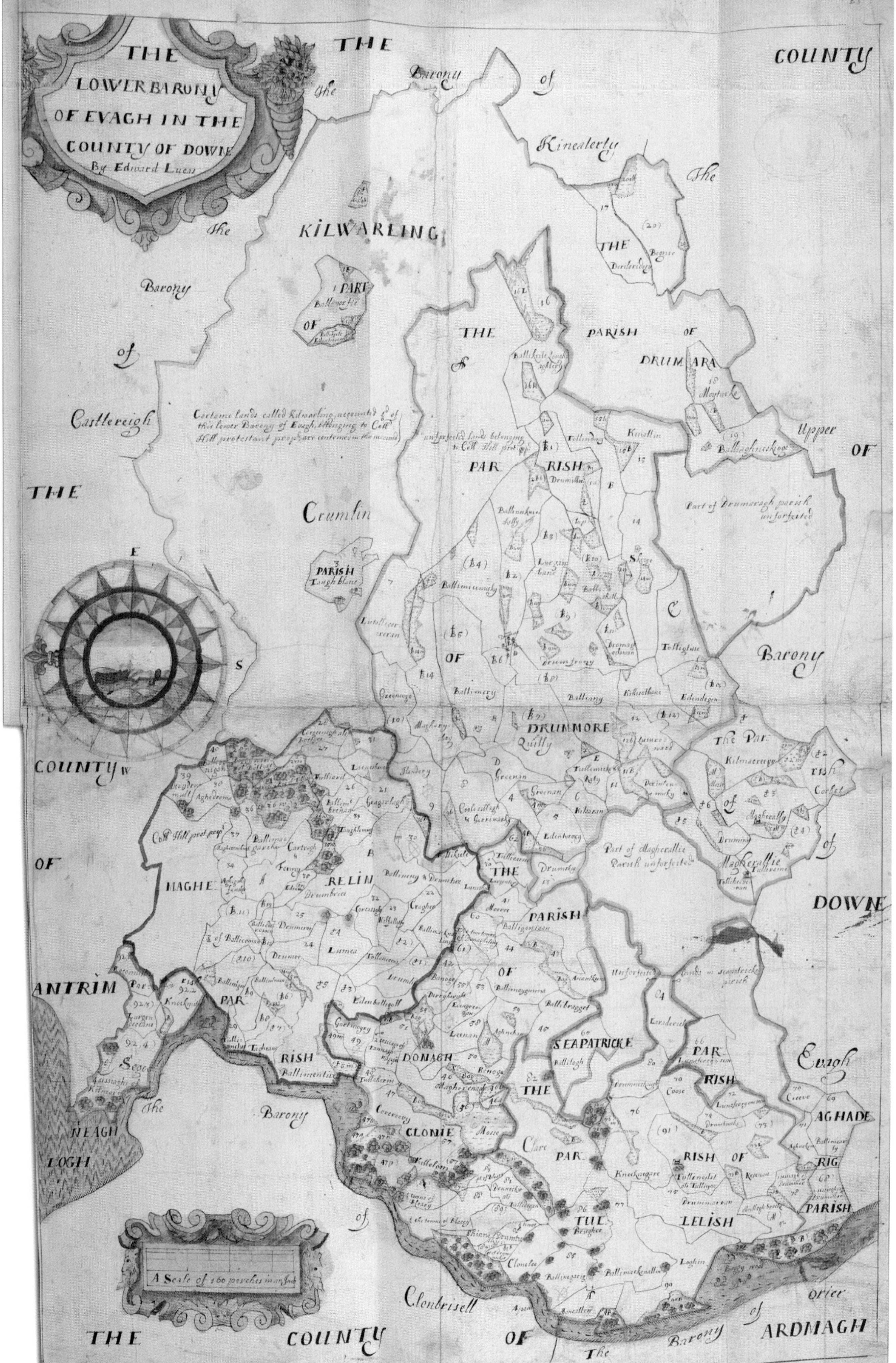

THE LOWER BARONY OF EVAGH IN THE COUNTY OF DOWNE
By Edward Lucas
THE Barony of Kinealerty
THE Barony of Castlereigh
THE PARISH OF DRUMARA
the KILWARLING
Certaine lands called Kilwarling, accounted p^t of this lower Barony of Evagh, belonging to Coll Hill protestant prop^r, are conteined in the surveie
Crumlin PARISH
Part of Drumaragh parish unforfeited
Upper Barony OF
PARISH OF DRUMMORE
The Parish of Kilmacrewe
Magheralli
Part of Magherallie Parish unforfeited
MAGHERELIN PARISH
THE PARISH OF DONAGHCLONIE
SEAPATRICKE
Unforfeited lands in seapatricke parish
THE PARISH OF TULLELISH
AGHADERIG PARISH
COUNTY OF ANTRIM
NEAGH LOGH
THE COUNTY OF DOWNE
Evagh
A Scale of 160 perches in an Inch
Clonbrisell
the Barony of Orier
THE COUNTY OF ARDMAGH

County Down, Northern Ireland

(1654–56)

As a consequence of the 1641 Irish Rebellion, which occurred around the time of the English Civil War (1642–51), large swathes of Irish Catholic lands were judged forfeit to the English Crown. In total 8,400,000 acres of land were identified for redistribution to the English, mainly Protestant soldiers and investors, thanks largely to one of the most significant colonial mapping projects in history. The 'Down Survey' was named after the fact that the measuring, surveying and drafting work, compiled in a mere four years between 1655 and 1659, was 'set down' on paper (the historian J.H. Andrews describes the title as an example of 'Cromwellian newspeak').

The main force behind the survey was William Petty (1623–87). Petty was an extraordinary figure: an army surgeon, Royal Society founding member, mathematician and pioneer of statistical analysis. 'Sceptical and droll' and fiercely ambitious, Petty drew on earlier Irish surveys and organised fresh ones, instructing the (mostly local) surveyors that they would need to 'ruffle with the severall rude persons of the country' in order to get the job done. He collected boundary and economic information into books and had hundreds of parish maps, barony maps and county maps produced. A commercially minded man, Petty charged a fee for his own set of maps to be consulted, and he had the country maps published as the atlas *Hibernia delineato* in 1685.

This is one of the barony maps, drawn by the surveyor Edward Lucas, showing the county of Uí Echach (Iveagh) in County Down. Though not outstanding artistically, it is a clinically efficient map which identifies forfeited land, provides its calculated area, and indicates whether the land is cultivated, woodland or bog. These were the most important things for the maps to show, a reduction of a place to its essential economic elements with disregard for any topographical or cultural detail. The Down Survey showcased a mapping mentality that would be developed in the mapping of British India during the following century.

As a result of their precise quality, Down Survey maps were assigned legal status as irrefutably true representations of land ownership in Ireland. Accordingly, they were in demand and numerous sets were copied. However, incidents in 1711 and 1922 led to the entire set of parish maps being destroyed, while Petty's own maps were stolen by a French privateer in 1707 and are now in the Bibliothèque nationale de France. This incomplete set, from the papers of Petty's descendants, reached the British Library in 1992.

France

(1636)

One of the key requirements of the modern European state of the seventeenth century was a good communications network. In order to exercise control, centralised governing authorities needed to be able to reach their subjects in outlying areas, and subjects needed to know that they could be reached. From the end of the sixteenth century Henri IV's (*r.*1589–1610) minister Maximilien de Béthune, Duke of Sully (1560–1641) had strengthened communications with France's frontier provinces and initiated infrastructure projects including the building of roads in order to facilitate central control from Paris. Roads were the principal lines of communication for transport, trade and the postal system.

This printed map is one of the earliest to show France's post-road network. It was produced in Paris in 1636 by Nicolas Berey (1610–65) after an earlier edition of 1632 by Melchior Tavernier (1594–1665), which was itself a copy of a manuscript map by Nicolas Sanson (1600–67). It was continually updated from lists to show new roads that had been built. Looking at it we can clearly see those major arteries running across France, with towns marked at regular intervals along them. Rivers, a principal obstacle (which Sully's project of bridge-building also addressed), are prominently shown. The coverage is uneven, with Brittany, for example, particularly poorly served. Roads meet at the capital, Paris, and at the major cities of Limoges, Toulouse, Bordeaux and Lyon. From Lyon we can see an unfinished road leading to the Italian border, reminding us that France was also part of the wider European network.

The map is decorated in the Dutch *carte à figure* style, with a profile scene of post riders and coaches along the top, and along the side and in the centre town profiles and bird's-eye views copied from the *Civitates Orbis Terrarum* of between 1572 and 1617 by Georg Braun (1541–1622) and Frans Hogenberg (1535–90). This decoration would have appealed to a discerning and increasingly mobile cosmopolitan audience. Nicolas Berey was a proactive French map publisher working during a period in which the French map trade was beginning to emerge from under the shadow of the dominant Dutch map industry. By the end of the century French maps would be the main force in European cartography. This is another way in which Berey's map informed France's national development.

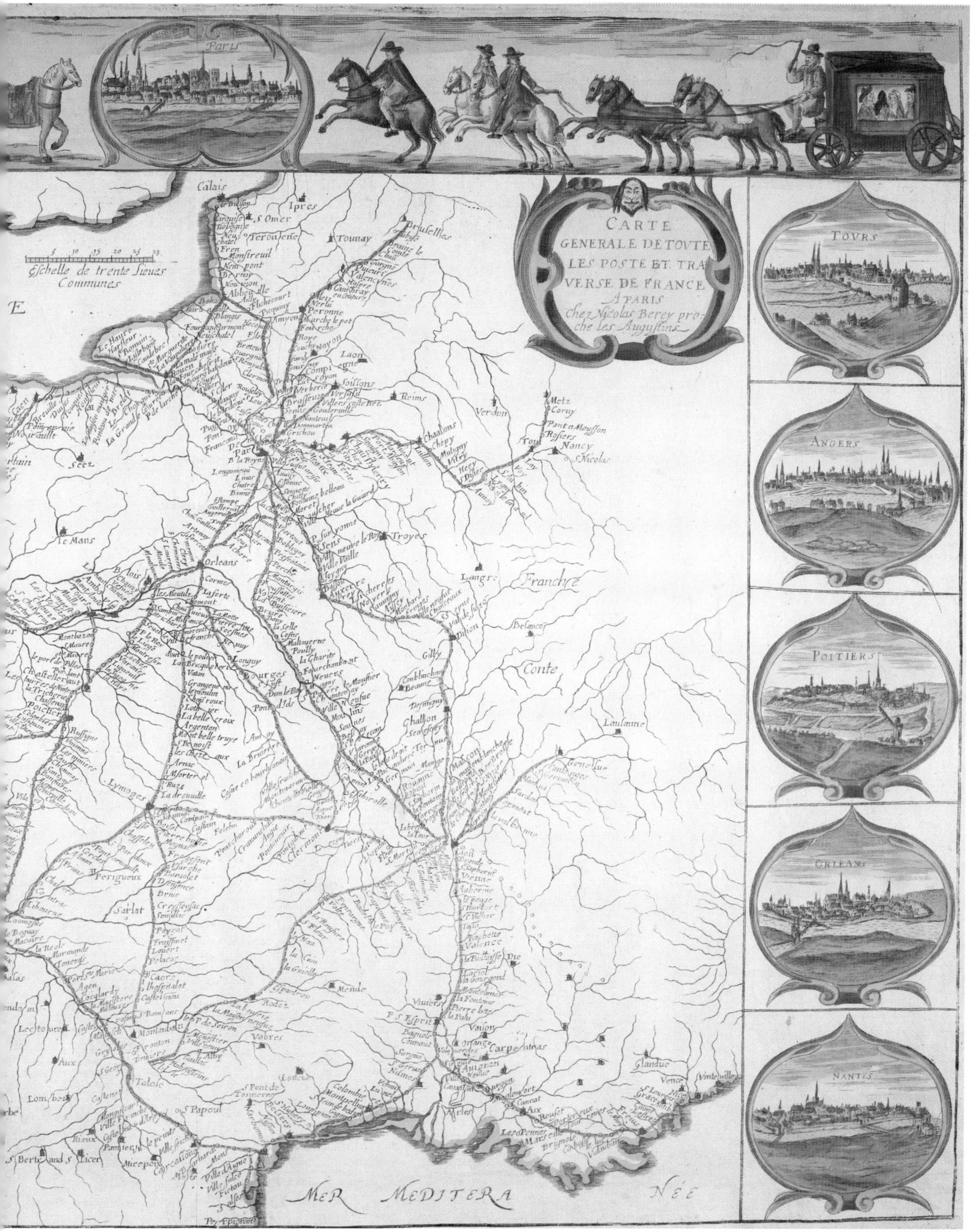

CARTE GENERALE DE TOVTE LES POSTE ET TRAVERSE DE FRANCE. A PARIS Chez Nicolas Berey proche les Augustins
Paris
TOVRS
ANGERS
POITIERS
NANTES
Eschelle de trente lieues Communes
Calais
Ipres
S. Omer
Tournay
Brusselles
Abbeville
Amyens
Peronne
Laon
Soissons
Reims
Verdun
Metz
Pont a Mousson
Nancy
S. Nicolas
Chaalons
Toul
Seez
Le Mans
Orleans
Blois
Troyes
Sens
Auxerre
Langre
Franche
Conte
Dijon
Beaune
Bourges
Lymoges
Perigueux
Sarlat
Lyon
Vienne
Valence
Mende
Rodez
Montauban
Tolose
Alby
Avignon
Carpentras
Nismes
Montpellier
Arles
Aix
Marseille
Narbonne
Carcassonne
Mirepoix
S. Papoul
Castres
Lausanne
Mer Meditera Née

PLAN, DE BOVLONIGNE
LA DVNNETTES
La ville Basse
A°. 1602
La Maison Rouge
Porte du havre
Porte
Le Tintellerie
Or.
Oc.
S.
M.
20 40 60 80 100
200
300

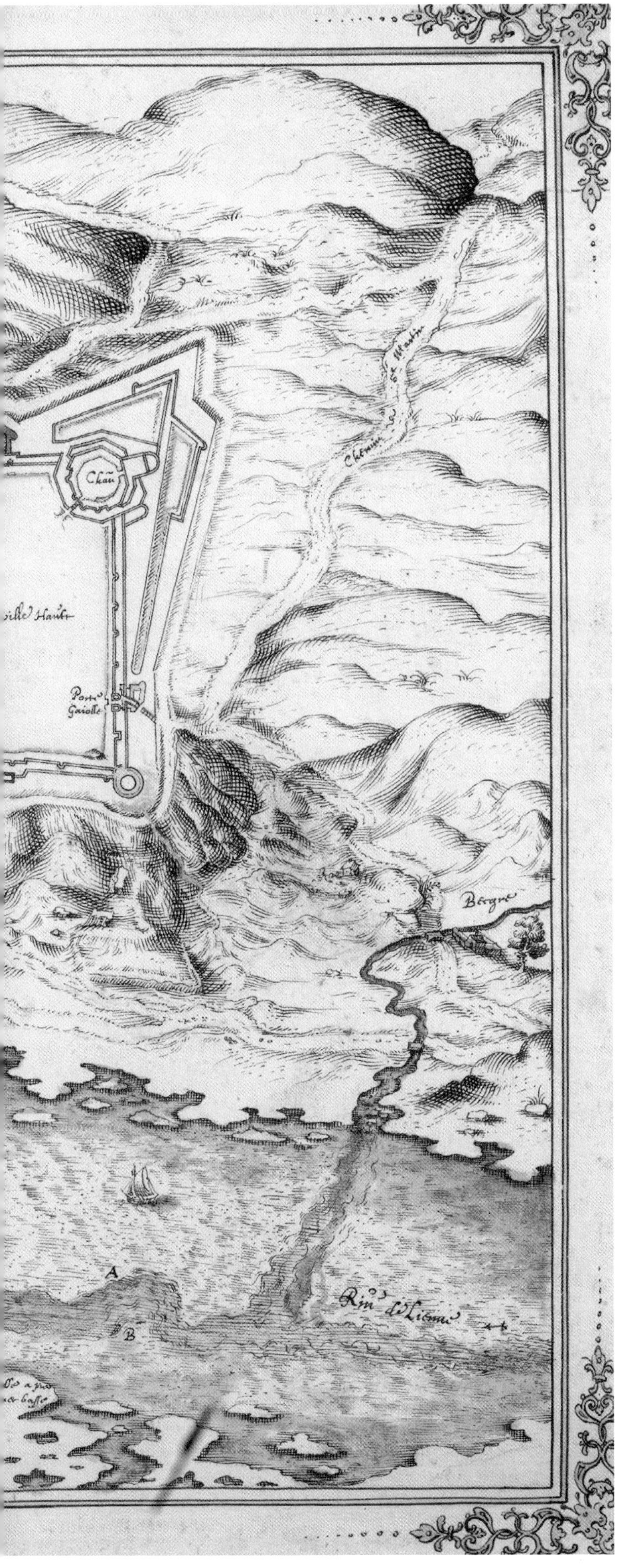

Boulogne, France

(c.1608)

The French Wars of Religion had subsided by 1600, and once internal tranquillity was attained, Henri IV could set about strengthening his kingdom. In order to advance his plan of a centralised and secure kingdom, Henri turned to his trusty lieutenant, master of artillery and superintendent of fortifications Maximilien de Béthune, Duke of Sully. Sully saw the French frontier provinces in the northeast, southeast and southwest (facing the Spanish Netherlands, Savoy and Spain) as the key, and he set about strengthening them and their ties to Paris.

Sully attached special royal engineers known as *ingénieurs du roi* to these frontier provinces. As *ingénieurs* they combined the roles of military surveyor, architect and cartographer, producing designs for the construction and repair of fortifications on the latest Italian principles, and regional maps of parts of France.

This map of Boulogne is from a collection of hand-drawn maps, plans and views of over 100 locations in the provinces of Dauphiné, Provence, Champagne and Picardy. It was drawn by the *ingénieur* of Picardy, Jean Errard (1554–1610). Others were produced by Errard's drawing master or *conducteur des dessins*, Jean Martellier, and other hands. Like the others, the Boulogne map is clear and informative, blending bird's-eye view and plan formats, prioritising relief, rivers, towns and roads with a scale. Its attractive appearance belies its practical military function.

The atlas is different to contemporary atlases because as well as including maps of forts, towns and provinces, there are also regional maps of towns' surrounding areas. The combination of maps of the different administrative and military areas within an atlas was an uncommon approach (Christopher Saxton's 1579 atlas of England and Wales, also originally produced for internal defence, consisted only of county maps). With their terrain, settlements and supply routes, these outlying zones were critical to the defence of the towns and therefore important to map, as Errard realised.

Errard and Martellier's strategic atlas of France's frontier provinces was kept in the engineer's drawing office in Paris, where it could be consulted, analysed and used for planning. Some of the first printed regional maps of France, by Christophe Tassin (d.1660), were copied from them. This defence manual facilitated centralised control during the early years of the Bourbon monarchy. When the Bourbons were overthrown during the French Revolution in 1792, the atlas was probably removed during the chaos, and found its way to the British Museum 70 years later.

Northeast France

(1918)

Few reputations have suffered as greatly as that of the commander-in-chief of the British armed forces from 1915 to 1918, Field Marshall Sir Douglas Haig (1861–1928). Although his stock was high in the period following victory over Germany in 1918, the longer view that the war was won at an unnecessary human cost laid the blame firmly at the generals' door. This map provides a fascinating insight into the mind of Haig.

Signed by him and presented to the British Museum in 1920, the map shows the Western Front, a strip of land stretching from the North Sea coast to Switzerland, which formed the principal arena during World War One (1914–18). The line divides the Allied French, British and (from April 1917) United States forces to the west from the German army in the east. Rectangular shapes represent divisions (units of around 10,000 troops), which are grouped into armies. The British and Empire armies occupy the northern area of the front, with the French and American forces to the south.

This was how the Western Front armies lined up on 25 September 1918, the day before the Allied 'Hundred Days' offensive which broke the German defences and secured victory. This was a significant moment and every Allied general wanted their army to be the one to make the decisive breakthrough. Rivalry and reputation went hand in hand. Animosity existed between Haig and General John 'Black Jack' Pershing (1860–1948), commander of the United States troops. Pershing criticised the British Army as lacking in morale and determination, noting them as being demoralised and unsuitable for leading an attack (this was repeated in his autobiography of 1931). Such an accusation would have struck at the heart of their commanding officer.

Through this map Haig could argue the contrary. It showed clearly that it was the British 4th army that was facing the area around the St Quentin Canal where the German line was first breached on 29 September. That this breach was one of a number of Allied attacks which ultimately ushered in the Armistice is less important than the evidence of the map to refute Pershing's accusation and to uphold the reputation of Haig and the British Expeditionary Force.

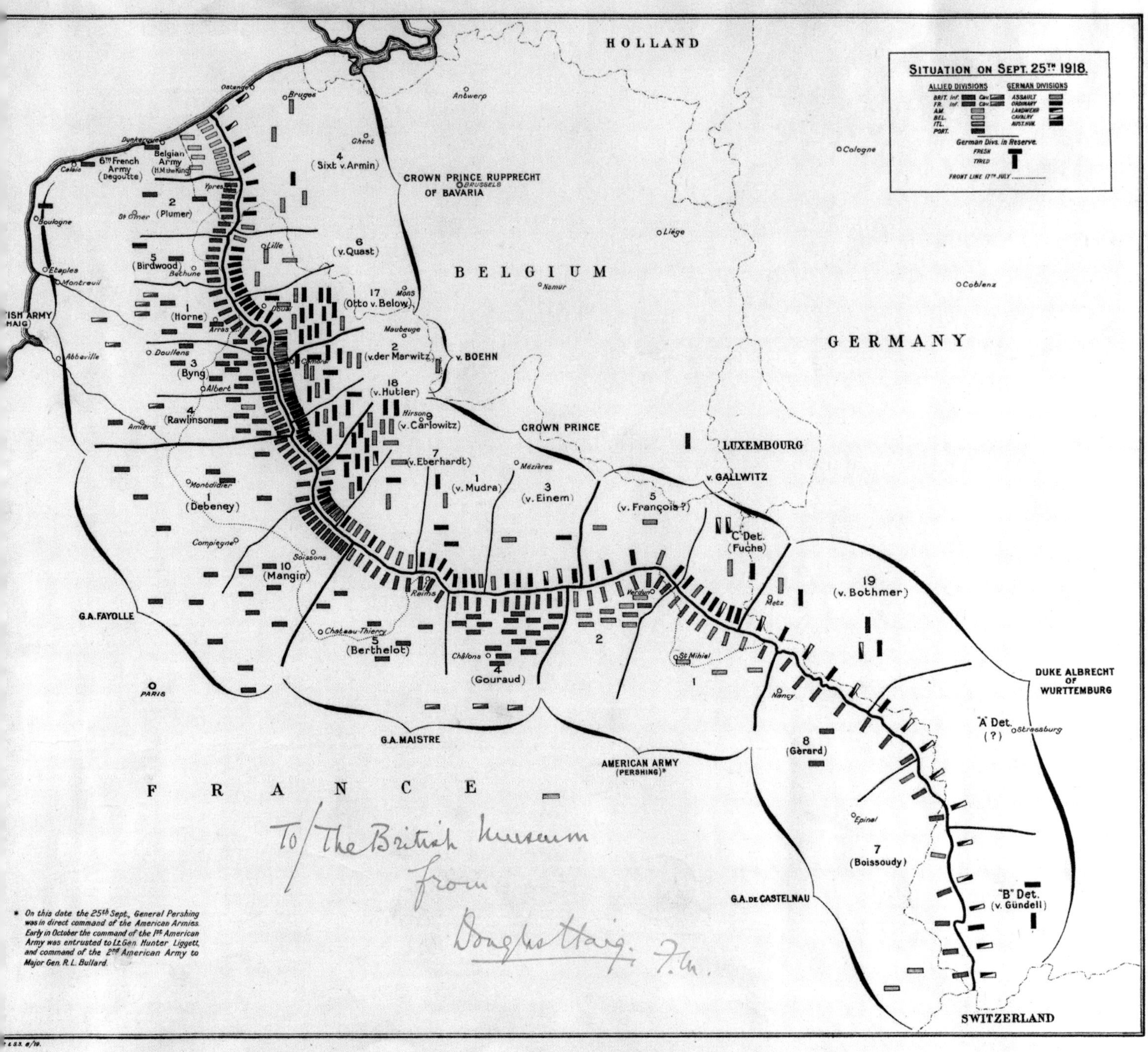

SITUATION ON SEPT. 25TH 1918.
ALLIED DIVISIONS
BRIT. Inf. Cav.
FR. Inf. Cav.
AM.
BEL.
ITL.
PORT.
GERMAN DIVISIONS
ASSAULT
ORDINARY
LANDWEHR
CAVALRY
AUST.HUN.
German Divs. in Reserve.
FRESH
TIRED
FRONT LINE 17TH JULY
HOLLAND
BELGIUM
GERMANY
LUXEMBOURG
FRANCE
SWITZERLAND
CROWN PRINCE RUPPRECHT OF BAVARIA
CROWN PRINCE
v. BOEHN
v. GALLWITZ
DUKE ALBRECHT OF WURTTEMBURG
G.A. FAYOLLE
G.A. MAISTRE
G.A. DE CASTELNAU
AMERICAN ARMY (PERSHING)*
6TH French Army (Degoutte)
Belgian Army (H.M. the King)
4 (Sixt v. Armin)
2 (Plumer)
6 (v. Quast)
5 (Birdwood)
17 (Otto v. Below)
1 (Horne)
2 (v. der Marwitz)
3 (Byng)
18 (v. Hutier)
4 (Rawlinson)
9 (v. Carlowitz)
7 (v. Eberhardt)
1 (v. Mudra)
3 (v. Einem)
1 (Debeney)
5 (v. François ?)
C Det. (Fuchs)
10 (Mangin)
19 (v. Bothmer)
5 (Berthelot)
4 (Gouraud)
2
1
"A" Det. (?)
8 (Gérard)
7 (Boissoudy)
"B" Det. (v. Gündell)
Ostende
Bruges
Antwerp
Ghent
Dunkerque
Calais
Ypres
BRUSSELS
Boulogne
St Omer
Lille
Cologne
Liège
Etaples
Montreuil
Béthune
Namur
Mons
Coblenz
Douai
Arras
Maubeuge
Abbeville
Doullens
Cambrai
Albert
Hirson
Amiens
Mézières
Montdidier
Compiègne
Soissons
Verdun
Metz
Reims
Chateau-Thierry
Châlons
St Mihiel
PARIS
Nancy
Strassburg
Epinal
* On this date the 25th Sept., General Pershing was in direct command of the American Armies. Early in October the command of the 1st American Army was entrusted to Lt. Gen. Hunter Liggett, and command of the 2nd American Army to Major Gen. R. L. Bullard.
To / The British Museum from Douglas Haig. F.M.

γ δ ε ς ζ η θ ι ια ιβ
μίνιος ποταμός
κλουνία κολωνία

Portugal

(c.1300)

The maps associated with Claudius Ptolemy, a second-century Greek geographer working in Alexandria in North Africa, are among the oldest we know about. These 'Ptolemaic maps' are derived from his work *Geographia* and usually consist of 26 regional maps of the regions of the ancient world. There are no Ptolemaic maps of America, Australia or anywhere much below the equator.

The story of Ptolemy's maps is complicated by the fact that although *Geographia* contained instructions on how to draw maps, no maps were originally included, and we aren't sure whether Ptolemy ever drew maps himself. What Ptolemy did do was collate a catalogue of places with co-ordinates – *Geographia* is a sort of gazetteer – and it is this information (along with his famous star catalogue, the *Almagest*) which was passed down over the centuries, from the Middle East and into Greece at the beginning of the fourteenth century. It was probably only at this point that scholars took the geographical lists and drew maps from them. One of the earliest of these Byzantine manuscripts is now in the Apostolic Library in the Vatican. The first printed version was published in Bologna, Italy, two centuries later.

The British Library has a number of hand-drawn versions of the *Geographia*, and the earliest is also the most intriguing. It is a 'fragment' of a once-complete manuscript consisting of 21 pages and maps of the world, the British Isles and half of a map of Portugal and Spain (illustrated here). The manuscript was probably produced in Constantinople (Istanbul) and once formed part of the library of the famous Vatopedi monastery on Mount Athos in Greece. During the sixteenth century it seems to have been in the collection of the scholar Nicolaos Sophianos (*c.*1500–51), but in around 1852 it was purchased by a Greek collector, dealer and sometime forger named Constantine Simonides (1820–90), who sold this portion of it to the British Museum the following year.

Despite its damaged appearance and patchy paintwork we can still make out the shape of Portugal and western Spain, with the Strait of Gibraltar at the bottom and various Atlantic islands to the left. The square castellated motifs are towns, only a few of which have been named. When Ptolemy compiled his *Geographia* Hispania was under the administration of the Roman Empire. In the early fourteenth century, when this map was drawn, the region remained at the western edge of the European world.

A Coruña, Spain

(1809)

In May 1808 British troops were sent to Portugal in support of Portuguese and loyalist Spanish forces against the invading French army. The Peninsular War (1808–14) was a struggle for Spanish independence and a distinct arena in the Napoleonic Wars (1803–15). The uncompromising terrain around the Portuguese and Spanish border was not well known to the British, and there was a lack of good maps of the area. In order to solve this problem the recently enlarged Quartermaster-General's Office (responsible for army logistics in the field) turned to the new and novel method of lithography to quickly produce clear maps.

Lithography was invented in 1796 by Alois Senefelder (1771–1834). It was far more expedient than intaglio printing from copper plates, for example, because instead of incising lines on to a plate, an impression was drawn on to a prepared stone (*litho* means stone in Latin). In 1807 promotors of Senefelder's invention visited the Quartermaster-General's Office at Horse Guards Parade in London, where a new Depôt of Military Knowledge had been assigned mapmaking duties four years earlier. Britain's first lithographic press was installed there, and the first map to roll off it was a map of Bantry Bay in southern Ireland, dated 1 May 1808.

That same year the Quartermaster-General, Sir George Murray (1772–1846), was sent to Portugal to organise the war campaign's logistics. Royal Staff Corps officers mapped roads and distances, provided itineraries, orders of march and plans of battles, collected topographical information and produced hand-drawn maps which were sent to London for printing and distribution. Around 50 maps followed the progress of the campaign as troops under Arthur Wellesley, Duke of Wellington (1769–1852) and Sir John Moore (1761–1809) pushed the French back into Spain. There, however, they were forced to retreat, fighting a rearguard action at the Battle of A Coruña on 16 January 1809 and successfully evacuating by sea.

This map was printed in London just ten days after the battle. It illustrates the British and French positions, the direction of British advances, and the hilly terrain around the port which caused both sides problems. The map provided military officials with a summary of the battle and would have been used for office reference. The experience during the Peninsular War, which culminated in the defeat of French forces at the Battle of Vittoria (21 June 1813), marked an important stage in the production of official British military mapping. The Quartermaster-General's Office also mapped domestic situations such as the Peterloo Massacre in Manchester of 1819. The map production of the Quartermaster-General's Office was assimilated by that of the Topographical and Statistical Depôt following the Crimean War (1853–56) in 1857.

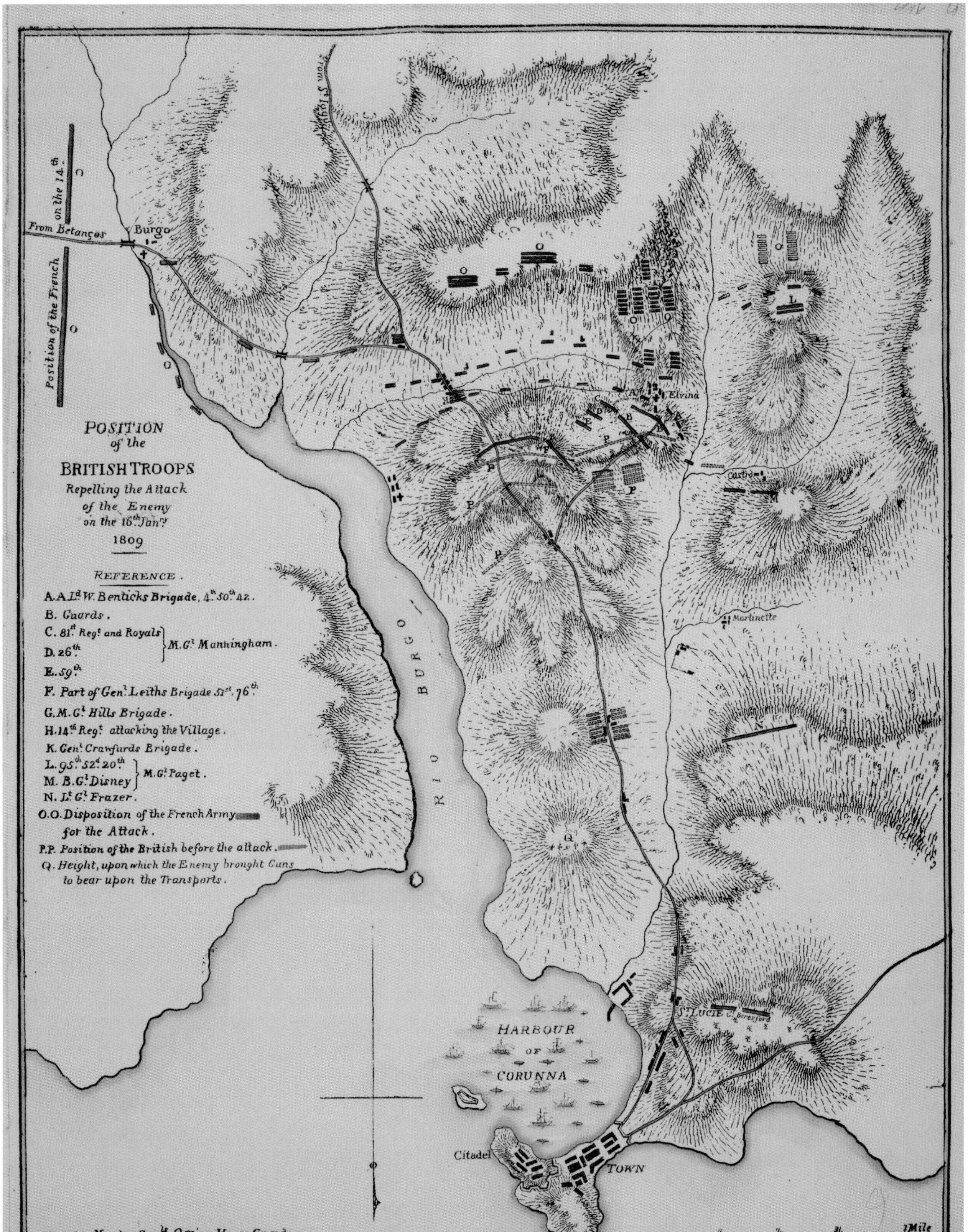

From Betanços
Burgo
Position of the French on the 14th
From St Iago
Elvina
Castro
Martinette
RIO BURGO
POSITION of the BRITISH TROOPS Repelling the Attack of the Enemy on the 16th Jan.ry 1809
REFERENCE.
A.A. Ld W. Bentick's Brigade, 4th 50th 42.
B. Guards.
C. 81st Regt and Royals } M.Gl Manningham.
D. 26th
E. 59th
F. Part of Genl Leiths Brigade 51st. 76th.
G. M.Gl Hills Brigade.
H. 14th Regt attacking the Village.
K. Genl Crawfurds Brigade.
L. 95th 52d 20th } M.Gl Paget.
M. B.Gl Disney
N. Lt Gl Frazer.
O.O. Disposition of the French Army for the Attack.
P.P. Position of the British before the attack.
Q. Height, upon which the Enemy brought Guns to bear upon the Transports.
HARBOUR OF CORUNNA
St LUCIE
Citadel
TOWN
1 Mile
Quarter Master Genl's Office Horse Guards Jan.ry 26th 1809

Italy

(c.1255)

The diagrammatic way in which this map shows a route as a line passing through a sequence of places is easily recognisable to a modern audience. The same clear and straightforward method appears in some motoring atlases and online route planners. This map, however, was drawn nearly eight centuries ago, showing how aspects of eras separated from each other by a great expanse of time can occasionally align in unpredictable ways.

This is one of the middle sections of a road between London and the Holy Land. The four strips are designed to be read from bottom to top and from left to right. We join the road as it passes through southeast France, over the Saône and Rhône Rivers at Lyon, and into Italy. Towns such as Turin, Cremona and Bologna are illustrated as detailed symbols, and there is sufficient variation between them to suggest the mapmaker knew what they looked like. Rivers, mountains, seas and occasional alternative routes are shown. This map wasn't intended to be taken on such a journey. Rather, we think that it was intended to act as a sort of visual guide for monks in the monastery of St Albans in Hertfordshire, where it was created around 1255. Such a guide would have helped its viewers meditate on the long and difficult journey as a form of virtual pilgrimage.

The map is included in a manuscript known as the 'Historia Anglorum', a history of England from the Norman Conquest by the Benedictine monk and chronicler Matthew Paris. A number of Paris's manuscripts survive in collections in the UK and Ireland, and they contain illustrations of animals, historical scenes, royal portraits and even a self-portrait. It is the maps, however, which impress with their originality. Road maps already existed by the thirteenth century, and Paris may have had a Roman map to work with, but the ribbon format is not known elsewhere until it was adopted by John Ogilby (1600–76) for his 1675 road atlas *Britannia*.

The diagrammatic nature of Paris's route maps is easier to understand as the product of an era in which the written word was more powerful than the drawn image. Look again at the itinerary and consider that it is simply a series of place names, correctly positioned in relation to each other, and linked by lines. It is a word diagram with some additional pictorial embellishment. Even Paris's maps of the British Isles are essentially word diagrams with coasts drawn around them. A modern map on the same lines is the 1932 London Underground map by Harry Beck. Paris's method of working anticipated an era in which maps had to be stripped down to their essential elements in order to function quickly and efficiently.

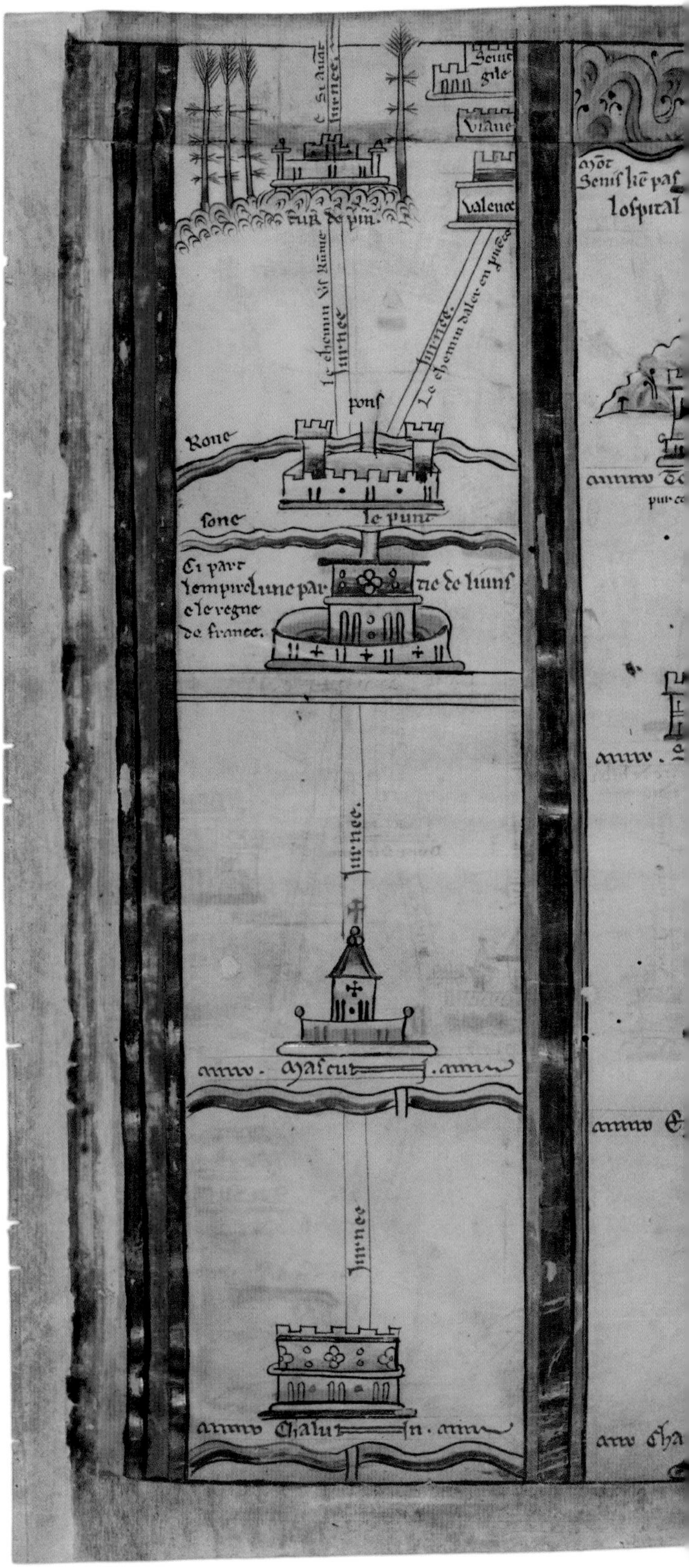

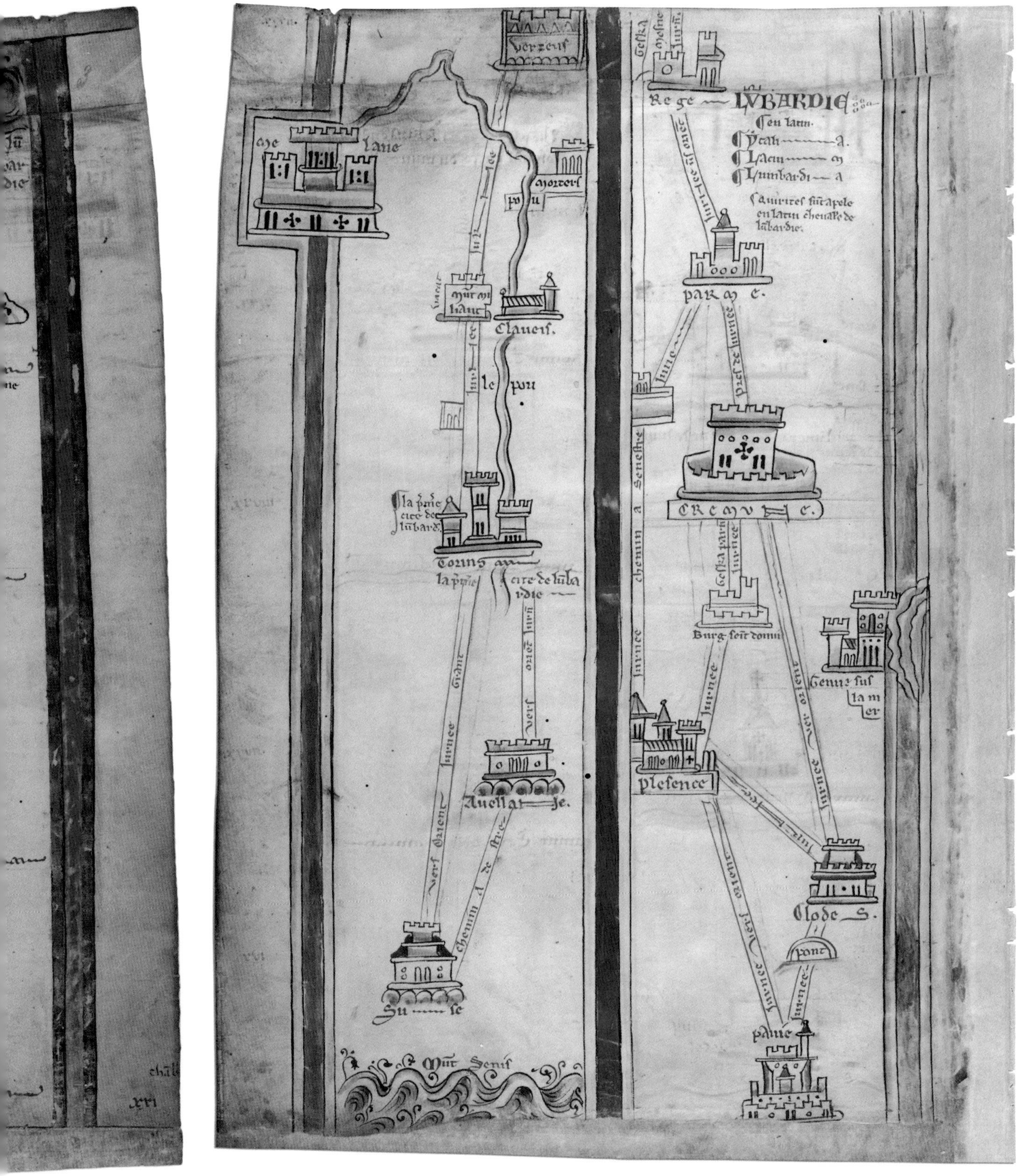

Verzeus
LVBARDIE
Clauers
le pou
Plesence
pont

Lucca, Italy

(1744 or 1745)

George III's Topographical Collection of maps and views is an important reminder of the synergy between what today are misleadingly divided between science (maps) and art (views). One effect of the utilitarian perception of map collections was that their artistic contents escaped the attention of art historians. Until a few decades ago this was the case with a set of four drawings of the Italian town of Lucca, drawn 1744–1745 by the landscape artist Bernardo Bellotto (1721–80).

Bellotto was primarily known as a student of Giovanni Antonio Canal, called Canaletto (1697–1768), but in recent decades he has emerged from the shadow of his more famous uncle and teacher. Not only has the perception of him as a mere imitator of Canaletto given way to a better appreciation of his individual qualities as an artist, but works previously attributed to Canaletto, including these drawings, have been reattributed to him.

After training in his uncle's workshop in Venice, but prior to his departure for northern Europe in 1747, Bellotto spent some years creating views (known as *vedute*) of various northern Italian cities.

His visit to Lucca occurred in 1744 or 1745. There he sketched the principal vistas including the cathedral and Piazza San Martino (the drawing on the right) as preparation for the oil painting now in York City Art Gallery (in which we can see what the art historian Charles Beddington described as Bellotto's 'scraped icing-sugar' clouds). F.J.B. Watson, writing in 1953, first identified the drawings as by Bellotto on account of the 'floppy headgear' of the people and the 'blobby' foliage, which had 'no exact parallel in Canaletto's drawings'.

Looking at this drawing we can appreciate how the sparingly applied brown inked lines create a view of real depth and distance. Virtuoso sketched areas, such as the large circular window of the church in the extreme left, enliven the straightforward architectural details such as the façade of the cathedral. Bellotto probably did not sketch this entirely from life, sitting in the piazza with his sketchbook. It was pointed out by Stefan Kozakiewicz that the cathedral tower is one storey shorter than it is in reality, using this to argue that Bellotto drew or at least completed it in his studio. It has also been suggested that Bellotto might have traced the image, which he could have created using a camera obscura or pinhole camera. In art as in cartography, virtuosity and practicality went hand in hand.

Landeskarte der Schweiz 1:25000
Zermatt
Zermatt
Unt. Gabelhorn
Oberrothorn
Unterrothorn
Breithorn
Klein Matterhorn
Theodulhorn
Furgghorn
Testa Grigia
Roccia Nera
Gobba di Rollin
Zwillinge
Castor
Felikhorn
Stockhorn
Gornergrat
I T A L I A
1:25000

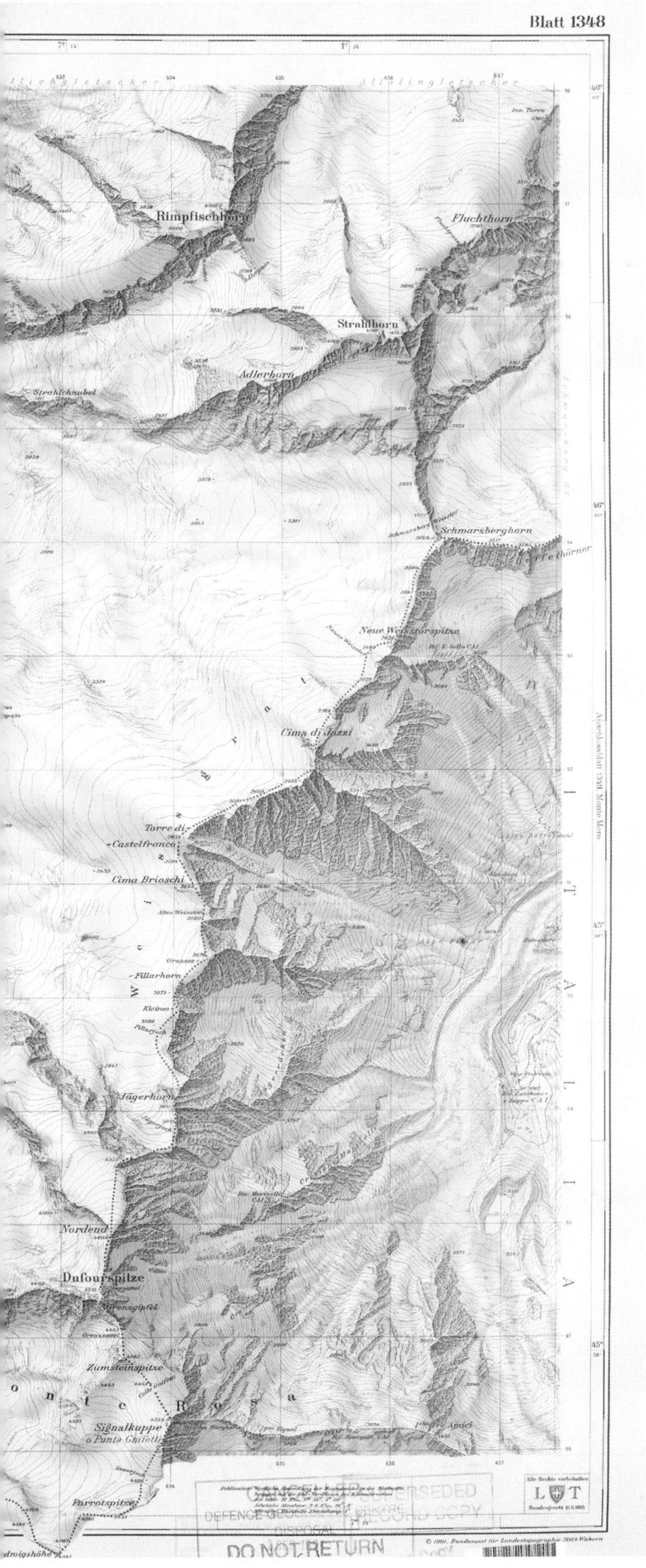

Zermatt, Switzerland

(1991)

Of all maps drawn on flat surfaces, the *Carte national de Suisse* (*Landseskarte der Schweiz* in German) comes closest to achieving the impossible goal of recreating the three-dimensional world on a two-dimensional surface. Because of this, as well as for its balanced and coherent design, it is often cited as the professional cartographer's favourite map. The *Carte national de Suisse* also unites those aspects of maps which we have been conditioned to view as polar opposites: the practical and the beautiful.

Switzerland's national topographical map is a series covering the Swiss state at various scales down to 1:25,000. Typically for a national map it was first inaugurated during the 1840s, at a time when European nation states were beginning to assume their modern identities.

Living among mountains made the Swiss especially good at mapping them. Guillaume Henri Dufour's (1787–1875) official map of Switzerland of 1845–65 was one of the first to convincingly capture the mountainous alpine territory. Dufour showed relief using a technique known as shadow hachuring, whereby tiny engraved lines were used to shade one side of a mountain, giving it definition and depth.

Over the nineteenth and twentieth centuries there were significant developments in the surveying and depiction of terrain. Aerial photography greatly facilitated the surveying process, while contour lines – ringed lines placed at increasing height intervals – became the preferred scientific method of recording terrain on maps. Unfortunately, contours cease to work for sheer or vertical heights such as rock faces (of which the Swiss Alps has many), because vertical height increase does not permit gaps between contour lines. The Swiss Topographical Bureau solved this problem by combining different methods, including the addition of rock drawing to represent rock forms and the steep faces of mountains. Though this form of drawing was rigidly developed, it added an element of naturalism and visual complexity to the maps.

Stepping back and looking at this sheet showing Zermatt and the Dufourspitze mountain (named after Dufour) and printed in 1991, it is possible to imagine for a moment that you are suspended high in the air looking down on the real thing. There is such tangible and illusionistic three-dimensionality that the glacier seems literally to burst free of the map's lower border.

Germany

(1500)

This grubby and unassuming piece of paper contains one of the greatest landmarks in the history of cartography. How deceptive appearances can be.

It is the first printed road map and the earliest map produced specifically for travellers. Published in Nuremberg in 1500 by Erhard Etzlaub (*c.*1455–1532), the south-oriented map shows a portion of Europe between Poland and eastern France, and Scotland and southern Italy. Hundreds of towns are marked along with rivers, mountain ranges and – key to the map – a series of dotted lines which converge on Rome. All roads lead to the Eternal City, the centre of Christianity in Europe and a place of pilgrimage. This map was made for the thousands of mainly northern Europeans who planned to travel to Rome to mark the jubilee year of 1500, one and a half thousand years after the birth of Christ. Its title is *Das ist der Rom Weg von Meylen zu Meylen* ('This is the way to Rome from mile to mile').

The map would have provided inspired guidance for the large numbers of people travelling beyond their localities, many surely for the first time. To begin with, the eight dotted routes leading from northern cities do not merely mark the way. Each dot is placed one German mile apart (around seven and a half kilometres) so that pilgrims would know how far they had travelled and how far they had to go. Additionally, marks in the map's left and right borders give the number of daylight hours available during the longest day at each latitude, which would have helped with planning and indicated when it was time to find somewhere to sleep. At the bottom of the map is a circular diagram which the traveller could align with a compass in order to help them decide which direction to take. All of this was explained by Etzlaub in clear vernacular German text.

Etzlaub was a scientific instrument maker based in one of the centres of Renaissance science. His expertise is evident from his map, yet it also displayed his keen business acumen. The map was surely a phenomenal bestseller, and we know this despite the fact that we know of only ten examples today. Through close inspection of these examples, former British Library map librarian Tony Campbell found minor but multiple differences between them. He concluded that this must have occurred through the deterioration of the woodblock used to print them, which could only have been caused by extensive and repeated use. You'd have to do a lot of printing to wear down a piece of wood. The *Rom Weg* must once have been as common as an AA route guide.

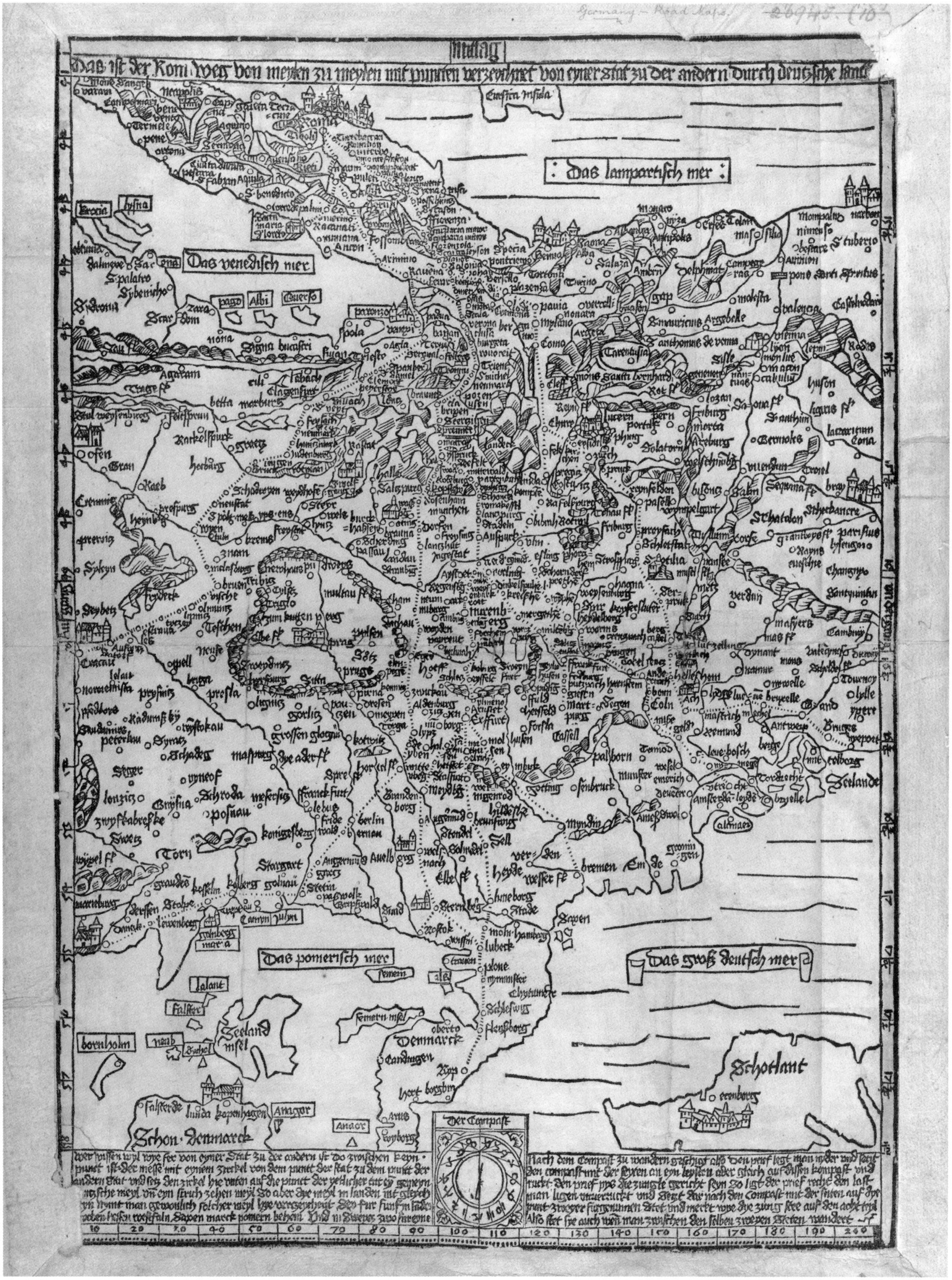
Mittag
Das ist der Rom weg von meylen zu meylen mit puncten verzeichnet von eyner stat zu der andern durch deutzsche lant
Das lampartisch mer
Das venedisch mer
Das pomerisch mer
Das groß deutsch mer
Schotlant
Zeeland insel
Denmarck
Schon denmarck
bornholm
Der Compast

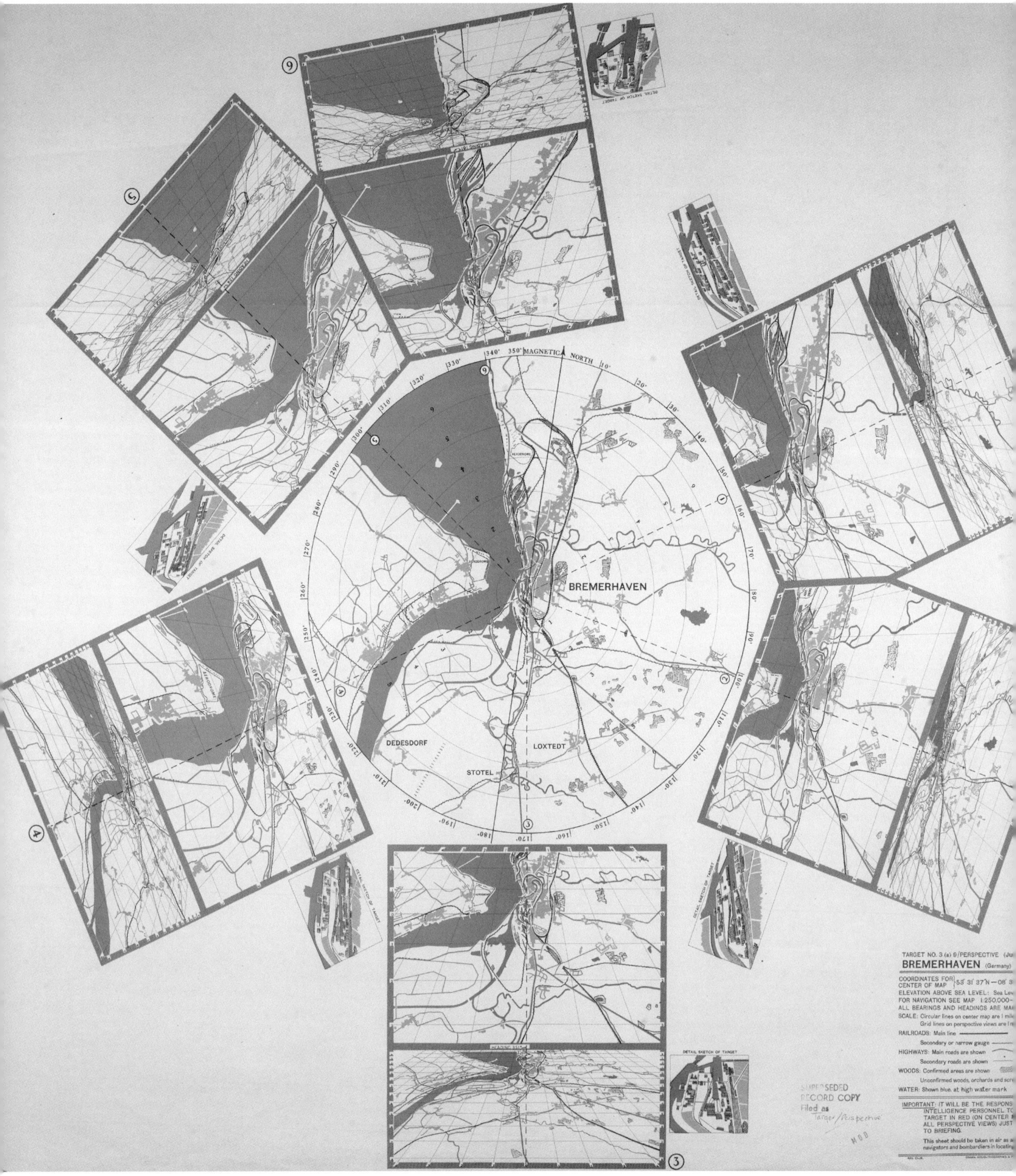
MAGNETIC NORTH
BREMERHAVEN
DEDESDORF
LOXTEDT
STOTEL
DETAIL SKETCH OF TARGET
TARGET NO. 3 (a) 9/PERSPECTIVE (Ju
BREMERHAVEN (Germany)
COORDINATES FOR CENTER OF MAP 53° 31′ 37″N — 08° 3
ELEVATION ABOVE SEA LEVEL: Sea Lev
FOR NAVIGATION SEE MAP 1:250,000-
ALL BEARINGS AND HEADINGS ARE MA
SCALE: Circular lines on center map are 1 mil
Grid lines on perspective views are I
RAILROADS: Main line
Secondary or narrow gauge
HIGHWAYS: Main roads are shown
Secondary roads are shown
WOODS: Confirmed areas are shown
Unconfirmed woods, orchards and scr
WATER: Shown blue. at high water mark
IMPORTANT: IT WILL BE THE RESPONS
INTELLIGENCE PERSONNEL T
TARGET IN RED (ON CENTER
ALL PERSPECTIVE VIEWS) JUST
TO BRIEFING.
This sheet should be taken in air as a
navigators and bombardiers in locatin
SUPERSEDED
RECORD COPY
Filed as

Bremerhaven, Germany

(1943)

This astonishing map of the town of Bremerhaven, with its clean crisp lines and its impressive aerial perspectives, is like an image from the future. In fact, it was produced in 1943 during World War Two (1939–45), one of hundreds of target perspective maps made for airborne Allied daylight bombing raids on German cities.

'Strategic bombing' raids were launched on German industrial and infrastructural targets such as factories, railways and docks, as well as military targets, by RAF Bomber Command from 1940, and by the 8th American Air Force from 1943, with the intention of disrupting Germany's war effort and the flow of civilian life. German raids on British towns (the Blitz) began in August 1940, for which special Luftwaffe *Sonderfolgen* booklets containing maps and aerial photographs were produced for navigators.

Daylight raids offered bombers the greatest chances of finding and hitting their targets, but aircraft simultaneously became easier targets themselves. The target perspective maps, also known as 'Geerlings maps' after their inventor, American Air Force Captain Gerald Geerlings (1897–1998), were designed to make target identification as efficient as possible. They were not to be taken into the air for fear of capture, so navigators had to memorise what they showed.

This map is centred on the docks of Bremerhaven, the port of the city of Bremen, one of Germany's crucial North Sea ports (and a port of embarkation for the returning American army after the war's end) and shows the typical layout of the maps. A circular map with the target at its centre is surrounded by a series of rectangular oblique perspective views of the area. These were calculated to correspond with views from the window of an aircraft approaching at different bearings. Large-scale sketches of the port have been placed in between. The simple, clear use of colour was designed to avoid any confusion in the mind of the navigator: the window of opportunity was short.

How were these astonishing perspective viewpoints arrived at? The answer is by a high level of intelligence in the form of aerial photography, which was transposed into map form using mathematical calculations, photographic transfer techniques and painfully precise penmanship. It is the quality of the drawing which places them years ahead of their time, and they are arguably on a par with the most sophisticated digital images. Geerlings was an architectural draftsman, artist and printmaker who produced striking images of New York City in the 1970s and 1980s.

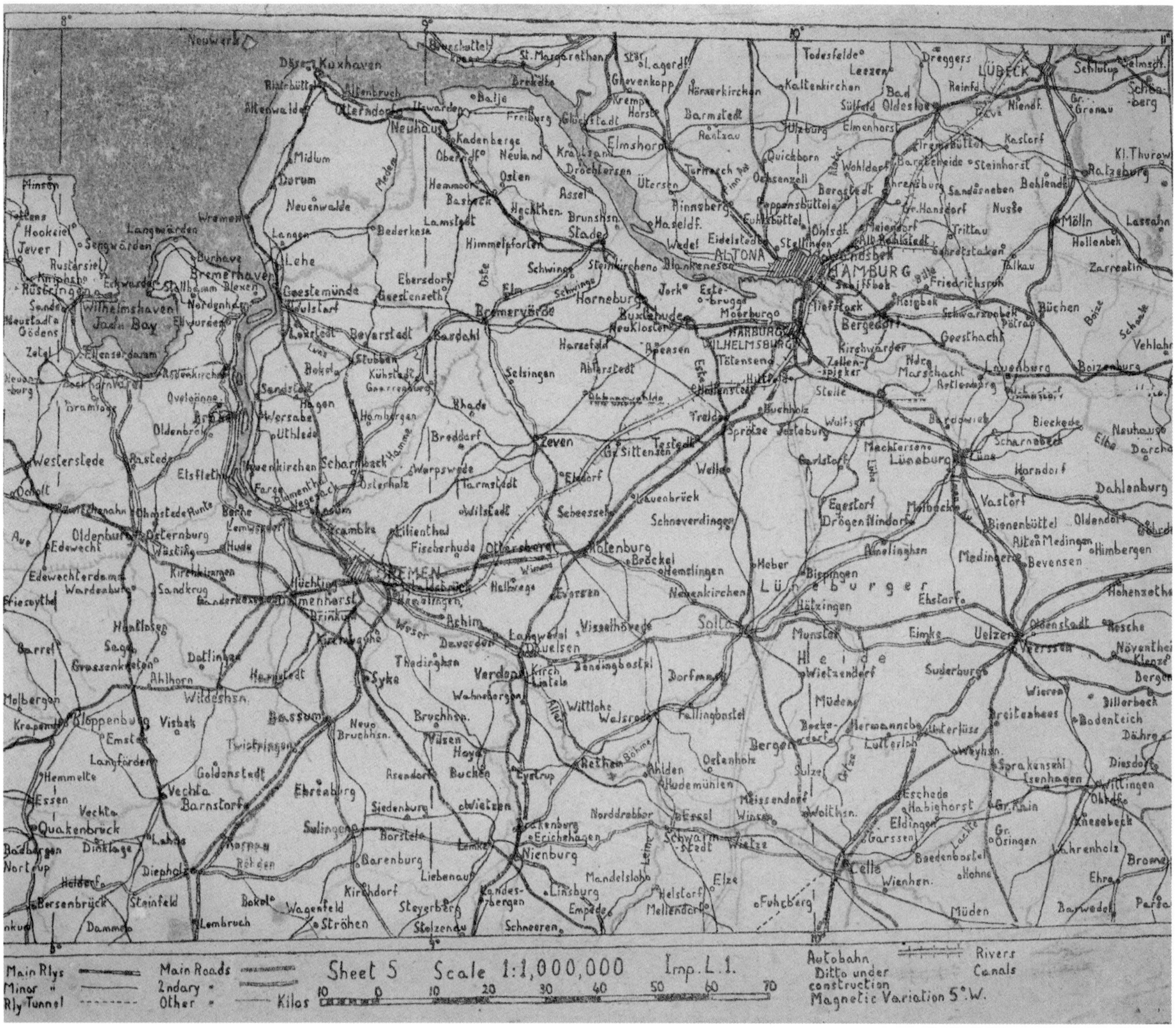

Querum, Germany

(1944)

Imagine you are a British prisoner of war (POW) in a camp near Braunschweig, in Germany, in 1944. Adolf Hitler has survived an assassination attempt and the war threatens to lurch into dangerous anarchy. Your days are spent between boredom and apprehension of what might happen to you, so you resolve to make some maps to help you escape.

The story of the secret British wartime mapping project has been compellingly told by the historian Barbara Bond. With the help of Waddingtons, the board game company, the mapmakers John Bartholomew & Son and the British special intelligence department MI9, a programme of escape and espionage map manufacture was established. Maps of parts of Germany were printed on to thin paper or silk and hidden in chess pieces and packs of cards to be smuggled into POW camps by organisations such as the Red Cross. Among the most famous is the map which enabled the British soldier Airey Neave (1916–79) to find his way across the German–Swiss border to safety after escaping from Colditz Castle in 1942.

Of the various tales of ingenuity and derring-do, one of the most irresistible is the story of two POWs named Philip Evans (1917–1992) and Wallis Heath (1916–2003), who were held from 1944 in a camp

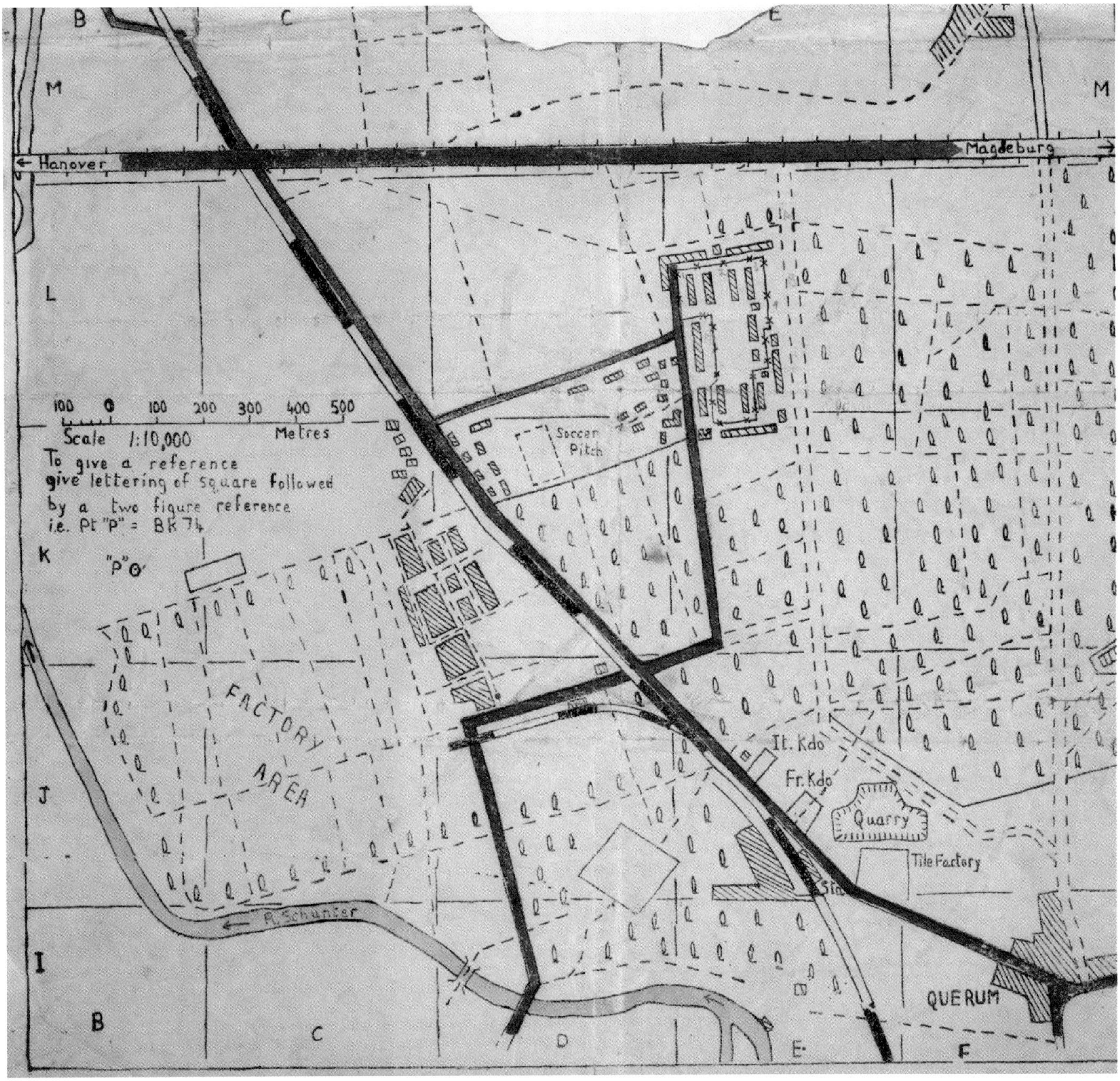

in Querum. They realised that the single maps smuggled in to them would not help an entire camp to escape, so they created their own printing press to reproduce the maps they had illicitly received, right under the noses of their captors.

These maps were eventually donated to the British Library by the heirs of Philip Evans, together with Evans's account of the whole clever process. The printing plates were sourced from roof tiles from a bombed building, the printing press was created out of floorboards, and the ink roller was made from a window bar. To make the ink, dirt was scraped from between paving slabs, boiled then mixed with margarine and pigment. Despite their being discovered and punished (with five days' solitary confinement), an astonishing 500 copies of four different maps of the vicinity of the camp were produced at different scales.

It isn't the content, skill or even artistry of these maps which make them worthy of praise. It is the circumstances surrounding their production, the light it sheds on a pivotal moment in twentieth-century history, and the ingenuity shown by a few people against significant odds.

The Low Countries

(1650–c.1720)

The Beudeker Atlas is a love letter by its compiler, the Amsterdam map collector Christoffel Beudeker (1675–1756), to his beloved country of the Netherlands and the city of Amsterdam. It is a compendious set of 24 (out of an original 27) volumes of printed and hand-drawn images relating to Belgium, the Netherlands and Luxembourg. There are over 2,500 maps, views, prints, scientific instrument engravings, genealogical tables, portraits and historical, allegorical and contemporary scenes dating from the late sixteenth to early nineteenth centuries, celebrating the region's illustrious past.

The atlas is a composite or 'extra illustrated' set of volumes formed largely between 1718 and 1749 by dis-binding and rearranging the contents of various books, principally Joan Blaeu's (1596–1673) Netherlands town atlas of 1649 and the relevant part of his *Atlas Maior* of 1662, together with separately issued material. The volumes are arranged by province and town, with additional volumes dedicated to general maps of the Low Countries, Dutch palaces and portraits of important figures. Complementing the atlas's impressive scale of conception is the quality of the prints, and in particular their spectacular colouring, which was applied by professional artists.

The atlas's many highlights include the 1650 *Leo Belgicus* (lion of Belgium) by Nicolaes Visscher (1618–79), a metamorphic map which shows a defiant lion superimposed on to the Seventeen United Provinces. The *Leo Belgicus* maps were invented by Michael von Aitzing (*c.*1530–98) in 1584 and originally functioned as a symbol of Dutch national consciousness and opposition to Habsburg rule, though some looked back nostalgically to the days when the North and South Netherlands had been united. Further highlights are battle scenes engraved by Romeyn de Hooghe, including the 1695 Siege of Namur during the Nine Years' War (1688–97) between the Dutch Republic and France (illustrated on the frontispiece of this atlas). The scene's sophisticated arrangement creates a swirling maelstrom of animated action.

The prints of Dutch palaces with their formal gardens (called 'Lusthoven' overleaf) are the true stars of the show, filling three volumes and showcasing Dutch Baroque culture at its most impressive. In the engravings of the palaces of Honselaarsdijk by Balthazar Florisz. van Berckenrode (1591–1645) from around 1640, and Huis ten Bosch by Anna Beeck (*fl.*1693–1717), we can see the principal elements of the gardens: carefully proportioned spaces designed to look like theatre sets, contrasts between formal and wild elements, classical references and inspired water features (the Dutch excelled in drainage and land reclamation). The gardens often contained political and allegorical messages.

It was partly in order to celebrate the splendour of these spaces that Beudeker constructed his atlas. Alongside other Dutch atlas collections of similar scale and conception, such as the *Atlas van der Hem* and *Atlas der Neederlanden*, it is a sublime monument to the culture of the Low Countries.

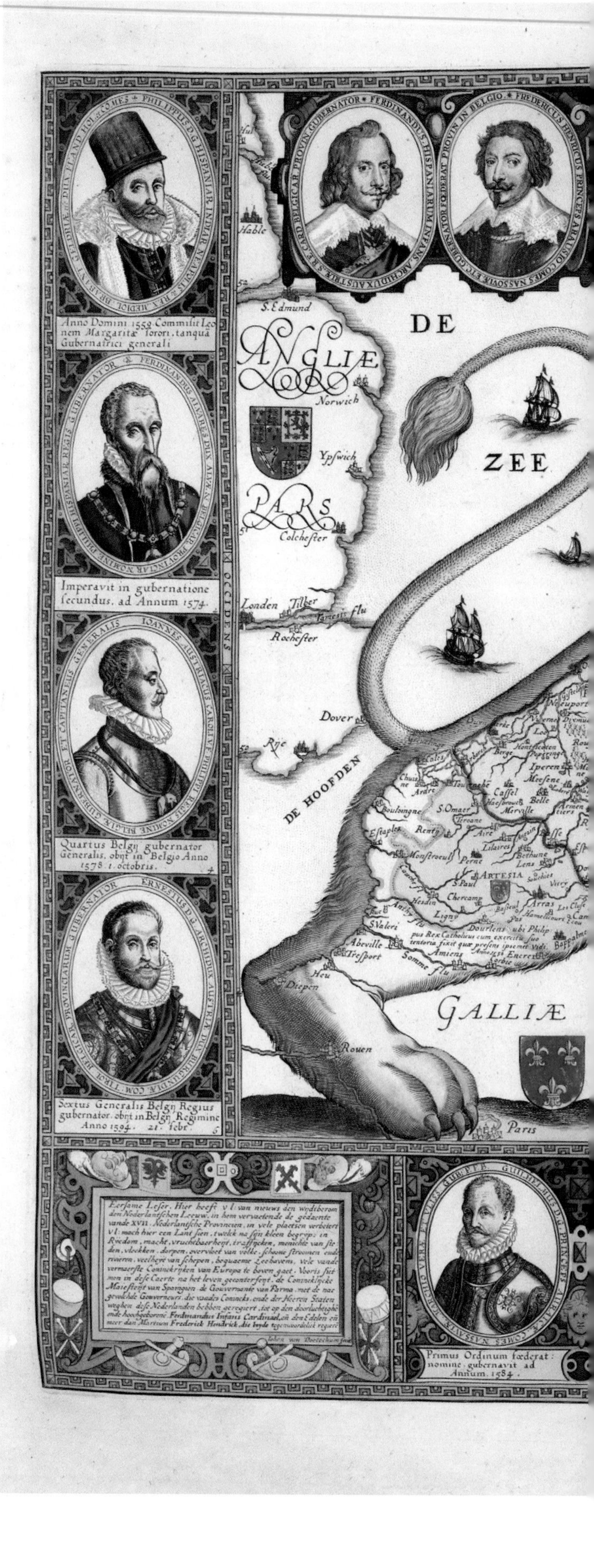

BEL
US
GER
MA NIÆ
PARS.
PARS
Artificiosa et Geographica tabula sub Leonis figura XVII inferioris Germaniæ Provincias repræsentans, cui addita sunt singularum insignia, una cum ordinaria Præfecturarum distinctione, Longè elimatius quam hactenus unquam expressa. Accesserunt & icones Gubernatorum Generaliũ qui utrinque Belgium, Gubernarunt.
Scala Milli: Germanic:
Catalogus Civitatum Pagorumq in singulis Provinciis
Gubernavit Leonem nomine Philippi fratris, ad Annũ 1567.
Tertius in gubernando Leone Belgico, obijt Anno 1576. 5.a Martij. in Belgio.
Quintus Regis Hispaniæ in Belgio Gubernator, gubernavit ad Annum 1592
Septimus Regius Belgij Generalis Gubernator gubernavit ad Annum 1621.
Palatium Bruxellense
Palatium Comitũ Holland
Vißcher Excudit Anno 1650
Ordinum fœderatorum nomine gubernavit. ab Anno 1586. ad Annum. 1588.
Ordinum fœderatorum nomine gubernavit ab Anno 1587 ad Annum 1625.
Ami Lecteur. Nous te presentons ici de nouveau Le tres-renommé Lion des Pays bas, comprenant en soy La figure des XVII Provinces, corrigé en Lieux infinis. Tu vois ici vn pays, qui au regard de son petit enclos, en richesses puissance, fertilité, trafique, grand nombre de villes, bourgades, et villages, abondance du peuple, et quantite innombrable de bateux, ports maritimes, surmonte plusieurs des plus renommez Royaumes de L'Europe. En oultre peut on veoir dans ceste carte Les pourtraitures de sa Maiesté d'Espagne et de La Gouvernante de Parma & d'aultres Gouverneurs suivans, contrefaits au vif, tant de ceux qui au nom dudit Roy comme aussi sous L'autorité de Mes Seigneurs Les Estats des Provinces Unies ont gouverné ces Pays bas, iusques au Tresillustre Ferdinand Hisp. Infant. & Le tres-noble. et plus que Martial F. Henric. Lesquels pour Le present en tiennent Le gouvernement.

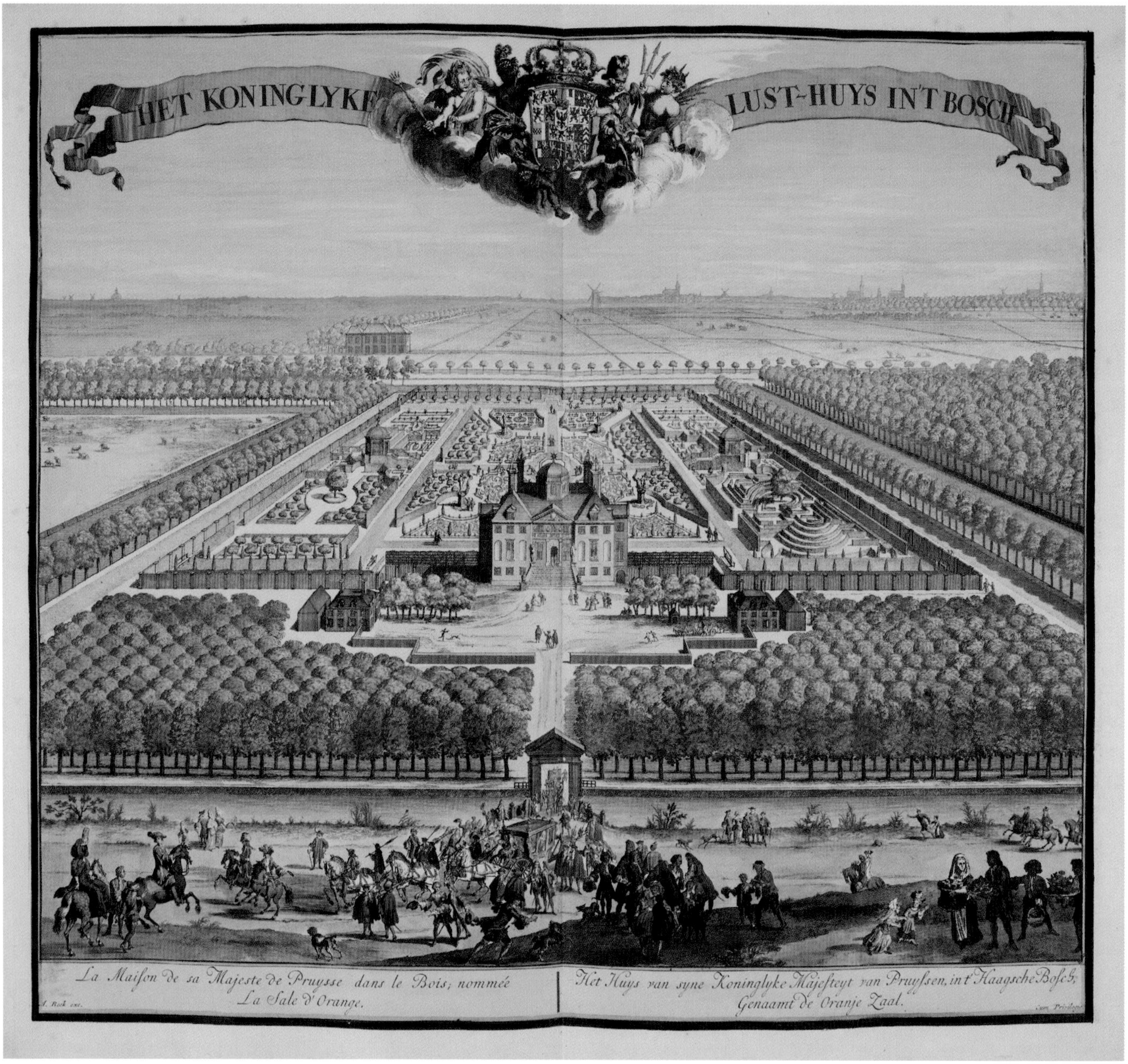
HET KONINGLYKE LUST-HUYS IN'T BOSCH
La Maison de sa Majeste de Pruysse dans le Bois, nommée
La Sale d'Orange.
Het Huys van syne Koninglyke Majesteyt van Pruyssen, in t' Haagsche Bosch,
Genaamt de Oranje Zaal.

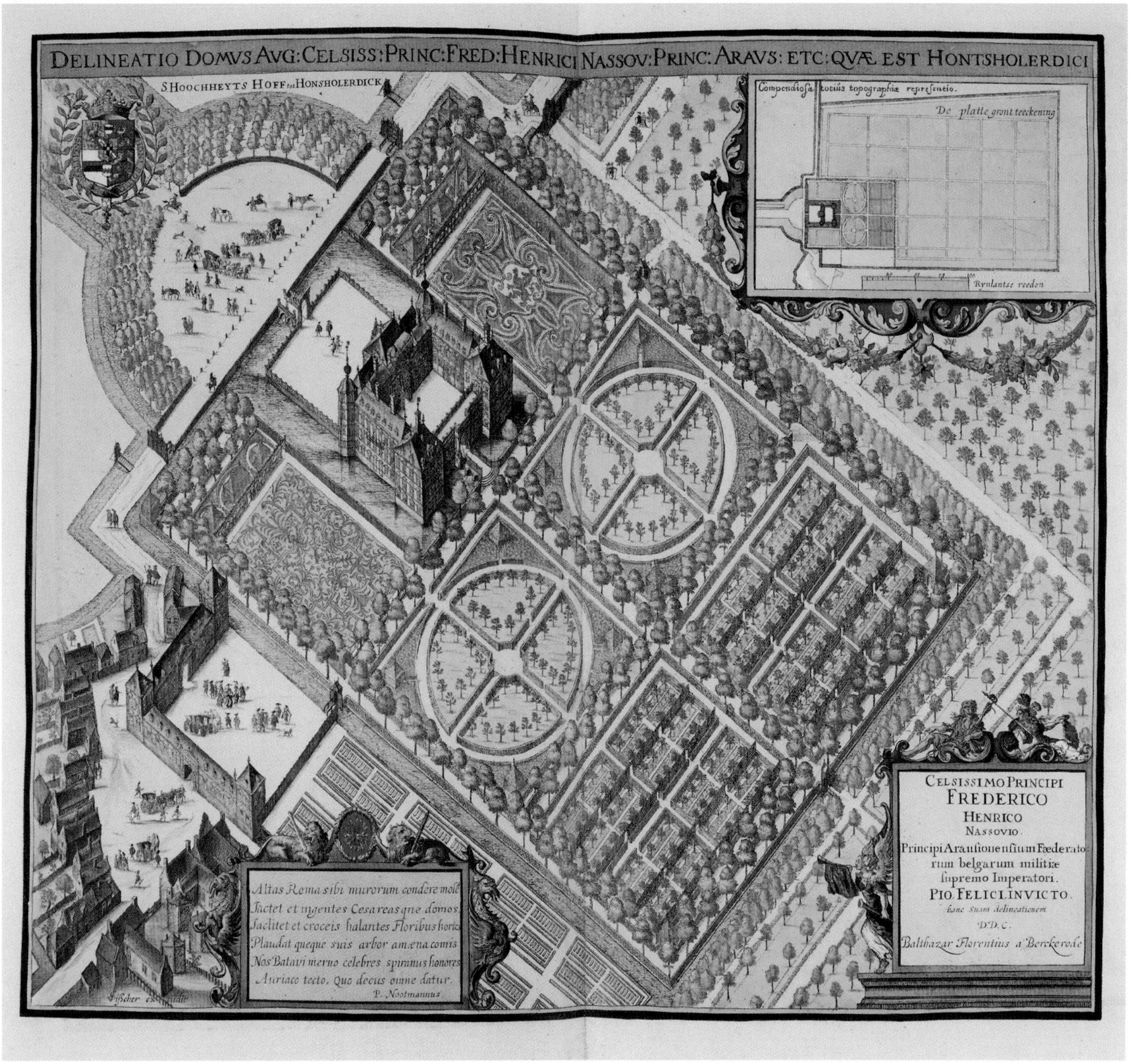
DELINEATIO DOMVS AVG: CELSISS: PRINC: FRED: HENRICI NASSOV: PRINC: ARAVS: ETC: QVÆ EST HONTSHOLERDICI
S HOOCHHEYTS HOFF tot HONSHOLERDICK
Compendiosa totius topographiæ representio.
De platte gront teeckening
Rynlantse roeden
CELSISSIMO PRINCIPI
FREDERICO
HENRICO
NASSOVIO
Principi Arausionensium Fœderatorum belgarum militiæ supremo Imperatori.
PIO. FELICI. INVICTO.
hanc Suam delineationem
D.D.C.
Balthazar Florentius a Berckerode
Altas Roma sibi murorum condere moles
Iactet et ingentes Cesareasque domos
Iactitet et croceis halantes Floribus hortos
Plaudat queque suis arbor amæna comis
Nos Batavi merito celebres spiramus honores
Auriaco tecto. Quo decus omne datur.
P. Nootmannus

Ypres, Belgium

(1917)

Among the extraordinary feats of mapping on the Western Front in World War One (1914–18), which included the first systematic aerial observations and printing of maps on the battlefield, are the relief maps known as 'Haig Models'. These hand-crafted models, named after the set used by the commander-in-chief of the British Army, Douglas Haig, now in the Royal Military Academy at Sandhurst, are an achievement as much for the labour involved in their construction as for their historical value.

From 1915 a more realistic and helpful strategic map of the Western Front was required for the British Army command, whose headquarters were stationed well behind the front line. The nature of trench warfare, in which two opposing sides dug lines of defences separated by a 'No-Man's Land', made elevation particularly important. Even the slightest increase in height could give the advantage to one side.

When the Western Front was formed at the end of 1914 the Germans occupied the most commanding spots. Terrain was a decisive feature of the battlefield, but the British Army's trench maps did not capture this feature adequately enough, even with contours and spot heights. So the Ordnance Survey set about creating three-dimensional models. In order to do it, they took 1:20,000-scale trench maps and, using a knife, cut around the contours and stuck them on to thick cardboard of the same shape, reassembling them and gradually building up a three-dimensional map of the area (with a vertical exaggeration of between 4:1 and 9:1). This was done for every trench map at that scale, covering the entirety of the British section of the Western Front from the North Sea to Lyon south of Paris, making an interlocking set of over 100 maps.

This map from the British Library's set shows the area around the Ypres Salient in Belgium, the scene of some of the war's most vicious and prolonged fighting. The town of Ypres was held obstinately by the British throughout the war, with the German army's high-ground locations virtually encircling it. Some of the other models show signs of use, having been annotated and drawn on, or had pins stuck in them to represent troop positions. In their attempt to create a more realistic impression in the minds of the military decision makers, the mapmakers, like the infantry troops on the front line, made a valiant effort.

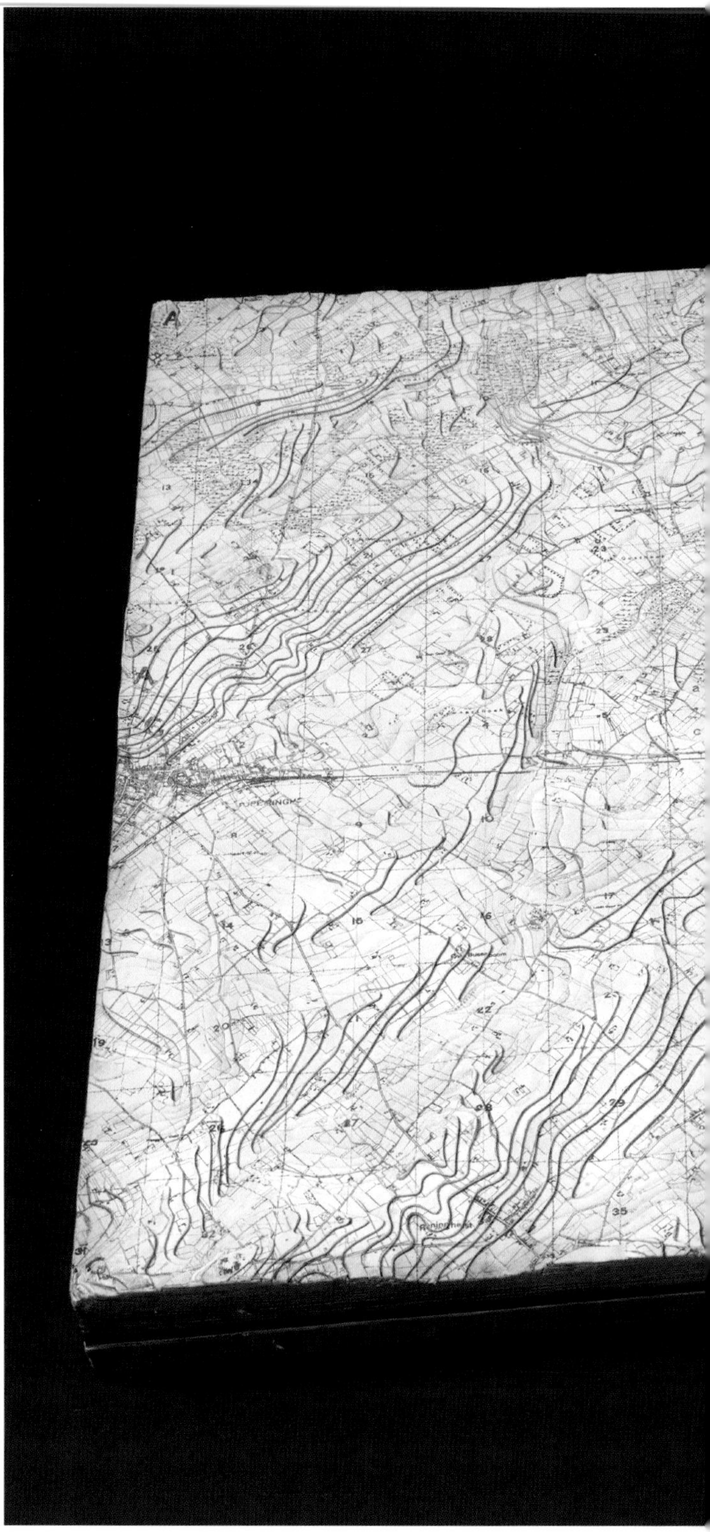

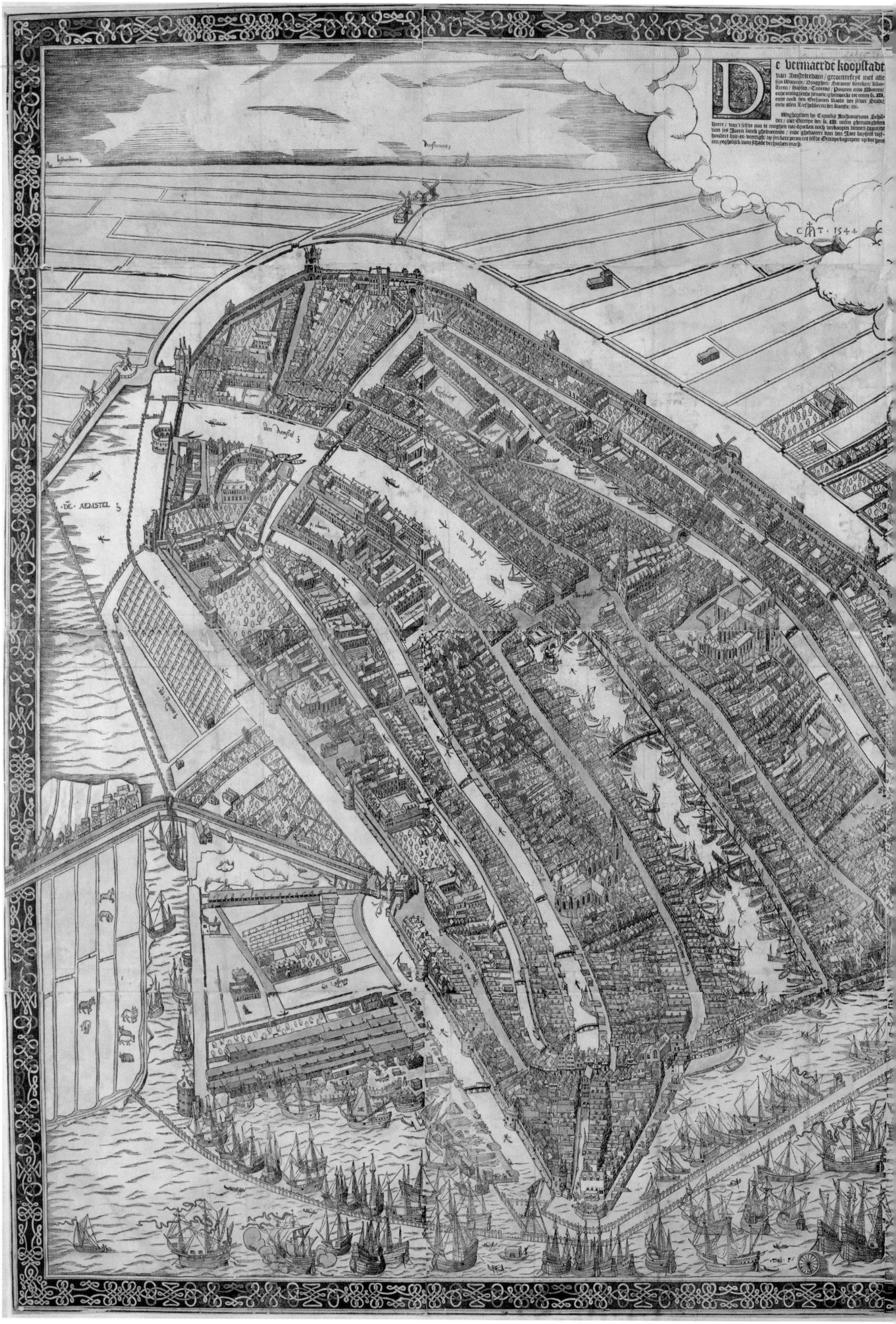
De vermaerde koopstadt
van Amstelredam / gheconterfeyt met alle
sijn Wateren / Bruggen / Straten / Kercken / Kloo-
steren / Huysen / Toorens / Poorten ende Muerren /
ende omleggende situatie / ghemaeckt ter eeren K. M.
ende oock den Eersamen Raedt der selver Stadt /
ende allen Liefhebberen der Konste / etc.
Wtghegeven by Cornelis Anthoniszoon Schil-
der / met Octroye der K. M. onsen ghenadighsten
Heere / van't selfde niet te moghen nae-drucken noch verkoopen binnen den tijdt
van ses Jaren lanck ghedurende / ende ghedateert van den Jare duysent vijf-
hondert drie-en-veertigh / op seeckere penen int selfde Octroye begrepen / op dat hem
een yeghelijck voor schade verhoeden mach.
1544
DE AEMSTEL

Amsterdam, the Netherlands

(1544)

The rise of the Western European city was one consequence of developing Atlantic commerce during the sixteenth century. Urban centres such as London, Seville, Lisbon and Antwerp grew in wealth and importance, acquiring commercial, ecclesiastical and administrative structures and very often a print and map trade. In order to promote their might, influential groups or individuals commissioned maps. These maps were often large, artistically accomplished and dramatic images, public statements of civic propaganda. Because they were very often printed as opposed to hand-drawn, these visions of commercial power could be transmitted far and wide through the numerous copies that were available.

By the first half of the sixteenth century Amsterdam, in the Habsburg Netherlands, had risen from a fishing port to a major centre of Baltic trade, principally grain. Its years of true greatness, as headquarters of the Dutch East India Company (from 1602), replacing Antwerp as the principal port of the Low Countries, were just around the corner. This map marked the town's arrival.

It is a woodcut bird's-eye view of the town on 12 joined sheets of paper produced in 1544 by the artist and mapmaker Cornelis Anthoniszoon (often shortened to Anthonisz., *c.*1505–53). Anthonisz. was an early producer of sea guides for pilots. The map is a copy of his painting of 1538, which was commissioned by the heads of the town as an expression of loyalty to the Habsburg Emperor Charles V (*r.*1530–56). The independence of the Dutch Republic was still some decades away. The map is, if anything, even more dramatic than the painting. The town appears to have been tilted up towards the viewer, beyond which the landscape falls away severely towards the horizon. There are a greater multitude of sailing vessels in the canals and harbour. Details capture lively, thronging streets and grim warnings – for example, the gallows in the bottom right-hand corner.

Probably the most dramatic feature of all is the benevolent figure of Neptune in the upper right, with the arms of the city in one arm and a trident in the other. This is one of the most obvious features which Anthonisz. has borrowed from his prototype, the 1500 woodcut map of Venice by Jacopo de' Barbari (see page 11). This was the first great printed urban propaganda map, pioneering the combined use of dramatic perspective, intricate key details and divine providence. Anthonisz.'s homage is surely not accidental, as it identified Amsterdam as the Venice of the North, successor to the great Mediterranean port in the new Atlantic era.

Scandinavia

(1572)

The *Carta Marina et Descriptio Septentrionalium Terrarium* or 'Maritime Map and Description of the Northern Lands' of 1539 is a woodcut map of Scandinavia produced by a Swedish scholar called Olaus Magnus (1490–1557). As you can see by looking at this smaller copperplate engraved copy of it from 1572 by Antonio Lafreri (*fl.*1544–77), the *Carta Marina* is not so much a geographical image as a visual encyclopedia of Scandinavia. It includes political information, portraits of rulers, bishoprics, scenes of historical battles, mining information, details of zoology and ornithology, fantastical sea monsters, natural and legendary phenomena, and a range of Scandinavian customs from religious observation to sport.

Magnus's map may have shared the same concept as earlier encyclopedic maps such as the medieval *mappae mundi*, but its description of the Scandinavian coasts surpassed anything then in existence, including in portolan charts. It therefore provided a valuable update to European mapmakers' knowledge of northern Europe.

Magnus had travelled to Italy in 1537 on business relating to his brother Johannes Magnus (1488–1544), the Catholic Archbishop of Sweden. The *Carta Marina* and its accompanying text was published in Venice (the Doge of Venice paid for the woodcuts to be made), where it came to the attention of Italian mapmakers and sellers. Italy was then the heart of commercial European mapmaking, centred on the competitive cities of Florence (the earliest to develop), Rome and Venice. Rome specialised in prints of classical Rome while Venice pioneered printed sea charts and island books known as *isolari*. Their high-quality copper engraved maps were available for a customer to select from and then have bound up into bespoke 'assembled-to-order' atlases.

These atlases have been inaccurately called 'Lafreri' atlases, and their makers termed 'Lafreri school' mapmakers, but Lafreri was just one of a number of mapmakers and print sellers, albeit a prolific one. He was a Frenchman who had moved to Rome in 1544 and struck up a formidable business partnership with Antonio Salamanca (1479–1562). As was usual, his maps were often copied from earlier examples. He would have seen the commercial potential in producing a smaller version of the nine-sheet *Carta Marina*, despite the fact that it was decades out of date, and so produced one to sell to his enthusiastic patrons. These included the unknown recipient of this, one of three Italian assembled-to-order atlases in the British Library.

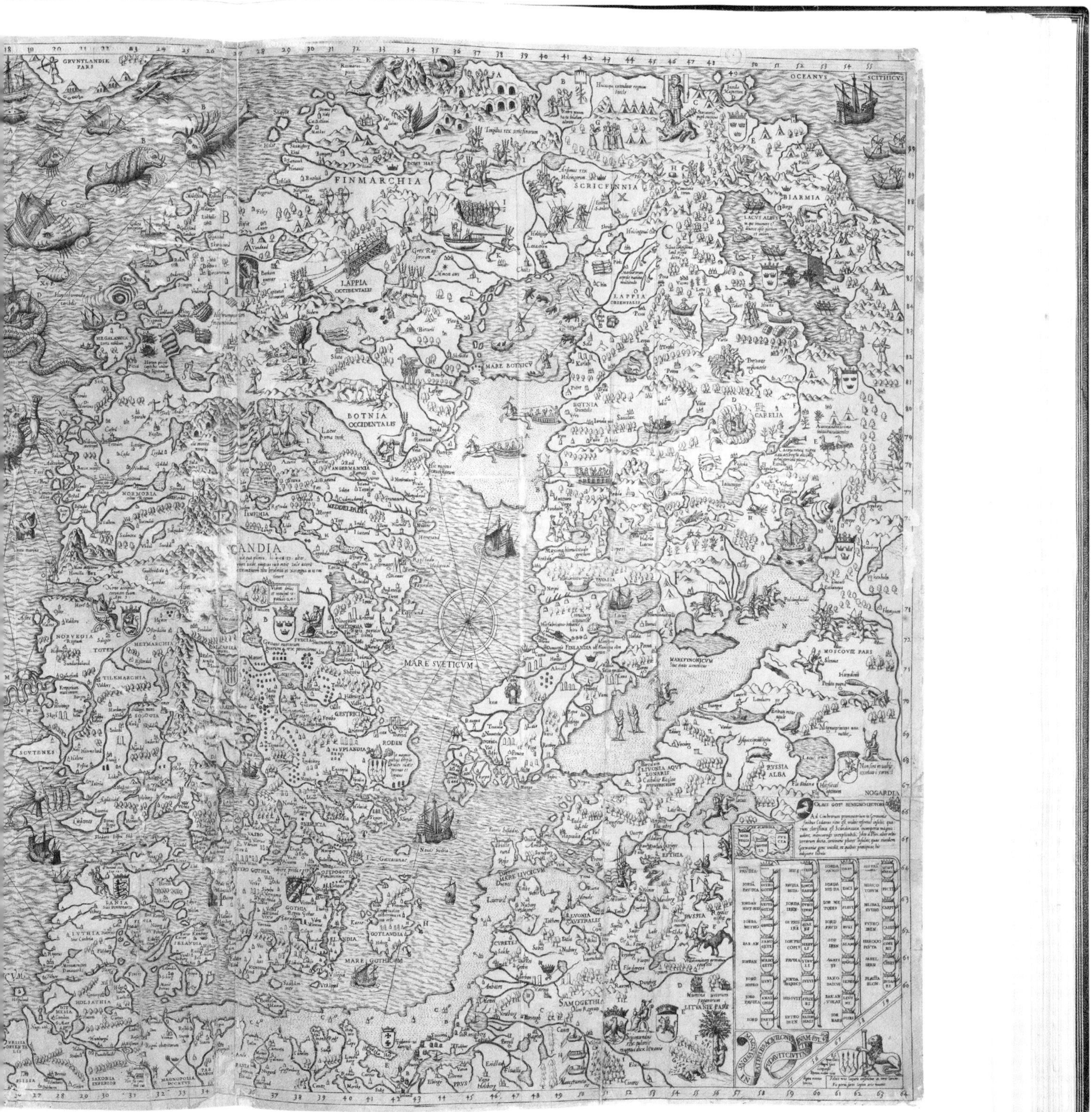
GRVNTLANDIE PARS
OCEANVS SCITHICVS
FINMARCHIA
SCRICFINNIA
BIARMIA
LACVS ALBVS
LAPPIA OCCIDENTALIS
LAPPIA ORIENTALIS
MARE BOTNICV
BOTNIA OCCIDENTALIS
BOTNIA ORIENTALIS
CARELIA
ANGERMANNIA
MEDDELPADIA
NORMORIA
CANDIA
NORVEGIA
TOTEN
HELSINGIA
FINLANDIA
MARE SVETICVM
MAREFINONICVM
MOSCOVIE PARS
GESTRICIA
VPLANDIA
RODIN
RVSSIA ALBA
NOGARDIA
LIVONIA AQVILONARIS
ESTHIA
GOTHIA
GOTLANDIA
ELANDIA
MARE GOTHICVM
LIVONIA AVSTRALIS
CVRETES
SAMOGETHIA
LITVANIE PARS
DANIA
SCANIA
HOLSATIA
SAXONIA INFERIOR

HONI SOIT QUI MAL Y PENSE
THE MARINERS MIRROVR
Wherin may playnly be ſeen the courſes, heights, diſtances, depths, ſoundings, flouds and ebs, riſings of lands, rocks, ſands and ſhoalds, with the marks for th'entrings of the Harbouroughs, Havens and Ports of the greateſt part of Europe: their ſeueral traficks and commodities: Together w.th the Rules and inſtrumēts of NAVIGATION.
First made & ſet fourth in diuers exact Sea Charts, by that famous Nauigator LVKE WAGENAR of Enchuiſen And now fitted with neceſſarie additions for the uſe of Engliſhmen by
ANTHONY ASHLEY.
Heerin alſo may be underſtood the exploits lately atchiued by the right Honorable the L. Admiral of Englād with her Ma.ties Nauie and ſome former ſeruices don by that worthy Knight
S.r FRA: DRAKE.
20 40 60 90

Southern Norway

(1588)

Given Britain's self-image as a proud, seafaring island nation, you would assume a long and equally proud tradition of marine charting. However, it was only with the creation of the post of Admiralty Hydrographer in 1795 that British charts could attain a consistently high standard. Prior to this, with some notable exceptions, English charts had flattered to deceive. Even the first printed English sea atlas, the *Mariner's Mirrour* of 1588, was a pirated copy of a Dutch original. Nevertheless it is a fantastic work which tells us a lot about English opportunism as well as the continuing reliance on the expertise of others.

In 1584 the Dutch navigator Lucas Janszoon Waghenaer (*c*.1533–1606) published his bestselling guide to the coasts of Western Europe, the *Spieghel der Zeevaerdt*. Waghenaer had sailed these coasts with Dutch trading vessels, and the *Spieghel* contained all of his knowledge and experience. It included distance tables, directions and diagrams to aid navigation using celestial objects, instructions on how to make a map, and a series of coastal maps stretching from Spain to Norway. The maps were clear and useful, with innovative features such as coastal profiles running the length of the maps, which sailors could match with what they saw at sea. The *Spieghel*'s first edition was in Dutch, not Latin, because it was for practical navigators as opposed to scholars.

By the 1580s Britain had its national survey (Christopher Saxton's atlas of England and Wales), but apart from the coastal maps commissioned by Henry VIII (*r*.1509–47) in the 1530s there were no consistently reliable maps of all British waters, and little in printed form. Britain was vulnerable to a seaborne invasion from Spain, and Elizabeth's Lord Chancellor Christopher Hatton (1540–91) saw the opportunity. With such a useful book of sea charts as Waghenaer's already in existence, why bother to make another afresh?

Hatton commissioned Anthony Ashley (1551–1628), clerk of the Privy Council, to translate Waghenaer's text into English and had fresh copies of the maps engraved by predominantly Dutch engravers including Theodore de Bry (1528–98) and Jodocus Hondius. It was an expensive process, but not nearly as expensive as having to start from scratch. As well as the useful defensive coverage of Britain's coasts which the atlas provided (particularly in the wake of the Spanish Armada earlier that year), it included the wider coasts of Western Europe including Norway (overleaf), which English merchants were then venturing into with greater confidence.

In many ways the *Mariner's Mirrour* was an inauspicious start to England's printed sea chart tradition. Britain may not yet have ruled the waves, but it was beginning to explore its means for doing so.

The Shewing of the land of Norway betweene Mardou & Langhesond, when you comme out of the East aboute
De vos van Mardou
De voort vā Trom
Mardou
Trom
Oxesfoort
Longen
West kiel
Oost kiel
Conincx hauen
Stadt
Sant voort
Tromsondt
Mieu hohnen
t'Eylandt van Mardou
Tgat van Oxsfort
Tgat van Longen
Tgat van west kiel
T'Hoffer landt
Tgat van Oost kiel
De baers
WEST
SOVTH
NO
Englishe Leagues 20 in a degree
Spanishe Leagues 17 ½ in a degree
Dutche Leagues 15 in a degree

Appearing of the Land of Langesond, foure Leagues of, Coning from the west
Long Sound
Debuij
Anslo
Kaeleers
Holm strant
Braecke
Lausondt
Bast
Poelsche gronden
Marie enboe
Neess
De nesse
Vuyle hoeck
Tonsbar
Haer wijck
De Laerwijck
Seynen
Farder
'tmonnicke Eylandt
De Slecht
De bodem
Elsanghe
Grasswijck
De Susters
I. Akersondt
Aker sondt
Tlandt van Noordt Oosten
Noorder Meu holm
Suyder holm
Boechscheer
RN SEA
The Sea Coastes of Norway And of the land of North: East, as they shewe and appeare betweene Mardou and Akersond, according unto their right situation

Russia

(1662 and 1680)

Joan Blaeu and Moses Pitt (*c.*1639–97) were two seventeenth-century mapmakers on a mission to produce big atlases. One fared considerably better than the other, but both of their grand projects are worthy of the highest accolades. Joan Blaeu was the head of one of the world's most successful mapmaking dynasties. His father Willem Janszoon Blaeu (1571–1638) had developed a strong reputation for the production of sea charts, sailing directions, maps and globes. On succeeding his father in 1633 as official chart maker to the Dutch East India Company, Blaeu Jr developed the company's commercial production of high-quality printed maps and atlases for a cosmopolitan European merchant class.

His most illustrious work was the set of wall maps included in the 1660 Klencke Atlas, but the most expansive was his *Atlas Maior* of 1662 and later. This was the atlas to beat all atlases, a set of 11 volumes containing nearly 600 maps of the world, its continents, its countries (his map of Russia is overleaf) and regions, translated into four languages. There was even a volume devoted to Scotland. The historian Jerry Brotton has described the atlas as a 'true baroque creation' that was 'driven by the market', because in order to compile it Blaeu collected information from as many maps as he could, sourcing them from far and wide. For example, his Scotland maps are based on regional maps drawn by Timothy Pont (*c.*1565–1614). Blaeu's main competitor, Jan Janssonius (1588–1664), was put out of business by his prolific rival.

The map printing plates of Janssonius were acquired by London-based print seller Moses Pitt. With the support of the Royal Society Pitt decided in 1678 to create a multi-volume world atlas on Blaeu's model. *The English Atlas* would announce Britain as a major player in commercial cartography. There had been no English translation of the *Atlas Maior*, and Pitt set out to ensure one was not required. Printed in the Sheldonian Theatre in Oxford, the quality of *The English Atlas* maps was magnificent, on high-quality paper and exquisitely coloured (his map of Russia is on the right). The British Library's example was presented to James, Duke of York (the future James II) with his portrait and tooled binding bearing his arms.

Unfortunately, things began to go wrong. Costs spiralled – £1,000 per volume according to Pitt. Property deals and partner disputes meant that with only four volumes produced Pitt was declared bankrupt in 1689. 'The whole design was blasted', according to the volume's author, William Nicholson. Pitt, however, did not go quietly, publishing an impassioned plea in the form of *The Cry of the Oppressed* from prison in 1691. Fate had dealt Pitt a bad hand, but his atlas can at least now be written about in the same vein as the masterwork he had striven so hard to emulate.

MOURMANSKOY MORE dicitur
Norvegicum et Danicorum Mare
quia Russi Norvegos et Danos Maurmans vocant
Noort Caep
Mourmanskoi leporie
Terschana wolochi
Bella More
NOVA ZEMLA
NIAREN MORE
Fretum Weygats
OBDORA
SAMOEDA
TINGOESI
TAR
BAIDA
SIBIRIA
LUCOMORYE
CONDORA
Pegaorda
DWINA
Czeremissi Logowoy
CASAN
Casan
BULGARIA
Bulgar
Czeremissi Nagornoy
Moscua
MOSCUA
RESANIA
POLE
Fossa Kamouz
ASTRACAN
OCRAINA
CRIMEA
TARTARIA PRZECOPEN
Cabarda
NAGAYSKI
PETIGORY
Mare delle Zabache
Taurica Chersonesus
Sonscha regio
CIRCASSI
MARE CASPIUM quod Russi vocant GUALENTSCHA MORE vocatur etiam MARE DE SALA vel de BACHU
Gilan
Baca
Scalthale
Arski Principes Pastihumski Cirkassi hic habitant
PERSIÆ CONFINIA
PONTUS EUXINUS
Rhutenis ZORNO MORE
NATOLIA siue ASIA MINOR
Iveria siue Grusinæ Imperium
Apud Janssonio-Waesbergios, et Mosem Pitt.

A. Kremelena-gorod, Aula Imperatoris
B. Kitay-gorod urbs media
D. Skorodom, urbs exterior
C. Tzar-gorod urbs Cæsarea
E. Streletska sloboda, vel vicus militaris.
a. Curia
b. Patriarcheion
h. Forum equarium
i. Balneæ publicæ
k. Forum lignarium
l. Viridarium Imperatoris
m. Equile
Moscua fluvius
MOSCUA
ad Architypum Foedori Borissowitsi
NOORDZEE
SWEDEN.
DANIA
MARE BALTICUM
LIEFLANT
PRUSSIA
LITTAW.
POLONIA
SEVERA
WOLYNIA
PODOLIA
MOLDAVIA.
WALACHIA.
BULGARIA.
ROMANIA.
CRIMEA
PALUS MEOTIS
PONTUS EUXINUS
NATOLIA.
ARCHIPELAGO
CAIANIA
CAREELIA.
CARGAPO
TABULA
RUSSIÆ
ex autographo, quod delineandum curavit Foedor filius Tzaris Boris desumta; et ad fluvios Dwinam, Zuchanam, aliaque loca, quantum ex tabulis et notitiis ad nos delatis fieri potuit, amplificata: ac
Magno Domino, Tzari et Magno Duci Michaëli Foedrowits omnium Russorum, Autocratori Wolodimeriæ, Moscoviæ et Novogardiæ, Tzari Cazaniæ, Tzari Astracaniæ, Tzari Sibieriæ, Domino Plescoviæ Magno Duci Smolenscoviæ, Otweriæ, Iugoriæ, Permiæ, Wiatkiæ, Bulgariæ etc: Item Domino et Magno Duci Novogardiæ Inferioris etc: Domino regionum Iveriæ Kartaliniæ et Grosiniæ Tzari etc:
dedicata ab
Hesselo Gerardo
M.DC.XIIII

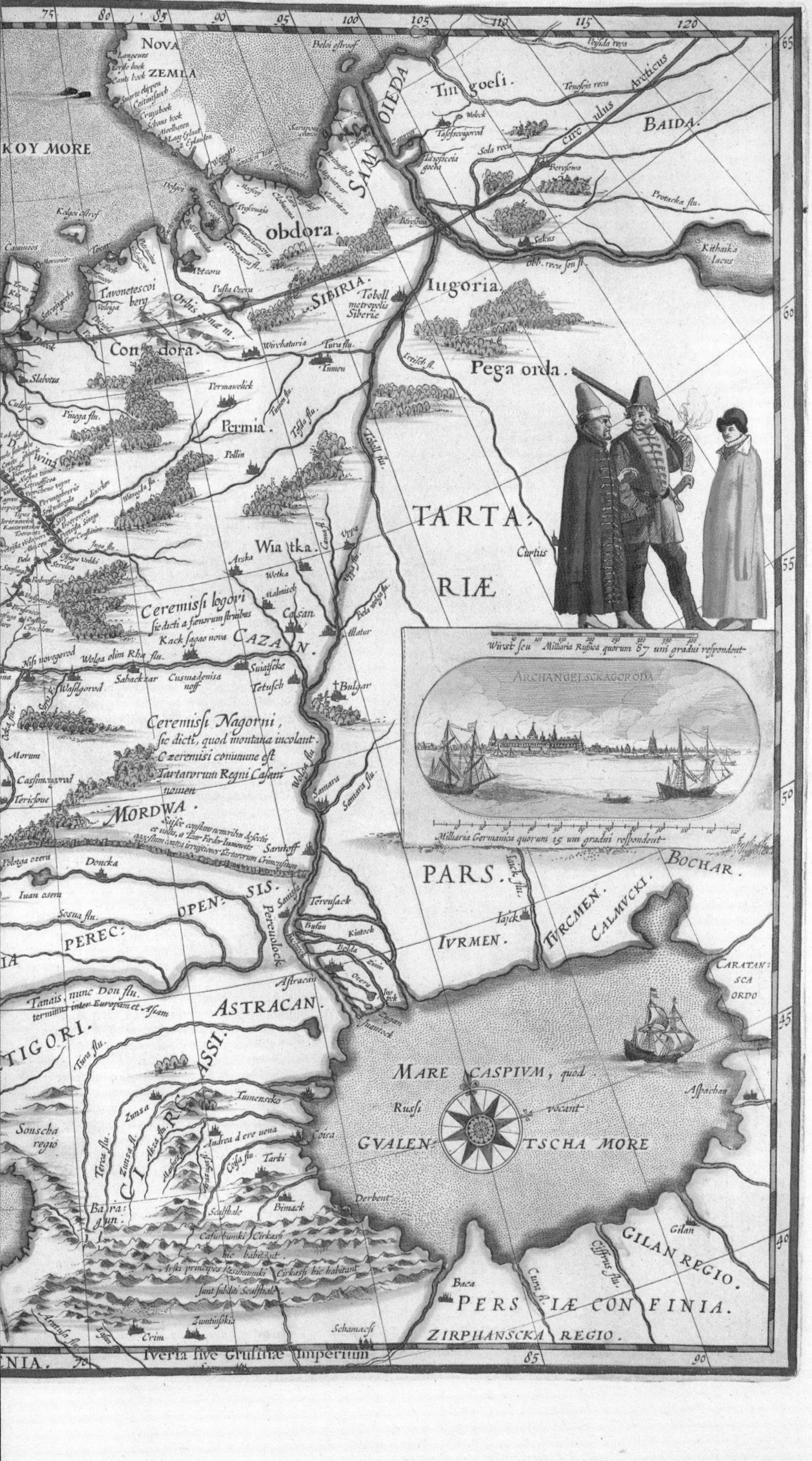
NOVA ZEMLA
KOY MORE
SAMOIEDA
Tingoesi.
BAIDA.
Circulus Arcticus
obdora.
SIBIRIA.
Tobell metropolis Siberie
Iugoria.
Kithaika lacus
Condora.
Pega orda.
Permia.
Wiatka.
TARTARIÆ
Curtius
Ceremissi logori sic dicti a fenorum struibus
Kack sagao nova CAZAN.
Wolga olim Rha flu.
Casan
Bulgar
Ceremissi Nagorni, sic dicti, quod montana incolant. Czeremissi commune est Tartarorum Regni Casani nomen
MORDWA.
Wirst seu Milliaria Russica quorum 87 uni gradui respondent
ARCHANGELSCKAGORODA
Milliaria Germanica quorum 15 uni gradui respondent
PARS.
BOCHAR.
Samara
OPEN: SIS.
PEREC:
IURMEN.
TURCMEN.
CALMUCKI.
CARATANSCA ORDO
Tanais nunc Don flu. terminus inter Europam et Asiam
ASTRACAN.
Astracan
TIGORI.
MARE CASPIUM, quod Russi vocant GUALENTSCHA MORE
Astrachan
Derbent
Sonscha regio
GILAN REGIO.
Gilan
PERSIÆ CONFINIA.
Baca
ZIRPHANSCKA REGIO.
Schamachi
Iveria sive Grusinæ Imperium

Ukraine

(c.1650)

During a visit to the cabinet of rarities of Charles II (*r.*1660–85) in November 1660, the English diarist John Evelyn (1620–1706) recorded seeing 'a vast book of mapps in a volume of neare 4 yards large'. This is the giant atlas of 41 wall maps known as the Klencke Atlas, commissioned by the Dutch sugar merchant Johannes Klencke (1620–72) and presented to the king in May 1660 as a gift to celebrate his restoration to the English throne following the English Civil War. The atlas, which is over two metres wide when open, is one of three giant atlases created during the mid-seventeenth century and presented to prominent European rulers.

Why make such a large and impractical atlas? The answer is, quite simply, for effect. If you are going to present a gift to a king you should make it a good one. The symbolism attached to the possession of a large book containing the entire world's knowledge would not have been lost on either monarch or gift giver. Klencke received a knighthood and perhaps even commercial privileges for his partners hoping to develop the Dutch trade in sugar within English territory.

The size of the atlas was not the only splendid aspect of it. Another was the quality of the cartography. The atlas contained the most sophisticated printed wall maps then available, the sort of wall

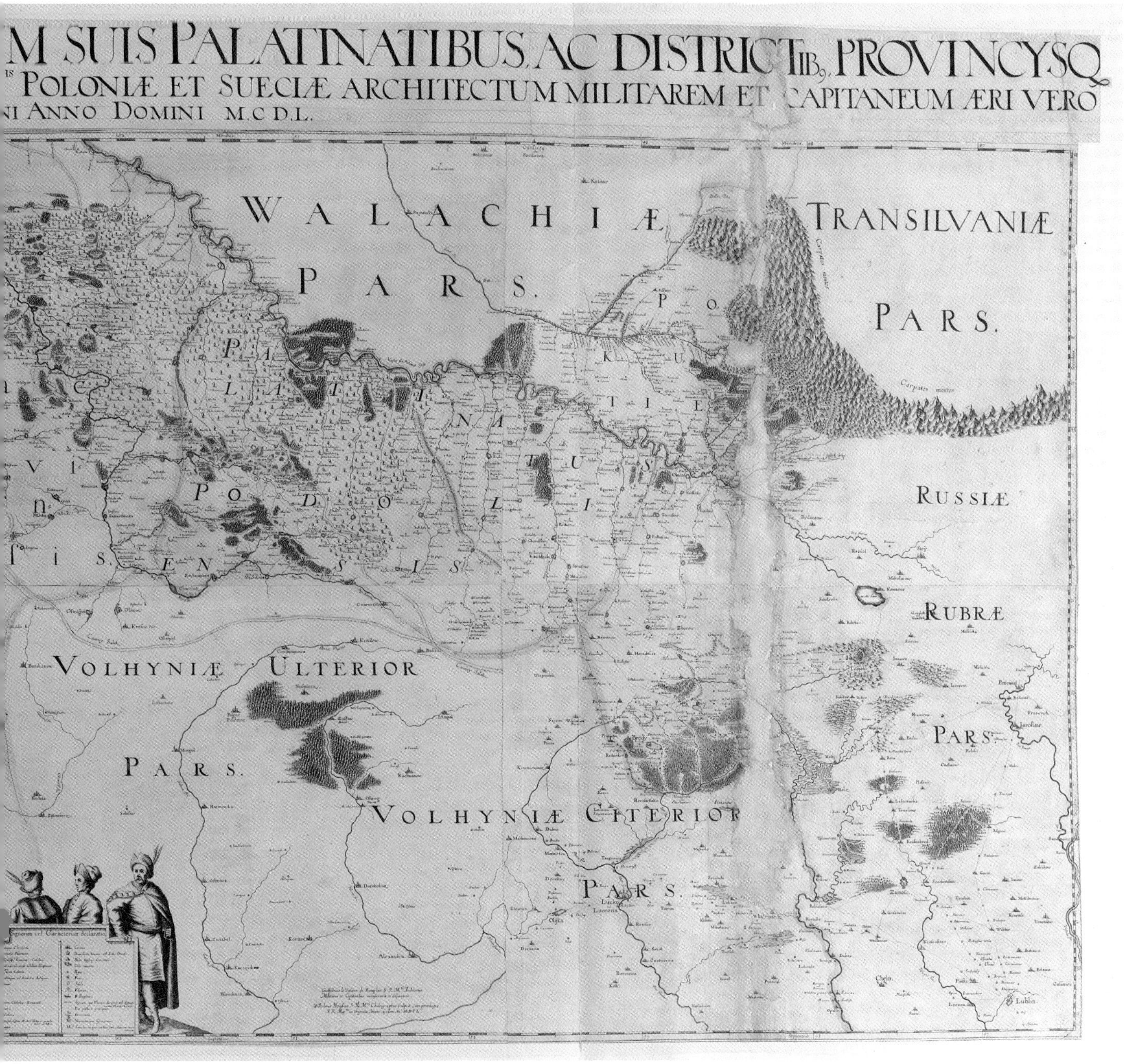

hangings which appear in oils of the Dutch artist Johannes Vermeer (1632–75). They were handpicked to interest and flatter Charles: maps of the British Isles and a map of North America with its British colonies.. The maps exhibited high-quality artistry. For example, the map of Italy contains engravings after Rembrandt's teacher, Pieter Lastman (1583–1633).

The maps also contained the latest commercial information about parts of the world under the influence of the Dutch East India Company (VoC) to whom the atlas's chief mapmaker, Joan Blaeu, was official chart maker. The map of Australia was the first to show the 1642 discoveries of Abel Tasman (1603–59), and the first to show both the east and west coasts of Australia together.

The Klencke Atlas may have been a monumental Baroque curiosity, but it also looked to the modern age. Many of the maps contained important scientific and practical information for administration, business and even war-making. The *c.*1650 map of Ukraine by Guillaume Le Vasseur de Beauplan (*c.*1600–73) was printed for the Polish king, Ladislaus IV (*r.*1634–48), to assist him in a military campaign against the Crimean Tartars. The distances between towns were measured by the mapmaker attaching an odometer to his horse and riding between them.

EYSTAT ANNO SALUTIS
XII KALENDIS AUGUSTI PERFECTUM
MARE OCEANUM GERMANIAE
MARE LIGUSTICUM
PARS MARE GALLICUM
MARE TYRHENU PARS
SAXONIA
ANTIQUA MARCHIA
POLONIA MAGNA
POLONIA IN TOTO
POLONIA MINOR
SILVA HERITYNIA
BOHEMIA
AUSTRIA
FRANCONIA
TURINCIA
HASSIA
WESTUALIA
BRABANDIA
FLANDRIA
POMERANIA
PRUSSIA
TRANSILVANIA
VENECIAE

Central and Eastern Europe

(1530)

The 'Cusanus map' is a map of Central and Eastern Europe dating from 1530. It is based on the travels of the German priest and scholar Nicolaus Kryffs (1401–64), known as Nicolaus de Cusa after his town of birth (now Bernkastel-Kues) in the German Rhineland. Its significance lies in the fact that it has claim to be the earliest modern map of Europe, based on first-hand travel accounts rather than ancient knowledge. It is also one of the earliest European copper-engraved maps and utilised new and ground-breaking production techniques. The map has had a long and convoluted history, spanning at least eight decades and involving key figures of the German and Italian Renaissance.

Nicolaus was a significant figure in philosophical and theological circles. He rose to the position of cardinal, and was also a papal envoy, travelling widely between Rome and German sovereign states. One such tour of Germany and the Low Countries between 1450 and 1452 probably furnished Nicolaus with the first-hand geographical information required to construct a map, which he supplemented with information on other places from his associates. For example, his housemate in Rome, Georg von Puerbach (1423–61) would have supplied information about his Austrian homeland. The map was therefore an assemblage of various sources with Nicolaus's knowledge at its core, capturing an impressive swathe of Europe from Belgium in the west to the Crimea in the east, taking in regions as far apart as the Baltic Sea and Istanbul.

Nicolaus's original doesn't survive, but it was copied by Nicolaus Germanus (*c.*1420–*c.*1490). This map formed the basis for others including the regional map in Hartmann Schedel's (1440–1514) 'Nuremberg Chronicle' of 1493. Nicolaus's map was also used for this further version, known as the Eichstätt map because the name of the southern German town and the date 1491 is given in the top margin. We now know that it was begun in Rome during the 1470s alongside the production of maps for the Rome edition of Ptolemy's *Geographia* (published 1478), partly because, in common with the Ptolemaic maps, the letters for the text have been punched into the plate rather than engraved.

The copper plate was taken to Germany and was in the possession of Konrad Peutinger (1465–1547), one-time owner of the thirteenth-century copy of a road map of the Roman Empire, the 'Tabula Peutingeriana'. Prior to this the map had been extended to include Italy and Greece; bizarrely, the map's old lower border is still plainly visible across its lower portion. The only extant copies of what the historian Peter Meurer has named 'the mysterious map' are from its fifth edition, printed in Basle in 1530. This is one of the surviving seven, which has been lavishly coloured with deep blues and greens, and tiny gold dots for settlements. It was once owned by Albrecht Dürer's (1471–1528) friend, the Bavarian lawyer Willibald Pirckheimer (1470–1530).

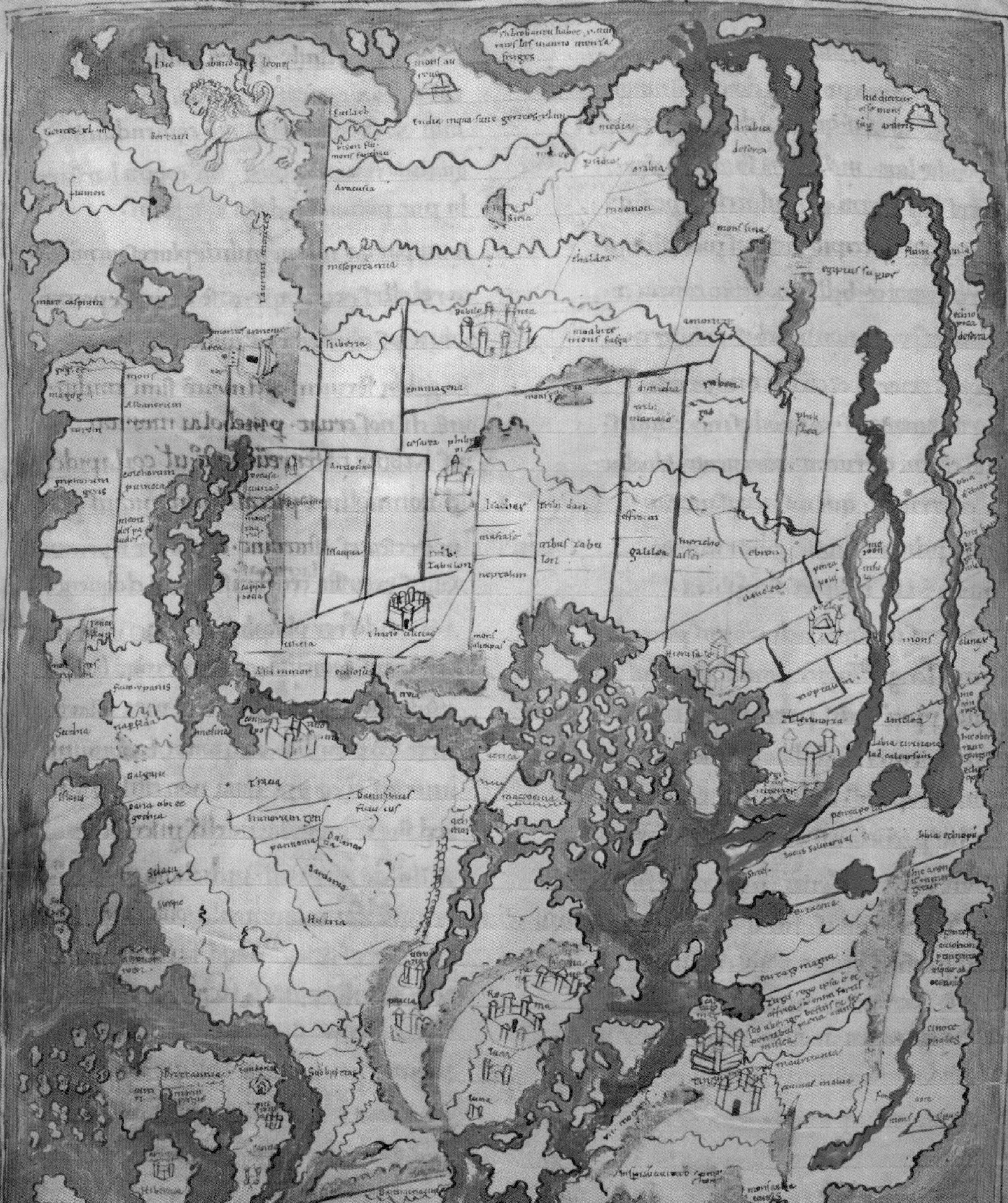

Hic abundant leones
mesopotamia
mare caspium
Hiberia
Commagena
Albanorum
Galilea
Ebron
media
arabia
chaldea
mons sina
egyptus superior
Tracia
Danubius fluvius
hunorum gens
pannonia
macedonia
pentapolis
cartago magna
mauritania
Britannia
Hibernia
Hispania citerior

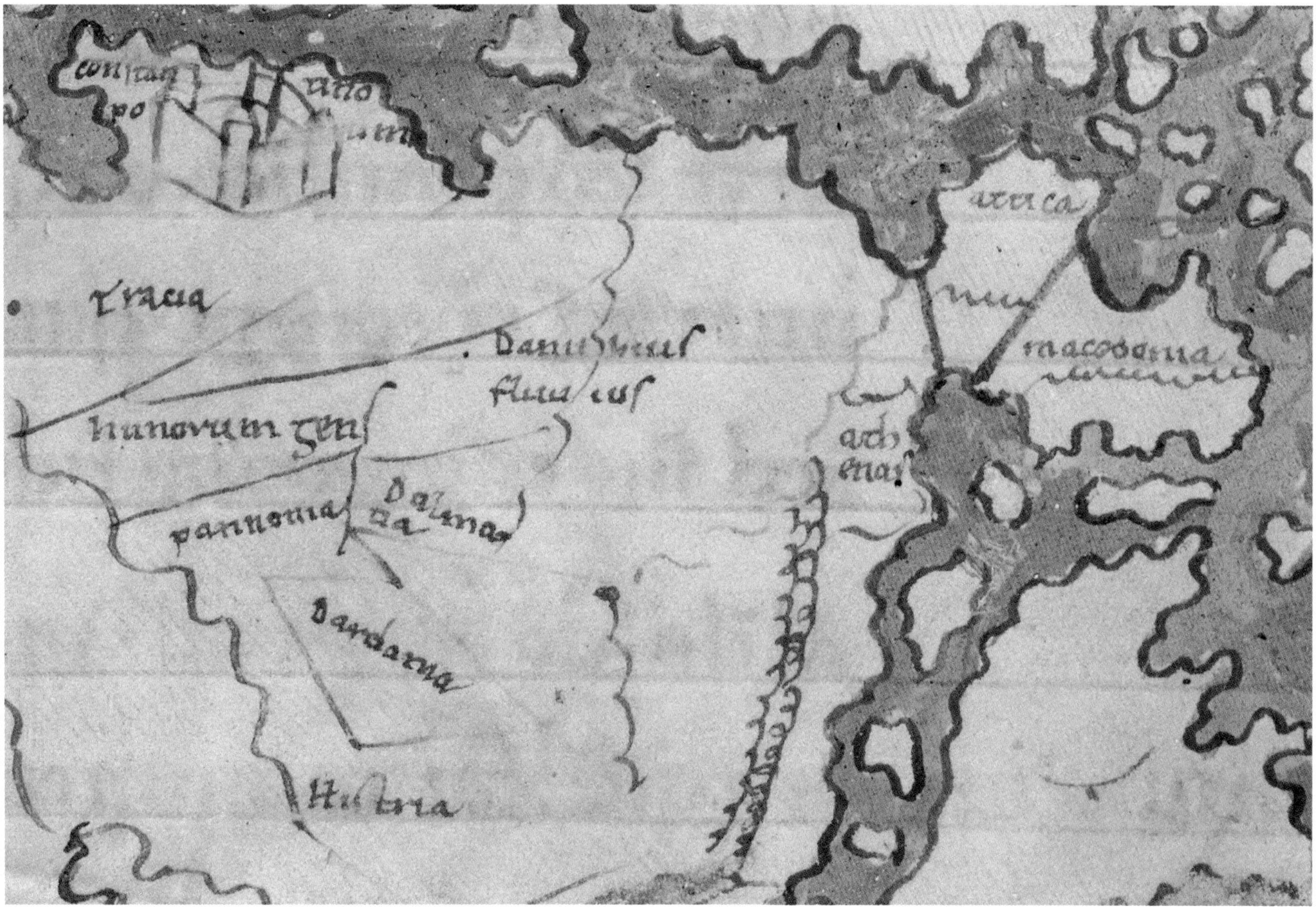

Southeaſtern Europe

(eleventh century)

Today we have a great deal of knowledge of Roman mapping through surviving examples. For inſtance, we can see symbolic mapping on Roman coins, practical mapping in the form of land survey diagrams (the 'Corpus Agrimensorum') and a massive plan of Rome (the 'Forma Urbis Romae') carved on to marble. There is also the Roman road map copy, the 'Tabula Peutingeriana'.

This small, squarish map is the beſt evidence we have of what a Roman world map would have looked like. We think it was drawn in the eleventh century in Anglo-Saxon England, which is extraordinarily early for a map with such a quantity of information. It is almoſt certainly a copy (perhaps even a copy of a copy) of an earlier map, possibly even a version of the world map of the firſt century BCE by Marcus Vipsanius Agrippa (63–12 BCE), based on a survey ordered by Julius Caesar (110–44 BCE) in 44 BCE.

Looking at the map itself, which is oriented with eaſt at the top, and with the islanded Mediterranean Sea running from the Strait of Gibraltar (note the Pillars of Hercules) up through the centre of the map, we can appreciate its Roman genesis. Features of Weſtern Europe and North Africa are clear, walled cities include Conſtantinople, Rome and Alexandria, while lines mark off the Roman provinces. Particularly prominent are the provinces of southeaſtern Europe, including Pannonia and Dalmatia which are shown in this detail. Britain, the island at the bottom left, is particularly well drawn, which has led us to conclude that it was drawn in Britain, probably at Canterbury.

Outside the bounds of the Roman Empire are features derived from legend, such as the lion-cum-monſter with the label 'here lions abound'. Such features are far more common in the later, larger and more detailed *mappae mundi*. This Anglo-Saxon map is a unique link between the world of the Romans and the makers of these medieval maps, who at any rate ſtill felt themselves to be living in the Classical era and not the so-called Dark Ages. The map, which is also known as the 'Cottonian map' because it was owned by Sir Robert Cotton, is bound in a miscellaneous manuscript containing Anglo-Saxon texts and illuſtrations produced between the eighth and fourteenth centuries.

Salzburg, Austria

(1570)

Gerhard Mercator is popularly credited with producing the first uniform book of maps (his posthumous *Atlas* of 1595), but in fact his associate Abraham Ortelius had produced an earlier one: the ground-breaking *Theatrum Orbis Terrarum* or 'Theatre of the World' of 1570. Although lacking a title as catchy as Mercator's effort, the *Theatrum* was an instant bestseller and is seen as inaugurating the 'Golden Age' of mapmaking in the Low Countries.

Its success was largely down to Ortelius himself. He was, like many of his contemporaries, a polymath, and the *Theatrum* was a consequence of his combining the roles of mapmaker, businessman, humanist scholar and man of letters. As a businessman Ortelius identified a market for a unified collection of maps. He financed the project himself, entering into a shrewd partnership with the great Antwerp printer and publisher Christoffel Plantijn (*c*.1520–89) from 1579. The 56 maps in the first edition were appealing, up to date and well sourced, with historical illustrations and commentaries, skilfully engraved and neatly packaged.

This map of the province of Salzburg in northern Austria is one of the *Theatrum*'s most inventive. It shows pictorially the mountainous region with snaking rivers, forests and mountains. Ortelius chose to create an illusion of the map by presenting it as a ragged map pinned to a frame. This *trompe l'œil* feature peels back to reveal glimpses of an expansive Alpine landscape behind it and a profile view of the town of Salzburg (derived from a woodcut view by Sebastian Münster). The map is an allegory on the temporal nature of human knowledge.

The cartography is based on an earlier woodcut map of 1551 by Marcus Secznagel (*c*.1520–*c*.1580) which Ortelius was able to discover thanks to his extraordinarily wide network – the 'who's who' of sixteenth-century European cartography. The majority of the *Theatrum* is similarly based on important regional maps already in existence, while for others Ortelius copied printed maps by Italian mapmakers such as Giacomo Gastaldi (*c*.1500–66) and Antonio Lafreri, which were by then readily available across Europe.

Ortelius's 'epoch-making' atlas became one of the bestselling books of the later sixteenth century, running to 33 full editions (of which the British Library's collection holds an impressive 26) in seven different languages. It expanded in size as new content was added, so that the final edition of the atlas in 1612 was three times larger than the first, containing over 160 maps.

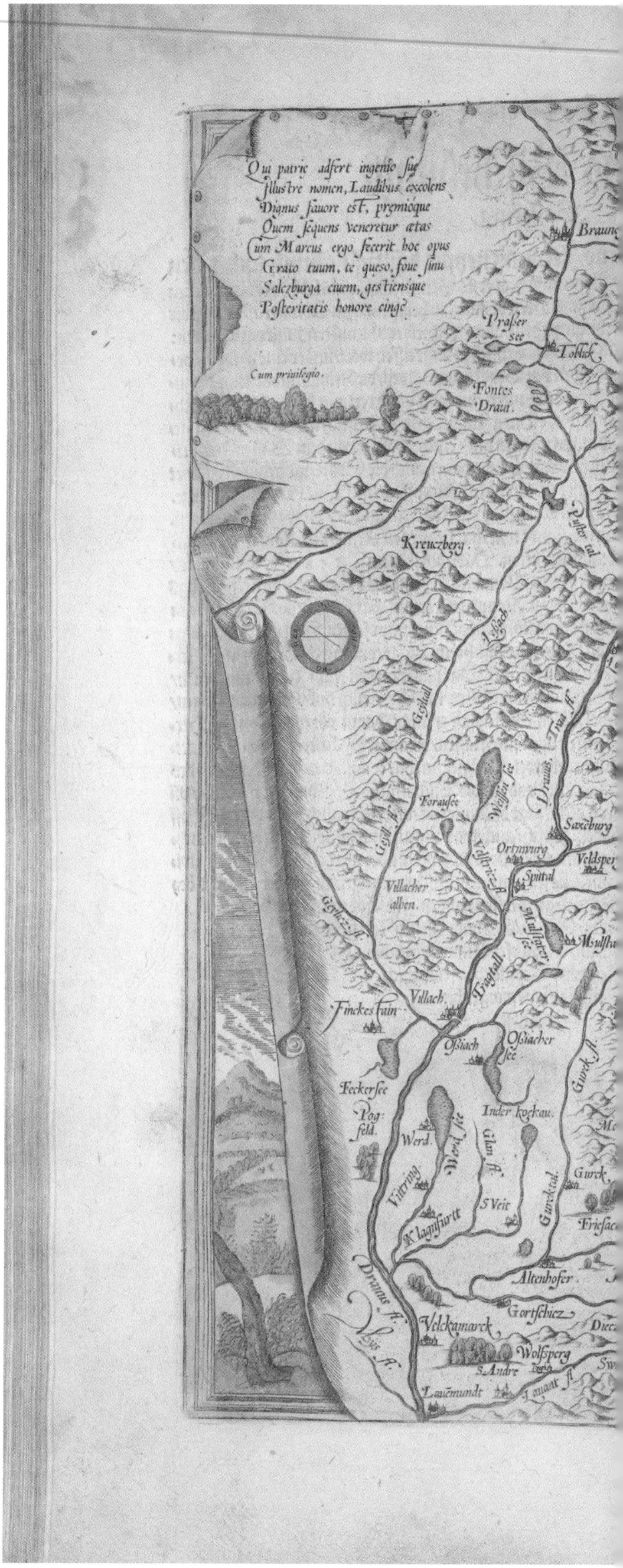

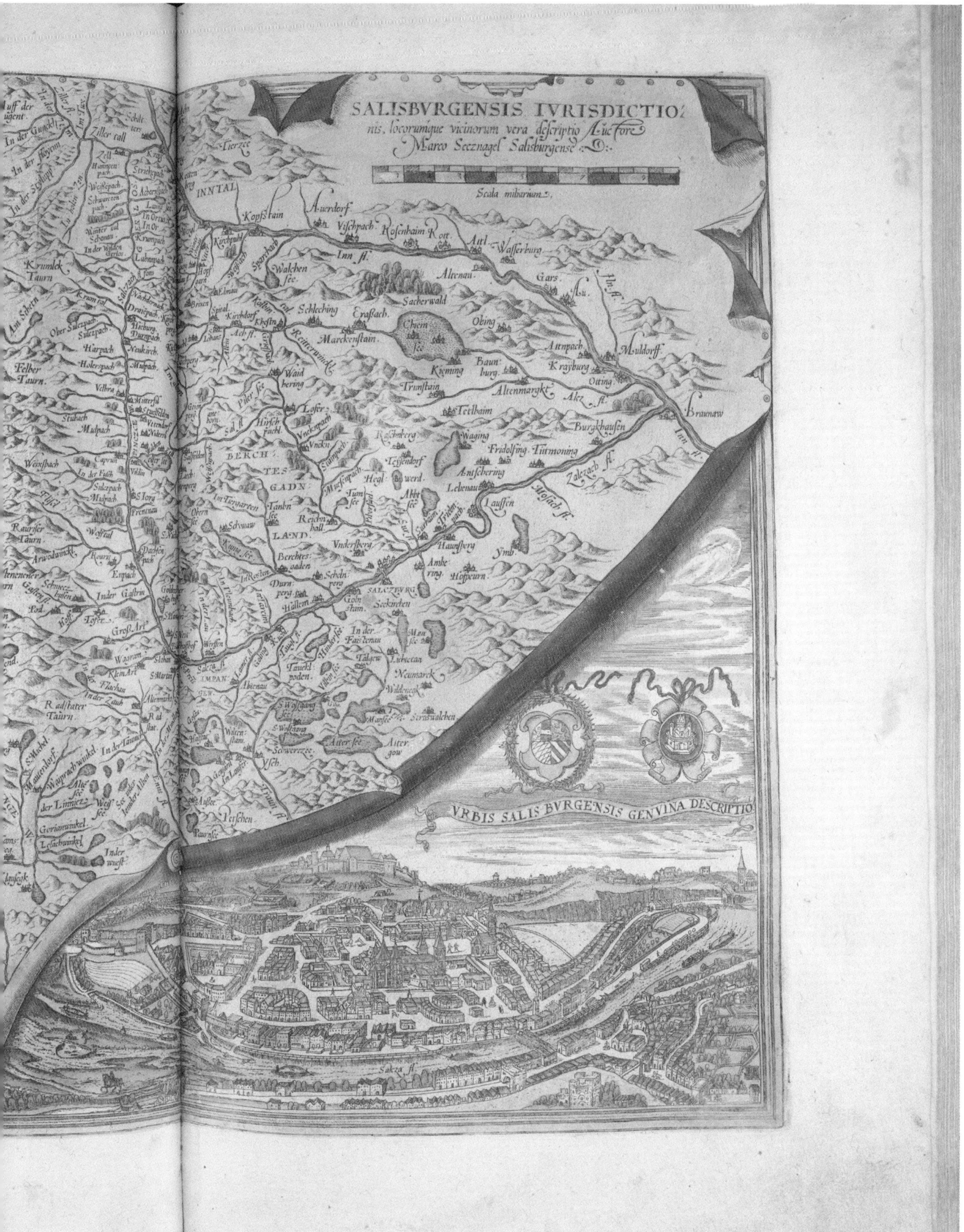
SALISBVRGENSIS IVRISDICTIO
nis, locorumque vicinorum vera descriptio Auctore
Marco Seeznagel Salisburgense
Scala miliarium
VRBIS SALIS BVRGENSIS GENVINA DESCRIPTIO
INNTAL
Kopfstain
Vischpach
Rosenhaim
Wasserburg
Inn fl.
Walchen see
Sacherwald
Chiem see
Marckenstain
Mulldorff
Kraybung
Altenmargkt
Braunaw
Burgkhausen
Tetlhaim
Waging
Fridolfing
Lauffen
Reichenhall
Berchtesgaden
LAND
Hallein
SALCZBVRG
Seekirchen
Neumarck
Salcza fl.

Euboa olim
egrypas dicta
nōiata nigrop

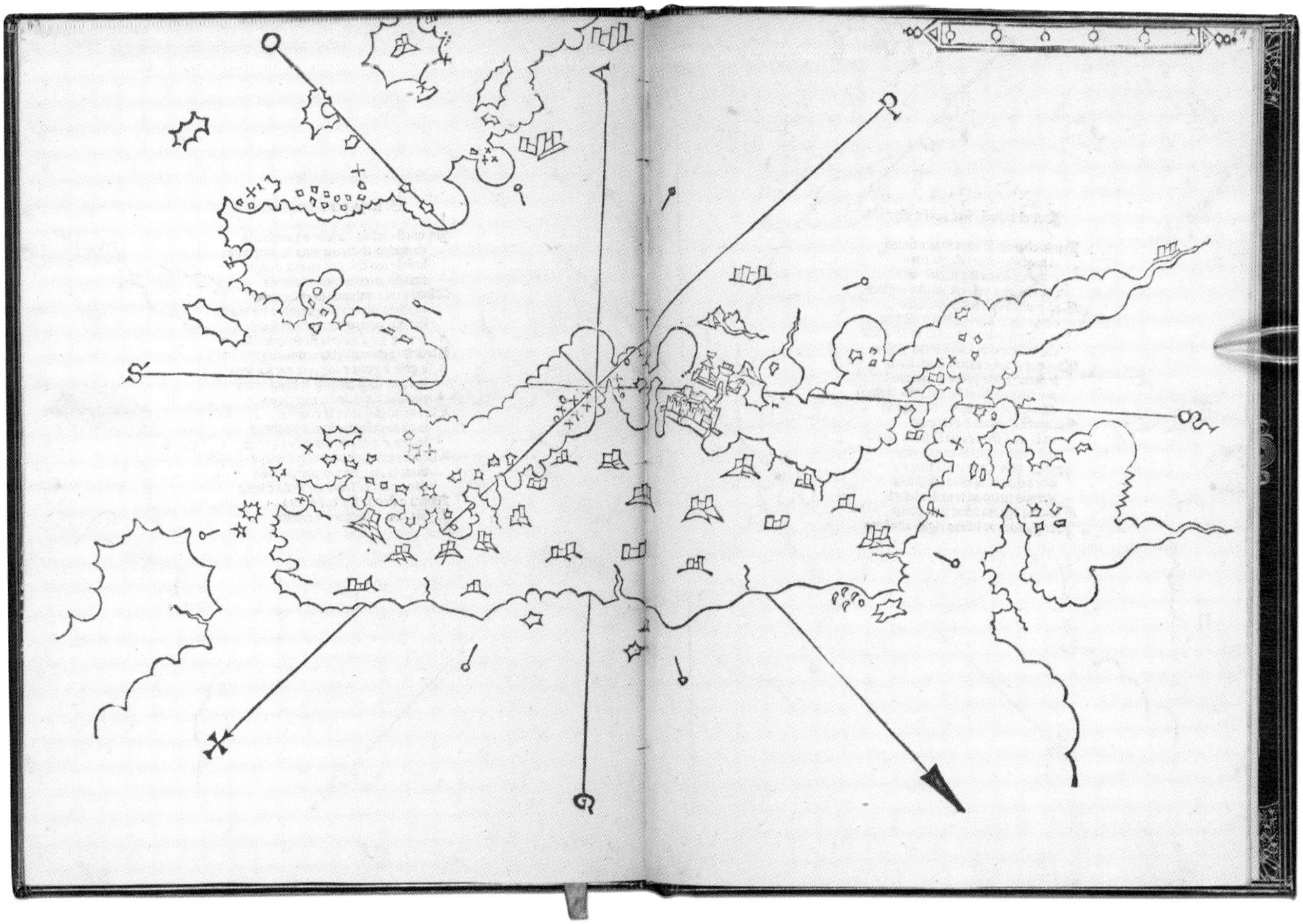

Euboea, Greece

(1480s)

The earliest European printed maps are incunables: prints produced before the year 1501. In these early maps it is fascinating to witness their early practitioners improving their engraving and printing skills. If we look at them against refined hand-drawn manuscript maps of the same time they can appear quite naïve. Yet there was novelty in this new form of map production, and fresh possibilities.

These two maps of the island of Negroponte (now Euboea) northeast of Athens are from books produced within no more than four years of each other. They are from a genre known as *isolarii*, or island books. The earlier of the two (left) is from a 1482 copy of the *Liber insularum archipelagi* or 'Book of the Islands of the [Greek] Archipelago', first produced in 1420 by the Florentine traveller Christoforo Buondelmonti (1386–*c*.1430). The *Liber insularum* is regarded as the first *isolario* and is basically a travel guide to the Aegean Sea and western Turkey, in which the author describes the history and geography of the area through a journey by sea, noting ancient remains and the legends attached to them. The exquisitely painted miniature map shows the ancient cities of Athens and Thebes, and the bridge which once crossed the strait, as if they have been rebuilt anew.

The later map of Euboea (above) was included in an *isolario* published in Venice *c*.1486 by a sailor called Bartolommeo (*fl*.1485). The map shows the island with north to the right. We can see the regularised shapes of the coastline, symbols marking shoals and other hazards, the cardinal directions and a nautical scale. In order to de-clutter the coastline of place names Bartolommeo has simply dispensed with names altogether. All of the accompanying textual description of the geography and history of the island is contained in a sonnet on an adjacent page, hence the nickname which has been given to the author: Bartolommeo 'dalli Sonetti'. The historian Tom Conley has described the relationship between the 'island of words adjacent to an island mapped' in terms of the reader's experience, comparing one with the other, reflecting on their contrasting forms and meanings.

This was an inventive and fresh approach for a new audience. The 1482 *Liber* was produced for the Abbot of St Bavo in Ghent in modern-day Belgium, but Bartolommeo's *isolario* was produced for the average Joe. Quite apart from being printed and thus less expensive than Buondelmonti's lavish hand-drawn work, the sonnets have been written in the 'racy vernacular': not Latin, but the words people actually spoke in their everyday lives.

pars Europa
ungaria
albarreal
lunbardia
Venecia
Roma
flum danoie
flum vecane

Atlantic Ocean

(c.1650)

Vellum (calfskin) is as tough as old boots. This makes it a great material on which to draw maps, particularly if the maps are likely to be heavily used. Vellum is also waterproof, so it isn't surprising that it was the principal material used for early sea charts. This 'plotting chart' of the Atlantic Ocean was produced by the Dutch cartographer Anthonie Jacobsz. (1606/7–50) in 1650. It is a copy of Willem Janszoon Blaeu's earlier bestselling chart which had appeared in 1630. What is unusual about it is that it is not hand-drawn but printed.

The introduction of printing to Europe in the fifteenth century and the production of the first printed maps there during the 1470s allowed maps to be reproduced without recourse to expensive and time-consuming hand-copying, but it did not mean that maps ceased to be hand-drawn overnight. On the contrary, manuscripts and in particular sea charts continued to be drawn by hand, not least because of the practical difficulties of printing on to vellum. Vellum's often large, uneven and undulating surface made it difficult to run through a printing press and capture a good impression from the printing plate.

Printed vellum maps were produced as a luxury product from the late fifteenth century, but it was the Dutch mapmakers of the seventeenth century who fine-tuned and upscaled the process for high-quality large printed vellum charts. They identified a business opportunity. Following Henry Hudson's 1609 expedition to maritime Canada, sponsored by the Dutch East India Company, the Dutch West India Company was established in 1621 to commercially exploit areas of the West Indies and the Atlantic coasts of America and Africa. As a consequence, map publishers such as Blaeu, Jacobsz. and others developed vellum-printed long-range plotting charts such as this *overzeiler* to help pilots navigate their ships across the Atlantic.

The map has been drawn using Gerhard Mercator's map projection, meaning that straight lines of equal bearing could be plotted on to it. Once the pilot had used it to get the ship across the expanse of sea, larger-scale coastal charts would then take over. Blaeu's 1630 map contained navigational information which he had privileged access to as head chart maker to the Dutch East India Company, for example the Le Maire Strait passing under South America, first charted by the Dutch in 1616 and appearing in Jacobsz.'s chart in the large inset positioned over South America.

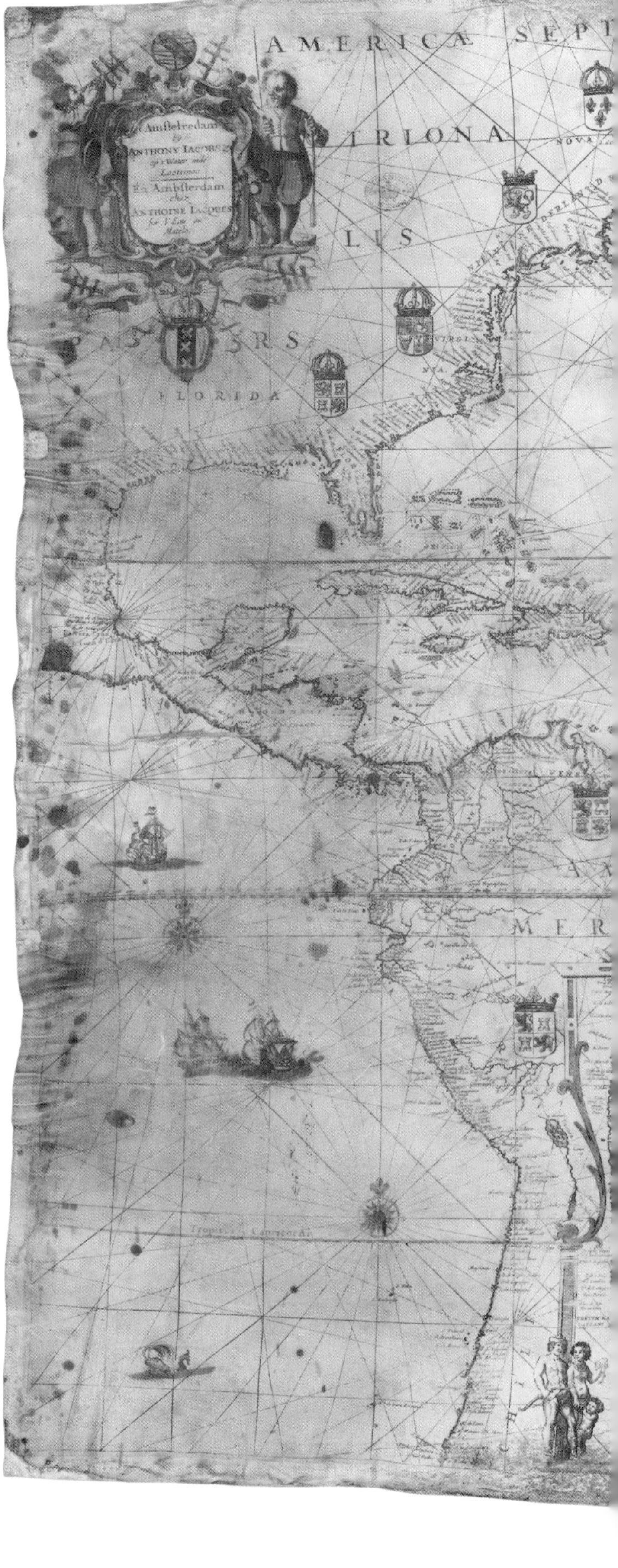

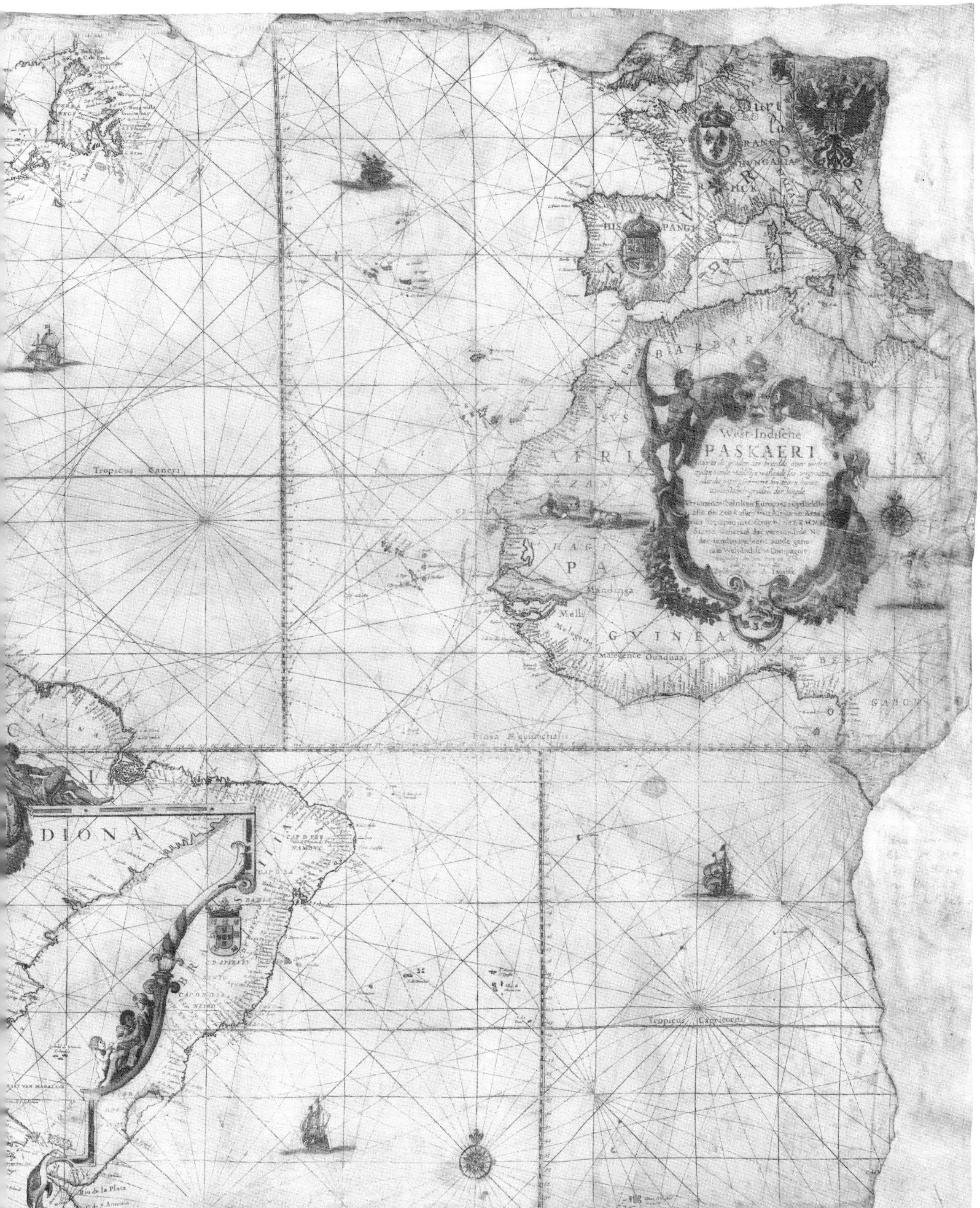
West-Indische
PASKAERT
Tropicus Cancri
Tropicus Capricorni
BARBARIA
GVINEA
BENIN
GABON
Mandinga
Melli
Rio de la Plata
DIONA

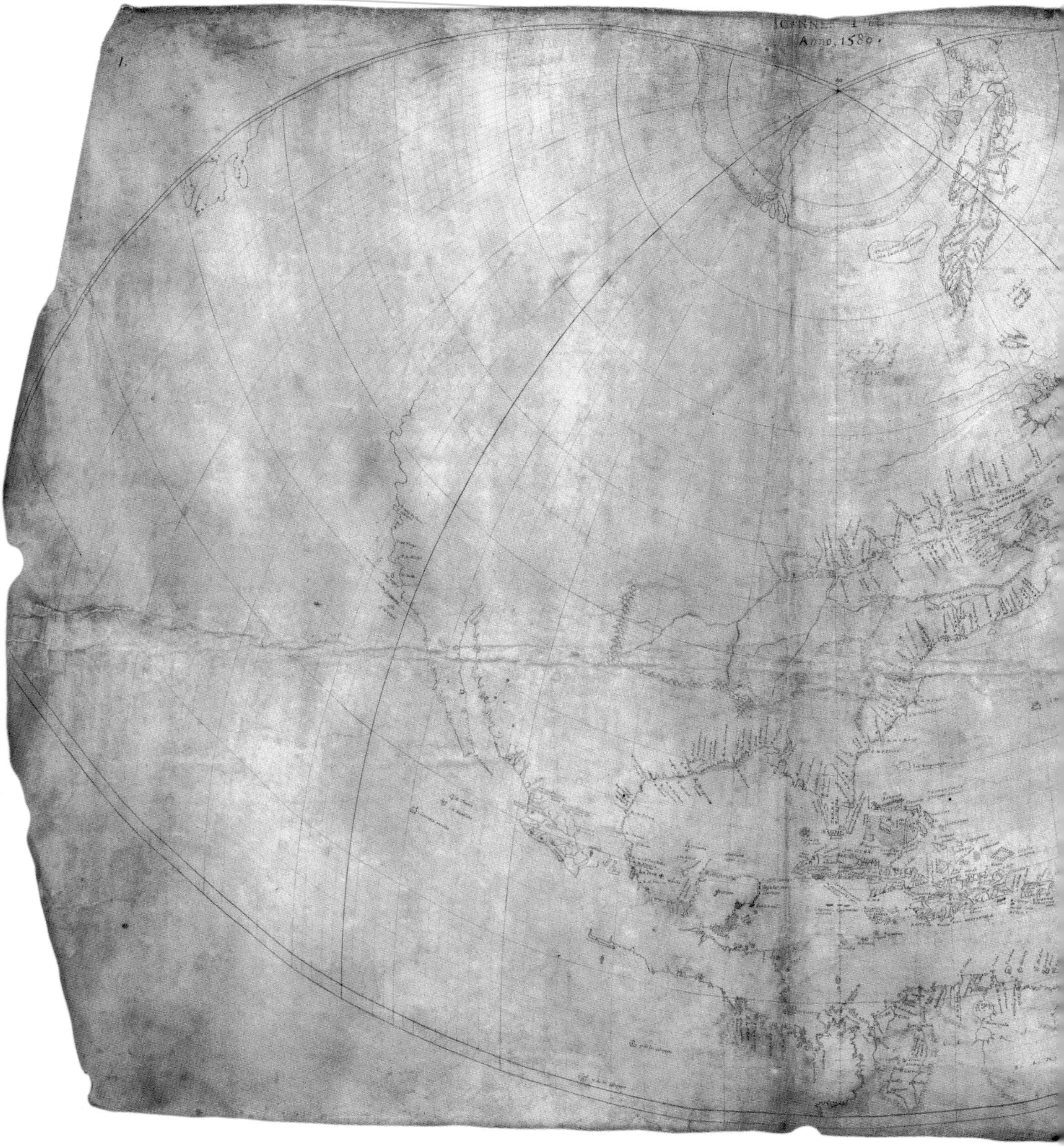
Anno, 1580.

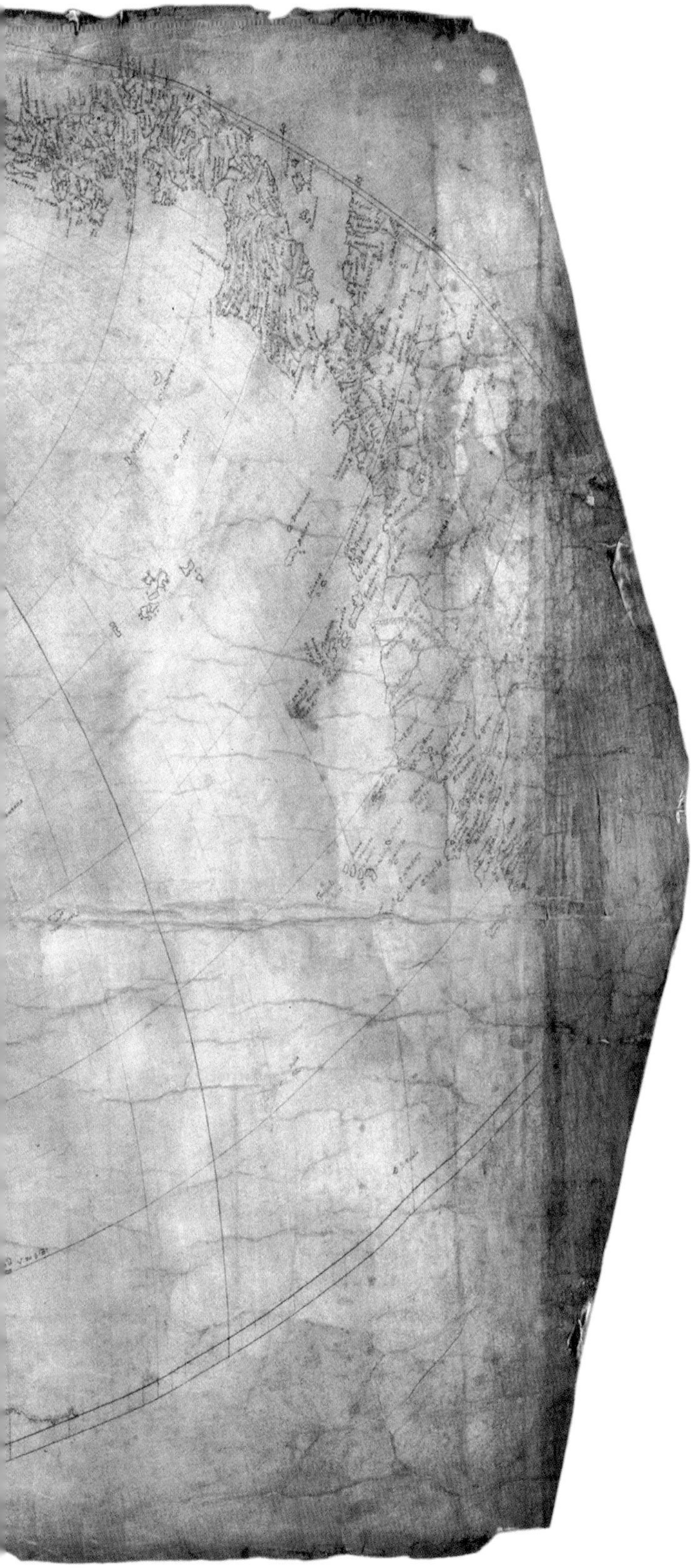

North Atlantic and Arctic Oceans

(1580)

There are few more enigmatic characters in British history than the Elizabethan John Dee (1527–1608/9). A figure who 'stood on that ground where the concerns of his age met and could not easily be distinguished', Dee was both mathematician and magician, astronomer and astrologer, advisor and philosopher. He was also a mapmaker. This chart of the Northern Hemisphere, including North America, the Arctic and Western Europe, was drawn by him in around 1580 and was probably presented to Elizabeth I.

The map is strongly associated with Tudor expansionism during Elizabeth's reign. Sir Francis Drake's circumnavigation of the world between 1577 and 1580 had brought confidence and prestige to England, but it remained in the shadow of the Spanish and Portuguese empires in the southern Atlantic and Pacific oceans. English explorers resolved to discover another route to the riches of the East Indies, via a Northwest Passage through the Arctic and over the top of what is now Canada.

This part of the world was not very well known in Europe, but John Dee set about discovering more about it. He contacted his associate, the mapmaker Gerhard Mercator, whose 1569 world map had shown some interesting features in the Arctic Northwest. Dee asked Mercator where this information had come from. Unfortunately, Mercator's reply was both late and vague. He cited an obscure fourteenth-century voyage account by an explorer named Jacob van Cnoyen which he had lent to someone and not received back.

Dee drew his map to resemble Mercator's as closely as he could, for example repeating the four curious large islands and the large magnetic rock at the North Pole. He also added discoveries that had already been made by the explorers Stephen Borough, Sebastian Cabot and Martin Frobisher. The rest could be filled in later.

On the back of the map Dee wrote what is regarded as one of the earliest statements expressing an ideology of an English Empire and of English foreign policy. The legend sets out 'the Queenes maiesties title royall to these foreyn regions and ilands'. The justification cites, among more recent explorers, King Arthur, who in the sixth century had supposedly conquered Iceland, Greenland and the area of modern Labrador. Further reasoning concludes that 'by the same order that other Christian Princes doo now a days make conquests upon the heathen people, we also have to procede herein'. Basically, everyone else is doing it and so will we.

North Sea

(1646–7)

The British Library possesses a number of engraved copper plates used to print early maps. They include a version of Christopher Saxton's England and Wales wall map of 1583, Wenceslaus Hollar's 1642 map of Hull and a number of Major James Rennell's *Bengal Atlas* maps of 1781 and later. Copper plates have a low survival rate, partly due to the heavy wear they suffer in the printing press, but also because there was no need to retain them once they had served their purpose. They were usually melted down and reconstituted, but very occasionally they were saved if their reverse side was used for another engraving or even a painting.

That is the reason for the survival of this plate, used to print half of a seventeenth-century sea chart of the Netherlands' North Sea coast (overleaf). In 1783 the Florentine artist Giuseppe Foraboschi engraved a copy of a fresco of the Annunciation in the Basilica della Santissima Annunziata on the reverse of it.

The chart was included in one of the most original atlases of the seventeenth century. The *Dell'Arcano del Mare* ('Secrets of the Sea') by Robert Dudley (1574–1649) was published in Florence between 1646 and 1647 and again in 1661. Robert Dudley was the illegitimate son of Robert Dudley, 1st Earl of Leicester (1532–88), an Elizabethan statesman and favourite of the Queen. Dudley junior was an explorer and engineer who in 1605, after unsuccessfully claiming his legitimacy at court, fled with his lover to Italy leaving his wife and family in England. Outlawed by James I, in Florence he assumed his father's title and became chamberlain to Maria Maddalena of Austria (1559–1631), wife of Cosimo II de Medici (*r.*1609–21), Grand Duke of Tuscany. He worked on engineering and military projects for the Duke.

His sea atlas, which took 12 years to produce, is the first printed sea atlas by an Englishman and the first to use Gerhard Mercator's projection. It was an exhaustive three-volume guide to navigation, with sections on longitude, existing sea charts' errors, even shipbuilding, illustrated with 372 engravings of which 142 were maps of the world's coasts. These engravings were the work of Antonio Francesco Lucini (*fl.*1661–75), who copied Dudley's manuscript maps (now in the Bayerische Staatsbibliothek in Munich) and wooden models of scientific instruments which Dudley had had specially made for the purpose (the models were used as firewood by German soldiers in World War Two).

As we can see from the map and the smooth engraved surface of the plate, Lucini was a fine engraver, particularly skilled at elaborate capital letters. In the dedication for the 1661 edition of the atlas, published after Dudley's death, Lucini wrote: 'I, for 12 years sequestered from the world in a little Tuscan village, have consumed no less than 5000 pounds of copper in engravings to illustrate it'. That is a substantial amount of copper, and this half-plate is now a rare survivor.

Carta particolare della costa di
Zelanda e Frislanda e Olanda che co-
mincia con il Porto di Newport e
Finisce con Messelwart
d'Europa Carta XXXVI
PAESE BASSO
Holanda

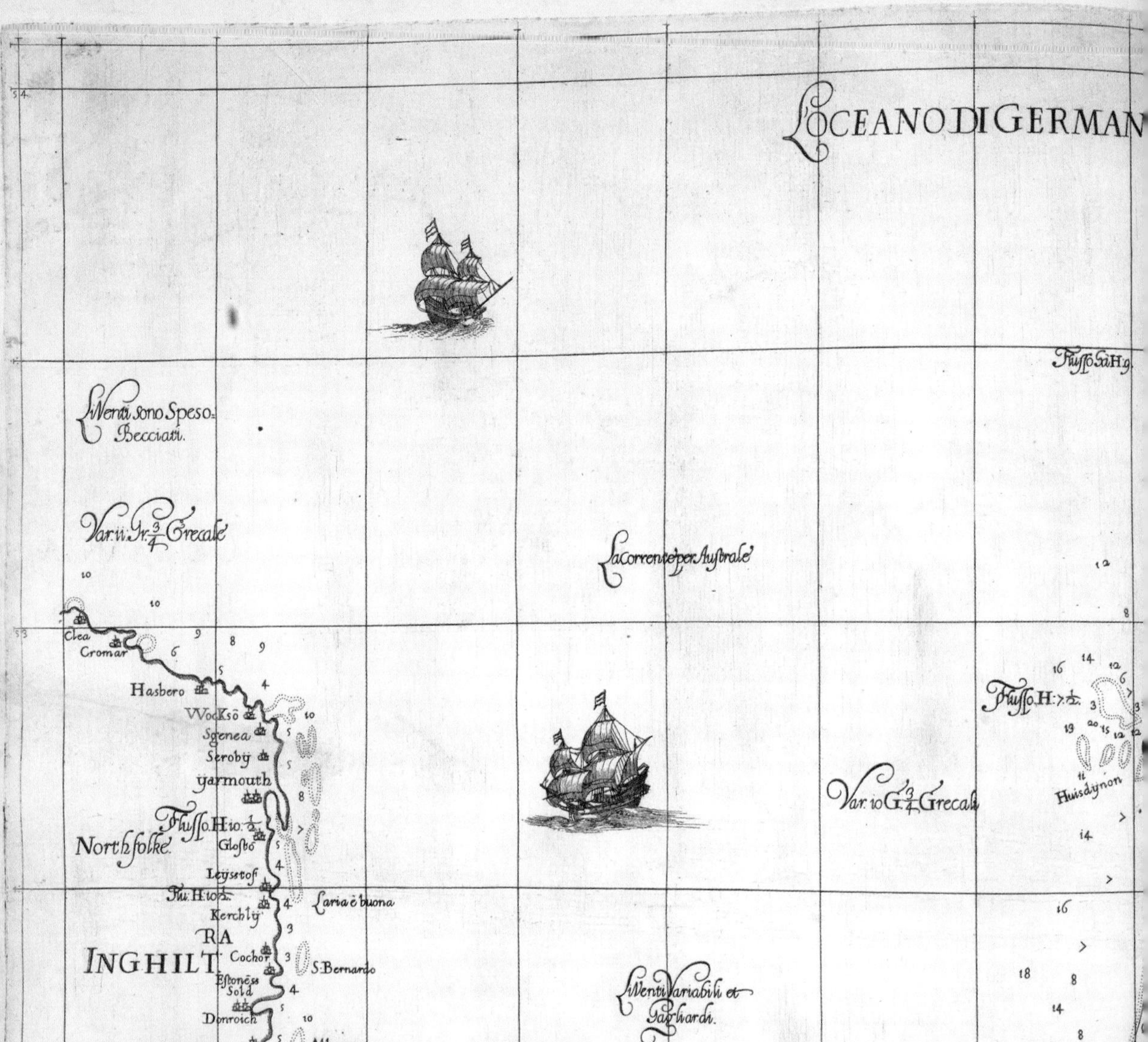
L'OCEANO DI GERMAN
Li Venti sono Speso Becciati
Var: ii Gr. 3/4 Grecale
La corrente per Australe
Var. 10 G. 3/4 Grecale
Flusso S.a H. 9
Flusso H: 7 1/2
Huisdynon
Clea
Cromar
Hasbero
Wockso
Sgenea
Seroby
yarmouth
Flusso H. 10 1/2
Northfolke
Glosbo
Leysetof
Flu: H: 10 1/2
L'aria è buona
Kerchly
INGHILTERRA
Cochor
S. Bernardo
Estoness
Sold
Donroich
Alborow
Alborow napps
Suffolek
Orford ness
Flu: H: ii 1/2
Orford
B. di Orford
Dover Cow
Wodbrige
Ipswig
Flu: ii H: 1/2
Essex
P. Harwid
Flu: H: ii 1/2
C. Nore
Li Venti Variabili et Gagliardi
Scheveling
Ter Hoy
Loos dunen
Ter heyd
Flu: H: 4 1/2
L'Aria è mal Sana la State
Il Mare d'Inghilterra
Flusso H: 1 1/2
Flu: H: 1 1/2
Bocca del R. Tamice
Rompot
Briel
S. Nuld. di Voorn
S. Schowe
Voorn
Overflacke
Dunland
Var. ii Gr. Grecale
S. Walkeren
Middelburg
Flusbing
Bancho Bianco
Tergoes
Beveland
Flusso ii H. 1/2
N. Forland
Flusso H: 12
S. Margerita
Querns
Brockes
Flu: H: 1 1/2
Tenet
Kent
Bocr Band
Innerweluck
Ne Sand
Sandwich
Goodwin Sand
Inghilterra
Le Dounes
S. Foreland
Flu: H: 12
Douer
Downes
New Port
Pd. Ostende
Blanken berg
Sluys
Vlies
Damme
Fiandra
Bruges
De Noese
La Punca
Flus. H: 12
Le Seccaie mutano assai ogni Anno
Tolen
Bergen opzome
Flu: H: 12

Var. 10 G. Grecale.
Li Venti Sono Spesso grerali & ouanti
Osse banch
Messelward
Flus: a H 12
Wedward
Leche
Li canali di q. Secc. Sai si allargano, e mutano ogni anno qualche cosa.
Gatt
Langer Oog
Wrangeroog
Weser
Juyst
Norderney
Keten
Kete Sand
Borkum
Rottom
Il Rancoel
Schiermonik
Ameland
Hesse Sand
Ruidt Watt
Opt Watt
Groat Holm
Esens
Shollech
Knyppers
Landkworde
Burbach
R: Weser
Strotto di Iade
I: Iade
I: Stollam
Norde
Dornu
Heppes
I: ScomKom
Lutzburg
Ossel
W: March
Duddibwrg
Godeas
Surgic
Vassel
I: Brioch
Stenbusch
Emden
Flusso Sa H. g.
I: Messerland
Borsu
Iarsiu
Oldersum
Wiwelsu
Larel
Knopk
Logo
Wthusem
Watum
Berum
Vlrum. o. Witlan
Flusso H. g.
Holwirda
Fauingum
Reijde
Weldendorpa
Swrdyck
Sexbierū
Engiuere
Flusso H. g.
Sansw
Midwold
Beert
Heilgerle
Bunde
R: Amaso
Proningam
Bonter garden
Winaem
Flusso H. g.
Dockam
G. Inondato
GERMANIA
Harlingen
Coorwere
Worcom
Hinlopen
Sloeten
Lemerhorn
Kuyder
Flusso H. g.
Blog
Vollenhoue
FRISIA OCCIDENTALE
L'Ariano è molto sana la State
Flusso H. 12
Emeloort
Brock
Encuse
Reuel Sand
VreK
Ens
Grasherst
Wilfte
Fl. H. 3.
Jl Mare d'Olanda
Var. g. Gr. ½ Grecale
Campen
PAESE BASSO
Elburg
Zuyderzee
Marck
Doer
Nunspeet
Harderwick
Muyden
Oud Narden
Fl. H. 3
Naerden
BARBANZI
Holanda
anda
EVROPA
Carta particolare della costa di Zelanda è Frislanda è Olanda che comincia con il Porto di Newport è Finisce con Messelward
La longitudine Comincia da l'Isola di Picho d'Asores.
di Europa Carta XXXVI.
Æ: Lucini Fece

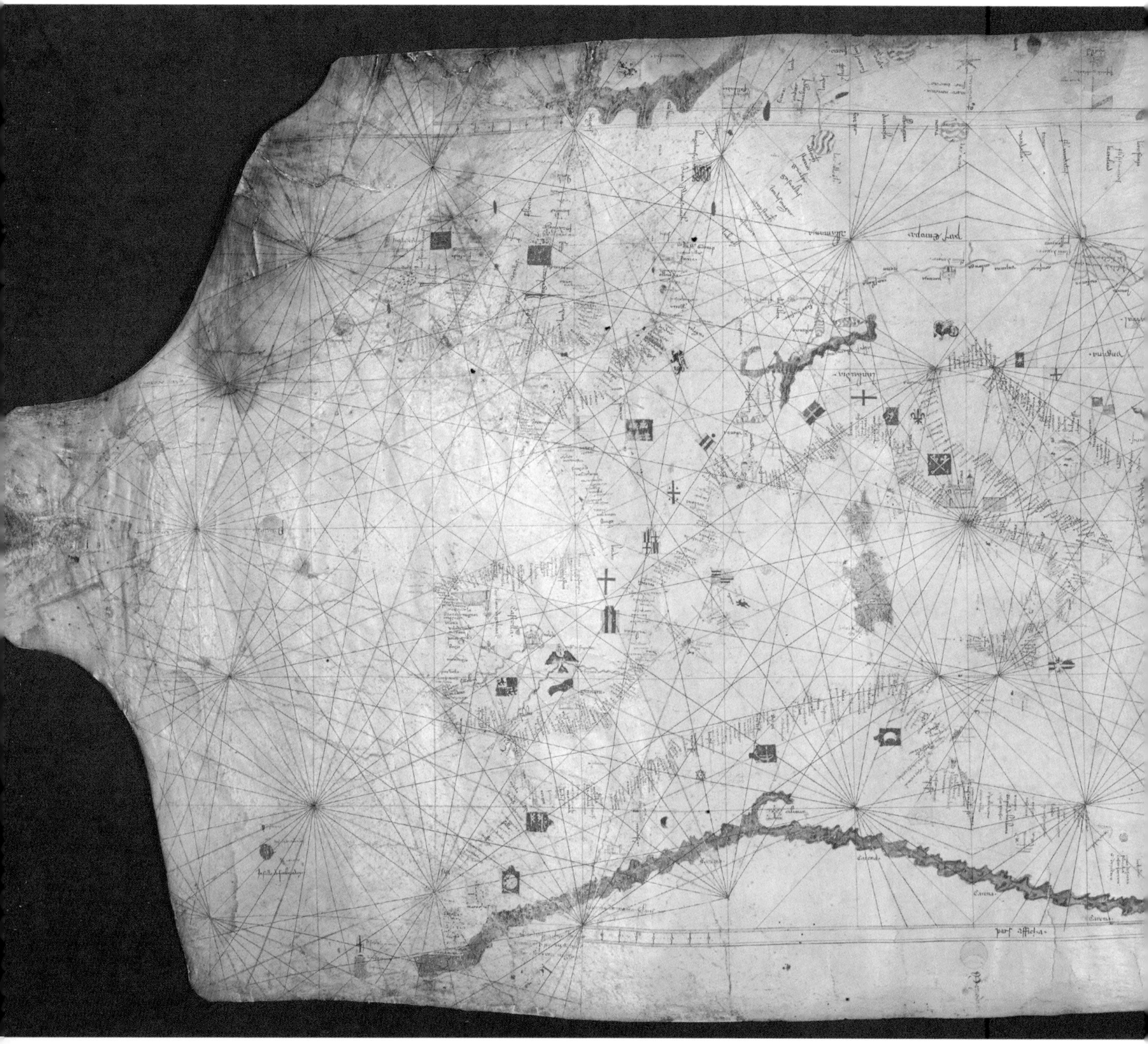

Mediterranean Sea

(c.1339)

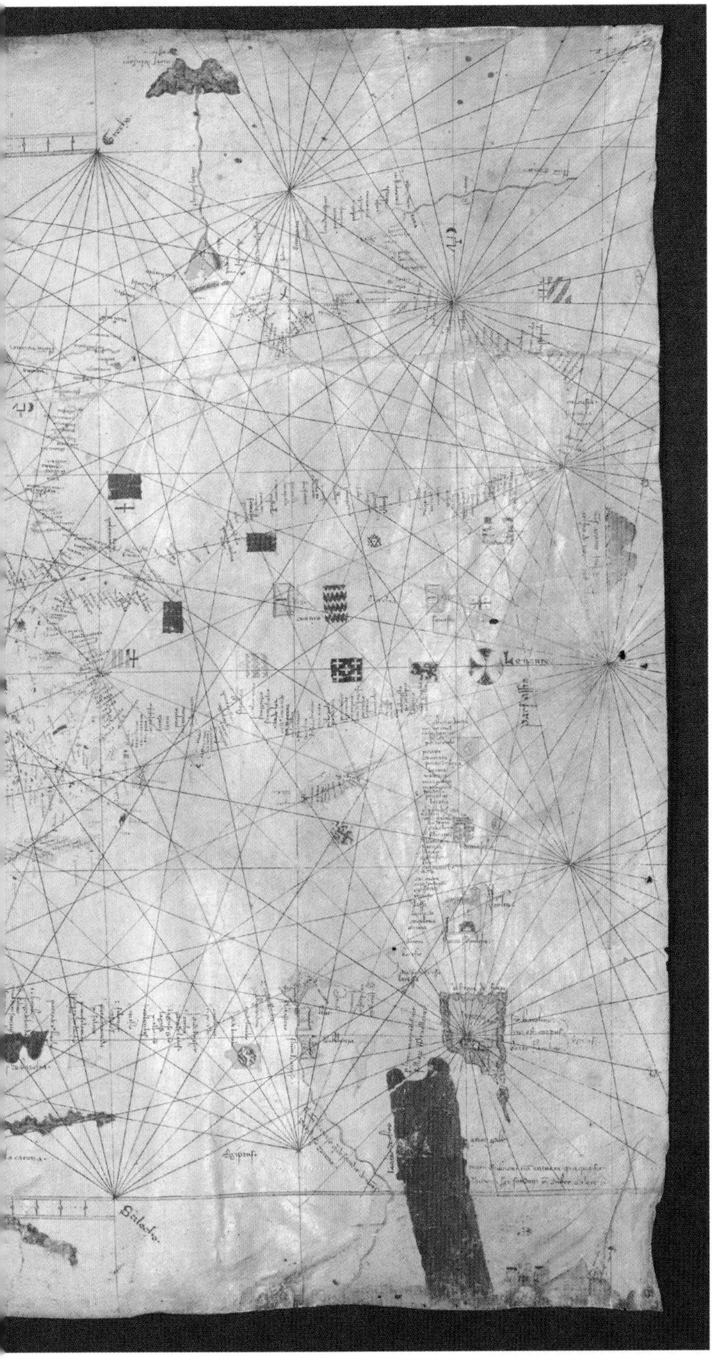

Early European sea charts known as 'portolan charts' continually amaze people. 'How were they able to be so accurate?' is often asked. It is true that portolan charts show the coast of the Mediterranean Sea with unnerving and impressive accuracy. If we look at this chart produced in around 1339 (the British Library's earliest portolan chart) we can perfectly well make out the Mediterranean, with Italy in the middle and faintly coloured Sardinia and Corsica to the left of it.

The coastlines look accurate because knowledge of them was developed and refined over many centuries by sailors who navigated them using the ancient method of 'dead reckoning' – basically educated guesswork to approximate one's position. We are not entirely sure when navigators decided to go from storing their knowledge of the Mediterranean in their heads and writing lists to drawing maps of it. The correlation in date between the earliest surviving portolan chart (the 'Carte Pisane' of around 1280) and the introduction of the marine compass in the thirteenth century may provide a clue, but the issue is hotly debated.

Portolan charts also strike a chord with a modern audience because of their practical navigational purpose (which led an author in 1905 to call them 'the first true maps'). However, some portolan charts do contain illustrations which are apparently superfluous to their utility. Their early study revealed two Mediterranean chart traditions: Catalan charts made in Majorca tended to include decorative features and pictures, while charts made in Italy, for example in Genoa, Venice and later Messina, are generally unadorned.

This chart was probably made in Palma by a chart maker called Angelino Dulcert (*fl.*1339). Though it is unsigned it bears similarities with a signed chart of 1339 in Paris. Looking beyond the coastlines, place names and rhumb lines, we can make out a variety of illustrations including mountains (the Atlas Mountains in North Africa, and the Alps) and rivers (the island-filled Danube). Switzerland's lakes are shown, and Mount Ararat appears as a green double-peaked hill in the far right. The Red Sea is coloured red, and a small line intersecting it represents the path of the Israelites escaping from Egypt. Churches have been drawn over the locations of Rome and Jerusalem, and the winged lion of St Mark hovers over Venice.

Although this information was not important for navigation, aesthetics, tradition and belief also played a part in people's lives and so they quite naturally found their way on to maps. Even pictorial features might have some practical use. Flags have been added in order to indicate who ruled a particular stretch of coast – anything but superfluous if it helped you avoid falling into the hands of enemies.

The Moon

(1978)

The moon has been the mapmaker's muse for centuries. The invention of the telescope at the beginning of the seventeenth century marked the modern era of lunar mapping, with greater magnification making its surface more accessible to cartographer–astronomers such as Galileo Galilei (1564–1642), Johannes Hevelius (1611–87) and Jean-Dominique Cassini (1625–1712). What they would have made of this geological map of a region on the far side of the moon is anybody's guess.

The map is one of a number of maps of the geology of the moon produced by the United States Geological Survey for inclusion in a lunar atlas. The map was created in 1978 by Desiree E. Stuart-Alexander (b.1930) and is based on lunar information in the form of photographs taken during NASA's Apollo missions and the Soviet Union's Zond programme – a rare moment of Cold War co-operation. Maps of the near side of the moon benefited from information derived from rock samples taken as part of the Apollo landings. As yet no human has set foot on the far side of the moon.

Despite the extraordinary type and distribution of colours in the map, quite a departure given that maps of only a few years earlier had been produced in monochrome, and which has elicited comparisons with psychedelia and Jackson Pollock paintings, this is one of the driest maps in this atlas. A comprehensive key, diagrams and an accompanying essay give it the tone of a research paper. The colours are certainly the key to the map, used to differentiate the incredibly complex and often overlapping lunar surface features of craters and basins from each other and representing the age of the impacts by asteroids or volcanic eruptions which caused them. Distinction is helped by the use of duller colours such as brown and beige for the older features, with brighter yellow, greens and blues for the younger ones. The pink features, in the middle of the colour scale, are thought to be around 3,800 million years old.

This role of colour is a key feature of geological mapping, a generally younger genre than lunar mapping. William Smith's (1769–1839) 1815 map of the strata of England and Wales differentiated geological types using colours, but their allocation was often naturalistic – for example, coal deposits were coloured black or grey. This map is a landmark in both genres and pays lip service to the traditions of each. But it is also very much of its time, in its palette, and in the names of many craters honouring prominent contemporary Russian and American scientists and astronauts.

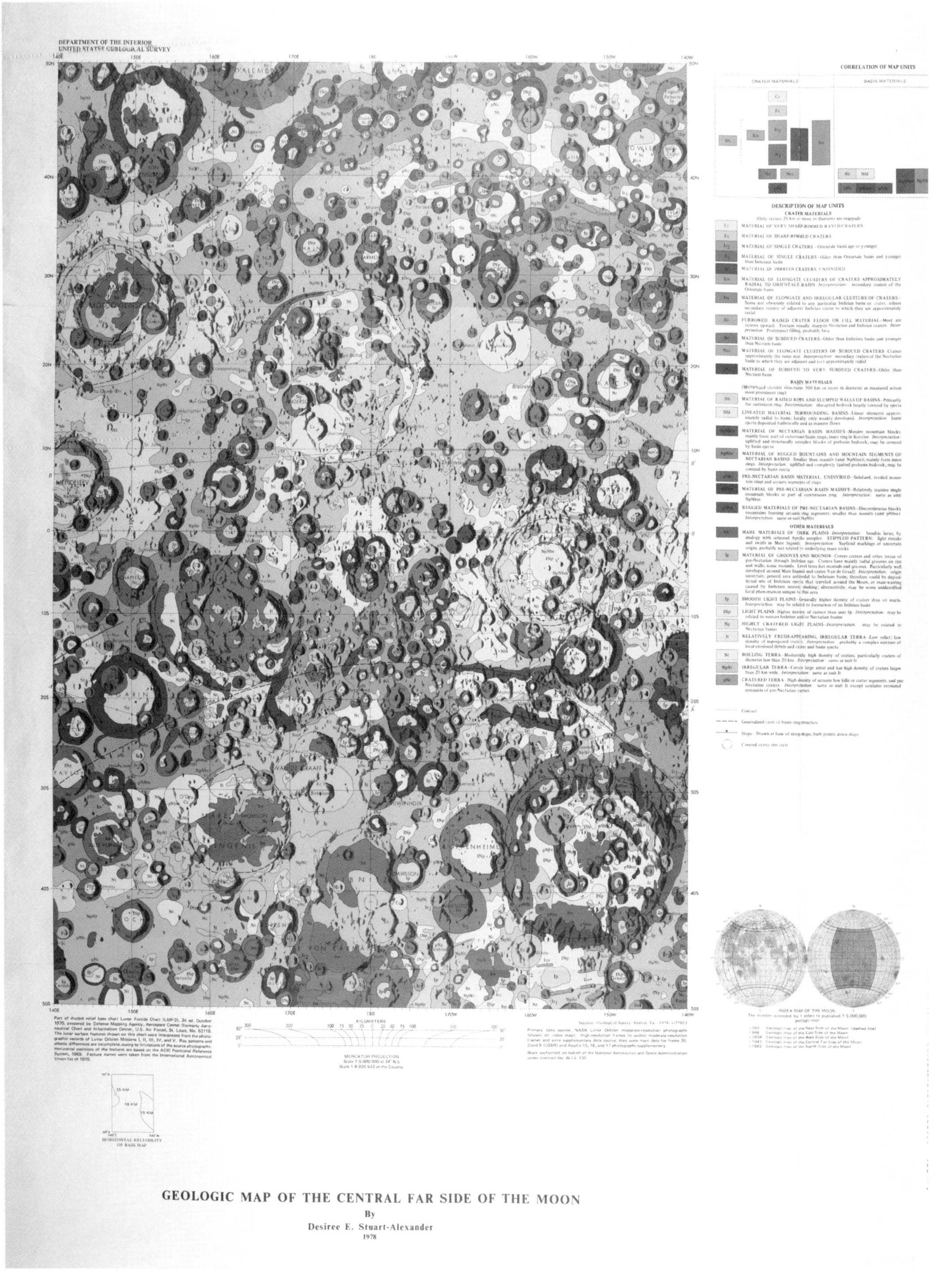
DEPARTMENT OF THE INTERIOR
UNITED STATES GEOLOGICAL SURVEY
CORRELATION OF MAP UNITS
DESCRIPTION OF MAP UNITS
CRATER MATERIALS
MATERIAL OF VERY SHARP-RIMMED RAYED CRATERS
MATERIAL OF SHARP-RIMMED CRATERS
MATERIAL OF SINGLE CRATERS
MATERIAL OF IMBRIAN CRATERS, UNDIVIDED
MATERIAL OF ELONGATE CLUSTERS OF CRATERS APPROXIMATELY RADIAL TO ORIENTALE BASIN
MATERIAL OF ELONGATE AND IRREGULAR CLUSTERS OF CRATERS
FURROWED, RAISED CRATER FLOOR OR FILL MATERIAL
MATERIAL OF SUBDUED CRATERS
MATERIAL OF ELONGATE CLUSTERS OF SUBDUED CRATERS
MATERIAL OF SUBDUED TO VERY SUBDUED CRATERS
BASIN MATERIALS
MATERIAL OF RAISED RIMS AND SLUMPED WALLS OF BASINS
LINEATED MATERIAL SURROUNDING BASINS
MATERIAL OF NECTARIAN BASIN MASSIFS
MATERIAL OF RUGGED MOUNTAINS AND MOUNTAIN SEGMENTS OF NECTARIAN BASINS
OTHER MATERIALS
GEOLOGIC MAP OF THE CENTRAL FAR SIDE OF THE MOON
By
Desiree E. Stuart-Alexander
1978

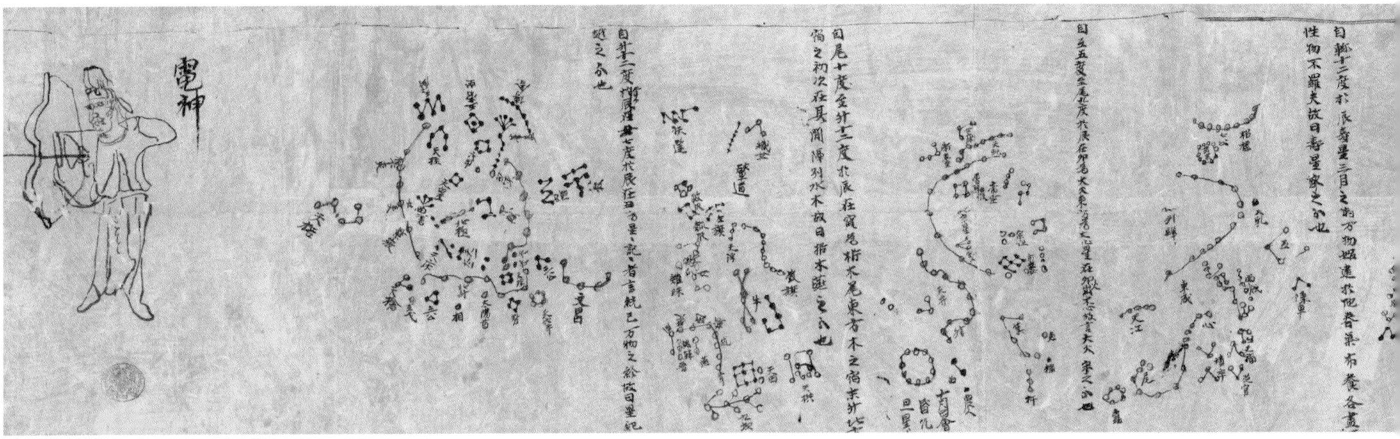

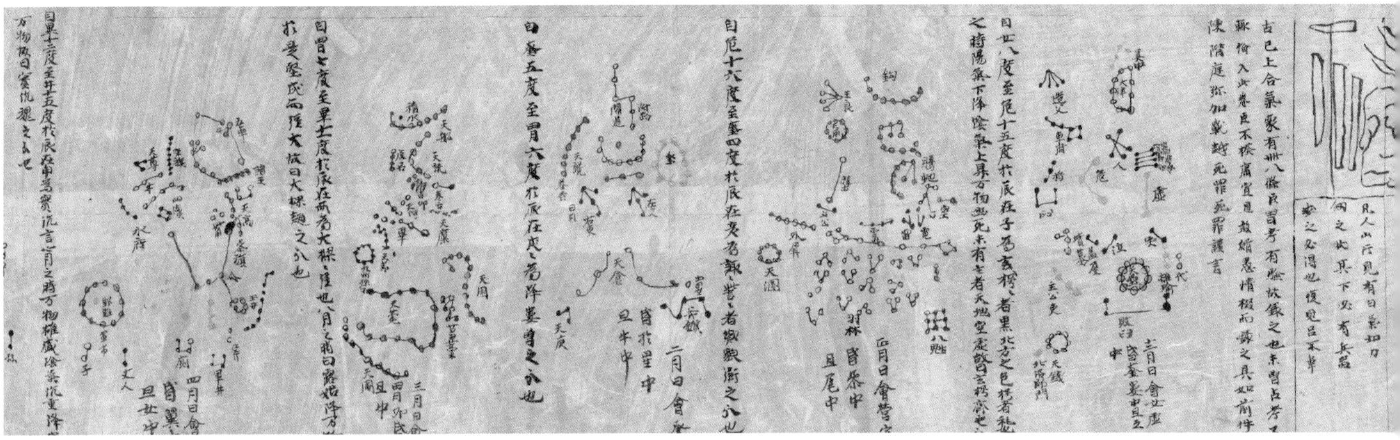

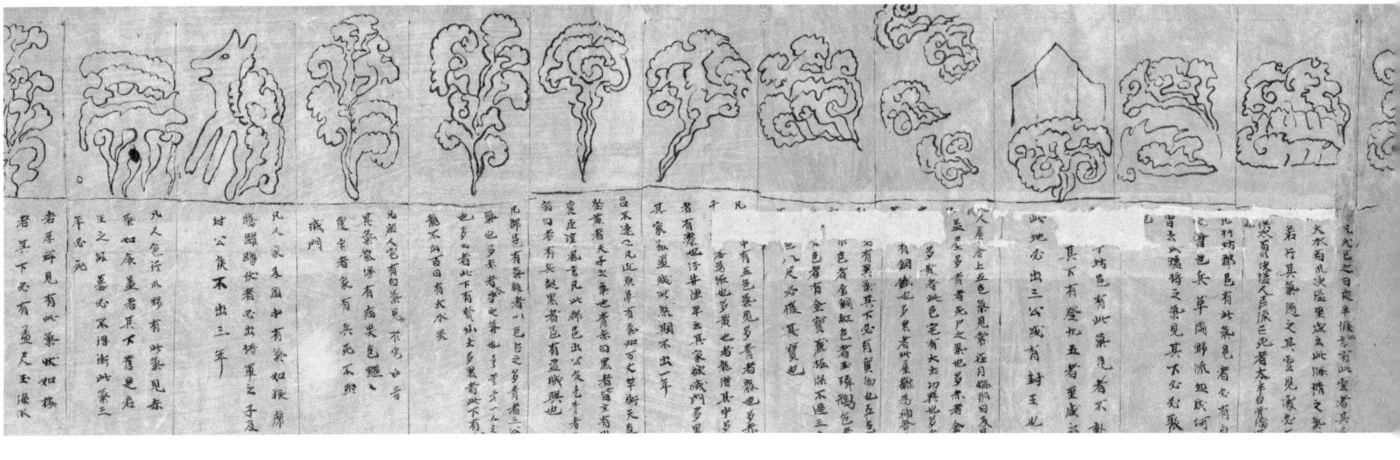

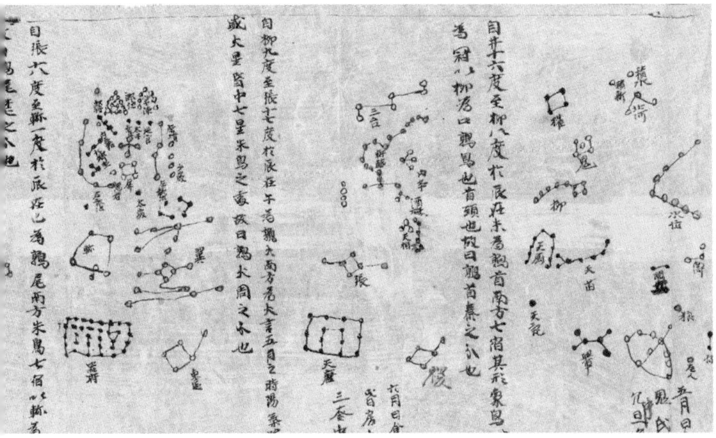

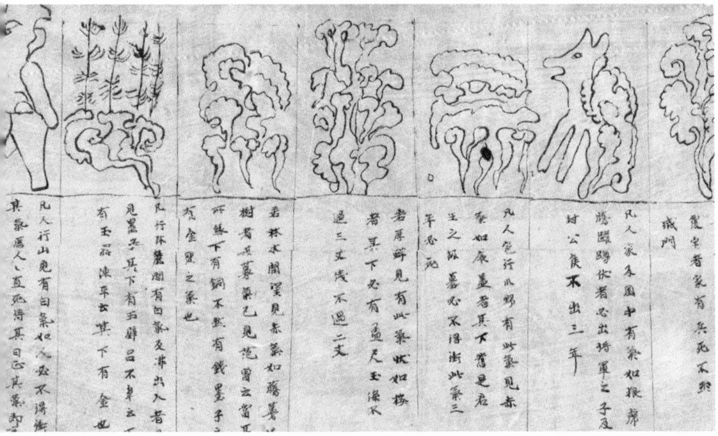

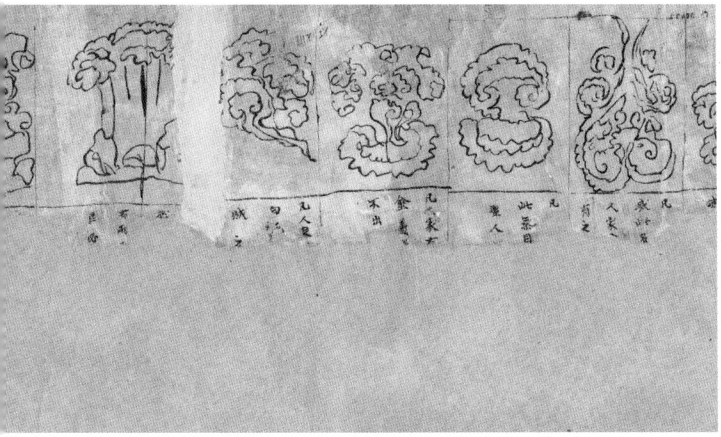

The Sky

(c.700)

Maps of the sky were produced before maps of the earth. In the ages before artificial light, the night sky had a more dominant presence in people's lives, and celestial objects played a greater role, for navigation and weather predictions as well as prophecies and storytelling.

These are the world's oldest surviving star charts of the whole of the night sky. They were drawn in China at the start of the eighth century and show well over a thousand stars visible in China, arranged into 13 vertical sections on a roll which is a metre and a half in diameter. The stars, which are named, have been drawn in three colours – red, yellow and black – with star groupings often sharing the same colour. Star patterns such as Orion's Belt, the Plough and the distinctive 'W' of Cassiopeia can be recognised.

Unlike on later Western charts, the constellations have not been overdrawn with the legendary stories that were attached to them. Yet Chinese culture did attach powerful significance to the movement of the heavens. The sky and its natural phenomena were felt to relate to the actions of the Chinese emperor and were used to predict political events. An eclipse, for example, could signify an imminent coup, and for this reason the emperor's astronomers kept a close eye on the sky.

The charts were found in 1900 by European sinologists including the Frenchman Paul Pelliot and the English-Hungarian Aurel Stein (1862–1943). They were discovered in a cave in eastern China along with around 40,000 other texts which once formed an ancient Buddhist library. The Dunhuang Library, which lay on the important Silk Road trade route network between China and the West, had been sealed and as a result was miraculously preserved around the turn of the first millennium.

Looking at these maps, it is astounding how fresh and innovative they appear, far more contemporary than many celestial maps which were produced after them. Although Greek geographers were making important astronomical observations concurrent with Chinese cultures in the second century (Claudius Ptolemy's second-century 'Almagest' is the basis for our modern star catalogue), charts were either not drawn from them, or have not survived.

Northern and Southern Skies

(1590)

The Elizabethans loved their maths. Over the course of the 1580s and 1590s a substantial number of mathematical books, treatises and education courses were published to cater for an expanded audience of merchants and professionals. This wasn't the pure mathematics taught in universities, but applied mathematics for practical purposes at a time when maths and magic were becoming distinct from one another and the former was necessary for commerce: algebra for business, arithmetic for bookkeeping, geometry for surveying.

One of the leading Elizabethan London mathematicians was a man named Thomas Hood (1556–1620). Hood wasn't a high-minded academic but a down-to-earth teacher who educated ordinary people about practical things such as arithmetic and the use of scientific instruments. Measuring and observational tools such as the quadrant, astrolabe and cross-staff were increasingly used by mariners travelling further afield for business and war. Instruments and maps were loosely associated, and a number of manufacturers, such as Augustine Ryther (*d.*1593), constructed both.

It was Ryther who engraved for Hood the two celestial charts which were issued with his 1590 book, *The use of the celestial globe in plano*. These are the first celestial charts to have been engraved in England, and not before time given that Albrecht Dürer's charts, which Hood followed closely, had been published three-quarters of a century earlier. Nevertheless, the charts were worth the wait. They are large, ornate and vividly coloured engravings, a northern and southern hemisphere chart with the northern one typically busier than the southern one because of the lack of European knowledge of the southern skies. Over a thousand major stars are marked, while the large though naively drawn constellations were designed to stick in the memory.

The accompanying book, based on one of Hood's public lectures, describes how to use the charts. It takes the form of a question-and-answer dialogue between a master and a precocious pupil. 'I tolde you even noew', the master complains at one point, clearly exasperated at having to impart such basic information as why some stars look different from others, and why the tail of the Great Bear is so long (Jupiter used the bear's tail to pull it up to the heavens, Hood explains). For navigators hoping to use the stars as locational reference points, however, the book is a simple and straightforward crash course.

PART OF
PRIVATE INCOME
LAND
Part of
Sports Island
OCEAN
Composer's Rocks
Playwright's Isle
Isles of Literature
Poets' Isle
Music Isle
Fiction Isle
Painting Isle
Pools Island
Science Isle
Designers Isle
Poison Pen Pt
Slander Pt
Libel Rocks
Gossips Isle
Brown Bread Head
Burnt Toast Bay
Lizard Bay
Lazy Rocks
White Bread Point
Bakers Town
FLOUR CITY
Dough Church
TELEVISION ROCK
EVENING
Rolls Head
Millers Town
Crispcrust Hotel
Sandwich Manor
Oven Croft House
Penny Bun Village
Crumb Church
Confectioners Village
Bun Point
Salmon Castle
Fresh Fish Town
Great Haddock Head
Plaice Village
Big Fin Inn
FISHERMANS CITY
Mackerel Town
Sturgeon's Castle
Sole Town
Herring Bay
Herring Town
Kipper Bay
TWILIGHT HOUSE
Cod Town
Kipper Village
Goldfish Hotel
Whitebait Point
Oatmeal Bay
Porridge Point
Scotts Town
Quaker Town
Weetabix Head
Shredded Wheat Bay
Recording Studio
Casino
Swimming Pool
Girl Sound
Attraction Island
Beauty Mountain
"Showing off" Island
Engagement Island
Jealousy Rocks
Honeymoon Isle
Reading in Bed Hills
Snorers Bay
Loud Snorers Rock
BEAUTY SLEEP DOWNS

PART OF
STATE INCOME LAND
Too big to show on this Map.
The One and only Original Map of Breakfast Island
indicating life & taste in Britain at the beginning of the 2nd Elizabethan Reign
An ever expanding terrain with increasing population despite Political strife and disease
LABOUR
PAY PACKET DEDUCTION ISLANDS
PAYE Isle
Nat Insurance Isle
Welfare Isle
Superannuation Isle
Employers Federation Board
Tin Plate
Textiles
Steel
Mustard Island
Kidney Head
Ketchup Pt.
Tomato Pt.
Relishes Castle
Piccalilli Village
H.P. Town
Perrins Inn
Gammon Sands
Sausage Village
Porkpie Town
WORCESTER CITY
Spice Town
SAUCES COUNTY
MEAT COUNTY
HAM CITY
Liver Town
BACON CITY
Bacon Hills
Sow Castle
Pig Mountain
O.K. Cottage
Clove Hill
BUS YARD
OPEN YARD
TRANSPORT COUNTY
AIR PORT
POLICE
CANTEEN
Rush Hour Circus
Pedal Cyclists
Motor Cyclists
Trolley Bus
Underground
THE "AFTER BREAKFAST" COUNTY
Strap-hangers Sanatorium
Load-shedding Control Point
PRIVATE CARS PARK
Taxi Rank
BREAKFAST CITY
MARMALADE HILLS
Orange Castle
Tangerine Lodge
Tinned Fruit Town
Jam Town
Plum Town
FRUIT COUNTY
Fruit Juice River
Grape Fruit Delta
Peach Head
STONE FRUIT CITY
Jelly Manor
HARD FRUIT CITY
Bottled Fruit Town
Pear Town
Apple Town
Greengage Village
Blackberry Hill
Strawberry Downs
SOFT FRUIT CITY
Tomato Town
Raspberry Village
Day Shift Sound
Safe-words Bay
Heifer Hills
CREAM VALLEY
Bottle Town
MILK COUNTY
Red Cow Hill
Rye Village
Milkmaid Village
Nestle Castle
JERSEY CITY
Duck Town
EGG COUNTY
Suspension Bridge
Good Pasture Inn
Canned Milk Village
Fried Egg House
HEN CITY
Pullet Town
Broody Ck
Flowers Egg Village
Chicken Houses
Boiled Egg Inn
Pepper Isle
Salt Isle
Alarm Clock Point
Alarm Clock Works
Barley Town
Malt Town
Butter Town
Goat Milk Village
DAIRY CITY
Baby Milk Town
GRAIN CITY
Packing Town
Roasting Village
Rice Town
SUGAR ISLAND
Tea River
FIRST POST ISLAND
O.H.M.S. Letters
Bills Point
Early Morning Tea Island
Fresh Egg Pt.
CHANNEL
Hangover Isle
M.A.N.B Head
Fearful Head
Cross Head
Gloom Head Bay
Bathroom Queue Point
Stay-in-bed Quicksands
Halfwit Head
Tea in bed Houses
Nightmare Lakes
Breakfast in bed Houses
Hangover Head
MORNING
Rice Crispies Bay
Good Crisp Hotel
All Bran Bluffs
Bright Morning Head
Grape Nut Rock
GULF OF DREAMS

The New Papal World

(1567)

This map of the Jaws of Hell is a biting satire on the indolence of the Tridentine Catholic Church which, almost five centuries on from its publication, still has the capacity to shock.

The *Mappe-monde nouvelle papistique* or 'Map of the new papal world', by the Italian Jean-Baptiste Trento (*c.*1523–*c.*1588) and the French artist Pierre Eskrich (*c.*1530–*c.*1590), was published in Geneva, Switzerland in 1567. Geneva was a key site of the Protestant Reformation and the particular branch known as Calvinism after its founder John Calvin (1509–64). This hotbed of religious struggle and anti-papist sentiment attracted figures such as Trento, an Italian convert who had fled the Inquisition. Protestant propaganda focused on the perceived failure of the Council of Trent (held between 1545 and 1563) to address the abuses and problems of the Catholic church that had given rise to the Reformation. Printed pamphlets, treatises and illustrations were produced in the town and sent across Europe.

In its size and complexity Trento and Eskrich's map has not been surpassed. It is a large multi-sheet print, originally accompanied by an explanatory booklet that was dedicated to the Protestant Queen of England, Elizabeth I. It shows the devil, open mouthed, within which is a map of an apocalyptic landscape arranged in provinces and incorporating a view of the Vatican being besieged by Reformation armies. These provinces have titles such as 'Sacrament Province', 'Pilgrimage Province' and 'Monks Province' after key areas of contemporary debate. Within them are multi-figured scenes which illustrate the Church's continuing hypocrisy.

For example, in the 'Province of Saintly Service' we see an area of church building with a large overturned barrel of money and labels such as 'The Stones of Scandal' and 'Temple of Ingratitude'. Elsewhere, the criticised practices of indulgences and the veneration of relics continue unabated following the Council's failure to limit them. In this detail from the top right of the map, next to the under-construction St Peter's Basilica, we can see Dame Verité (Lady Truth) being murdered by a cohort of abbots and cardinals. The careful organisation of these complex numbered scenes, which are described in the exhaustive text around the map's edge (see overleaf), was designed to assist the viewer in contemplating and memorising the map's lessons, following Renaissance rhetorical practice.

This is combative cartography at its finest, but there is also humour in it (for example, the holy hermits which have metamorphosed into habit-wearing goats), which likens it to modern political cartoons. In this respect the map chimes with modern map use. To those looking at it during the height of Reformation fervour it must have appeared as powerful a weapon as the brutal devices of Hell in the map's bottom right corner. The British Library's example, one of only five surviving, is missing two sheets in its lower left portion.

26.Seig.EVANGILE
Gusanus Cardinal boul.
P.PERTVSA
Concile de Constance bouleu.
du Royaume
Euesque.
Abbé.
Cardinal de Lor.
Co. de Basle
du Pape.
Cō. Latrā.
BELVIDERE.
25. Dame VERITE.
Retraict de meschanceté.
Courtisans du Pape.
Monsieur de Haine.
Monsieur le Traistre.
Trōpeur
27.Astarot pe du Pape.
28.Perditiō mere.
32.PAPE.
29.Dame Pecune nourrice.
30.D.Menterie.
Bras Seculier.
D.Guerre.
76.BENEDICTINE,cité 45.
74.HIERONIMIANE,cité 43.
75.AVGVSTINIANE,cité 44.
Soldats de Danie, Suesse, Liuonie & Russie.

MAPPE-MONDE NOUV

L'ORIGINE ET COMMENCEMENT de ceste Mappe-Monde nouuelle Papistique, & comment elle a esté trouuee.

POVR mieux entendre l'origine & le contenu de ceste Mappe-Monde Papale, ...

LES DAMES DE LA COVRT

LES COVRTISANS DV PAPE

LA COVRT DV ROY FRANCARBITRE

LE PAPISTIQVE

Breakfast Island

(1953)

The funny thing about so-called 'fantasy' maps is that they often say a whole lot more about the real world than any other type of map. 'Breakfast Island' is no exception.

In the early 1950s Britain was emerging from an era of austerity forced on it by World War Two (1939–45). In the years following the end of the war, rationing of food and other materials had not only continued but had become even stricter, with bread, not rationed during wartime, controlled between 1946 and 1948. Things improved gradually, however, and it was surely the end of rationing of tea (1952), and eggs and sugar (1953) which motivated Cyril Phillips to produce this breakfast tray adorned with his *One and Only Original Map of Breakfast Island indicating life and taste in Britain at the beginning of the 2nd Elizabethan reign*.

If we look at the geography we can see Breakfast Island as the large landmass at the centre of the map. It is divided into counties – 'Fish County', 'Bread County', 'Fruit County' – and contains geographical features including 'Sausage Downs', 'Burnt Toast Bay' and 'Kellogg Castle'. We can almost imagine somebody sitting up in bed one Saturday morning to receive their breakfast on the tray and exclaiming: 'Look at all the lovely things I can have to eat!'

The satire turns more biting when we move beyond the breakfast table to the spaces beyond it. To the left is 'Private Income Land, a diminishing area subject to severe erosion … plentiful ruins and fine relics'. This includes, besides the 'Sea of Leisure' and 'Gossips Isle', the 'Duke of A's castle, National Trust Property, Duke now rents a flat in it from National Trust'. To the right is 'Wage Earner's land', described as 'an increasing area: subject to severe attacks of inflation and deflation despite all planning to contrary'. In addition to the various trades, it provides features such as 'Pay Packet Deduction Islands' and 'State Income Land (too big to show on this map)'.

This is a map of the situation of post-war Britain, specifically the decline of the upper class and the rise of the state. It suggests that, at least to Cyril Phillips, despite the return of the most important meal of the day and a new young monarch on the throne (Elizabeth II was crowned in the year of Breakfast Island's production), Britain's prospects were not yet set entirely fair.

PART OF STATE INCOME LAND
Too big to show on this Map.
The One and only Original Map of Breakfast Island
indicating life & taste in Britain at the beginning of the 2nd Elizabethan Reign
An ever expanding terrain with increasing population despite Political strife and disease
LABOUR
PART OF WAGE EARNERS
an increasing LAND area: subject to severe attacks of inflation and deflation despite all Planning to contrary.
PAY PACKET DEDUCTION ISLANDS
PAYE Isle
NAT. INSURANCE Isle
Welfare Isle
Superannuation Isle
Government Direction Board
Employers Federation Board
Wages Conciliation Board
T.U.C. Council
Official Strikes Com'ttee
Un-official Strikes Com'ttee
Mining
Textiles
Steel
Transport
Coal, Electricity & Gas
Cars, Tractors, Etc.
Earthenware
Hardware
Agriculture
Fishery
Meat
Losers Pt
Stale Bread Point
Burnt Toast Bay
Sausage Downs
Gammon Sands
Mustard Island
Kidney Head
H.P. Town
SAUCES COUNTY
WORCESTER CITY
Spice Town
MEAT COUNTY
Porkpie Town
HAM CITY
Liver Town
BACON CITY
Bacon Hills
Sow Castle
Pig Mountain
Dough Church
Crumpet Village
FLOUR CITY
Sandwich Manor
Confectioners Village
John-dory's Folly
Shell Fish Town
Halibut Cottages
Whalemeat Hill
FLAT FISH CITY
Turbot Town
Sole Town
Barley Town
Distillery
Brewery
Malt Town
CEREALS COUNTY
Scotts Town
OATS CITY
Quaker Town
GRAIN CITY
Packing Town
Rice Town
Rice Crispies Bay
Harvest Church
WHEAT CITY
Kelloggs Castle
Corn Town
All Bran Bluffs
Grape Nut Rock
Corn Flake Head
CHANNEL
SOUND SLEEP BAY
Midnight oil Burners Cottage
BREAKFAST CITY
Orange Castle
MARMALADE HILLS
FRUIT COUNTY
Tangerine Lodge
Jam Town
Plum Town
STONE FRUIT CITY
HARD FRUIT CITY
Jelly Manor
Bottle Town
Pear Town
Apple Town
Bottled Fruit Town
GREENGAGE Village
Blackberry Hill
Strawberry Downs
Raspberry Village
SOFT FRUIT CITY
Tomato Town
Peach Head
MILK COUNTY
CREAM VALLEY
Heifer Hills
Red Cow Hill
JERSEY CITY
Nestle Castle
DAIRY CITY
Baby Milk Town
Butter Tower
EGG COUNTY
Duck Town
Fried Egg House
HEN CITY
Pullet Town
Broody Ck
Chicken Houses
Boiled Egg Inn
Poached Egg Pt
Salt Isle
Pepper Isle
Fresh Egg Pt
FIRST POST ISLAND
Early Morning Tea Island
SUGAR ISLAND
Hangover Isle
MORNING CHANNEL
Fearful Head
Cress Head
Halfwit Head
Hangover Head
Nightmare Lakes
Tea in bed Houses
Breakfast in bed Houses
Bright Morning Head
GULF OF DREAMS
Baby's Feed Wakeup Hill
SLEEP
Gloom Head Bay
Bathroom Queue Point
Stay-in-bed Quicksands
The Sluggard's Delight Castle
TRANSPORT COUNTY
Rush Hour Circus
THE "AFTER BREAKFAST" COUNTY
Load-shedding Control Point
Underground
Marmalated Jay Walkers Refuge
subject to tidal submersion
Hooters Point
STRAITS
VICIOUS TIDES
DANGEROUS CURRENTS
RUSH HOUR BASIN
Grape Fruit Delta
Hooters Echo
The "Early Bird" Pt
caught worms Bay
"FIRST UP FIRST SERVED" HILL
Grey Dawn Head
Bright Dawn Head
Lorry Drivers Club
DAWN ISLAND
Rooks Parliament
All night Canteen
Police Stn
Telephone Calls Exchange
Safe worms Bay
Day Shift Sound
Night Shift Sound
Alarm Clock Works
Alarm Clock Point
Cock-crow Island
Cock Crow Light
N
S
W
E
Scale: Strictly according to tastes
COPYRIGHT RESERVED
FIRST PUBLISHED IN 1953

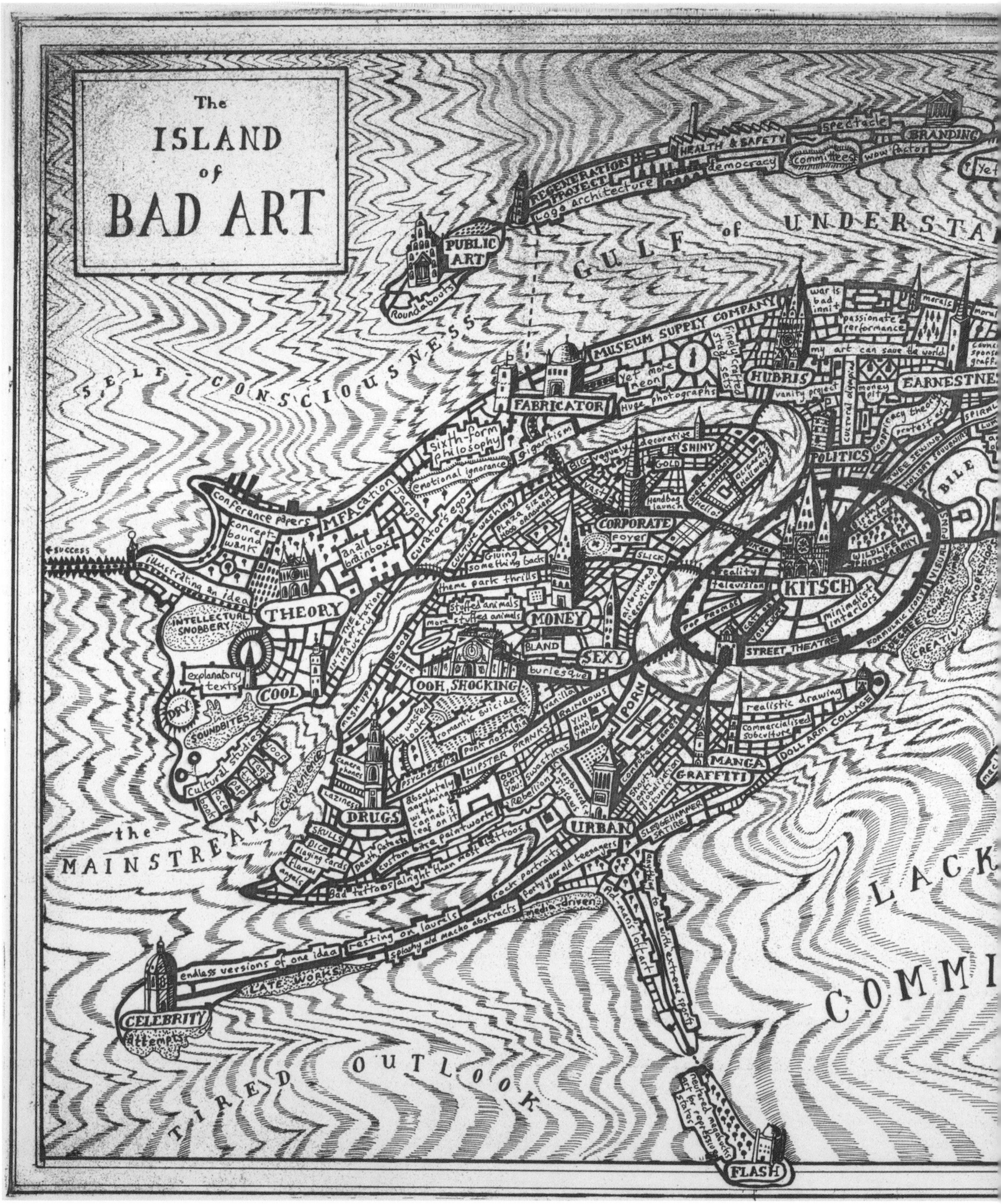

The ISLAND of BAD ART
GULF of UNDERSTA
SELF CONSCIOUSNESS
the MAINSTREAM
TIRED OUTLOOK
LACK
COMMI
PUBLIC ART
Roundabouts
REGENERATION PROJECT
Logo architecture
HEALTH & SAFETY
democracy
committees
spectacle
wow factor
BRANDING
MUSEUM SUPPLY COMPANY
FABRICATOR
yet more neon
Huge photographs
HUBRIS
war is bad innit
passionate performance
my art can save the world
vanity project
POLITICS
SHINY
CORPORATE
foyer
SLICK
KITSCH
reality television
minimalist interiors
STREET THEATRE
sixth-form philosophy
gigantism
emotional ignorance
conference papers
MFAcation
jargon
concept-bound wank
anal brainbox
curator's egos
culture washing
Giving something back
theme park thrills
illustrating an idea
THEORY
INTELLECTUAL SNOBBERY
explanatory texts
COOL
DRY
SOUNDBITES
cultural studies
stuffed animals
more stuffed animals
MONEY
BLAND
SEXY
burlesque
OOH, SHOCKING
romantic suicide
punk nostalgia
HIPSTER PRANKS
vanilla
RAINBOWS
YIN AND YANG
PORN
realistic drawing
commercialised subculture
DOLL ARM COLLAGE
MANGA
GRAFFITI
Rebellion
DRUGS
laziness
camera phones
Convenience
SKULLS
DICE
playing cards
flames
angels
custom bike paintworks
Bad tattoos
rock portraits
forty year old teenagers
URBAN
SLEDGEHAMMER SATIRE
Ad-man's loft art
to do with extreme sports
resting on laurels
splashy old macho abstracts
media driven
endless versions of one idea
LATE WORKS
CELEBRITY
attempts
FLASH
success
BILE
WILDLIFE PHOTOGRAPHY
CREATIVITY WORKSHOP
VISUAL PUNS
FORMULAIC IRONY
protest art
cultural olympiad
Handbag launch
BIG
vast
vaguely decorative
GOLD

The Island of Bad Art

(2013)

The genre of satirical mapping is alive and well in the twenty-first century. Indeed, throughout the past few centuries, from the hypocrisies of the Roman Catholic Church of the sixteenth century to the grim realities of twentieth-century post-war Britain, it has found a great deal to be satirical about. Yet satirical mapping is often seen as a niche area in cartography, subordinate to maps' practical and navigational functions. When practised by artists such as Grayson Perry (b.1960), however, we can appreciate its rich communicative capacity.

Grayson Perry works in a variety of traditional artistic mediums including tapestry, pottery and printmaking, the latter including maps of hypothetical places. What is interesting about his mapwork is that it often emulates historical cartographic genres or modes. For example, his *Map of Nowhere* (2008) references a medieval *mappa mundi*, while his *Map of an Englishman* (2004) is a fortification plan. In each case the form and content are vehicles for communicating Perry's feelings about the world.

The Island of Bad Art is an etching in the style of a sixteenth-century printed town plan. It shows an urban island which is shaped like a cat but gives more than a passing nod to Venice, location of the world-famous two-yearly art festival or Biennale. This map is a satire on the art world. Names have been substituted for labels, slogans and statements associated with art. For example, churches are named 'Kitsch' and 'Just Plain Ugly'. The surrounding sea has 'the Mainstream' and the 'Gulf of Understanding'.

Especially clever is how Perry has grouped similar themes into spatial zones, in doing so adding an extra layer of complexity which people like to savour in maps. In the west an area recalls the theoretical side of art: 'Conference Papers', 'Cultural Studies' and 'Curator's Egos'. The 'Just Plain Dull' zone contains 'Village Hall Watercolours' and 'Sorry, but most children's art too'. In the north we have a description of a 'Huge Contemporary Public Museum' with its extensions, further extensions, planned extensions, shop, café and education wing. 'Success' lies somewhere beyond the map.

Of course, it will not escape anyone, especially not the art critic Jonathan Jones, critical of Perry's 'snarky, obvious, holier-than thou' work, still less the artist himself, that Perry is a Turner Prize-winning artist whose work is collected by the same huge contemporary public museums. Though not yet having had the honour of designing Britain's Venice pavilion, Perry is part of the bad art hypocrisy. That is yet another twist in the tale of the map, and ultimately why it is such a good one.

Image © Grayson Perry

Acknowledgements

This book would not have been possible without the knowledge, advice and support of the following people: Abbie Day, Robert Davies, Sally Nicholls, Liz Jones and Rebecca Nuotio from British Library Publishing; Peter Barber, Ashley Baynton-Williams, Pinda Bryars, Tim Bryars, Tony Campbell, Ken Field, David Gaylard, Paul Harvey, Mike Heffernan, Alex Johnson, Nicholas Krebs, Diana Lange, Yasuyo Ohtsuka, Magdalena Peszko, Malini Roy, Sarah Tyacke, Jonathon Vines and Frances Wood.

I would also like to express my sincere thanks to Ben Hennig and Tina Gotthardt for creating the bespoke cartograms for the atlas.

This book rests upon years of scholarship on the maps of the British Library. Much of this has been communicated through the pages of *Imago Mundi: The International Journal for the History of Cartography*, the voice for the discipline of map studies and a clearing-house for the latest research on early maps. This research, and a great deal else, is synthesised in the ongoing University of Chicago Press *History of Cartography* project.

The research in these and other publications has only been possible because of the continuing accessibility of the British Library's map collection for public use, and its ongoing acquisition of maps and views to facilitate and anticipate current and future research needs. The quality and extent of its holdings is attributable in no small part to the successive visions of those who have steered it, and for that reason I would like to dedicate this book to the Map Librarians of the British Museum and British Library.

List of Maps

The Universe and the World

'Aḍhāīdvīpa' [Northern India, 1830]. Add. Or. 1814.

Beatus of Liébana, [Commentary on the Apocalypse, Liébana, 1109]. Add. MS 11695, ff. 39v–40.

'The Psalter World Map' [London, *c.*1265]. Add. MS 28691, ff. 9–9v.

Pietro Vesconte, [World map in the style of a portolan chart] in Marino Sanudo, 'Secreta fidelium crucis; sive de recuperatione terrae sanctæ libri tres' [Venice, *c.*1325]. Add. MS 27376*, ff. 187v–188.

Peter Apian, *D. Domino Leonardo ab Eck ... P. Apianus ... mathematicus hanc universaliorem cogniti orbis tabulam ex recentibus observationibus confectam dedicat.* Ingolstadt, 1540. Maps C.7.c.16.

Haci Ahmed (Giacomo Gastaldi?), *Kemāl ile Naks Olinmis Cümle-I Cihān Nemunesi.* [Venice, 1559–60 (1795)]. Maps STW.97.

Claes Janszoon Visscher, *Orbis terrarum typus de integro in plurimis emendatus, auctus, et icunculis illustratus.* Amsterdam: Nicolaus Ioannis Vischerrius tabellam hanc execudit, Amstelodam ad intersigne piscatoris Via Vitulina [between 1614 and 1618]. Maps CC.5.b.96.

Nicolò Longobardo and Manuel Dias, [Terrestrial Globe, 592 mm in diameter. Beijing, 1623]. Maps G.35.

Africa

John Spilsbury, *Africa in its principal divisions,* London: Spilsbury, engraver, map & print seller in Russel Court Covent Garden, 1767. Maps 188.v.14.

Jonas Moore, *A mapp of the citty of Tanger; with the straits of Gibraltar.* London, 1664. Maps K.Top 117.79.2.TAB.

Sir Walter Raleigh, [Notebook for a projected history of the world, consisting of a historical gazetteer, library lists, notes etc. London, 1606–8]. Add. MS 57555.

Vice-Admiral Horatio Nelson, 'Sketch of the battle of Aboukir'. London, 18 February 1803. Add. MS 18676.

Diogo Homem, 'The Queen Mary Atlas' [London, 1558]. Add. MS 5415A.

Pedro Barreto de Resende, 'Mombaca', in 'Livro do Estado da India Oriental… ' [Lisbon[?], 1640–46]. Sloane MS 197, f. 103v–104.

A. Richardson and E.G. Fenning, *Uganda, upper part (sheet 86 U I).* Uganda: War Office, 1903–05. WOOS/13/5/1/1/1.

Thomas Baines, 'Track of the Ma Robert up the Zambesi River' in [Tracings of maps of southern and south-central Africa, chiefly illustrating the travels of David Livingstone on the Coanza and Zambesi Rivers from 1849 to 1864. London, *c.*1865]. Add. MS 31356, f. 58.

Chas. E. Goad Ltd., *Insurance plan of Johannesburg, Transvaal Province, South Africa.* London, January 1937. Maps C.15. vol. 12.(9.).

America

Diego Gutierrez, *Americae, sive quartae orbis partis, nova et exactissima descriptio* [Antwerp: Hieronymus Cock, 1562]. Maps *69810.(18.).

John Mitchell, *A Map of the British colonies in North America ...* [London]: publish'd by the Author Feb.ry 13.th 1755 according to Act of Parliament: Printed for Jefferys & Faden Geographers to the King at the corner of St. Martins Lane Charing Cross London, [about 1775]. Maps K.Top 118.49.b

William Baffin, [A map of Hudson Strait and part of Hudson Bay] in 'True Relation of his Fourth Voyage for the discovery of a north-west passage, in the year 1615.' Add. MS 12206.

James Cook, 'A Plan of the traverse or passage from Cape Torment in to the south channel of Orleans'. [Orleans, 1759]. Add. MS 31360, f. 17.

Elizabeth Posthuma Simcoe, 'Sketch of Upper Canada' [Ontario, *c.*1795]. Maps K.Top 119.15.A.

Elizabeth Posthuma Simcoe, 'Navy Hall opposite Niagara' [Ontario, *c.*1792]. Maps K.Top 119.15.AA.

Elizabeth Posthuma Simcoe, 'Castle Frank near York' [Ontario, *c.*1794]. Maps K.Top 119.15.E.

George Sproule, 'A plan of the coast from Kennebeck River to round pond on the west side of Muscongus bay, including the islands, rivers, &c. within that extent'. [Portsmouth, New Hampshire?]: Deputy Ensign George Sproule of His Majesty's 59th Regiment, 1772. Maps K.Top 120.20.

'A description of the towne of Mannados or New Amsterdam as it was in September 1661 lying in Latitude 40 de: and 40,: Anno Domini 1664'. London, 1664. Maps K.Top 121.35.

[Map showing the position of the Indian tribes to the north-west of South Carolina copied from a painting on deer-skin by an Indian chief, and presented to Sir Francis Nicholson]. Carolina[?], *c.*1719. Add. MS 4723.

Joseph de Urrutia, 'Plano dela vila de Santa Fee capital del reino de Nuebo Mexico' in [A collection of 21 maps of Spanish Mexico], New Mexico, *c.*1766–67. Add. MS 17662.(13.).

Culiacan / NG–13. Washington, DC: American Geographical Society, 1935. Maps 920.(294.).

Giovanni Matteo Contarini, *Mundu spericum ... cognosces diligentia Joani Mathei Contareni.* Florence: Franceso Rosselli, 1506. Maps C.2.cc.4.

Jean Rotz, [A map of North and Central America and the West Indies] in 'This Boke of idrography ... made by me Johne Rotz sarvant to the Kingis mooste exellent Majeste ...' [Dieppe and London, *c.*1535–42]. Royal MS 20.E.IX, ff. 23v–24.

Thomas Jefferys, *The Virgin Islands from English and Danish surveys, by Thomas Jefferys Geographer to the King, Corrected and Improved by Captn. James Waring 1797.* London: Laurie & Whittle, 1797. Maps 188.o.2.(1.).

Bartholomew Sharpe, [A profile showing the volcano of Guatemala to R. Sonsonate] in 'This Wagoner of the Great South Sea …' London: Guilielmo Hack Delineavit, Anno 1682. Maps 7.TAB.123.(15–16.).

Taddeus Hänke, 'Partidos de la nueva yntendencia de S.ta Cruz de la Sierra.' [Cochabamba, *c.*1800]. Add. MS 17671.cc.

Sir John Narbrough, 'The land of Patagonia: &c. The draught of Magellan straits drawen by Captain John Narbrough: ann^{o}: 1670: on board his maiestis shipp sweepstaks as I pased and repased the straits'. [London, 1671–2]. Maps K.Top 124.84.8.TAB END.

Thomas Boutflower, 'The pengwin and albitrose towns in the N. side of Saunders's Island during the egg season at Port Egmont'. [West Falkland, 1769]. Add. MS 60333 E.

Thomas Boutflower, 'The sea lion party on Burnt Island in Byron's Sound'. [West Falkland, 1769]. Add. MS 60333 D.

Thomas Boutflower, 'The mullet and trout fishery at the E. End of Byron's Sound'. [West Falkland, 1769]. Add. MS 60333 B.

Thomas Boutflower, 'The wild geese chace or progging party on Keppels Island at Port Egmont'. [West Falkland, 1769]. Add. MS 60333 C.

Asia

[A map of Asia] in 'Tabula geographica ex opusculis S. Hieronymi descripta'. Tournai, *c.*1190. Add. MS 10049, f. 64r.

Royal Geographical Society, *Map of Eastern Turkey in Asia, Syria and Western Persia*. London, 1915. Add. MS 88906/25/6.

William Camden, [A map of the Holy land after Matthew Paris]. [London, *c.*1600]. Lansdowne MS 253, ff. 194v–195.

Igor Ivanovich Chirikov, *Carte topographique de la frontière Turco-Persane par des officiers Russes et Anglais sous la direction des commissaires-médiateurs Tchirikow et Williams – sheet XIII*. [Saint Petersburg: Corps Topographique Impérial, 1869]. Maps S.T.T.a.13.

[A map of Shahjahanabad or Old Delhi]. Delhi, *c.*1858. IOR/X/1659.

James Rennell, 'The southern part of Dacca, and low lands of Tiperah: with the islands in the mouth of the Ganges. Surveyed by Rennell, Ritchie, Martin & Richards, 1764 to 1773'. [Dacca]: I. Rennell fec.t, 1773. IOR/X/995/8.

Vitus Bering, 'Diese charte über Siberien nimt ihren anfang zu Tobolske Ostwerts bis an die euserste Grentze von Sukotskij gemacht unter dem Commendo des Capt: Co͞mandeurs Bering Ao: 1729'. Maps K.Top 114.43.1.

Katsushika Hokusai, [*Gakyō rōjin Manji toshi hachijū-ichi* / A map of China drawn in perspective]. [Edo: Seiundō, 1840–1]. Maps 188.v.3.

Matteo Ripa, [A map of China and surrounding lands, known as the K'ang-hsi map]. [Beijing, *c.*1719]. Maps K.Top 116.18.1-d.2.TAB.

[A pictorial map of part of Tibet, from 'The Wise Collection', 1857–8]. Add. Or. 23016, f. 3.

William Alexander, [View of the city wall of Pao-ying-shien], 1793. Maps 8.TAB.c.8.(6.).

[An atlas of Jiangxi province, 1682–91). Add. MS 16356.

[Panoramic view of Canton from the sea]. [Guangzhou, 1760–70]. Maps K.Top 116.23.

William Farquhar, 'Plan of the island of Singapore including the new British settlement and adjacent islands' [Singapore, *c.*1823]. IOR/X/3347.

William Farquhar, [A map of Singapore town and harbour, Singapore, *c.*1823]. IOR/X/3346.

Pedro Murillo Velarde, *Carta hydrographica y chorographica delas yslas Filipinas*. [Manila]: en Manila año de 1734 de orden d' su magd., [1734]. Maps K.Top 116.37.2.

Antonio Fernandez de Roxas, *Topographia de la ciudad de Manila: capital de las yslas Philipinas, Fundada en la de Luzon nuevo Reyno de Castilla* [Manila, *c.*1739]. Maps K.Top 116.40.

[Bankoku sōzu]. [Nagasaki, 1645]. Maps *920.(485.).

Nagasaki ezu [An illustrated map of Nagasaki], Nagasaki, *c.*1680. Or.75.g.25.

Australasia

H.T. Hawes, 'Australia and New Zealand relief' [London, 1956]. Maps CC.7.a.36.

HB., *A Gum Leaf From the Golden South* [Sydney[?], *c.*1906]. Maps C.1.a.9.(360.).

Western Australia (*c.*1980). Maps C.12.c.1.(1421.).

Valentine's Series, *New Zealand ... Pohutuaroa Mountain*, [London[?], *c.*1900]. Maps C.1.a.9.(91.).

New Zealand. Hastings: Pictorial Publications Ltd., [*c.*1990]. Maps 211.a.1.(991.).

Fernando Brambila, [View of Sydney Cove from the North-West]. [Sydney, 1793]. Maps K.Top 124.Supp, f. 43.

James Cook[?], [A map of islands in the Pacific Ocean centred on Tahiti]. [Tahiti, *c.*1769]. Add. MS 21593C.

Europe

Gerhard Mercator, 'The Mercator Atlas of Europe'. [Duisburg, 1570–72]. Maps C.29.c.13.(1.).

Howard T. Fisher, Carl Steinitz et al., [Examples of computer mapping according to the Synagraphic Mapping System (SYMAP)] [Cambridge, MA: Laboratory for Computer Graphics and Spatial Analysis, Harvard University, 1969]. Maps 950.(286.).

J. & C. Walker, *England & Wales, founded upon the grand trigonometrical survey ...* 'coloured according to the distribution of hand loom labours'. London: J. & C. Walker, [1835]. Maps C.44.d.77.

Christopher Saxton, *Westmorlandiæ et Cumberlandiæ Comit: nova ... descriptio ... 1576. C. Saxton descripsit. A. Ryther Anglus sculpsit.* [London], 1576. Royal MS. 18.D.III, f. 75.

J. Sowerby, 'Plan of property belonging to the Friends in the township of Darlington in the county of Durham' [Darlington, 1849]. Add. MS 64816.

Francis Matthew, *This Navigable passage from London to Bristoll and else where set forth by Francis Matthew ...* [London, 1668]. Maps C.44, f. 20.

Emanuel Bowen, 'An accurate map of Buckingham ...' from *The Royal English Atlas*, [London, *c.*1764]. Maps *1530.(5.).

Norton, Trist, Watney and Co., *Higham, near Rochester. Kent. A very valuable and beautiful freehold property known as 'Gadshill Place,' for many years the favorite abode of Charles Dickens.* London: T.W. Nicholson, 5 August 1870. Maps CC.5.c.2.

Nicholas Hawksmoor, [An outline ground plan of Christ Church Spitalfields, with variations]. [London, 1714]. Maps K.Top 23.11.h.

Nicholas Hawksmoor, [Elevation, in outline, of the west front and tower of Christ Church Spitalfields]. [London, between 1714 and 1720]. Maps K.Top 23.11.o.

Nicholas Hawksmoor, [Side elevation of Christ Church, Spitalfields]. [London, *c.*1714]. Maps K.Top 124.Supp, f. 47.

Thomas Jefferys, *A new plan of the city and liberty of Westminster, exhibiting all the new streets & roads: with the residences of the principal nobility, public offices, &c. Not extant in any other plan.* [London, 1766]. Maps Crace Port. 4.128.

John Speed, 'Glamorgan Shyre; With the situations of the chiefe towne Cardyff and ancient Landaffe described', in *The theatre of the empire of Great Britaine ...* [London, *c.*1607]. Maps C.7.c.5.(20.).

Robert Dawson, 'Part of Caernarvonshire'. [Caernarfon[?], 1816]. Maps OSD 306.

John Harding, [A map of Scotland] in [The chronicle of John Harding in metre, 1437]. Lansdowne MS 204, f. 226v.

William Roy, [Fair copy of the military survey of Scotland at 2 inches to the mile, 1747–55]. Maps CC.5.a.441, sheet 15 (part).

The Englishe victore agaynste the Schottes by Muskelbroghe 1547. [London: Thomas Geminus[?], *c.*1547]. Maps CC.5.a.409.

Baptist Boazio. *Irlandiae accurata descriptio*. [London, 1599]. Maps C.2.cc.1.

Edward Lucas, 'The Barony of Lower Eveagh', from *The Down Survey, volume E, containing surveys of the province of Ulster* [1655–6]. Add. MS 72871.(E.3.).

Nicolas Berey, *Carte generale de toute les poste et traverse de France. A Paris: chez Nicolas Berey proche les Augustine* [*c.*1636]. Maps CC.5.a.565.

Jean Errard, 'Boulogne', from [A collection of maps, plans and profiles of parts of France, Paris, 1602–9]. Add. MS 21117, no. 38.
Sir Douglas Haig, 'Map of the situation in France and Flanders, 25 Sept. 1918, the eve of the breaking, of the Cambrai-St. Quentin line 1918 trenches' [London, 1918]. Add. MS 39928.
Claudius Ptolemy, [The left half of Europa Tabula II showing Portugal and part of Spain], from 'Geographica', [Istanbul, *c.*1300]. Add. MS 19391, f. 21v.
Position of the British troops repelling the attack of the enemy on the 16th Jan.ry 1809. [London]: Quarter Master Gen.l's Office Horse Guards Jan.ry 26th 1809. Maps C.18.m.1.(9.).
Matthew Paris, [Part of an itinerary map showing France and Italy], from 'Historia Anglorum'. [St. Albans, *c.*1255]. Royal MS 14.C.VII, ff. 3–3v.
Bernardo Bellotto, [Duomo and Piazza San Martino, Lucca]. [Lucca, 1744–45]. Maps K.Top 80.21.a.
Bernardo Bellotto, [Lucca Cathedral from the Palazzo dell' Arcivescovado]. [Lucca, 1744–5]. Maps K.Top 80.21.c.
Switzerland. Bundesamt für Landestopographie, *Landeskarte der Schweiz ... Zermatt ... Blatt 1348*. Wabern-Bern, 1991. Maps 24405.(138.).
Erhard Etzlaub, *Das ist der Rom Weg von Meylen zur Meylen ...* [Nüremberg, 1500]. Maps C.2.a.7.(2.).
Target No. 3 (a) 9 / Perspective (June 1943) Bremerhaven (Germany), London, 1943. Maps MOD TP.
Philip Radcliffe Evans and Wallis Heath, [Map of Querum PoW camp and surrounding area, 1:10,000]. [Querum, 1944]. Maps C.25.a.23.
Philip Radcliffe Evans and Wallis Heath, [Map of part of Northern Germany, 1:1,000,000]. [Querum, 1944]. Maps C.25.a.23.
Nicolaes Visscher, *Leo Belgicus, artificiosa et geographica tabula sub leonis figura XVII. Inferioris Germaniae provincias representans ... J. van Doetechum fecit*. Amsterdam: Claes Janszoon Visscher, 1650. Maps C.9.d.1.(6.).
Balthazar Florens von Berckenrode, *Delineatio domus Aug: celsiss: Princ: Fred: Henrici Nassou: Princ: Araus: Etc: quae est Hontsholerdici.* Amsterdam: Claes Janszoon Visscher, *c.*1640. Maps C.9.e.8.(24.).
Het koninglyke lust-huis In't Bosch. Amsterdam: Anna Beeck, 1717. Maps C.9.e.8.(15.).
Western Front, trench maps, 1:20,000. Southampton: Ordnance Survey, 1916–17. Maps C.19.a-g.
Cornelis Anthoniszoon, *De vermaerde de Koopstadt van Amstelredam* [Amsterdam, 1544]. Maps STA.29.
Antonio Lafreri, *Olaus Magnus, Gottus Upsalensis, quo melius universis geographia studiosis satisfaceret, septentrionalium suarum partium* [Rome, 1572]. Maps C.7.e.2.(19.).
Lucas Janszoon Waghenaer, 'The sea coastes of Norway and the land of north east ... between Mardov and Akersond ...' in *The Mariners mirrour, wherin may playnly be seen the courses, heights, distances, depths, soundings, flouds and ebs, ...* [London: Henry Haslop, 1588]. Maps C.8.b.4.(29.).
Joan Blaeu,'Tabula Russae ex autographo ...' in *Atlas maior, sive Cosmographia Blaviana, qua solum, salum, cœlum, accuratissime describuntur*. Amsterdam, 1662. Maps C.4.c.1. vol. 1.
Moses Pitt, 'Russia vulgo Moscovia', in *The English atlas. volume I. Containing a description of the places next the North-Pole; as also of Muscovy, Poland, Sweden, Denmark, and their several dependances.* Oxford: printed at the Theater, for Moses Pitt at the Angel in St. Pauls-Church-Yard, London. MDCLXXX [1680]. Maps 1.TAB.16.
Guillame Vasseur de Beauplan, 'Delineatio specialis et accurata Ukrainæ cum suis palatinatibus ac districtibq provincysq adiacentibus bono publico erecta' [Gdańsk: Willem Hondius, 1650] in 'The Klencke Atlas', 1660. Maps K.A.R.(32.).
Nicolaus de Cusa, 'The Eichstätt map'. [Basle[?], 1530]. Maps C.2.a.1.
The 'Cottonian' or 'Anglo-Saxon' map. [Canterbury, *c.*1100]. Cotton MS Tiberius B.V., f. 56v.
Abraham Ortelius, 'Salisburgeusis Jurisdictionis, locorumque vicinorum vera descriptio / Auctore Marco Secznagel Salisburgense' in *Theatrum orbis terrarum*. [Antwerp: Christoffel Plantijn, 1597]. Maps C.49.e.58.
Christoforo Buondelmonti, [A map of Euboea] in 'Liber insularum archipelagi'. Ghent, 1482. Arundel MS 93, f. 159r.
Bartolommeo dalli Sonetti, [A map of Euboea] from [Isolario]. [Venice: Guilelmus Anima Mea, Tridinensis[?], 1485]. G.6587.(47.).

Seas and Oceans

Anthonie Jabobsz. *West-Indische Paskaert, waer in de graden der breedde over wederzyden vande middellyn wassende soo vergrooten, dat die geproportioneert syn tegen hunne nevenstaende graden der lengde ...* [Amsterdam, *c.*1650]. Maps ST.1.
John Dee, [A map of the North Atlantic and Arctic Oceans]. [London, 1580]. Cotton MS Augustus I.i.1.
Antonio Francesco Lucini. [Copper plate used to print one half of 'Carte particolare della coste di Zelande è Frislande è Olanda…'] Florence: A. Lucini fece, [c. 1640]. Maps 177.j.3.
Robert Dudley, 'Carte particolare della coste di Zelande è Frislande è Olanda che comincia con il porto di Newport è Finisce con Messelword ... carta XXXVI' in *Dell' Arcano del Mare* [Florence, 1646–7], G.7266.(55.).
Angelino Dulcert, [Portolan chart of the Mediterranean Sea]. [Parma, *c.*1339]. Add. MS 25691.

Celestial Maps

Desiree E. Stuart-Alexander, *Geological Atlas of the Moon: Central Far Side of the Moon*. United States Geological Survey, 1978. Maps Y.81.
[A set of star charts, Central China, *c.*700]. Or. 8210/S.3326.
Thomas Hood, [North / South celestial hemisphere charts] in *The use of the celestial globe in plano set foorth in two hemispheres ... by Thomas Hood, Mathematicall Lecturer in the citie of London, etc.* London: John Windet for Tobie Cooke, 1590. Maps 184.h.1.

Fantasy Worlds

Jean-Baptiste Trento, *Mappe-monde nouvelle Papistique.* [Geneva, 1566]. C.160.c.7.
Cyril Phillips, *The One and Only Original Map of Breakfast Island Indicating Life and Taste in Britain at the Beginning of the 2nd Elizabethan Reign.* [London[?], 1953]. Maps 188.v.40.
Grayson Perry, *The Island of Bad Art*. London, 2013. Maps CC.5.c.3.

BIBLIOGRAPHY

Akerman, James R. and Robert W. Karrow (eds.), *Maps: Finding Our Place in the World* (Chicago: University of Chicago Press, 2007).

Andrews, J.H., *Plantation Acres: An Historical Study of the Irish Land Surveyor and his Maps* (Ulster Historical Association, 1985).

Andrews, J.H., 'Colonial Cartography in a European Setting: The Case of Tudor Ireland' in David Woodward (ed.), *The History of Cartography Volume Three: Cartography in the European Renaissance, Part 2* (Chicago and London: University of Chicago Press, 2007), 1670–83.

Arbel, Benjamin, 'Maps of the World for Ottoman Princes? Further Evidence and Questions Concerning the Mappamondo of Hajji Ahmed' in *Imago Mundi* 54:1 (2002), 19–29.

Bagrow, Leo, 'The Vitus Bering First Voyage Map' in *Anecdota Cartographica* IV (Copenhagen, 1950).

Bagrow, Leo, *A History of Russian Cartography up to 1800* (Wolfe Island, ON: The Walker Press, 1975).

Baigent, Elizabeth, 'Baines, (John) Thomas (1820–1875)' in *Oxford Dictionary of National Biography*, 23 September 2004. https://doi.org/10.1093/ref:odnb/1095 [accessed 25 January 2018].

Barber, Peter, 'The Manuscript Legacy: Maps in the Department of Manuscripts' in *The Map Collector* 28 (1982), 18–24.

Barber, Peter, 'Five Unusual Maps of the Falklands' in *The Map Collector* 20 (1982), 50–51.

Barber, Peter, 'Riches for the Geography of America and Spain: Felipe Bauzá and his Topographical Collections, 1789–1848' in *British Library Journal* (1986) http://www.bl.uk/eblj/1986articles/article3.html [accessed 15 January 2018].

Barber, Peter and Michelle P. Brown, 'The Aslake World Map' in *Imago Mundi* 44:1 (1992).

Barber, Peter, 'Malaspina and George III, Brambila and Watling: Three Discovered Drawings of Sydney and Parramatta by Fernando Brambila' in *Australian Journal of Art* XI (1993), 31–53.

Barber, Peter, 'George III and his Geographical Collection' in Jonathan Marsden (ed.), *The Wisdom of George the Third. Papers from a Symposium at the Queen's Gallery, Buckingham Palace. June 2004* (London: Royal Collection, 2005), 282–93.

Barber, Peter, *Commentary on the Queen Mary Atlas* (London: Folio Society, 2005).

Barber, Peter, 'Medieval Maps of the World', in P.D.A. Harvey (ed.), *The Hereford World Map: Medieval World Maps and their Context* (London: British Library, 2006), 4–8.

Barber, Peter, 'Mapmaking in England, ca. 1470–1650' in David Woodward (ed.), *The History of Cartography Volume Three: Cartography in the European Renaissance, Part 2* (Chicago and London: University of Chicago Press, 2007), 1589–1669.

Barber, Peter and Tom Harper, *Magnificent Maps: Power, Propaganda and Art* (London: British Library, 2010).

Barnard, Toby, 'Petty, Sir William (1623–1687)' in *Oxford Dictionary of National Biography*, 3 October 2013. https://doi.org/10.1093/ref:odnb/22069 [accessed 1 February 2018].

Barr, James, *A Line in the Sand: Britain, France and the Struggle that Shaped the Middle East* (London: Simon & Schuster, 2011).

Baynton-Williams, Ashley, *Maps of War* (London: Quercus, 2007).

Beaglehole, John Cawte, *The Life of Captain James Cook* (London: A. and C. Black, 1974).

Beddington, Charles, 'Bernardo Bellotto and his Circle in Italy, Part 1: Not Canaletto but Bellotto' in *Burlington Magazine* 146, no. 1219 (2004), 665–74.

Bendall, Sarah, 'Draft Town Maps for John Speed's *Theatre of the Empire of Great Britaine*' in *Imago Mundi* 54 (2002), 19–45.

Bodart-Bailey, Beatrice M. (ed.), *Kaempfer's Japana: Tokugawa Culture Observed* (Honolulu: University of Hawai'i Press, 1999).

Bond, Barbara, *Great Escapes: The Story of MI9's Second World War Escape and Evasion Maps* (London: Times Books, 2015).

Bonehill, John and Stephen Daniels, *Paul Sandby, Picturing Britain* (London: Royal Academy of Arts, 2009).

Bower, David I., 'Speed's Town-mapping Itineraries' in *Imago Mundi* 66:1 (2014), 95–104.

British Library, *Catalogue of Map Postcards* (London: British Library Map Library, 1995).

Brotton, Jerry, *A History of the World in Twelve Maps* (London: Penguin, 2012).

Bryars, Tim and Tom Harper, *A History of the Twentieth Century in 100 Maps* (London: British Library, 2014).

Buisseret, David, 'French Cartography: The Ingénieurs de Roi, 1500–1650' in David Woodward (ed.), *The History of Cartography Volume Three: Cartography in the European Renaissance, Part 2* (Chicago and London: University of Chicago Press, 2007), 1504–21.

Campbell, Tony, 'The Drapers' Company and its School of Seventeenth-Century Chart-makers' in Helen Wallis and Sarah Tyacke (eds.), *My Head is a Map: Essays and Memoirs in Honour of R.V. Tooley* (London: Francis Edwards, 1973), 81–106.

Campbell, Tony, *The Earliest Printed Maps, 1472–1500* (London: British Library; Berkeley: University of California Press, 1987).

Campbell, Tony, 'Portolan Charts from the Late Thirteenth Century to 1500' in J.B. Harley and David Woodward (eds.), *The History of Cartography Volume One: Cartography in Prehistoric, Ancient and Medieval Europe and the Mediterranean* (Chicago and London: University of Chicago Press, 1987), 371–463.

Chambers, Ian, 'A Cherokee Origin for the "Catawba" Deerskin Map (c.1721)' in *Imago Mundi* 65:2, 207–16.

Conley, Tom, 'Early Modern Literature and Cartography: An Overview' in David Woodward (ed.), *The History of Cartography Volume Three: Cartography in the European Renaissance, Part 1* (Chicago and London: University of Chicago Press, 2007), 401–11.

Cook, Andrew S., 'Major James Rennell and "A Bengal Atlas" (1780 and 1781)', [London]: Foreign and Commonwealth Office, 1976.

Cook, Andrew S., 'Rennell, James (1742–1830)' in *Oxford Dictionary of National Biography*, 23 September 2004. https://doi.org/10.1093/ref:odnb/23369 [accessed 10 January 2018].

Crace, Frederick, *A Catalogue of Maps, Plans and Views of London, Westminster & Southwark. Collected and arranged by Frederick Crace. Edited by his son J.G. Crace* (London, 1878).

Crane, Nicholas, *Mercator: The Man Who Mapped the Planet* (London: Weidenfeld & Nicolson, 2002).

Cutter, Donald C., *With Tadeo Hänke Aboard the 'Descubierta'.* http://ametas.homepage.t-online.de/tadeo/cutter.htm [accessed 10 January 2018].

Delano-Smith, Catherine and Roger J.P. Kain, *English Maps: A History* (London: British Library, 1999).
Delano-Smith, Catherine, 'Map Signs' in Peter Barber (ed.), *The Map Book* (London: Wiedenfeld & Nicolson, 2005).
Downes, Kerry, *Hawksmoor* (London: Thames & Hudson, 1969).

Edney, Matthew H., *Mapping an Empire: The Geographical Construction of British India, 1765–1843* (Chicago and London: University of Chicago Press, 1997).
Edson, Evelyn, *The World Map, 1300–1492: The Persistence of Tradition and Transformation* (Baltimore: Johns Hopkins University Press, 2007).
Ehlers, Eckhart and Thomas Krafft (eds.), *Shahjahanabad/Old Delhi: Tradition and Colonial Change* (New Delhi: Manohar, 2003).
Englisch, Brigitte, 'Erhard Etzlaub's Projection and Methods of Mapping' in *Imago Mundi* 48:1 (1996), 103–23.

Finney, Ben, 'Nautical Cartography and Traditional Navigation in Oceania' in Malcolm G. Lewis and David Woodward (eds.), *The History of Cartography Volume Two, Book Three: Cartography in the Traditional African, American, Arctic, Australian and Pacific Societies* (Chicago and London: University of Chicago Press, 1998), 443–92.
French, Josephine (ed.), *Tooley's Dictionary of Mapmakers: Revised Edition, A–Z* (Tring: Map Collector Publications, 1999).
French, Josephine (ed.), *Tooley's Dictionary of Mapmakers: Revised Edition, E–J* (Riverside, CT: Early World Press, 2001).

Gerry, Tom, 'Extremes Meet: Elizabeth Simcoe's Birchbark Landscapes' in *Queen's Quarterly* 106:4 (Winter 1999), 588–601.

Harley, J.B., 'The Map and the Development of the History of Cartography' in J.B. Harley and David Woodward (eds.), *The History of Cartography Volume One: Cartography in Prehistoric, Ancient and Medieval Europe and the Mediterranean* (Chicago: University of Chicago Press, 1987), 1–42.
Harper, Tom, 'An Extraordinary Atlas: The Klencke Atlas at the British Library' in *IMCoS Journal* 122 (Autumn 2010), 35–39.
Harper, Tom (ed.), *Maps and the Twentieth Century: Drawing the Line* (London: British Library, 2016).
Harper, Tom, 'Nineteenth Century Map Collections' in Roger J.P. Kain (ed.), *History of Cartography Volume Five: Cartography in the Nineteenth Century* (Chicago: University of Chicago Press, forthcoming).
Harris, Michael, 'Pitt, Moses (bap. 1639, d. 1697)' in *Oxford Dictionary of National Biography*, 3 January 2008. https://doi.org/10.1093/ref:odnb/22331 [accessed 20 January 2018].
Harris, P.R., *A History of the British Museum Library, 1753–1973* (London: British Library, 1998).
Harvey, P.D.A., *Medieval Maps of the Holy Land* (London: British Library, 2012).
Hewitt, Rachel, *Map of a Nation: A Biography of the Ordnance Survey* (London: Granta, 2010).
Hiatt, Alfred, 'Beyond a Border: The Maps of Scotland in John Hardyng's Chronicle' in Jenny Stratford (ed.), *The Lancastrian Court: Proceedings of the 2001 Harlaxton Symposium* (Donnington: Shaun Tyas, 2003), 78–94.
Hibbert, Christopher, *Nelson: A Personal History* (London: Viking, 1994).
Hodson, Donald, *County Atlases of the British Isles Published After 1703: Volume III, Atlases Published 1764 to 1789 and their Subsequent Editions* (London: British Library, 1997).
Hodson, Yolande, *Ordnance Surveyors' Drawings 1789–c.1840: The Original Manuscript Maps of the First Ordnance Survey of England and Wales from the British Library Map Library* (Reading : Research Publications, 1989).
Hoff, Bert van t', 'Provisional Description of the Maps in the Klencke Atlas in the British Museum' (unpublished typescript, 1957).

Jewitt, Crispin, *Intelligence Revealed: Maps, Plans and Views at Horse Guards and the War Office, 1800–1880* (London: British Library, 2011).
Johnson, Alexander, *The First Mapping of America: The General Survey of British North America* (London: I.B. Tauris, 2017).

Kain, Roger J.P. and Catherine Delano-Smith, *English Maps: A History* (London: British Library, 1999).
Karrow, Robert W., *Mapmakers of the Sixteenth Century and their Maps: Bio-bibliographies of the Cartographers of Abraham Ortelius, 1570* (Chicago: published for the Newberry Library by Speculum Orbis Press, 1993).
Koeman, Cornelis, Günter Schilder, Marco van Egmond and Peter van der Krogt, 'Commercial Cartography and Map Production in the Low Countries, 1500–ca. 1672' in David Woodward (ed.), *The History of Cartography Volume Three: Cartography in the European Renaissance, Part 2* (Chicago and London: University of Chicago Press, 2007), 1296–1383.
Kohl, J.G., 'Substance of a Lecture Delivered at the Smithsonian Institution on a Collection of the Charts and Maps of America' in *Smithsonian Institution. Annual Report, 1856* (1857).
Kozakiewicz, Stefan, *Bernardo Bellotto* (London: Elek, 1972).
Kruger, Herbert, 'Erhard Etzlaub's "Romweg" Map and its Dating in the Holy Year of 1500' in *Imago Mundi* 8 (1951), 17–26.

Lange, Diana, *Journey of Discovery: An Atlas of the Himalayas by a Nineteenth-Century Tibetan Lama* (forthcoming).
Lestringant, Frank and Alessandra Preda, *Mappe-monde nouvelle papistique: histoire de la Mappe-Monde papistique, en laquelle est déclairé tout ce qui est contenu et pourtraict en la grande table, ou carte de la mappe-monde* (Geneva: Droz, 2009).
Lewis, G. Malcolm, 'Maps, Mapmaking, and Map Use by Native North Americans' in Malcolm G. Lewis and David Woodward (eds.), *The History of Cartography Volume Two, Book Three: Cartography in the Traditional African, American, Arctic, Australian and Pacific Societies* (Chicago and London: University of Chicago Press, 1998), 51–182.
Lewthwaite, Gordon R., 'The Puzzle of Tupaia's Map' in *New Zealand Geographer* 26:1 (1970), 1–19.
Lo, Andrew, Frances Wood et al., *Da ying tu shu guan te cang zhong guo qing dai wai xiao hua jing hua [Chinese Export Paintings of the Qing Period in the British Library]* (Guangzhou: Guangdong People's Publishing House, 2011).
Lynam, Edward, *The Mapmaker's Art: Essays on the History of Maps* (London: Batchworth Press, 1953).

Ménage, V.L., 'The Map of Hajji Ahmed' and its Makers' in *Bulletin of the School of Oriental and African Studies* 21:2 (1958), 291–314.
Meurer, Peter H., *Corpus der älteren Germania-Karten: Ein annotierter Katalog der gedruckten Gesamtkarten des deutschen Raumes von den Anfängen bis um 1650* (Alphen aan den Rijn: Canaletto, 2001).
Meurer, Peter H., 'Cartography in the German Lands, 1450–1650' in David Woodward (ed.), *The History of Cartography Volume Three: Cartography in the European Renaissance, Part 2* (Chicago and London: University of Chicago Press, 2007), 1171–1244.

Nicholls, Mark and Penry Williams, 'Ralegh, Sir Walter (1554–1618)' in *Oxford Dictionary of National Biography*, 17 September 2015. https://doi.org/10.1093/ref:odnb/23039 [accessed 15 November 2017].
Nolan, Mike, 'American Target Perspective Maps of the Second World War' in *Sheetlines: The Journal of the Charles Close Society for the Study of Ordnance Survey Maps*, 105 (April 2016), 54–58.

O'Donoghue, Yolande, *William Roy 1726–1790: Pioneer of the Ordnance Survey* (London: British Museum Publications, 1977).
Orde, Anne, *Religion, Business and Society in North-East England: The Pease Family of Darlington in the Nineteenth Century* (Stamford: Shaun Tyas, 2000).

Papelitzky, Elke, 'A Description and Analysis of the Japanese World Map Bankoku sōza in its Version of 1671 and Some Thoughts on the Sources of the Original Bankoku sōza' in *Journal of Asian History* 48:1 (2014), 15–59.
Pearson, Alastair W., 'Relief Depiction' in Mark Monmonier (ed.), *The History of Cartography Volume Six: Cartography in the Twentieth Century* (Chicago and London: University of Chicago Press, 2007), 1260–72.
Pearson, A.W. and Michael Heffernan, 'The American Geographical Society's Map of Hispanic America: Million-scale Mapping between the Wars' in *Imago Mundi* 62:2 (2009), 215–43.
Pearson, Alastair W. and Michael Heffernan, 'Globalising Cartography? The International Map of the World, the International Geographical Union and the United Nations' in *Imago Mundi* 67:1 (2015), 58–80.
Peaty, John, 'Haig's Relief Maps' in *Royal Engineers Journal*, 121:2 (August 2007), 127–33.
Pennington, Richard, *A Descriptive Catalogue of the Etched Work of Wenceslaus Hollar 1607–1677* (Cambridge: Cambridge University Press, 1982).
Plumb, John Harold, *The Commercialisation of Leisure in Eighteenth-century England* (Reading: University of Reading, 1973).
Popper, Nicholas, *Walter Ralegh's 'History of the World' and the Historical Culture of the Late Renaissance* (Chicago and London: University of Chicago Press, 2012).
Pujades, Ramon J., *Les Cartes Portolanes: La Representació Medieval d'una Mar Solcada* (Barcelona: Institut Cartogràfic de Catalunya: Institut d'Estudis Catalans: Institut Europeu de la Mediterrània, 2007).

Roberts, R. Julian, 'Dee, John (1527–1609)' in *Oxford Dictionary of National Biography*, 25 May 2006. https://doi.org/10.1093/ref:odnb/7418 [accessed 9 January 2018].
Rowley, Glyn, 'Goad, Charles Edward (1848–1910) in *Oxford Dictionary of National Biography*, 25 May 2006. https://doi.org/10.1093/ref:odnb/41105 [accessed 5 February 2018].

Schilder, Günter, *Monumenta Cartographica Neerlandica, Volume VI: Dutch Folio-sized Single Sheet Maps with Decorative Borders, 1604–1660* (Alphen aan den Rijn: Canaletto, 2000).
Schilder, Günter and Marco van Egmond, 'Maritime Cartography in the Low Countries during the Renaissance' in David Woodward (ed.), *The History of Cartography Volume Three: Cartography in the European Renaissance, Part 2* (Chicago and London: University of Chicago Press, 2007), 1384–1432.
Schmidt, Allan H.,' SYMAP (software)' in Mark Monmonier (ed.), *The History of Cartography Volume Six: Cartography in the Twentieth Century* (Chicago and London: University of Chicago Press, 2015), 1477–9.
Schofield, Richard, 'Narrowing the Frontier: Mid-nineteenth Century Efforts to Delimit and Map the Perso–Ottoman Border' in Roxane Farmanfarmaian (ed.), *War and Peace in Qajar Persia: Implications Past and Present* (Routledge, 2008), 149–73.
Schwartzberg, Joseph E., 'Cosmological Mapping' in J.B. Harley and David Woodward (eds.), *The History of Cartography Volume Two, Book One: Cartography in the Traditional Islamic and South Asian Societies* (Chicago and London: University of Chicago Press, 1992), 332–87.
Schwartzberg, Joseph E., 'Maps of Greater Tibet' in Harley, J.B. and David Woodward (eds.), *The History of Cartography Volume Two, Book Two: Cartography in the Traditional East and Southeast Asian Societies* (Chicago and London: University of Chicago Press, 1994), 607–88.
Scott, Valerie (ed.), *Tooley's Dictionary of Mapmakers: Revised Edition, K–P* (Riverside, CT: Early World Press, 2003)
Scott, Valerie (ed.), *Tooley's Dictionary of Mapmakers: Revised Edition, Q–Z* (Riverside, CT: Early World Press, 2004).
Shannon, William and Michael Winstanley, 'Lord Burghley's Map of Lancashire Revisited, *c.*1576–1590' in *Imago Mundi* 59:1 (2007), 24–42.
Shefrin, Jill, *Neatly Dissected: For the Instruction of Young Ladies and Gentlemen in the Knowledge of Geography: John Spilsbury and Early Dissected Puzzles* (Los Angeles: Cotsen Occasional Press, 1999).
Shefrin, Jill, *Such Constant Affectionate Care: Lady Charlotte Finch, Royal Governess & the Children of George III* (Los Angeles: Cotsen Occasional Press, 2003).
Shirley, Rodney W., *The Mapping of the World: Early Printed World Maps, 1472–1700* (Riverside, CT: Early World Press, 1993).
Shirley, Rodney W., *Maps in the Atlases of the British Library: A Descriptive Catalogue AD 850–1800* (London: British Library, 2004).
Simcoe, Elizabeth, *Mrs Simcoe's Diary, Edited and with an Introduction by Mary Quayle Innis; Foreword by Michael Gnarowski* (Toronto: Dundurn Press, 2007).
Simoni, Anna E.C., 'Terra Incognita: The Beudeker Collection in the Map Library of the British Library' in *British Library Journal* 11 (1985), 143–75.
Skelton, R.A., *Explorers' Maps* (London: Routledge & Kegan Paul, 1958).
Skelton, R.A., *County Atlases of the British Isles, 1579–1850. A Bibliography* (London: Carta Press, 1970).
Skempton, A.W. (ed.), *Biographical Dictionary of Civil Engineers in Great Britain and Ireland* (London: Thomas Telford; ICE Publishing, 2002–[2014]).
Slater, Michael, 'Dickens, Charles John Huffam (1812–1870)' in *Oxford Dictionary of National Biography*, 25 September 2014. https://doi.org/10.1093/ref:odnb/7599 [accessed 29 December 2017].
Smith, Richard H.P., 'Peninsular War Cartography: A New Look at the Military Mapping of General Sir George Murray and the Quartermaster General's Department' in *Imago Mundi* 65:2 (2013), 234–52.

Stephenson, F. Richard, 'Chinese and Korean Star Maps and Catalogs' in J.B. Harley and David Woodward (eds.), *The History of Cartography Volume Two, Book Two: Cartography in the Traditional East and Southeast Asian Societies* (Chicago and London: University of Chicago Press, 1994), 511–78.

Sumira, Sylvia, *The Art and History of Globes* (London: British Library, 2014).

Taylor, E.G.R., 'A Letter dated 1577 from Mercator to John Dee' in *Imago Mundi* 13 (1956), 56–68.

Thomas, H.B. and A.E. Spencer, *A History of Uganda Land and Surveys and of the Uganda Land and Survey Department* (Entebbe: Government Press, 1938).

Tolias, George, 'Isolarii, Fifteenth to Seventeenth Century' in David Woodward (ed.), *The History of Cartography Volume Three: Cartography in the European Renaissance, Part 1* (Chicago and London: University of Chicago Press, 2007), 263–84.

Tyacke, Sarah and John Huddy, *Christopher Saxton and Tudor Mapmaking* (London: British Library Reference Division, 1980).

Van den Broeke, Marcel, Peter Van der Krogt and Peter Meurer (eds.), *Abraham Ortelius and the First Atlas* (t'Goy-Houten: HES, 1998).

Van Dyke, Paul. A., *Merchants of Canton and Macao: Politics and Strategies in Eighteenth-Century Chinese Trade* (Hong Kong: Hong Kong University Press, 2011).

Van Houts, Elisabeth M.C., 'Camden, Cotton and the Chronicles of the Norman Conquest of England' in *British Library Journal* (1992). http://www.bl.uk/eblj/1992articles/article9.html [accessed 16 January 2018].

Wallis, Helen and E.D. Grinstead, 'A Chinese Terrestrial Globe A.D. 1623' in *British Museum Quarterly*, XXV (1962), 83–91.

Wallis, Helen, 'The Influence of Father Ricci on Far Eastern Cartography' in *Imago Mundi* 19:1 (1965), 38–45.

Wallis, Helen, 'The Map Collections of the British Museum Library' in Helen Wallis and Sarah Tyacke (eds.), *My Head is a Map: Essays and Memoirs in Honour of R.V. Tooley* (London: Francis Edwards, 1973).

Wallis, Helen, 'The Rotz Atlas: A Royal Presentation', *The Map Collector* 20 (1982), 40–42.

Wallis, Helen, 'A Banquet of Maps' in *Map Collector* 28 (September 1989).

Wallis, J.P.R., *Thomas Baines: His Life and Explorations in South Africa, Rhodesia and Australia, 1820–1875* (Cape Town: A.A. Balkema, 1976).

Wardington, Lord, 'Sir Robert Dudley' in *The Book Collector* 52 (2003).

Watalet, Marcel (ed.), *The Mercator Atlas of Europe: Facsimile of the Maps by Gerhardus Mercator Contained in the Atlas of Europe, circa 1570–1572* (Pleasant Hills, OR: Walking Tree Press, 1998).

Watson, F.J.B., 'A Group of Views of Lucca by Bellotto' in *Burlington Magazine* 95, no. 602 (1948), 166–9.

Westfall, Richard S., 'Charting the Scientific Community' in Kostas Gavroglu, Jean Christianidis and Efthymios Nicolaidis (eds.), *Trends in the Historiography of Science: International Conference: Selected Papers* (Dordrecht; Boston: Kluwer Academic, 1994).

Williams, Glyn, *Arctic Labyrinth: The Quest for the Northwest Passage* (Toronto: Viking Canada, 2009).

Wood, Frances, 'Closely Observed China: From William Alexander's Sketches to his Published Work' in *British Library Journal* (1998), 98–121.

Woodward, David, 'Some Evidence for the Use of Stereotyping on Peter Apian's World Map of 1530' in *Imago Mundi* 24 (1970), 43–48.

Woodward, David (ed.), *Five Centuries of Map Printing / The Kenneth Nebenzahl, Jr., Lectures in the History of Cartography at the Newberry Library* (Chicago and London: University of Chicago Press, 1975).

Woodward, David, 'Medieval Mappaemundi' in J.B. Harley and David Woodward (eds.), *The History of Cartography Volume One: Cartography in Prehistoric, Ancient and Medieval Europe and the Mediterranean* (Chicago and London: University of Chicago Press, 1987), 286–370.

Woodward, David, *Maps as Prints in the Italian Renaissance: Makers, Distributors & Consumers / The Panizzi Lectures*, 1995 (London: British Library, 1995).

Woodward, David, 'The Italian Map Trade, 1480–1650' in David Woodward (ed.), *The History of Cartography Volume Three: Cartography in the European Renaissance, Part 1* (Chicago and London: University of Chicago Press, 2007), 773–803.

Worms, Laurence, 'Jefferys, Thomas (*c.*1719–71)' in *Oxford Dictionary of National Biography*, 3 January 2008. https://doi.org/10.1093/ref:odnb/14696. [accessed 9 March 2018.

Worms, Laurence and Ashley Baynton-Williams, *British Map Engravers: A Dictionary of Engravers, Lithographers and Their Principal Employers to 1850* (London: Rare Book Society, 2011).

Yee, Cordell D.K., 'Chinese Maps in Political Culture' in J.B. Harley and David Woodward (eds.), *The History of Cartography Volume Two, Book Two: Cartography in the Traditional East and Southeast Asian Societies* (Chicago and London: University of Chicago Press, 1994), 71–95.

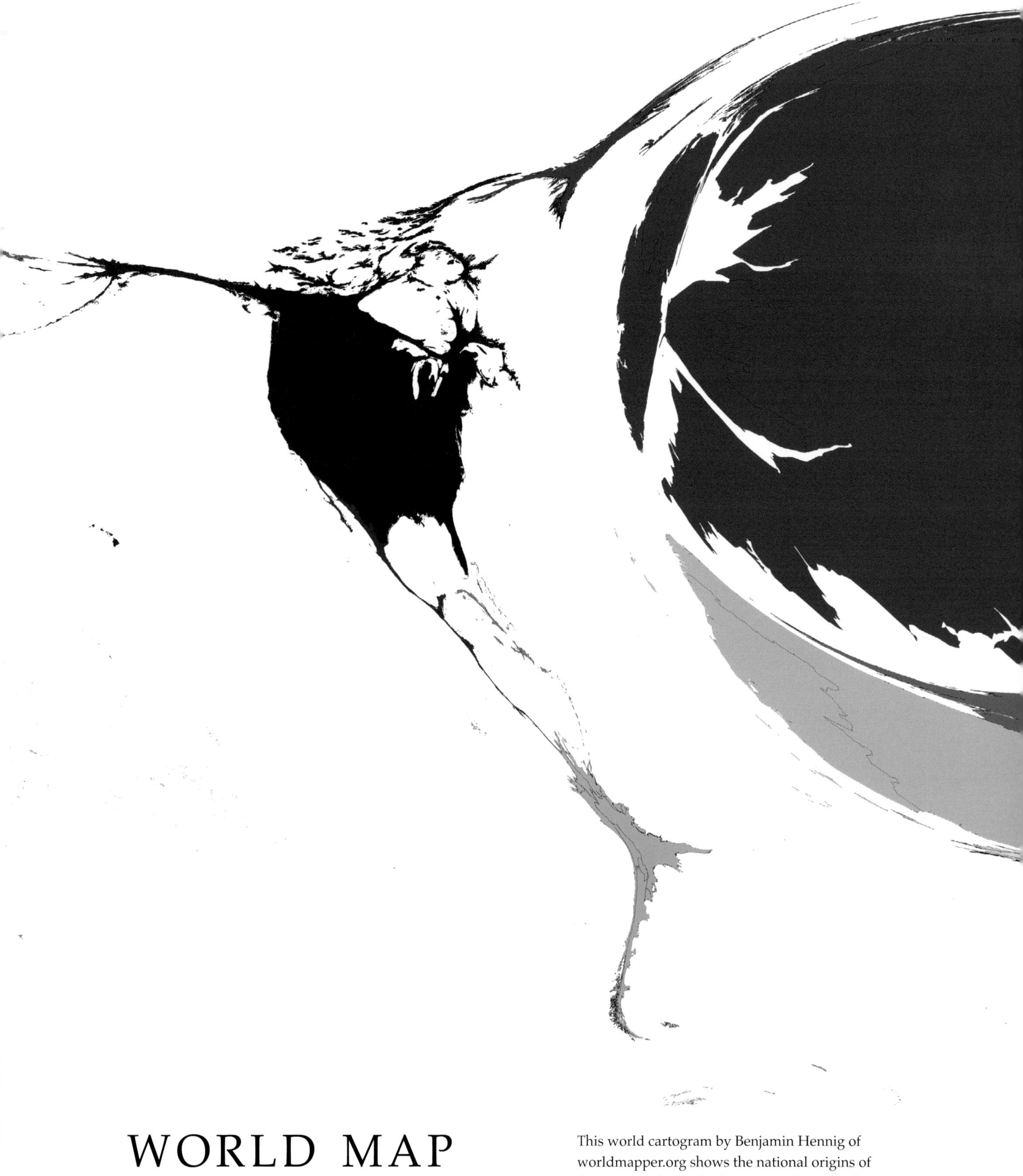

WORLD MAP

ORIGINS OF THE MAPMAKERS INCLUDED IN THIS ATLAS

This world cartogram by Benjamin Hennig of worldmapper.org shows the national origins of the people who made the maps included in this atlas. The territories with the most mapmakers are visualised as bigger in size.

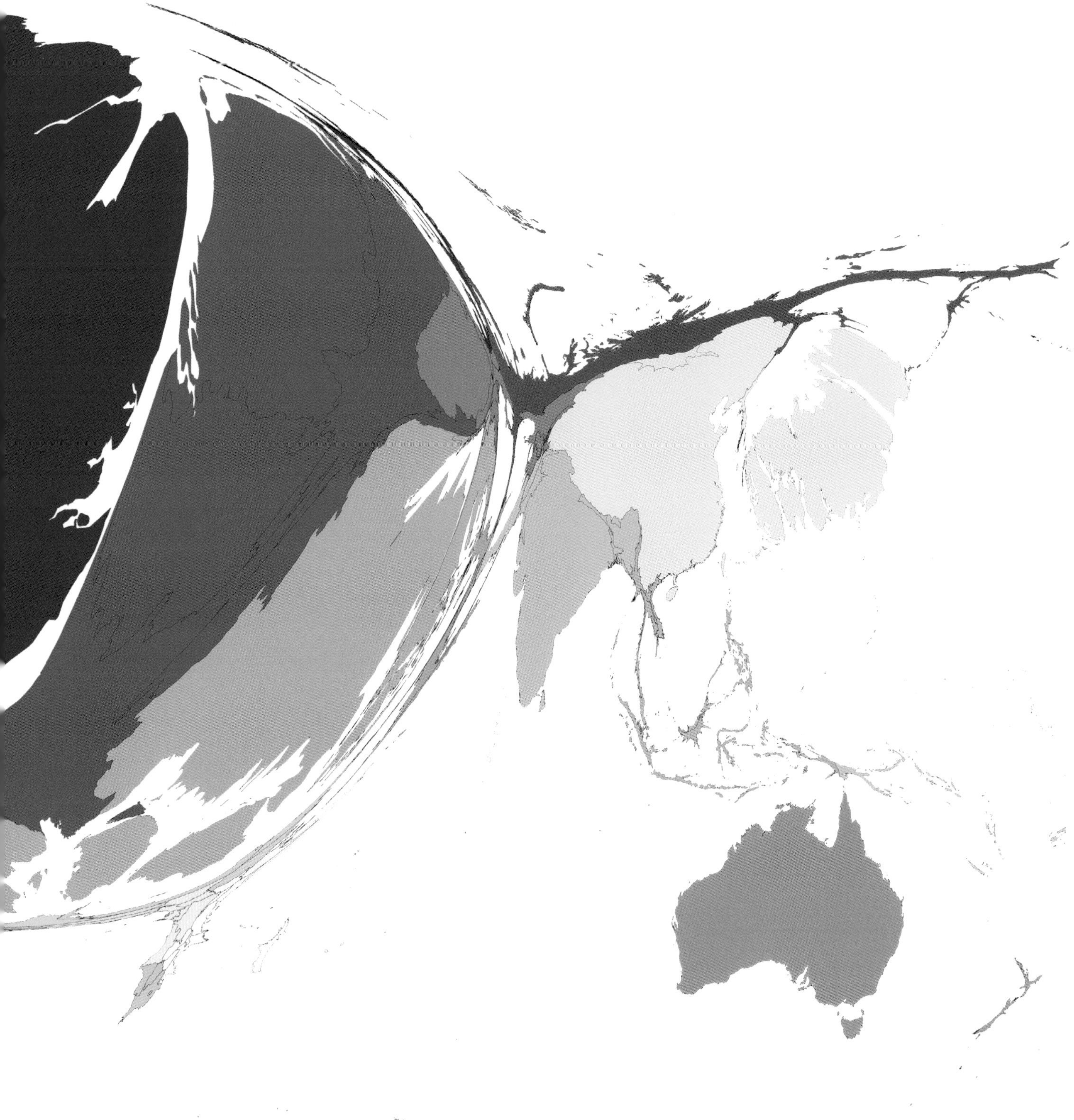

INDEX

Italic page numbers indicate illustrations.